MAROON SOCIETIES
Rebel Slave Communities in the Americas

Maroon Societies:

REBEL SLAVE COMMUNITIES IN THE AMERICAS

EDITED BY RICHARD PRICE

1973

ANCHOR BOOKS
ANCHOR PRESS/DOUBLEDAY
GARDEN CITY, NEW YORK

Anchor Books Edition: 1973

ISBN: 0-385-06508-6
Library of Congress Catalog Card Number 73-83603

TABLE OF CONTENTS

Contents

For the Saramaka, and their children

INTRODUCTION

Maroons and Their Communities

With the fleet of Governor Ovando, bound for Hispaniola in 1502 to reinvigorate the faltering colony that Columbus had left behind the previous year, sailed "a few Negroes . . . brought out by their masters" (Parry and Sherlock 1965:16). Among them was the first Afro-American maroon, an anonymous slave who "escaped to the Indians" in the mountainous interior soon after setting foot in the New World (Guillot 1961:77). Today, some 470 years later, there still lives in Cuba a man named Esteban Montejo, who escaped from slavery in his youth and lived for years in the forests, and who must be the last surviving exemplar of this desperate yet surprisingly frequent reaction to slavery in the Americas —flight or *marronage* (Montejo 1968; Salkey 1971).

For more than four centuries, the communities formed by such runaways dotted the fringes of plantation America, from Brazil to the southeastern United States, from Peru to the American Southwest. Known variously as *palenques, quilombos, mocambos, cumbes, ladeiras,* or *mambises,* these new societies ranged from tiny bands that survived less than a year to powerful states encompassing thousands of members and surviving for generations or even centuries. Today their descendants still form semi-independent enclaves in several parts of the hemisphere, remaining fiercely proud of their maroon origins and, in some cases at least, faithful to unique cultural traditions that were forged during the earliest days of Afro-American history.[1]

[1] The English word "maroon," like the French *marron,* derives from Spanish *cimarrón.* As used in the New World, *cimarrón* originally referred to domestic cattle that had taken to the hills in Hispaniola (Parry and Sherlock 1965:14) and soon after to Indian

During the past several decades, historical scholarship has done much to dispel the myth of the "docile slave." The extent of violent resistance to enslavement has been documented rather fully—from the revolts in the slave factories of West Africa and mutinies during the Middle Passage to the organized rebellions that began to sweep most colonies within a decade after the arrival of the first slave ships (see, for example, Herskovits 1958:86–109; Mannix and Cowley 1962: 104–30; Pope-Hennessy 1969; Genovese 1967; Kilson 1964; Moura 1959; Schuler 1970b; and Synnott 1971). And we are finally beginning to appreciate the remarkable pervasiveness of various forms of "day to day" resistance—from simple malingering to subtle but systematic acts of sabotage (see, for example, Bauer and Bauer 1942; Blassingame 1972; Bryce-Laporte 1971; Fredrickson and Lasch 1967; and Mintz 1971). Flight or *marronage*, however, has received much less attention, at least from North American scholars— in part no doubt because so much of the relevant data are in languages other than English but also because publications on maroons and their communities have so often been couched in what Curtin has called the "parochial tradition of ethnocentric national history" (1969:xv).

Yet maroons and their communities can be seen to hold a special significance for the study of slave societies. For while they were, from one perspective, the antithesis of all that slavery stood for, they were at the same time everywhere an embarrassingly visible part of these systems. Just as the very nature of plantation slavery implied violence and resistance, the wilderness setting of early New World plantations made *marronage* and the existence of organized maroon communities a ubiquitous reality. Throughout Afro-America, such communities stood out as an heroic challenge to white authority, and as the living proof of the existence of a slave consciousness that refused to be limited by the whites' conception or manipulation of it.

From a European perspective, *marronage* appeared to be "the chronic plague" of New World plantation societies (Peytraud 1897:373). Within the first decade of most colonies' existence, the most brutal punishments had already been

slaves who had escaped from the Spaniards as well (Franco 1968:92). By the end of the 1530s, it was already beginning to refer primarily to Afro-American runaways (Franco 1968:93; see also Guillot 1961:38), and had strong connotations of "fierceness," of being "wild" and "unbroken" (Friederici 1960:191–92).

reserved for recaptured runaways, and in many cases these
were quickly written into law. An early eighteenth-century
visitor to Surinam reported that

> if a slave runs away into the forest in order to avoid work
> for a few weeks, upon his being captured his Achilles ten-
> don is removed for the first offence, while for a second of-
> fence . . . his right leg is amputated in order to stop his
> running away; I myself was a witness to slaves being pun-
> ished this way [Herlein 1718:112, translated in R. van
> Lier 1971:133].

And similar punishments for *marronage*—from castration to
being slowly roasted to death—are reported from many different regions in the selections included in this book.

Yet *marronage* did not have the same meaning in all colonies at all times. As long as the numbers of slaves who took
to the hills remained small, only the least skilled slaves were
involved, and they did not interfere directly with plantation
life, the maroons' existence might be tolerated or largely ignored, as Debien suggests for some of the French islands
(1966b:7–9). Moreover, throughout the Americas, planters
seem to have accepted as part of the system the common
practice of *petit marronage*—repetitive or periodic truancy
with temporary goals such as visiting a relative or lover on a
neighboring plantation. For example, temporary flight of this
type was clearly an everyday part of plantation life in the
southern United States; the pattern is vividly brought to life
in several of Faulkner's stories (for example, "Was," "Red
Leaves"), and is more dryly attested to by Mullin's statistics
on the "motives" of Virginia runaways (1972:108–9).

It was marronage on the grand scale, with individual fugitives banding together to create independent communities of
their own, that struck directly at the foundations of the
plantation system, presenting military and economic threats
that often taxed the colonists to their very limits. In a remarkable number of cases throughout the Americas, the whites
were forced to bring themselves to sue their former slaves for
peace. In their typical form, such treaties—which we know of
from Brazil, Colombia, Cuba, Ecuador, Hispaniola, Jamaica, Mexico, and Surinam—offered maroon communities
their freedom, recognized their territorial integrity, and made
some provision for meeting their economic needs, demanding

in return an agreement to end all hostilities toward the plantations, to return all future runaways and, often, to aid the whites in hunting them down (see, for example, Kent 1965:172; Escalante 1954:226–29; Franco 1968:100; Debbasch 1961/62:188–89; Edwards 1796; Davidson 1966:249–50; King 1958). Of course, many maroon communities never reached this stage, being crushed by massive force of arms; and even when treaties were proposed they were sometimes refused (Escalante 1954:226–27) or quickly violated (Kent 1965:172; Escalante 1954:229). Nevertheless, new maroon communities seemed to appear almost as quickly as the old ones were exterminated, and they remained the "chronic plague," "the gangrene," of many plantation societies right up to final Emancipation (Debbasch 1961/62:124).

It is important to keep in mind that maroon societies arose in reaction to *colonial* slavery, an institution significantly different from that of the ante bellum South, which until recently served so many North American scholars as *the* implicit model of plantation slavery (see Engerman, et al., 1972). Colonial slave systems in the various parts of the Americas were much more similar to one another at the outset than they were to become later on, after locally born slaves came to predominate, and as whole plantation systems became more differentiated economically, legally, and politically. Early colonial systems shared, for example, a particularly high proportion of native Africans (with all that this implies culturally), a sex ratio heavily skewed in favor of males, and considerable craft specialization among the slaves. As Mullin concluded in a recent study, such factors made colonial slave populations "more alike than not and therefore highly comparable" (1972:xi). And it is this comparability that is the ultimate justification for a hemispheric approach to maroon societies.

This book is, in a sense, an extended argument that maroon societies form a class or type that can yield unique insights about the Afro-American experience. By juxtaposing a large number of particularistic case studies drawn from throughout the Americas, I try to suggest that those rebels who attempted to create communities of their own faced largely similar problems and arrived at broadly comparable solutions. I must admit at the outset that both personal and professional biases lead me to slight somewhat the European or colonial perspective, in favor of attempting to come to grips with maroon societies as much as possible on their own terms. Two years of field research with the largest surviving maroon group, the Saramaka "Bush Negroes" of Surinam, failed to prepare me for the frustrations of trying to achieve a "maroon perspective" on other communities, seen only through the screen of Eurocentric histories. Yet in spite of the difficulties, the effort seems well worth making. Since I have been unable to find any generalizing work on maroons and their communities from this perspective, I will try in the remainder of this Introduction to survey some of the major themes and common problems and to point to topics for future investigation.

To be viable, maroon communities had to be almost inaccessible, and villages were typically located in inhospitable, out-of-the-way areas. In the southern United States, isolated swamps were a favorite setting (Aptheker 1939); in Jamaica, the most famous maroon groups lived in the unbelievably accidented "cockpit country," where deep canyons and limestone sinkholes abound but where water and good soil are scarce (for photos of this terrain, see Robinson 1969:49); in the Guianas, seemingly impenetrable jungles provided a home for the maroons; and numerous other such "extreme" environments are mentioned as settings for communities throughout this book.

It is worth suggesting that such locales were often inhospitable not only to pursuing troops (about which so much has already been written) but also to the original runaways themselves. Reading Edwards (1796) on Jamaica or Stedman (1796) on Surinam one gets a romantic picture of sons and daughters of Africa perfectly adapted to an environment that generously provides water, crops, and game. But the maroon viewpoint, as we know it from a few precious accounts, suggests instead that the harsh natural environments of early communities at first presented terrifying obstacles, and that it was only with a great deal of suffering, and by bringing to bear the full range of their collective cultural experience and creativity that the remarkable adaptations that inspired Edwards and Stedman were finally achieved. In discussing their early history with Saramaka maroons in Surinam, I was often struck by the way that they emphasized their initial difficulties in fighting the environment (with few of the key tools—axes, hoes, guns—that they had known on the plantations) almost as much as they did their problems with pursuing troops. Something of the utter "alienness" of their new jungle home as it must have appeared to eighteenth-century Saramakas may be seen in a story still told today; the band of runaways who, after months of wandering, reached the Gaánlío (a river far in the interior along which they live today) were unable to drink the water because it was filled with tiny worms. It was only after performing major rituals, under the protection of what was to become the central oracle-deity of the region, that they were able finally to purify the river and to settle by its banks.

Successful maroon communities learned quickly to turn the harshness of their immediate surroundings to their own advantage for purposes of concealment and defense. Paths leading to the villages were carefully disguised, and much use was made of false trails replete with dangerous booby traps. In the Guianas, villages set in swamps were approachable only by an underwater path, with other, false paths carefully mined with pointed spikes or leading only to fatal quagmires or quicksand (see, for example, Pinckard 1806, II:246–47; Stedman 1796, II:116–17). In many regions man traps, and even dog traps, were used extensively in village defenses (see, for example, Schwartz 1970:329–31; Pérez de la Riva 1952:23). And the villages themselves were often surrounded by a strong palisade (whence the generic name for hispanic maroon communities: *palenques*). The extensive use of natural features for defense is well illustrated by this account of the Leeward Maroons of Jamaica:

[The Maroon] men were placed on the ledges of rocks that rose almost perpendicularly to a great height, on a ground which, compared to those precipices, might be called a plain, the extremity being narrowed into a passage, upon which the fire of the whole body might bear. This passage contracted itself into a defile of nearly half a mile long, and so narrow that only one man could pass along it at a time. Had it been entered by a line of men, it would not have been difficult for the Maroons from the heights to have blocked them up in the front and in the rear, by rolling down large rocks at both ends, and afterwards to have crushed them to death by the same means. . . . The entrance was impregnable, the continuation of the line of smaller cockpits rendered the rear inaccessible, and Nature had secured the flanks of her own fortification. In this dell were secured the Maroon women and children, and all their valuable things deposited. On the open ground before the defile the men had erected their huts, which were called Maroon town, or Cudjoe's town, whence, in case of an alarm, the people could fly in a minute to the ledges of the rocks at the mouth of the cockpit [Dallas 1803, I:49–50].

It is interesting that Saramakas, in Surinam, used a similar stratagem in building a palisaded village atop a hill and digging a single, sunken path as the only means of approach to its entrance. As the colonial troops advanced up this path, the maroons rolled large logs down it, crushing them (according to the account of an old Saramaka, recorded in 1968). In some places, maroons depended even more heavily on man-made defenses, of which the most formidable were probably those erected in the final years of Palmares in Brazil, at the end of the seventeenth century. An eyewitness wrote:

The line of defense was very strong, of 2,470 fathoms, with parapets of two fires at each fathom, complete with flanks, redoubts, redans, faces, sentry-boxes, . . . and the exterior terrain so full of caltrops [pointed stakes] and of pits full of them, at all levels—some at the feet, others at the groin, others at the throat—that it was absolutely impossible for anyone to come close to the said line of defense at all from any angle. . . . Nor was it possible for them [the soldiers] to make approaches, such was the density and the thickness of the underbrush in the woods; and indeed this factor had made it impossible for them to dig trenches [from a document in the Arquivo Histórico Colonial, translated in Ennes 1948:209].

Maroon men throughout the hemisphere developed extraordinary skills in guerrilla warfare. To the bewilderment of their European enemies, whose rigid and conventional tactics were learned on the open battlefields of Europe, these highly adaptable and mobile warriors took maximum advantage of local environments, striking and withdrawing with great rapidity, making extensive use of ambushes to catch their adversaries in crossfire, fighting only when and where they chose, depending on reliable intelligence networks among

nonmaroons (both slaves and white settlers), and often communicating by horns. The two most detailed reports of actual
battle tactics, from Jamaica and Surinam, describe strikingly
similar evasive maneuvers of great ingenuity (Edwards 1796,
I:541; Stedman 1796, II:97–99). Since it was imperative to
maximize the effect of what little firepower they possessed,
early maroon survival depended heavily on such general
tactics. Many bands had only a few usable firearms, and the
shortage of ammunition sometimes led to the use of buttons,
coins, and pebbles instead of shot (see Debbasch 1961/62:
109; Mirot 1954:254; Stedman 1796, II:114). In many areas,
maroons used bows and arrows extensively as weapons, as
well as home-made spears and Amerindian warclubs, and
even, in some cases, "crooked stick[s] shaped something like
a musket" to frighten the whites by their apparent force of
arms (see Stedman 1796, II:89).

The contrast between maroon and European styles of
fighting can be seen in two accounts from Jamaica. A nineteenth-century writer, with the advantage of hindsight, noted
that:

> The [British] troops marched in their proper regimentals,
> as if they were going to fight a regular and civilized enemy,
> and sometimes had even the absurdity to traverse the
> mountainous roads with drums beating. . . . The custom-
> ary accoutrements were too clumsy and burdensome for
> traversing the woods and clambering over the rocks, and
> the red coats were too conspicuous an object to the Ma-
> roon marksmen, who seldom missed their aim. . . . The
> regular soldiers . . . disdained for a time to have recourse
> to rocks and trees as a shield against their enemies' fire,
> accounting it base and unmanly in a soldier thus to shrink
> from danger [Stewart 1823:316–18].

Meanwhile, the Maroons, using classic guerrilla tactics,

> disposed of themselves on the ledges of the rocks on both
> sides [of a canyon] . . . through which men can pass only
> in a single file. . . . [They] lay covered by the underwood,
> and behind rocks and the roots of trees, waiting in silent
> ambush for their pursuers, of whose approach they had al-
> ways information from their out-scouts. [The troops]
> . . . after a long march, oppressed by fatigue and thirst,

advance toward the mouth of the defile. . . . A favorable opportunity is taken [by the Maroons] when the enemy is within a few paces to fire upon them from one side. If the party surprised return the fire on the spot where they see the smoke of the discharge . . . they receive a volley in another direction. Stopped by this, and undecided which party to pursue, they are staggered by the discharge of a third volley from the entrance of the defile. In the meantime, the concealed Maroons, fresh, and thoroughly acquainted with their ground, vanish almost unseen before their enemies have reloaded. The troops, after losing more men, are under the necessity of retreating; and return to their posts, frequently without shoes to their feet, lame, and for some time unfit for service [Dallas 1803, I:41–42].

Maroons not only faced superior firepower, but were almost always heavily outnumbered. Local European militias were often supplemented with imported mercenaries (see, for example, Stedman 1796). Indians were hired by colonists to track down and to fight maroons in many areas—for example, Brazil, Dominica, Guatemala, the Guianas, Mexico, and the United States (Schwartz 1970:324; Debbasch 1961/62:100; Gage 1958:196; Nassy 1788:93; Synnott 1971:112–13; Davidson 1966:252; Aptheker 1939). In Jamaica, the government went so far as to import several shiploads of Miskito Indians from the Central American mainland for this purpose (Dallas 1803, I:38), and Indians were relocated by colonists attempting to deal with maroons in Brazil, and elsewhere as well (Schwartz 1970:324; see also Hart 1950:67). In addition, black troops—known variously as "rangers," "*chasseurs*," "black shot," etc.—were used widely by the Dutch, English, French, and Spanish (Stedman 1796, I:77–80; Dallas 1803, I:38; Debbasch 1961/62:145–46; Franco 1961:120). Composed of slaves and freedmen, or sometimes of slaves who were promised freedom in return for military service, these troops were considered far and away the most effective of all the antimaroon forces (see, for example, Stedman 1796, I:77–80). And finally, the maroons in some areas (for example, Cuba and Jamaica) had to contend with trained dogs (see, for example, Philalethes 1856:34–42, and Edwards 1796, I:560–69).

Reports by outsiders give only glimpses of what must have been the paramount importance of religious beliefs and practices to the fighting maroons themselves. We are told that in Cuba, attacking soldiers came upon "magical paraphernalia" (Pérez de la Riva 1952:23); that in Jamaica, Nanny was able to attract and catch bullets between her buttocks, where they were rendered harmless (Scott 1968:49; Hart 1950:54) and that Tacky "caught all the bullets fired at him in his hand, and hurled them back with destruction upon his foes" (Long 1774, II:451–52); and finally that in Surinam, as in Haiti, Jamaica, and elsewhere, warriors underwent complex rites and wore amulets intended to make them bulletproof (see, for example, Stedman 1796, II:107–8, 138–39). Saramakas, recounting to me their ancestors' battles with colonial troops, made quite clear that as far as they were concerned, it was their gods and obeahs that spelled the ultimate difference between victory and defeat.

The economic adaptations of maroons to their new environments were just as impressive as their military achievements. Living with the ever-present fear of sudden attack, they nevertheless succeeded in developing a wide range of innovative techniques that allowed them to carry on the business of daily life. Swidden horticulture was the mainstay of most maroon economies, with a similar list of cultigens appearing in reports from almost all areas—manioc, yams, sweet potatoes, and other root crops, bananas and plantains, dry rice, maize, groundnuts, squash, beans, chile, sugar cane, assorted other vegetables, and tobacco and cotton. These seem to have been planted in a similar pattern of intercropping—for example, vegetables scattered in a field of rice—from one end of the hemisphere to the other. Making gardens was one of the first tasks for each newly formed maroon group; only nine months after having established a new village, Yanga's people in Mexico "had already planted many seedlings and other trees, cotton, sweet potatoes, chile, tobacco, corn, beans, sugar cane, and other vegetables" (Davidson 1966:247). And pursuing troops, fully understanding the maroons' dependence on their gardens, often made their destruction the first order of business when attacking settlements (see Stedman 1796, II:116; Dallas 1803, I:38; Davidson 1966:248; and, for a maroon viewpoint, King 1958). It should be noted, however, that in a few areas, communities seem to have been unable to achieve this degree of economic independence or were uninterested in seeking it, and instead lived directly off plantation society—for example, the economically "parasitic" *mocambos* around Bahia (Schwartz 1970:322).

Maroons learned to exploit their environment in many other ways as well—from hunting and fishing to the development of a varied pharmacopoeia. Captain Stedman, who was positively awed by the environmental knowledge of his maroon adversaries in Surinam, provides several illustrations.

Inconceivable are the many expedients which these people employ in the woods. . . . Game and fish they catch in great abundance, by artificial traps and springs, and preserve them by barbacuing; while their fields are even overstocked with rice, cassava, yams, plantains, &c. They make salt from the palm-tree ashes. . . . We have found concealed near the trunk of an old tree a case-bottle filled with excellent butter, which . . . they made by melting and clarifying the fat of the palm-tree worms; this fully answers all the purposes of European butter, and I found it in fact even more delicious to my taste. The pistachio or *pinda* nuts [peanuts] they also convert into butter, by their oily substance, and frequently use them in their broths. The palm-tree wine they have always in plenty; they procure it by making deep incisions of a foot square in the fallen trunk, where the juice being collected, it soon ferments by the heat of the sun; it is not only a cool and agreeable beverage, but sufficiently strong to intoxicate. The manicole or pine-tree [a palm] affords them materials for building; they fabricate pots from clay found near their dwellings; the gourd or callebasse tree procures them cups; the silk-grass plant and maurecee-tree supplies materials for their hammocks, and even a kind of cap grows naturally upon the palm-trees, as well as brooms; the various kinds of nebee supply the want of ropes; fuel they have for cutting; and a wood called *bee-bee* serves for tinder, by rubbing two pieces on each other; it is also elastic, and makes excellent corks; candles they can make, having plenty of fat and oil; and the wild bees afford them wax, as well as excellent honey [1796,II:114–15].

A great many of these techniques for dealing with the environment clearly were learned, directly or indirectly, from American Indians. It is not yet possible to say how many had some sort of antecedents in the African homeland as well

(but see Lindblom 1924). I would suggest, however, that a
good deal of maroon technology must have been developed
on the plantations during slavery. Throughout Afro-America,
Indians interacted with slaves, whether as fellow sufferers, as
trading partners, or in other capacities. Indian technologies—
from pottery making and hammock weaving to fish drugging
and manioc processing—were taken over and, often, further
developed by the slaves, who were so often responsible for
supplying the bulk of their own daily needs. Life as maroons
meant numerous new challenges to daily survival, but it was
on a base of technical knowledge developed in the interaction
between Indians and blacks on plantations that most of the
remarkable maroon adaptations were built.

Yet in spite of their remarkable achievements in wresting a
living from an alien environment, maroons remained unable to
manufacture certain items that were essential to their continued existence. As long as the wars went on, the need for
such things as guns, tools, pots, and cloth (as well as for
new recruits, particularly women) kept maroon communities unavoidably dependent on the very plantation societies
from which they were trying so desperately to isolate themselves. This inability to disengage themselves fully from their
enemy was the Achilles heel of maroon societies throughout
the Americas.[2] Whether located at a marching distance of
several weeks from colonial centers (as were the early Saramakas or the Palmaristas) or within a few miles of major cities (as were the Bahian *mocambos* or André's village in
French Guiana [Mirot 1954]), successful communities
worked out fairly extensive economic relations with colonial

[2] In some cases, at least, maroon groups may have been less the
victims of economic necessity than these statements imply. There is
evidence that in some settings they could have survived physically
with considerably less contact with colonial society than was the
rule. For example, the Spanish maroons in Jamaica lived in vir-
tual isolation for years without guns and most other Western manufactures (Barbara Kopytoff: personal communication). But even
though some maroon groups could make their own cloth, pots, and
so forth (see, for example, Mirot 1954, King 1958), they seem to
have *preferred* Western manufactures and to have been willing to
risk a good deal to obtain them. To some extent at least, then, the
"economic dependence" of maroons on colonial society was a matter of choice, and it bespeaks a kind of "Westernization" which,
though limited in scope, is more profound than simply the knowledge of new skills picked up on the plantation.

societies. Such relations ranged all the way from the guerrilla raids on outlying plantations (which were especially frequent in Surinam) or the extortion tactics common around Bahia, to the quasi-institutionalized clandestine exchange of goods and services that took place in many other parts of the Americas. Two points deserve special emphasis: the extent of maroon dependence on colonial society for certain essential items, and the surprising amount of collusion by members of almost all social classes with the rebels, whenever it served their individual self-interest.

While colonial governments, which were charged with protecting the plantation system, were generally in a position of outright enmity toward maroon communities, a large number of individual members of these societies found the maroons useful suppliers of goods and services and had few scruples about supplying them, in return, with the items they needed. Selected plantation slaves, who often included relatives and friends, were important allies of maroons in most areas. In Guadeloupe, slaves smuggled arms to maroons (Debbasch 1961/62:107); in Cuba, slaves (as well as freedmen) served as their middlemen, selling their beeswax, honey, and leather in urban markets and supplying them, in return, with tools and firearms (Pérez de la Riva 1946:103–4, 109); and in Jamaica, slaves not only helped the maroons economically, but provided crucial intelligence information as well (Patterson 1970:303). Trade with white settlers was also common in most areas. Many Cuban communities traded directly with neighboring whites (Pérez de la Riva 1952: 24); Spanish middlemen sold game and fish in the towns of Saint-Domingue for the maroons of le Maniel, obtaining for them guns, powder, and tools (Debbasch 1961/62:108); the settlers around Palmares carried on an extensive and complex illegal trade with the *quilombos,* exchanging guns for silver and gold taken by the Palmaristas on their raids closer to the coast (Kent 1965:170–71); and in the southern United States the maroons of the Dismal Swamp carried on an active trade with the surrounding white populace (Aptheker 1939: 168).

In general, the social environments in which nascent maroon communities found themselves were as new and challenging as their natural surroundings, and success at survival depended in large part on how they responded to them. The colonial New World was a volatile social arena with many types of competing interest groups, and successful maroon communities were often able to play one off against another. In turn, of course, maroons often found themselves being used as pawns in struggles among the great European powers as well as among more special European or colonial interest groups. In eighteenth-century Amsterdam, for example, certain business interests periodically spread "false rumors about the imminent threat of violence from maroons . . . [causing] artificial drops in the prices of shares in Surinam on the stock market, for purposes of speculation" (R. van Lier 1971:40–41, 57).

One of the strangest of the "alliances of convenience" that arose in this setting was that between maroons in the Spanish territories and the pirates who represented Spain's enemies. This often close relationship was intermittent and based on opportunism by both sides; pirates were often slave traders or owners (see Masefield 1925:85–102; I. Wright 1929, 1932), and something of their general opinion of maroons might be inferred from the etymology of the verb "to maroon," which "came to mean the form of punishment meted out [by the pirates] to backsliders from their own numbers" (Woodbury 1951:130). Yet for three centuries, beginning in the early 1500s, there were maroons who fought alongside pirates in their naval battles, guided them in their raids on major cities, and participated with them in widespread, illicit international trade. We know that some maroons rose high in the pirate ranks; for example, the Cuban runaway Diego Grillo became Capitán Dieguillo, serving as an officer under the notorious Dutchman Cornelis Jol ("Kapitein Houtbeen"— "Captain Pegleg"), until the former maroon was convicted of illicit slaving along the coasts of Central America (Franco 1968:97; Diez Castillo 1968:37). The most famous collaboration between maroons and pirates, shrouded in legend like so much else about the man, involved Sir Francis Drake. On one major Panama adventure we are told that local maroons served him as hunters, carpenters, masons, nurses, scouts, and archers, providing him with thirty of his forty-eight fighting men. And, in return for helping him capture nearly thirty tons of Spanish silver and as much gold as each man could carry, Drake gave the maroon chief a "fair gilt scimitar" that had once belonged to the late French king, Henri II (Masefield 1925:21–77).

In many areas, maroons lined up even more directly with

the European rivals of their former masters. In Jamaica, the Spanish maroons joined the British and played a decisive role in driving the Spaniards from the island (Patterson 1970: 296); on Hispaniola, the maroons of le Maniel played off the French against the Spanish for decades (Debbasch 1961/62: 73–77, 185–91); in Florida, the Spaniards welcomed maroons from the British and American colonies, and used them against their former masters (K. Porter 1932:323); many other such examples could be cited.

Maroons in most parts of the Americas also found themselves dealing with native Americans—the Indians who were so often their reluctant neighbors. But while relations with Indians were a fact of life for most communities, such relations were diverse, varying from successful cooperation to all-out war. In a number of cases, groups of Indians and maroons "fused," both culturally and genetically, but their relative positions varied. The Miskito Indians of Honduras and Nicaragua, for example, kept a large group of maroons as domestic slaves in the seventeenth century, intermarrying with them and gradually absorbing them into their general population (see Helms 1971 for further reading on the Miskito). In contrast, the Island Carib, who had also kept maroons as slaves initially, soon found themselves dominated by the blacks in terms of power, and later genetically as well; in the twentieth century, one ethnographer went so far as to describe the culture of these Black Carib, rather misleadingly, as "an African cake with Amerindian ingredients" (Taylor 1951:143; additional references on the Black Carib will be found in the bibliographical note for Part Two of this book). Seminoles and maroons, during their long history of close collaboration and intermarriage, maintained their separate identities more clearly; they fought side by side but in separate companies against the whites, and maroons (even while being "domestic slaves") served as trusted advisers and counselors of Seminole chiefs (for references on Black Seminoles, see the bibliographical note for Part Three). Cases of close military cooperation between maroons and Indians occurred in many other areas as well—for example, Mexico, Colombia, and Surinam (Davidson 1966; Acosta Saignes 1967; Buve 1966). And throughout Brazil, groups of maroons and Indians merged in a wide variety of political and cultural arrangements (Bastide 1961:131–33).

Though relationships as close as those of maroons with

Miskitos, Island Caribs, or Seminoles were not the rule, maroons and Indians did carry on commerical relations in many parts of the hemisphere, and maroon men, suffering from a shortage of women, often took Indian wives (see below). In at least one case, maroon-Indian trade has continued unabated for over two centuries; the Trio Indians of Surinam

> received all types of manufactured goods [acquired by the "Bush Negroes" from the whites], but in particular axes, knives, machetes, and beads, and the Bush Negroes collected in exchange dogs, cassava squeezers, pets, and basketwork. [Hunting] dogs were and still are the most valuable trade item; . . . in 1964, I saw a hunting dog sold for two axes, two machetes, a big knife, a metal canister with padlock, a litre bottle of salt, two mirrors, a pair of scissors, and a metal basin [Rivière 1969:53–54].

However, in other areas (and in many of these same areas at different periods) hostile relations were common, often encouraged by local whites (see, for example, Willis 1963). In British Guiana and parts of Brazil and Virginia, it was probably the mere presence of hostile Indians in large numbers that prevented the establishment of viable maroon communities (van der Elst 1970:61–69; Schwartz 1970:322; Klein 1967:71), and, as mentioned earlier, Indians were commonly employed by the whites both to hunt down individual runaways and to serve as troops in major battles against maroon communities.

The internal organization of maroon societies has received relatively little scholarly attention. Yet enough is known to allow some generalization and to point to problems that deserve special attention in the future.

Early maroon societies, whether organized as centralized states (like Palmares), loose and shifting federations (like the Windward Maroons of Jamaica), or isolated bands (like that of André in French Guiana), were communities at war, fighting for their very existence. The state of continuous warfare strongly influenced many aspects of their political and social organization.

To assure the absolute loyalty of its members, each community had to take strong measures to guard against desertion and the presence of spies. New members, particularly those slaves liberated during raids, posed a special threat to security. We know that precautions were often taken to make it impossible for such people to return to their plantations and betray the group. In French Guiana, for example, new recruits

> are brought to the village . . . by way of numerous detours without going on any real paths, so that once they are there, they cannot find their way back [Mirot 1954: 253].

And in maroon communities throughout the Americas, new recruits served probationary periods, often in some kind of domestic slavery. For example, in Cuba, new maroons underwent a two-year trial period during which they were not allowed out of the village (Pérez de la Riva 1952:23); in Palmares, men freed on raids became slaves of the maroons until they succeeded in finding a substitute on another raid (Kent 1965:169); among Chief Boni's men in Surinam, none "were trusted with arms until they had first served him some years as slaves, and given him unquestionable proofs of fidelity and resolution" (Stedman 1796, II:174); the Leeward Maroons of Jamaica kept new recruits in a type of isolation during which "They would not Confide in them, until They had served a time prefixed for their Probation," which was sufficiently trying to make some of them wish to return to their masters (James Knight, "The natural, moral and political history of Jamaica . . . ," n.d., C. E. Long papers, British Museum Additional Manuscript 12419, p. 96); and the Windward Maroons obliged new recruits

> to be true to them by an oath which is held very sacred among the negroes, and those who refuse to take that oath, whether they go to them of their own accord or are made prisoners, are instantly put to death ["Further Examination of Sarra . . ." enclosed in Hunter/Bd. of Trade, October 13, 1773, Calendar of State Papers, Vol. 40, pp. 215–16].

Throughout the hemisphere, desertion was commonly punished by death. In Palmares,

> when some Negroes attempt to flee, he [the king] sends *crioulos* after them and once retaken their death is swift and of the kind to instill fear [Kent 1965:167].

In Cuba, the rebels "had the custom of killing those who deserted the maroon bands, and those who did not defend themselves against their pursuers" (Franco 1968:104), and the same penalty obtained among the Windward maroons of Jamaica (Patterson 1970:302), in French Guiana (Mirot 1954:253), le Maniel (Moreau de Saint-Méry 1958:1135), and elsewhere. Moreover, I can report that even today, the theme of fear and distrust of new runaways crops up repeatedly in Saramaka oral accounts of their own early history.

Internal dissension of any sort could also pose a fatal threat to a small community at war. In the absence of developed institutions to maintain social control, early maroon communities allowed a great deal of power and authority to accrue to their leaders, and they learned to live with very harsh sanctions on internal dissension. In Palmares, the "king rules . . . with iron justice" (Kent 1965:167) and "robbery, adultery, and murder were punished uniformly with death" (Southey 1817–22, III:24–25). At the other extreme in terms of size, André's small group in French Guiana also exhibited considerable centralization of authority and strong internal discipline (cf. Mirot 1954). In Jamaica, Cudjoe's concern with maintaining absolute authority is stressed by all observers; he went so far as to execute some of his own men who had murdered some whites contrary to his orders (Patterson 1970:309), and at one point refused to allow a fleeing group of Eastern Maroons to join his own group because

> He had an absolute command of His People . . . [while the eastern group] were Independent of Him, and Subject only to their own chiefs, who would not Submit to Him [Knight n.d., 12419:97].

In Surinam, the great maroon leader Boni "maintained the strictest discipline amongst his troops: he was . . . absolutely despotic, and had [recently] executed two of his men . . . only upon suspicion of having hinted some few words in favour of the Europeans" (Stedman 1796, II:173). Finally, according to the missionaries among the eighteenth-century Saramaka, the "choicest tortures," including dismemberment and burning at the stake, were used for those convicted of serious crimes (Staehelin 1913–19, III [2]:268–69).

Perhaps the most serious threat to the internal peace of early maroon societies involved rights over women. During the early colonial period throughout the Americas, there was a severe imbalance of male to female slaves (Curtin 1969:19, 41, Engerman et al. 1972:26, 31), and this proportion was further increased among the original bands of runaways because a disproportionately large number of men successfully escaped from plantation life. Moreover, polygyny was the prerogative of important maroon men in many areas (for example, in Jamaica, French Guiana, Surinam, and Palmares), further reducing the number of wives available for the rest of the community (Edwards 1796, I:539; Mirot 1954:250–51; Staehelin 1913–19, III[2]:262; Kent 1965: 168). Many groups tried to solve this problem by capturing Indian women (as in Mexico, Panama, Colombia, Brazil, and Peru [Pérez de Ribas 1896:284; Diez Castillo 1968:55; Palacios de la Vega 1955:39, 105; Bastide 1961:129; Millones 1971:611]). But until they were able to raise their own children to maturity, almost all groups had to live with a severe shortage of women. Maroon men were well aware that fights over women could have the most serious consequences. We know, in fact, of one community in French Guiana that split up in the wake of just such a dispute (Debbasch 1961/62:105). And where we have information on the penalty for adultery in early maroon communities, such as in Palmares or among the Windward Maroons of Jamaica, it is invariably death (Southey 1817–22, III:24–25; "Further Examination of Sarra . . . ," op. cit., p. 215). One additional and most unusual report about the regulation of rights in women deserves mention. It claims that among the Leeward Maroons of Jamaica, there were carefully codified rules regulating the sharing of one woman by more than one man, allotting each a specific number of nights with her, controlling rights in the offspring, and so forth (anon. "Account of the Maroons and the late war . . . ," n.d., C. E. Long papers, British Museum Additional Manuscript 12431, p. 99). Though from a cultural viewpoint such practices might seem anomalous in the context of Afro-America, they give some indication of the severity of the shortage of women and of the recognition of the need for preventing it from rending communities apart.

A great deal can be learned by comparing maroon societies in a time perspective. For example, the date of a community's original formation as well as the length of its survival seem everywhere to be major influences on the form of its political organization. Communities formed in the sixteenth or seventeenth centuries seem to have differed from those formed later, both in the types of men they chose as leaders and in the models used to legitimize their authority. Before 1700, the great majority of maroon leaders on whom we have data were African-born. Moreover, four of the six major leaders (Ganga Zumba, Domingo Bioho, Yanga, and Bayano) claimed to have been kings in their African homelands. During this period, models of monarchy were frequently appealed to; in addition to the well-known case of Palmares, where King Ganga Zumba and his relatives formed a dynasty (see Kent 1965), the Venezuelan maroon leader, "el Rey Miguel," "formed a royal court with his cabinet and royal family . . . his mistress Guiomar was made Queen, and their son became the Heir Apparent" (Arboleda 1950:86); Domingo Bioho in Colombia was styled "Rey del Arcabuco" [King of the Craggy Spot] or "Rey Benkos" (Escalante 1954: 228–29; Arboleda 1950:82); and in Panama King Bayano "was regarded with the reverance and obedience due a lord and natural king" (Aguado 1919, II:197).

In contrast, after the beginning of the eighteenth century, maroon leaders only very rarely claimed princely descent from Africa, tending instead to style themselves captains, governors, or colonels rather than kings. Moreover, a striking number of leaders during this period were Creoles, quite out of proportion to the number of American-born men in the general slave population.

I would like to suggest, particularly for this period, that the nature of maroon (and colonial) society made the person who was skilled at understanding whites, as well as his fellow maroons, especially valuable as a leader. Although many Creole slaves—taught special skills and treated relatively well—may have disdained the company of African-born field hands, there were at least some who managed to achieve high status in the eyes of both planters and common slaves (for example, Toussaint l'Ouverture in Haiti or many of the rebel leaders in British Guiana [see Synnott 1971:60–61]). It was that trusted servant who was wise in the ways of the whites, but who also maintained close ties with the mass of slaves and could understand and use "African" modes of thought and action, who was particularly suited for maroon leadership. In fact, looking back over the historical records in Surinam, I find that almost all successful tribal chiefs possessed just this unusual combination of skill at handling whites and knowledge of "African" traditions. Even today in Saramaka, neither a man who is too Westernized in experience and attitudes nor one who is too exclusively committed to traditional, "African"-type values is considered appropriate for this office; within the system, the former receive little respect, while the latter typically take on important but specialized advisory or priestly roles.

Few maroon societies outlived their turbulent wartime years. However, those that did manage to survive for long periods represent case histories of special sociological significance, since their complete evolution from initial formation to full development can often be reconstructed. This developmental aspect of maroon societies has barely begun to be explored and presents one of the most challenging problems for future research.

It seems clear, for example, that wherever maroon communities survived for long periods, important aspects of their early social and political organization were altered as new institutions developed. In some cases, such as Yanga's group in Mexico or San Basilio in Colombia, documentation of these developments is scanty (see Davidson 1966; Escalante 1954). In others, such as the "Bush Negroes" of Surinam or the Jamaican Maroons, the outlines are already beginning to emerge. For example, in Saramaka—the society I know best —the power and authority of early wartime leaders was gradually diffused into a number of developing institutions. Reading the reports of missionaries living with the Saramaka in the late eighteenth century (Staehelin 1913–19), I get the distinct impression that kinship networks, which had existed in only attenuated forms during the earliest years of the society, were playing a major organizational role and determining to a large extent the distribution of authority; legal institutions, including "councils," ordeals, and other standardized judicial mechanisms, were operating smoothly; a complex but integrated system of ritual and belief held an important place in social and political control; and the harsh sanctions that typified early maroon societies were at least beginning to give way to more subtle pressures against deviance—the moral force of the community as a group and the threat of supernatural sanctions. And there was a still more general tendency during this period for the focus of religion (especially for men) to shift away from cults that stressed individual power and protection to ones having a stronger ethical component—a trend vastly accelerated by increasing contact with coastal society during the late nineteenth century (cf. R. Price 1973c: Chapter 3).

Understanding the nature of long-range changes in the political ideology of maroons is a task for the future, but such studies are almost certain to throw light on current debates about the nature of "slave personality" (see, for example, Elkins 1959; Genovese 1967; Lane 1971; Patterson 1967: 145–81). The same immense difficulties that face the student trying to reconstruct slaves' thoughts and motives confront the student who is trying to interpret apparent shifts through time in the way maroons defined themselves vis-à-vis outsiders. Patterson touches on this problem (1970:315–16) in reviewing the famous confrontation between Cudjoe, the fierce war leader of the Western Maroons of Jamaica, and Colonel Guthrie, the white commander sent to make peace. And he suggests that Cudjoe's "contradictory" behavior—humbling himself at the white's feet—must be understood in the light of the essentially contradictory nature of slave personality more generally; he adds, however, that there may be a strong element of role-playing involved (ibid.).[3] The complexities of interpretation become intensified when a time perspective is added. Following the treaties, these same Jamaican Maroons bought, sold, and owned substantial numbers of slaves, hunted new runaways for a price, managed to gain the hatred of much of the slave population, and in many respects may have deserved their common post-treaty nickname, "the King's Negroes" (Kopytoff 1972; post-treaty Maroons cooperated in hunting down new runaways in Hispaniola, parts of Surinam, and elsewhere as well). But we know almost nothing about the reality or the extent of changes in accompanying underlying attitudes or self-image. From reports of encounters between Saramakas and outsiders

---

[3] It is worth noting that Cudjoe's kissing of Guthrie's feet may be less revealing of his personality than of the standard symbolic behavior of the era (see Kopytoff 1972). Foot-kissing was a common symbol of the relationship between vassal and lord, and appears matter-of-factly in a later incident involving the then-pacified Jamaica Maroons during a performance of martial skills for Governor Lyttelton in 1764. After going through their maneuvers, the Maroons approached the governor with their muskets "and piled them in heaps at his feet, which some of them desired to kiss, and were permitted" (Long 1774, II:349).

after the treaties, it is my own impression that there was less ambivalence or contradiction and more conscious role-playing than in Jamaica; until the late nineteenth century at least, most Saramakas seem to have retained a fairly firm belief in their own moral superiority over whites as well as coastal blacks and tended to view all relations with outsiders instrumentally. One is tempted to suggest that Saramakas were privileged by their greater isolation to live with less ambivalence toward Western society and with greater self-esteem than the Jamaican Maroons, who were subject to strong pressures for creolization as early as the mid-eighteenth century (see the introduction to Part Five, below). But we cannot be certain. Considerably more field work among surviving maroons, as well as more sophisticated analysis of documentary sources, will be necessary before speculations of this sort can be converted into intellectually interesting and testable propositions. The importance of the broader issues, however, suggests that the effort is well worth making.

Maroon societies possess an unusually "synthetic" character because of the special, largely shared historical circumstances in which they were forged. In this final section, I want to turn from the consideration of external contingencies on their form—such as alien environments or pursuing troops —to a discussion of the cultural ideas and models that maroons brought with them to the forests and that were the ultimate determinants of the unique shape that their societies took on.

It is essential at the outset to underscore the diversity of values and points of view that must have been represented in most of the original maroon groups. Not only were African tribal affiliations quite diverse, but a wide range of slave adaptations was represented as well. Marronage was not a unitary phenomenon from the point of view of the slaves, and it cannot be given a single locus along a continuum of "forms of resistance." The meaning of marronage differed for slaves in different social positions, varying with their total perception of themselves and their situation, and this in turn was influenced by such diverse factors as their country of birth, the period of time they had been in the New World, their task assignments as slaves, and the particular treatment they were currently receiving from overseers or masters, as well as more general considerations such as the proportion of blacks to whites in the region, the proportion of freedmen in the population, the opportunities for manumission, and so forth.

Because of such considerations, the frequency of marronage differed significantly among different types of slaves. Although the relevant statistical data have only just begun to be explored, certain generalizations are already emerging that seem to hold throughout the Americas (see Debbasch 1961/62; Debien 1966a and 1966b; Debien et al. 1961–67; Fouchard 1972; Mullin 1972; Schuler 1970b). First, the least acculturated slaves were among those most prone to marronage, often escaping within their very first hours or days on American soil, and often doing so in groups, sometimes in a vain attempt to find their way back to Africa. Second, native-born Africans who had spent some time in the New World were not particularly prone to flight, and when they did run off it was most often temporarily, in *petit marronage*. Finally, an unusually high proportion of Creoles and highly acculturated African-born slaves ran off, though it was less often to maroon communities than to urban areas, where their independent skills and relative ease in speaking the colonial language often allowed them to masquerade as freemen.

The typical early maroon community was, then, composed of Africans who were often literally just off the ships, unskilled plantation slaves born in Africa but who had lived for years in the Americas (and who, because of their numerical preponderance in colonial slave populations made up the bulk of most maroon communities), and some Creoles or highly acculturated Africans. We know, moreover, that this first group probably included an unusually high proportion of middle-aged men (Debien 1965:794), which must have enhanced its influence on the shaping of maroon cultures and societies; that the second group included a large number of especially embittered slaves, since those slaves who had made some kind of long-range adjustment to the system tended to take definitive flight only when they had been victims of brutality considered excessive even by the ordinary standards of the plantation, or after being torn from their normal social context, for example by sudden sale to a new master (see, for example, Debien 1966b:33–42); and that the third group probably included many people with particularly strong ideological commitments against the slave system itself, since most of these skilled slaves who joined maroon groups could have chosen the easier course of melting unobserved into urban populations.

Yet such generalizations tell us tantalizingly little about the actual processes of culture-building that must have gone on in these new societies. Such slave "types" as the newly arrived African or the Creole are abstractions which, though useful on one level, must be viewed with genuine caution. The alternatives open to slaves of any such category were much greater than has usually been supposed, and the individual adjustments achieved were often extremely complex. I doubt, therefore, that our understanding of "slave personality" can be furthered by attempts to force real individuals onto a unilinear gradient from "accommodation" to "resistance" to slavery. As Mintz reminds us, "the house slave who poisoned her master's family by putting ground glass in the food had first to become the family cook. . . . And the slaves who plotted armed revolts in the marketplaces had first to produce for market, and to gain permission to carry their produce there" (1971:321). In this context, it seems significant that some of the most "creolized" of maroon societies—those with the heaviest overlay of Catholicism, European language, Western dress, and so forth—seem to have been composed of a particularly high proportion of native-born Africans (for example, many of the sixteenth-century communities in the Spanish territories). We are dealing, then, with phenomena of great complexity, whose comprehension demands both considerably more facts than we currently have at our disposal and analytical thought of greater subtlety than has yet been brought to bear (see Mintz and Price 1973).

To my knowledge, Roger Bastide is the only scholar who has tried to come to grips with these broad issues, speculating on the dynamics of the formation of maroon cultures and societies and attempting to characterize their uniqueness (1972:46–71—a chapter filled, incidentally, with a great deal of factual misinformation on these groups). Bastide views maroon societies as somehow anomalous, perceiving in them a fundamental "split between the infra- and superstructures" (1972:67).

Whereas in Africa there exists a functional connection between the various levels of what G. Gurvitch has termed "sociology in depth", and all strata—from the ecological to those embodying social values or group conscience—form part of the same continuum, in these maroon communities a quite different state of affairs prevails. Here, environmental determinism and the claims of collective memory come into direct conflict [1972:68].

Moreover, he argues that, in examining maroon societies, "we find ourselves everywhere confronted with 'mosaic' cultures," with "one [African] culture predominant . . . [though] this still allows the coexistence of whole enclaves based on other civilisations" (1972:69).

It seems to me that, in these passages, Bastide oversimplifies the processes that contributed to the formation of maroon cultures and societies, misconstruing the nature of the principles that served to integrate them, and considerably underestimating the maroons' creative resources. The notion of a "collective memory," apparently viewed as some sort of repository of African culture, does not cope adequately with the reality represented by the total cultural equipment brought by maroons to the forests. As we have seen, this equipment was in fact quite diverse, including contributions by Africans just off the ships who represented a variety of languages and cultures, as well as by long-term (African-born) slaves and Creoles with a wide range of individual adjustments to slavery, orientations to reality, and ways of handling problems. What the majority of these people did share was a recently forged Afro-American culture and a strong ideological (or at least rhetorical) commitment to things "African." Though the environments in which maroons found themselves were alien and hostile in many respects, these people were far from being completely unequipped to deal with them; as suggested above, much of the basic cultural knowledge necessary for the maroons' physical adaptation had already been developed throughout the New World on local plantations. The image of an unrelenting tension in maroon societies between the claims of "collective memory" and the necessity for new environmental adaptations is misleading, then, on several counts: its failure to recognize adequately the cultural diversity of the Africans involved; its confusion of ideological commitment to things African with the putative possession of some sort of generalized African culture; and its complete omission of nascent but already powerful plantation-forged Afro-American cultures.

Bastide's belief that these are "cultures in mosaic" or "mosaic cultures" is also misleading, and contains more than a hint of old-fashioned, mechanistic thinking about the nature of Culture itself (as Herskovits himself, late in life, recognized; see his 1958:xxiii). Nor does Bastide's corollary image of "cultural enclaves" within a "dominant [African] culture" stand up to close scrutiny. I would suggest that by focusing on the diverse African origins of various "culture-traits" considered in isolation, Bastide has failed to see the principles that integrate these societies and gave them their characteristic shape. In studying maroon societies, I have always been struck by the earliness and completeness of their "functional integration," by very much the kind of fit between levels that Gurvitch writes of. And this remarkably rapid formation by maroon groups of whole cultures and societies was made possible, as I have suggested, by the previous existence throughout the hemisphere of rather mature local slave cultures combined with a widely shared ideological commitment to things African.

The development of rich, local slave cultures (which shared a great many features in the different colonies) is just beginning to receive the attention it deserves (see, for example, Goveia 1965; Mullin 1972; Patterson 1967; Rawick 1972), but it is already clear that Africans in the New World, who at first often shared little more than a common continental origin and the experience of enslavement, developed distinctively Afro-American ways of dealing with life from the very beginning. We know, for example, that the national language of Surinam (Sranan, an English-based creole) was already "firmly established" within the first sixteen years of the settlement of the colony (Voorhoeve 1971:307). Further, I can cite as evidence for the early and rich development of Afro-American cults on plantations the fact that today, particular groups of Saramakas commonly visit, worship, and exchange ritual information with certain non-Bush Negroes—in each case, precisely those who are the descendants of the slaves who lived on the same plantation from which the ancestors of that particular group of Saramakas fled over two and a half centuries ago. Moreover, some characteristic modern forms of Afro-American social relations are conterminous with the Middle Passage itself; Saramaccan *máti* and *síbi*—forms of "ritual kinship" implying strong solidarity—referred originally to the experience of having shared passage on the same slave ship (cf. Bastide 1961: 118–19 on the similar *malungo* relationship in Palmares). Far from being limited to the environmental realm, then, the contribution of plantation culture to maroon societies touched almost all areas of life.

Yet slave culture was restricted in certain key respects, providing maroons with few models, for example, for higher-level social or political organization. (There were important attempts at tribal-based political organization among slaves in British Guiana, Jamaica, and elsewhere, sometimes culminating in major revolts [Patterson 1970; Ramos 1939; Schuler 1970a, 1970b; Synnott 1971], but for the hemisphere as a whole, these were the exception rather than the rule.) And slave culture provided maroons with only attenuated models for the arts, religion, and certain other aspects of culture of which full expression was impossible in the setting of the plantation. The uniqueness of maroon societies in the context of Afro-American culture stems in large part from the ways in which they overcame these particular limitations, and it is here that Bastide's "mosaic" metaphor seems weakest.

Maroons indeed drew on their diverse African heritages in building their cultures. But unlike other Afro-Americans, who were unable to pass on integrated patterns of traditional culture, maroons could and did look to Africa for deep-level organizational principles, relating to cultural realms as diverse as naming their children on the one hand, or systems of justice on the other. We still know almost nothing about the actual culture-building processes that took place. It seems likely, however, that such factors as the geographical range in Africa of particular cultural principles (or at least their mutual compatibility), and their potential adaptiveness for the special conditions of early maroon life influenced the outcomes. And the generally shared commitment to a "homeland" ideology must have been the cement that allowed practices and beliefs from different areas to be incorporated more or less harmoniously into these developing systems. (Bastide himself has written elsewhere that marronage involved more of a "nostalgia for Africa" than an attempt at exact reconstitution of it [1961:134].)

Those scholars who have examined maroon life most closely seem to agree that such societies are often uncannily "African" in feeling, even if devoid of any directly transplanted systems. However "African" in character, no maroon social, political, religious, or aesthetic *system* can be reliably traced to a specific tribal provenience; they reveal, rather, their syncretistic composition, forged in the early meeting of peoples bearing diverse African, European, and Amerindian cultures in the dynamic setting of the New World. The political system of Palmares, for example, which Kent has characterized as an "African" state, "did not derive from a particular central African model, but from several" (Kent 1965:175). In the development of the kinship system of the Djuka of Surinam, "undoubtedly their West-African heritage played a part . . . the influence of the matrilineal Akan tribes is unmistakable, but so is that of patrilineal tribes . . . and there are] significant differences between the Akan and Djuka matrilineal systems" (Köbben 1967b:14). And painstaking historical research has recently revealed that the woodcarving of the "Bush Negroes" of Surinam, long considered "an African art in the Americas" on the basis of many formal resemblances, is a fundamentally new, Afro-American art "for which it would be pointless to seek the origin through direct transmission of any particular African style" (Hurault 1970:84; see also R. Price 1970b and 1972).

Of course, maroon cultures do possess a remarkable number of direct and sometimes spectacular continuities from particular African tribes, ranging from military techniques or defense to recipes for warding off sorcery. These are, however, of the same type as can be found, if with lesser frequency, in Afro-American communities throughout the hemisphere. In stressing these isolated African "retentions" (which, taken together, are probably what make maroon cultures look like "mosaics" to Bastide) there is, I believe, a danger of ignoring cultural continuities of a far more significant kind. Bastide himself has divided Afro-American religions into those *en conserve* ("preserved" or "canned")—like Brazilian *Candomblé* or Cuban *Santería*—and those that are *vivantes* ("living")—like Haitian *Vaudou*. The former, he claims, represent a kind of "defense mechanism" or "cultural ossilization," a fear that any small change may bring on the end; while the latter are more secure of their future and freer to adapt to the changing needs of their adherents (1972: 28–51). I think it can be shown more generally that tenacious fidelity to "African" forms is, in many cases, an indication of a culture finally having lost meaningful touch with

the vital African past. Certainly, one of the most striking
features of West African cultural systems is their internal
dynamism, their ability to grow and change. The cultural
uniqueness of the more developed maroon societies rests
firmly, I would argue, on their fidelity to "African" principles
on these deeper levels, to underlying cultural principles—
whether aesthetic, political, or domestic—rather than on the
frequency of their isolated "retentions" (see R. Price 1972:
Price and Price 1972a and 1972b; Mintz and Price 1973).
With a rare freedom to extrapolate African ideas and adapt
them to changing circumstance, maroon groups include
what are in many respects both the most meaningfully African and the most truly "alive" of all Afro-American cultures.

Finally, a few words about this book itself. It should be
clear by now that the organization of selections by geographical areas was dictated by the particularistic nature of
maroon scholarship to date. I have prefaced each section with
a few paragraphs intended to relate it to the broader themes
discussed in this introduction, and provided suggestions for
further reading on each area in the bibliographical notes
that appear at the end of the book. In several selections I
have modified or eliminated those footnotes that give general
background references on maroons, unnecessary here; I have
altered the form of certain footnotes and references to achieve
stylistic uniformity; but I have had to leave unchanged
many incomplete references (for example, with missing dates,
publishers, place of publication, or page numbers) for want
of time to track them down. At the end of the book, I have
provided a General Bibliography, which includes all references cited in the general introduction, the section introduc-
tions, and the bibliographical notes. For the remainder of the
book, references cited are given at the end of each article,
except that those already cited in the General Bibliography
are not repeated.

ACKNOWLEDGMENTS

My ideas about maroons and their societies have been influenced by many friends, students, and colleagues. The Saramaka people, as whose guests my wife and I lived for nearly two years in Surinam, deserve our fullest gratitude for their hospitality, cooperation, and friendship; this book is dedicated to them. During 1972, I benefited from the original and stimulating work of the Yale College students in my seminar on maroons, and would like to thank, in particular, Virginia Dominguez, Ira Lowenthal, Gary McDonogh, Scott Parris, Ken Robinson, and Drexel Woodson. Professors Sidney W. Mintz and Barbara Klamon Kopytoff spent a great deal of time criticizing my introductory materials, and I am extremely grateful for their help and encouragement. Professor A. J. F. Köbben contributed to the early planning of the book and, had it not been for the press of other obligations, would have been a joint editor. I am particularly grateful to my wife, Sally Price, who lent her critical judgment to this project at every stage.

Special library research in preparation for my course on maroon societies was supported by the Paul Moore Memorial Fund of Yale College. Yale's Afro-American Studies Program helped finance some of the translations that eventually found their way into this volume. I would like to thank M. Broekhuysen, Virginia Dominguez, and Christine Reno for their translations (from the Dutch, Spanish, and French, respectively), which I then revised and edited, often extensively; as they stand all translations are fully my own responsibility. Finally, I would like to thank Cecile Doty, Blair Jackson, and Helen Kyrcz for the care and good humor with which they typed the manuscript.

PART ONE

The Spanish Americas

It was in the Spanish Americas that marronage began and ended, spanning nearly four tumultuous centuries. It was there that maroons struck up their first alliances with Indians and pirates, and there that most of the great maroon kingdoms were established—by Yanga in Mexico, Bayano in Panama, Miguel in Venezuela, Domingo Bioho in Colombia and, undoubtedly, by others of whom we still know nothing.

The selections that follow present a broad sampling of scholarship on marronage and the colonial reaction to it in the Spanish territories, and they require little special introduction.

First, the Cuban scholar José L. Franco surveys maroon communities in the whole of Hispanic America in this excerpt from his general book on Afro-America. Then, his compatriot Francisco Pérez de la Riva offers some pointed generalizations about *palenques* in Cuba. Next, in an excerpt from the letters of a North American traveler in mid-nineteenth-century Cuba, "Demoticus Philalethes" paints a chilling portrait of the type of men who made their living by hunting maroons for a price and, inadvertently, reveals something of the moral contradictions and weaknesses implied in being a "Yankee." The Venezuelan historian Miguel Acosta Saignes then presents the case history of one small community, destroyed in 1771, in this excerpt from his general book on slavery in Venezuela. Aquiles Escalante, a Colombian anthropologist, is represented by an excerpt from his ethnographic monograph on San Basilio, a modern community whose inhabitants are the descendants of seventeenth-century maroons. And finally, David M. Davidson, a North American historian, offers a comprehensive review of maroon activity in Mexico, setting a high standard of scholarship and demonstrating, incidentally, the exciting possibilities for future investigators interested in doing similar work in any of the many still unsurveyed areas of the Spanish Americas.

Suggestions for further readings on maroons in the Spanish Americas are found in the bibliographical note for Part One, at the end of this book.

CHAPTER ONE

Maroons and Slave Rebellions in the Spanish Territories

JOSÉ L. FRANCO

The first slave rebellions were contemporaneous with the beginning of the slave trade and the introduction of slavery into the Americas. The first insurrection took place on December 26, 1522, in Santo Domingo, on the sugar plantation owned by Admiral (also Governor) Diego Colón. The rebels fought courageously against the Spaniards but were nonetheless defeated. The Admiral had most of the survivors hanged. In 1529, in what is now Colombia, rebel slaves destroyed Santa Marta. In 1531, Panamá reported several disturbances related to the persistent protests of the slaves.

In 1537, Mexico City saw its first slave massacre. This was provoked by the rash and careless behavior of the colonists who killed a couple of dozen slaves on account of their rebellious attitude, and on the grounds that they were allegedly planning to rise up in arms [Aguirre Beltrán 1946].

The Spaniards sent thousands of Negroes from Santo Domingo, Puerto Rico, and Cuba to the mainland territories of Mexico, Honduras, Guatemala, Nueva Granada, and Vene-

From José L. Franco, *Afroamérica*. La Habana: Publicaciones de la Junta Nacional de Arqueología y Etnología, 1961. Translated from pp. 115–31, 141, 161–62. Some of these sections have been rearranged here, for the sake of continuity. Translated and reprinted with the permission of the author.

zuela, mainly for work in the gold mines. In 1548, the slaves
of San Pedro, Honduras, rebelled and the Spaniards had to
send reinforcements from neighboring colonies in order to
suppress them.

In the middle of the sixteenth century, about 80 Negroes
were transferred to the Buría mines near Barquisimeto;
they were the first to rise up in arms against their masters.
Miguel, who was one of these slaves and who was quite
proficient in Spanish and well-versed in cunning tricks,
escaped in 1555, and began to persuade other slaves and
Indians to follow his example in order to be free from
Spanish tyranny. Many individuals joined him. They
named him their King, his mistress Queen, their illegitimate
son Prince, and another Negro Bishop. Miguel founded a
capital, organized an army, and ordered an attack on
Barquisimeto (where there were only 40 Spanish settlers).
But these settlers sent for help in El Tocuyo, and Captain
Diego de Losada, accompanied by a group of armed men,
destroyed the Negroes' kingdom and killed their king
[Fortoul 1942].

The Spaniards frequently used Negroes and Indians as
shock troops in their own internal wars. There were slaves
accompanying the forces of Vaca de Castro, Viceroy of Peru,
when he defeated Diego de Almagro in 1542 in the valley of
Chupas. Hundreds of Negro slaves were also used by the
authorities to suppress the antiroyalist movement led by the
Contreras brothers, who killed the bishop and marched on to
Panama. With the help of the Negroes, the authorities were
finally able to defeat the forces of Juan Bermejo, one of the
most courageous of the rebel captains.

In Peru—according to Saco (1938)—where conflicts and
civil wars among the Spaniards were common, there was an
uprising in 1553, which lasted for over a year. Francisco
Hernández Girón, an impatient and proud man, placed himself at the head of this rebellion against the royalist authorities. As in previous cases, belligerent Negro slaves were
called on to help by both sides. Two hundred fifty of them
joined Hernández de la Nazca, and this number later increased to over three hundred slaves armed with hoes and
guns. In the Battle of Pucará, those Negroes sacked the

dwellings of the royalist forces, where there were few soldiers, and finding little resistance, killed them as well as those who had been left behind because of illness. They all fled, however, when Hernández Girón was defeated. Some of those serving on the royalist side were employed by the colonial government of Peru as spies. Their job was to pretend they had the authorization to pardon the rebels and to try to persuade them to return where they would be captured. However, they were caught, and Francisco Hernández Girón had their hands cut off, after which they were hanged by their necks along with their faked documents granting amnesty, and were sent back to the royalist camp.

In Lima, the slaves rebelled when Drake's fleet approached the Peruvian coast. In Santiago de Chile, during the 1647 earthquake, a Negro slave proclaimed himself King of Guinea, and called for vengeance against the whites. Four hundred Negroes followed him, armed with sticks and weapons they had taken from the ruins. The rebellion was suppressed and their king was hanged. Bishop Villarroel told his frightened congregation at the central square in Lima that this Negro insurrection was a warning from God. When the earth trembles and the slaves rebel, God "is saying we have sinned against His Divine Majesty and against his humblest creatures, who are the Negroes of Angola."

The slave insurrections of 1532 in Coro and of 1555 in the mines of Buría (Miguel's rebellion) were followed in Venezuela

by the uprisings of Andresote in 1732 at Puerto Cabello and Capaya; by Miguel Luengo's rebellion in 1747 in the land of Yare; by the uprising of the Caucagua and Capaya districts in 1794 on the issue of slavery; by the most important of all, led by José Leonardo Chirinos in the Sierras de Coro in 1795; by the rebellion of Maracaibo in 1799, led by the Second Lieutenant of the Negro militias, Francisco Javier Pirela; and there must have been many others. All these rebellions were the inevitable corollary of a social context which was defined by the principles of slavery and racial prejudice [Liscano 1950].

The abuses of slavery must have been almost limitless; Ortiz (1916) wrote that it included the practice of cas-

trating recaptured maroons, just as they had done to Indians.
And a royal decree of April 15, 1540 (contained in the
Leyes de Índias, ley XXIII del título 5 del Libro 7) found it
necessary to assert that

> Maroons are to be punished according to the laws and
> statutes of this book, and at no time shall such punishments
> be replaced by the amputation of those parts of the body
> which, in all decency, cannot be named.

The Edict of 1685 signed by King Louis XIV of France,
known as *Le Code Noir,* recommends the following formula
for punishing maroons:

> A Negro who is absent for a month shall have his ears
> cut off and shall have a *fleur de lys* branded on his left
> shoulder. If he again runs away, his knees shall be lac-
> erated and his other shoulder shall be branded. Finally, if
> he runs away for a third time, he shall be sentenced to
> death.

In line with such barbarism, Napoleon Bonaparte issued a
statute for the colonies on June 10, 1802 in which he stipulated that free Negroes would lose their own freedom and
the freedom of their families if caught harboring runaway
slaves (Schoelcher 1948).

On March 16, 1542 Archdeacon Alvaro de Castro of
Santo Domingo answered the inquiries of the Council of the
Indies regarding the Negroes of La Española stating

> that he believed that there were more than 25,000 or
> 30,000 Negroes there compared to no more than 1,200
> settlers on the plantations or at the mines; and that he
> thought there were over 2,000 or 3,000 runaway slaves hid-
> ing on the Cape of San Nicolás, in the Ciguayos, on the
> Samaná Penninsula, and on the Cape of Igüey. . . . There
> is much trade going on among them, based on articles
> stolen from farms and ranches which they raid. We have
> reached a point where every Negro, regardless of how
> new he is to the territory, steals something every day,
> sometimes even gold. Some do this so that they may pay
> the daily fee that they owe their masters [for the privilege

of hiring themselves out]; others, to give it to their women
or to buy clothes. This stolen property finds its way into
the hands of the 200 or 300 female Negroes called *gana-
doras* who walk the streets of this city earning money
with which to pay their masters' daily, monthly or yearly
fees, but keeping whatever is left over for themselves. They
travel all over the island stealing, transporting and secret-
ing their merchandise. These Negroes are so richly dressed
and decorated with gold that, in my opinion, they have
more freedom than we have [quoted in Saco 1938].

The Audiencia of Santo Domingo informed the Emperor
on July 23, 1546 of the activities of maroons and of the
measures taken to prevent slaves from fleeing or rebelling.
There were at that time more than seven thousand maroons
in the forests and mountains of the island—the island that is
now divided between Haiti and the Dominican Republic.
The documents sent by Cerrato, a lawyer, to the Emperor

seem to show that there was a group of 200 to 300 male
and female Negroes in the Baoruco region . . . and that
there was a similar one in Vega made up of 40–50 individuals. They had spears which they had made themselves
as well as some weapons which they had stolen from
fallen Spaniards, whose bodies they had covered with
bullhide. They were so dangerous that no one dared to
venture out unless he was in a group of fifteen or twenty
people. And since there were 12,000 Negroes on the island
who could revolt at any time, it seemed best to try to deal
with this dangerous evil head on. The situation worsened
with the flight of quite a few Negroes from San Juan de la
Maguana. These individuals joined a group led by a Negro
captain and rebel called Diego de Guzmán, and raided the
town, burned part of a neighboring sugar mill, and engaged
the Spaniards in battle. One of the Spaniards and two of
the Negro captains were killed in the confrontation. Such
being the situation, a military officer was sent out with 30
men. They found the Negroes in the Baoruco, killed Captain Guzmán as well as another rebel who was even worse
than he, plus another 17 Negroes. Of the Spaniards, one
was killed and 16 were wounded, including their leader.
Consequently, two other captains accompanied by the in-

fantry and the cavalry were ordered to exterminate the
maroon Negroes throughout the island, and were told they
could not return to the city until this was accomplished.

Ten years had passed since the Negro Diego de Campo
had made himself leader of the maroons. A handful of
men was sent out to attack him in his base of operations at
la Vega. He fled from there to San Juan de la Maguana,
destroying property on two sugar plantations along the
way and taking about 100 Negroes with him from those
plantations and from Azúa. They then went to Baoruco,
then to San Juan burning parts of the sugar refineries, and
damaging other property. The Admiral Governor then set
out with 150 infantry and cavalrymen to go against the
maroons himself. But he reached a peaceful agreement
with them and returned to the city. The Negroes, however,
disregarded the agreement, returned to San Juan and
Azúa, burned down refineries, stole Negro men and women,
and killed 3 mestizos. Once again, new forces were sent
after them, killing and capturing many of the maroons.
Those captured were either exiled, hanged, burned, or
tortured, or had their feet cut off. The severity of these
punishments reveals the harshness and cruelty with which
the rebellious slaves were typically treated during that
period [Saco 1938].

Diego de Campo, betraying his fellow maroons, surrendered to the Spaniards and cooperated with them in pursuing and capturing maroons. Cerrato, the lawyer, returned to
Spain in 1548 with the belief that the maroon uprisings had
been completely suppressed, but a new rebellion began
shortly after his departure.

There were two bands—that of Captain Lemba, made up
of 140 Negroes, and another one which had been discovered at the beginning of May in the Province of Higüey,
and which had existed unnoticed for more than 15 years
in the mountains by the sea. An expedition was sent to
defeat the first band. Most of the fugitives were either
captured, killed, or brought to justice, so that Lemba was
left with fewer than 20 men. However, despite the reduction of his forces, he continued his highwayman tactics.
He was finally killed in September. Only 6 or 7 of his men

escaped, and these probably joined the 15 who had just
rebelled in la Vega [Saco 1938].

Meanwhile, on the mainland, the

maroons of Darien elected a king whom they called Bayano
(according to Herrera, who probably was thinking of
Vallano, the name of their capital). . . . Viceroy Cañete
sent an expedition after them, but, at the Negroes' urging,
concluded a peace treaty with them which included provisions that were even rather generous. The maroons would
be free, providing they refused to admit any newcomers
and returned them to their rightful owners. Any Negro
who was mistreated by his master would be allowed to
buy his freedom for the same price that his master had
paid for him. And finally, the maroons would be free men
but would be bound, like every Spaniard, to the statutes
of the *Laws of the Indies* [de Madariaga 1950].

Cuban slaves rebelled against slavery from the very beginning of the colonial period. They would flee to the mountains in order to defend themselves from slave hunters,
called *rancheadores*, who used fierce hunting dogs to find
them even in the most sheltered *palenques* [maroon communities, literally "palisades" or "stockades"]. The punishments
were terrible. In 1553, Governor Manuel de Rojas captured
and killed four maroons in the mines of Jobabo. "He took
their corpses to Bayamo, where they were cut up and their
heads were placed on tall stakes, according to a report from
Rojas to the Emperor on November 10, 1534" (Ortiz 1916).
Whenever they saw an opportunity to avenge their ill
treatment, the slaves would join the forces of Spain's enemies.
For instance, the slaves helped French pirates sack the city
of Havana in 1538. Moreover, slaves of southwestern sugar
plantations rebelled and proclaimed their freedom when the
English Viceadmiral, Hossier, sailed past the port of Havana
in 1726. In 1731, as a result of the serious maltreatment of
slaves by the administrators and supervisors of the governors
of Santiago de Cuba, there was a slave uprising at the Cobre
mines, where they proclaimed their freedom.

Colonel Pedro Giménez was governor of Santiago de Cuba
at the time of this uprising. And even though the rebellion

was suppressed, they never gave up the desire to be free, and so continued for many years to disturb the peace and tranquility of that province until they were finally granted total freedom. . . . [Saco 1938].

In Cuba, the *palenques* were, for many years, the only signs of resistance to the colonial system . . . a virile protest against the infamies of slavery. Already by 1788, according to Baron Alejandro de Humboldt in *Ensayo Político sobre la Isla de Cuba,* "there were large numbers of maroons on the Jaruco mountains living in *palenques* surrounded by trenches and stockades which served as a means of protection."

According to the minutes of the Cabildo of Santiago de Cuba on February 28, 1815, a council member reported that maroons had formed a *palenque* of over 200 cabins near the city. The most famous maroon in Santiago de Cuba was undoubtedly Ventura Sánchez, nicknamed Coba. His influence was so strong that the *Morning Chronicle* (Archivo Nacional, Correspondencia de los Capitanes Generales, Legajo 239, No. 1), an English newspaper, reported on September 20, 1819, that 320 Negroes had assembled and had asked for their freedom and for some property rights. It claimed "that the Governor had consented to these demands" and, moreover, that the rebels' slogan was *Tierra y Libertad!* ["Land and Liberty!"].

The truth is that Brigadier Eusebio Escudero, governor of Santiago de Cuba, sent a priest (the parish priest J. L. Manfugás) to talk with Ventura Sánchez, the leader of the rebels. Sánchez had organized a full-scale operation with hundreds of runaway slaves or *apalencados,* who subsisted mainly by the sale of wax and other articles, which were sold in Jamaica and Haiti with the help of white merchants. Through Father Manfugás, Sánchez asked the governor to recognize the freedom of the rebel slaves and to give them land for themselves and for their families. A delegation of maroons traveled to Santiago de Cuba in order to seal the agreement. The authorities of the city were in charge of caring for them and housing them. With faith in Governor Escudero's word, Sánchez relaxed his personal security, and a band of slave hunters was able to surprise him in December 1819. However, he chose to commit suicide rather than return to slavery. His head was taken to Baracoa where it was displayed in an iron cage at the entrance to the city. Brigadier Escudero immediately reported to the military governor of the island (Juan Manuel de Cagigal) what he thought was a victory over the Negro rebels. The following is de Cagigal's acknowledgment of having received Escudero's report on January 24, 1820:

I have received your notice (no. 700) and an attached copy by the Lieutenant Governor of Baracoa announcing the capture of the supreme leader of the maroons, Ventura Sánchez (alias Coba), and of one of his companions, who chose to drown in the Quiviján River rather than surrender [Archivo Nacional, Correspondencia de los Capitanes Generales, Legajo 141, No. 1].

One of those white merchants who traded with the *palenques* in the eastern region of Cuba—according to a report on July 31, 1819, written by Luis de Arrúe, lieutenant governor of Baracoa—was an Italian named Luis Rufo, a native of Genoa. With a small boat, he would take clothes, shoes, hats, machetes, and other articles to a place on the coast called Sagua, in order to sell his merchandise to the maroons. There was a *palenque* there that had been organized under the leadership of Manuel Griñán (alias Gallo). Gallo used to deposit the money, which he obtained from his trade with Rufo and from the sale of crops from the maroons' gardens, with Juan Sabón, another white merchant from Santa Catalina who chartered boats to Haiti (ibid., Legajo 139, No. 1).

Since it was easy for the masses of slaves in the Caribbean to maintain contact with each other, the authorities always feared the spread of the periodic attempts at rebellion throughout the Caribbean. For instance, Francisco de Zayas, lieutenant governor of Holguín, wrote back to the governor of Santiago de Cuba on March 22, 1824, saying the following:

Taking note of your preventive order issued this past February (which was generated by some well-founded fears that slaves who participated in the revolutionary conspiracy attempted on the island of Jamaica would be illegally brought to Cuba), I have ordered the Captains of the Coastal Districts to be especially aware of this possibility [ibid., Legajo 179, No. 4].

One lived in constant fear. Almost any news at all generated panic among the owners of the coffee and sugar plantations. They would send for help at the drop of a hat, because they feared the just revenge of the oppressed against their barbaric practices. For example, the rumor reaching Santiago de Cuba on April 28, 1827, that the slaves on the San Cayetano plantation—belonging to Juan Angola—were playing the drums for six continuous hours on holidays as well as on workdays, and that meetings of more than forty Negroes were being permitted, caused the governor to dispatch special orders by post to Captain Tomás Betancourt Ferrer to prevent such occurrences (ibid., Legajo 204, No. 1).

The *palenques* of Bumba and Maluala grew so rapidly that on June 11, 1830, Antonio León, military commander of Mayarí, summoned a meeting of settlers and slave owners where, among other things, he reported that

> there are 4 main *palenques* (to our knowledge) in the central area of the Río Seco and Piloto valley, and there are many more located between Cabonico and Sagua and their surroundings. . . . Less than two months ago, 30 Negroes had the audacity to come to this town and walk as far as the Ingenio San Gregorio. . . .

In the same month of July, the already familiar Commander Antonio de León recounted the military operations carried out against these maroons:

> Anxious to explore the *palenque* which Ramón Hernández had described to me, I looked for someone to supply me with 50 pesos with which to equip my forces; and armed with some gunpowder, lead for our bullets, and the few guns of varied caliber which our troops already had, I considered myself ready for the expedition. . . . On July 4, I sent out a group to keep a watch on all the neighboring roads so that the Negroes would not be able to send for help. At 2:00 P.M. on July 5, I fired a cannonball, and chose 50 of my men to accompany me en route to the *palenque*. We left at 3:00 P.M. and stopped to sleep at Bengan Sábalos—approximately 3 leagues from here. On the morning of the sixth, I left, rested at Arroyo Seco at 4 leagues from Bengan Sábalos, and at 3:00 P.M. continued on foot through cliffs and rugged mountains. We

arrived at Arroyo de Naranjo at dusk and stayed there for the night. At 2:00 P.M. on the seventh, we continued the march with the thought of surprising the *palenque* at dawn. But after walking for an hour with great effort, we got lost and could not proceed. We then waited till sunrise, and followed the banks of a tributary of the Río Frío. At seven, we saw the *palenque*—which must be located two leagues from Naranjo—and we approached it until we could distinctly hear what the Negroes were saying (even though we could see neither them nor their huts). I then sent Lieutenant Ignacio Leyte Vidal with two scouts and 30 men for the rearguard, reserving the frontal assault for myself. I hid long enough for the lieutenant to emplace himself, and in a half hour I began the attack. A few steps forward and I found myself in a ditch full of pointed sticks. However, we overcame this first obstacle without being heard. The second obstacle seemed insuperable: this was the climbing of a steep, rugged hill, covered with *tibisí*, which had two very narrow, winding paths that we followed, endlessly. We had already climbed a good third of the way, when at a turn of the path we encountered a Negro who, armed with a machete, attacked the first man in line. The latter, having already loaded his gun, fired a shot, whose report was heard throughout the rocky area. The Negro tried to run away but was too badly wounded and bleeding to go far. The sound of the shot caused the other Negroes on the hill to disperse. These then fled to the opposite side of the hill overcoming cliffs that have to be seen to be believed. We redoubled our pace, but when, out of breath and tired we reached the top, the only traces of them we could find were the pieces of cloth caught on the thorns in the bushes. After having walked through most of the area and having cleared numerous obstacles, Lieutenant Vidal found himself ready to retrace his steps, since he did not want to attack the *palenque* by himself. He then joined me at the first Negro cabin which we were already occupying. Leaving 10 of my men there, I ordered the rest to spread out in groups of four in order to explore the territory. They found up to 17 huts containing about 30 beds. We stayed there until 3:00 o'clock when I called a false retreat thinking I would hide on the hill and then return to the *palenque* at night, dividing the group up according to the information we had already gathered. But within a short while, we heard them talking in their huts, so I sent a group of men down there. They were able to capture one of the two Negroes they saw. The other escaped by way of one of their secret paths, and even though we fired a few shots we never found out whether or not we had hit him. Twenty men stayed there all night long while I returned to Naranjo. The captured Negro insisted on helping us capture the other Negroes, told our men where to stand for greater efficiency, and used a whistle to call his fellow maroons. They answered his call but did not come out. Due to a lack of food, the twenty men retreated to Arroyo Seco at dawn on July 8, where they met me some time before noon that day. We went to Bengan Sábalos to spend the night, and finally arrived here without any further incidents. The *palenque* is almost invulnerable if the Negroes get the firearms (which they now lack) in order to defend it. As I have already said, it is located on a hill covered with very thick *tibisí*; the huts are so spread out that it is only possible to surprise 2 or 3 at one time. They are so low that they cannot be seen over the bushes and cannot be detected except at a very close distance. Each hut has 2 doors with a small clearing on each side. The last-captured Negro calls himself Josef Antonio and belongs to the Countess of Santa Ignes. He says that this *palenque* is called Bumba, and that its inhabitants are related by kinship to those of the *palenque* of Maluala. Between these two *palenques,* there are three others called Rincón, Tibisial, and la Palma, which they commonly use as resting places. He has not told us the exact number of Negroes living in Bumba, but has given us the names of those he remembers. . . . He added that some of them traded with Don Rafael Peregrín from Arroyo Seco, and others with people at the Hacienda de Lagunita. They take their wax to these places to exchange them for the supplies they need. He said that three of his companions were now there trading. He has offered to take our men to these *palenques* and situate them so strategically that no Negro could escape. He offers to do this in exchange for his freedom. El Peregrín has confessed to me that they have traded wax with his son in exchange for clothes and tobacco, and that while he was there, nearly 40 of them offered to weed the banana grove and do other chores. . . . But he refused . . . [ibid., Legajo 230, No. 2].

On October 4, 1830, a few months after these events, Antonio de León, military commander of Mayarí, raided and burned down the *palenque* of Bumba after having extensively explored the Platanal de Naranjo and the Montes de Río Frío. The inhabitants of the *palenque* then sought refuge in the *palenque* of Moa (ibid.).

In a pamphlet entitled *Palenques de Negros Cimarrones* (which serves as an introduction to the diary of maroon hunter Francisco Estévez during the period 1837–42), Cirilo Villaverde describes the westernmost region of Cuba, where there were a number of *palenques* at that time. He also describes how Dr. Lucas Villaverde, his father, and rancher Máximo Arozarena strove to help Estévez persecute maroons in San Diego de Núñez (Villaverde 1890).

The major concern of the colonial government of Cuba was the persecution of maroons and the destruction of *palenques,* even after the first half of the nineteenth century. The Royal Consulate and the Executive and Permanent Military Commission of the Island of Cuba devoted most of their time and energy to suppressing slave rebellions and to preventing the development, among the masses of free and enslaved Negroes, of any ideas of freedom or advancement from the miserable living conditions that they bore. The Royal Consulate, from 1795 to 1801, made studies concerning "security measures for the Negroes in general, and in particular for those who had been brought to Cuba from foreign colonies" (Archivo Nacional, Real Consulado 6 Junta de Fomento, Legajo 492, No. 18, 659). From 1797 to 1846, the Office for the Capture of Maroons, an affiliate of this organization, reported the existence of thousands of runaway slaves, the capture of many of these, and their incarceration in special *Depósitos* [prisons] for Maroons (ibid., Legajo 140, No. 6, 888).

On February 17, 1820, the Government Council of the Royal Consulate in Havana agreed to give ten thousand pesos to support the plans proposed by the governor of Santiago de Cuba, Brigadier Eusebio Escudero, to destroy the numerous *palenques* in the eastern mountains (Archivo Nacional, Correspondencia de los Capitanes Generales, Legajo 142, No. 1). The Royal Consulate financed the official expeditions sent out to attack the hundreds of *palenques* in existence throughout the island. In the west alone they included: Lomas de Guane, El Rubí, El Brujo, Sierra de Villalta, Cuzco, San Diego de Núñez, Cayajabos, and others, in Piñar del Río; Guatao, Jaruco, Guanabo, Camoa, Rincón de Sibarimar, Ciénaga de Cajío, Guanimar, and others, in the province of Havana; Ciénaga de Zapata, Ensenada de Cochinos, Corral Nuevo, Guamacaro, Guamutas, Hanábana, and many others in Las Villas and Matanzas. The eastern mountains, however, harbored more permanent *palenques*, including the Moa, Maluala, Bumba, and Tiguabos *palenques*, which lasted till the beginning of the first War of Independence in 1868, when the maroons joined en masse the ranks of the Cuban Liberation Army. Between 1852 and 1854, one of the mountain *palenques* in the district of Baracoa forced the Spanish authorities to mobilize their military forces to destroy it (ibid., Legajo 146, No. 7, 229). Finally, the importance and influence on slaves of the indomitable rebelliousness of the maroons—guardians of the flag of liberation—forced the Royal Consulate to adopt extraordinary measures from 1848 to 1853 to attempt the extinction of *palenques* (ibid., Legajo 146, No. 7, 166).

REFERENCES NOT CITED IN GENERAL BIBLIOGRAPHY

Fortoul, José Gil
    1942 *Historia constitucional de Venezuela* (3re edición). Caracas.
Liscano, Juan
    1950 *Folklore y cultura.* Caracas.
de Madariaga, Salvador
    1950 *Cuadro histórico de las Indias.* Buenos Aires: Editorial Sudamericana.
Saco, José Antonio
    1938 *Historia de la esclavitud de la raza Africana en el nuevo mundo.* La Habana: Colección de Libros Cubanos.
Schoelcher, Victor
    1948 *Esclavage et colonisation.* Paris.
Villaverde, Cirilo
    1890 *Palenques de negros cimarrones.* San Antonio de los Baños.

CHAPTER TWO

Cuban Palenques

FRANCISCO PÉREZ DE LA RIVA

The flight of those oppressed by slavery, Indians and Negroes alike, began with the introduction of slavery itself. . . .
In their search for a sanctuary where they would be safe
from persecution, capture, and punishment, runaway slaves
sought refuge in the least familiar wilderness areas, in the
most remote places. At first, they led a nomadic-style existence, but later they began to settle down in more permanent
communities. These were protected by a series of covered
traps and all sorts of other obstacles that helped to camou-
flage these wilderness settlements. The existence of any particular community could only really be confirmed when the
betrayal of one of its inhabitants led to a surprise attack.
Such a conglomeration of dispersed huts became known as a
palenque [see Ch. One].

The stockades surrounding these *palenques* were hidden
and not out in the open, and there were always other means
of protection as well, which made the *palenques* almost inaccessible. There were few traces of Indians left in the later
palenques, since the aboriginal race was destroyed soon after
the conquest. The few who survived were so intermixed with
the whites and Negroes that they lost their native traits and
customs.

However, during the numerous Indian uprisings that occurred while Diego Valázquez was governor (and perhaps
later as well), some of them were able to flee to remote sites

From Francisco Pérez de la Riva, *La habitación rural en Cuba*. La
Habana: Contribución del Grupo Guamá, Antropología No. 26,
1952. Translated from pp. 20–28.

and found hidden settlements, with huts dispersed in such a way that they could resist attacks by Spanish *conquistadores* even when they were outnumbered. There are many documents describing these uprisings. In 1543, a letter from Hernando de Castro of Santiago de Cuba reads as follows:

> During the 20 years I have lived in Cuba we have had to spend money each year to pacify and conquer wild or maroon Indians. They go to the wilderness each year and come out at Christmastime, which is in the dry season, burning ranches, killing Spaniards as well as domesticated Indians, and stealing women.

In an even earlier report, in 1530, Lucas Vázquez de Ayellón transcribed an eyewitness declaration testifying that "there is a settlement of rebellious Indians in Trinidad as well as others near Bayamo, Baracoa, and Santiago." Other documents state that the Indians living in these communities practiced agriculture, a fact that implies that there must have been fairly permanent settlements shared by Indians and Negro maroons. The minutes of the Cabildo meeting held in Santiago de Cuba in 1529 refer to an uprising in which seven honest Spanish settlers and *conquistadores*, as well as some Indians and Negroes, lost their lives. Several estates and herds of cattle were also destroyed. There is a reference in the minutes of the Cabildo of 1530 stating that Guamá, an Indian from Baracoa who lived with many other Indian runaways, "had quite a few cultivated lands in the wilderness."

A plan that was called "the Experiment" was devised with the thought of trying to incorporate the Indians into the life of the colony. It entailed placing them in settlements that would prevent their being dispersed throughout the territory. This gave birth to the towns of Guanabacoa, Jiguarí, Caney, and so forth, and gave rise to the distinction between what was called a town of "domesticated Indians" [*indios mansos*] and a hamlet of "wild or maroon Indians" [*indios bravos o cimarrónes*]. From then on, the endeavors to destroy the hamlets never ceased. However, because of their extreme degree of mobility, the hamlets increased in number with the influx of runaway slaves and criminals, and with the passage of time they became permanent communities. These eventually gave rise to nuclei of the Cuban peasant population of today, which is dispersed throughout the most distant areas

of the country, despite having lost in most cases all traces of
its Indian heritage.

In 1541, the growth in the number of rebel Indians and
the increasing difficulty of finding them in their mountain
hideouts led to the conclusion that the best way to fight them
was to organize bands of free, loyal Indians who, for this
purpose, would be even more efficient than the Spanish
troops. The Indians serving in these bands received monthly
salaries. One of their chiefs, killed in action, was highly
honored in Santiago de Cuba in 1542. The government
proctors of this city said "that he had acquired much prestige by destroying an Indian hamlet located in the rugged
sierra where, in a trying battle, he had killed many of its
inhabitants, had captured others whom he had taken back
to the city where they were tried."

Despite the fact that we do not know what these [early]
hamlets looked like (because we have not found any description of them in the literature), we suppose that they did not
differ much from those built by the maroon Negroes later on
and that were called by the generic name *palenque*. . . .

Once the island had been pacified and the aboriginal population had almost been destroyed, the hamlets of the wilderness began to be nourished with the influx of runaway
Negro slaves. The existence and proliferation of these settlements began to worry the colonists as early as the late eighteenth century.

While the *palenques* in the western provinces or depart-
ments were at first few in number and short-lived due to the
existence of more efficient security measures by the colonial
government and to the smaller size of the maroon population
there, the *palenques* of the east were more fortified and
better hidden because of the inefficiency and carelessness of
the estate administrators in that area, as well as because of
the existence of frequent contact between the runaways and
plantation slaves (which was condoned by the overseers and
others left by absentee masters to care for their estates).

The first step in organizing these *palenques* was the election of a captain or a chief. This leader was then placed in
complete charge of life in the *palenque*, and behaved as if
he were its owner and master. He was elected on the grounds
that he was the most courageous, the most cunning, or the
one who was most familiar with the region. After selecting the
site for the settlement, these leaders or captains then pro-

ceeded to plan the defense of the *palenque*. Brigadier Escudero, in charge of their persecution in the east, said they had the custom of opening false paths (leading to their *palenques*), which were sown with very sharp stakes of *cuaba* wood. Each stake was ringed horizontally by a crack, which allowed the top to separate from the main body (which was implanted in the ground) whenever someone pricked himself with it. The stakes were covered with hay so that they could not be pulled out except by using some sort of tool. The use of these protective devices spread throughout the island, but it was more typical at the larger *palenques*. Captain Ramón Flores de Apodaca, while pursuing maroons on the southern coast near Patabano where the "Ingenio Morenita" is located, was able to surprise a *palenque* that was

> built with such art and so many obstacles that it was impossible for them to keep the Negroes from making their escape, despite having done everything in their power to cut off their flight. They, nevertheless, captured 2 maroons who had been attacked by the Spaniards' hunting dogs,

taking fourteen spears, four machetes, four large straw baskets with magical paraphernalia and other trivia, and killed Mariano Mandinga, one of the Negro leaders who had been living in *palenques* for years.

These traps of sharp stakes were easily recovered and saved by the Negroes when they escaped, even though they were an embarrassment and an obstacle to their pursuers, for they were located in dug-out pits covered with hay at intervals along the paths. It was easy for the Negroes to recover the stakes because they were not only extremely speedy in their flight, but they were also familiar with their surroundings. Their pursuers, on the other hand, had to pick their way about with utmost care, always fearing with every step they took that they—horse, rider, and hunting dog alike—might fall into one of the pits and be seriously hurt by the sharp prongs.

Once the *palenque* was formed, the leader selected the men who would make up his band, instituting the system of killing any maroon who would not defend himself from pursuers in order to eliminate any possibility of betrayal. The maroons also would not let anyone leave the *palenque* until he had spent at least two years in their company following his escape from the plantations. According to the information gathered by the captain of the district of Cayajabo, who was in charge of their persecution in Vuelta Abajo, the maroons would even kill newborn babies to insure that they would not be discovered by the babies' crying.

The *palenque* itself consisted of fifteen to twenty huts made of twigs and mud, which often grew into larger, somewhat dispersed settlements built and hidden in the bush, to the extent that it was possible to walk right by one of them without even noticing its existence. They practiced horticulture near the huts and in natural or man-made clearings, and nourished themselves with their produce. Manioc and sweet potato were preferred, and meat was secured through the theft of cattle from neighboring estates. When the Negroes went to battle, they would always leave a few of their men behind in the *palenque* to take care of the crops, to cover for them in case of retreat, or to inform the others in case of a surprise attack. The maroons' raids were basically aimed at getting gunpowder and weapons as well as at creating panic in the district, which would make the owners leave their estates, and would give the maroons time to trade freely with the overseers and other white people of questionable reputation who were spread throughout the countryside. They would later return to the *palenque* because of the security they felt there and because they had a better knowledge of the terrain—not because they claimed any sovereign title over the land or because of any preconceived over-all plan.

The main commerce of the *palenques* was the sale of virgin wax and honey, which they got by cutting the honeycombs from beehives in the forest, and exchanging them for sugar, clothing, gunpowder, weapons, and other tools they lacked, through the overseers of the neighboring farms, who accepted the transactions despite the fact that they knew where the goods were coming from. Sometimes the maroons could not barter directly, since the things they needed the most, such as gunpowder for their guns, had to be bought in the towns or at roadside stores, which were rarely visited by the *apalencados*. In those cases, trade was carried out by means of slaves on neighboring plantations who agreed to pick up the wax and the honey at a predetermined site and to deposit, at the same site, the money made on the sale. This money was handed over to the captains of the *palenques* who, in turn, buried it in earthen jugs or demijohns where no one else would know about it. Frequently, this money was lost when the leader died or the *palenque* was hastily abandoned. This gave birth to the legend, now well known throughout the farms in Cuba, that there is buried money somewhere on each farm. Many people have actually found such "burials" [*entierros*], as the peasants still call them, and treat the matter with prudence and circumspection. In many cases, these discoveries can be attributed to the burial practices of the liberating armies that bivouacked in the countryside, or of families who had to vacate their homes because of war or even pirates. But most of the time, they are simply a testimony to the one-time location there of an ancient *palenque*. The commercial transactions and the transfer of money were carried out with the highest degree of honesty due to fear of denunciation or of the always fierce reprisals of the *apalencados*.

Some of these *palenques* grew strong and lasted for many years, later becoming centers of urban population, which gave rise to several of our contemporary rural towns. A specific example is the Poblado del Cobre in Oriente Province. It is inhabited by the descendants of those slaves who were seized in 1637 by the Real Hacienda following the administration of Eguily, who had been a concessionaire of the copper mines. The governor of Santiago de Cuba, Don Pedro Jiménez, forced the inhabitants of this town to work in the mines, since he regarded them as descendants of those slaves who had become royal property upon their capture. These people revolted in 1731, taking possession of the Sierra del Cobre, where they remained until 1781 with the help of machetes, whips, and guns. By 1781, the original slaves had multiplied and reached a population size of 1,065, which was dispersed throughout the sierra forming scattered villages, as well as maintaining a stable nucleus, which is now the town of El Cobre. Once the Council of the Indies decided to end the long series of claims and the strange situation created by those who were considered to be descendants of Eguily's slaves, it sent a report to the King on October 31 of that year (approved by the royal letter of April 7, 1800) in which the inhabitants of El Cobre, the descendants of slaves, were declared free. They, however, remained living in the town and on the surrounding land leading the same type of life that they had led for generations. . . .

Another *palenque* that achieved fame because of its duration and its leaders' resistance was Bumba, near Santiago de Cuba [see also Ch. One]. Its captains, Cobas, Agustín, and Gallo, were even able to force Governor Escudero to sign a treaty with them offering them freedom and the right to continue working the land on which they lived, in exchange for their agreement to hand over other maroons. This treaty was not observed by either side, and the betrayal of one of the leaders of the *palenque* led to the execution of its captains, who were captured by the authorities. Bumba was so well organized that it was able to trade not only with neighboring estates but even with the adjoining islands of Santo Domingo and Jamaica by way of small boats, whose owners maintained contact with them.

In Oriente, other equally famous *palenques* at the beginning of the nineteenth century were the great *palenque* of Moa or El Frijol (mentioned by Bacardí in his *Chronicles of Santiago de Cuba*) and others in the Ciénaga de Zapata, where one can still find rocks bearing the names of various Negroes.

During the first half of the nineteenth century a new factor, namely piracy, brought life to the *palenques*. Some of those near the coast were used as sanctuaries for the wounded and as hideaways for stolen merchandise. Others were founded with better organization than before, and often with the knowledge of corrupt local authorities. Father Varela described the situation throughout the Island of Cuba in the following way:

The government of Cuba, whether weak or indifferent (for I do not dare call it an accomplice, which is what some people suspect), does not put an end to this evil which grows each day . . . to the point where it seems that the pirates have now become a feared nation, even if they have not yet been recognized by any government. It is generally known that the pirates are not the only ones to go out to sea. They are accompanied by the buyers of the products, who stimulate these enterprises with their greedy and criminal conduct. Everyone knows who these buyers are—except for the government, which is only concerned with recapturing slaves, who refuse to recognize that they are, in fact, slaves.

Some pirates—Lafitte, for instance—built their own *palenques* along the coast, as can be inferred from a May 15, 1822, letter written by Juan Xavier de Arrambarri, a colonist from Puerto Príncipe who used to know Lafitte. This letter (which was found by historian José Luciano Franco) was attached to a report sent to Nicholás Mahy, the captain general. Among other things, it states:

The question of whether Lafitte received help from anyone and, if so, the place where he found it, can be answered easily, since it is public knowledge that he left Nuevitas with a number of men and, with a small boat, boarded an English schooner, taking with him a cannon, a sail, and other objects. He likewise took an American schooner en route from Cayo de Sal to Guanaja, completely sacking it. The reports now say that he has settled on land, building himself a *palenque* armed with two cannons, and maintaining a fleet of 5 small boats with which he will undoubtedly bring much harm, especially if he captures a seaworthy ship—which is possible.

According to Franco, the historian,

the end of piracy, which was due to the impossibility of maintaining organized high-seas robbery, led these men, with all their repulsive cruelty, to engage, in great numbers, in slave trading. They raised this commerce in contraband human flesh and the practice of bribing the captains of slave ships to the category of a lucrative, official activity which enriched the colonial administrators and their lackeys. The beaches, keys, and bays which the pirates had used throughout the first 30 years of the nineteenth century for their illegal transactions must have later been turned into unloading stations for the large cargoes of men and women which they stole on African soil, once they became slave-dealers and had bought the backing of the Cuban and Puerto Rican authorities. By participating in the slave trade, the pirates of the Caribbean prolonged for another 30 years the most extraordinary history of sea adventurers in modern times.

During this whole period, the *palenques* functioned as centers for their activities and as sanctuaries and storage places for their illegal trade.

The Archivo Nacional has numerous reports and communications which describe the *palenques* with their scattered cabins, their plots of cultivated land hidden in the surrounding wilderness, and their defense based on pits full of forked poles of hard wood with very sharp points placed at short distances from each other. Life there was very rudimentary and primitive. Men and women lived in absolute promiscuity and were dominated by their leaders (whom they called captains) and by the sorcerer or *santéro*, who would at times function as witchdoctor.

Neither all the leaders nor all the inhabitants of *palenques* were Negroes. Even though the *palenques* consisted mostly of runaway Negroes or maroons, they also served to harbor fugitives from justice, habitual criminals, and pirates involved in smuggling and trading. In some cases, the heads of *palenques* were either whites or Yucatecan Indians. A fact which supports this contention is that in 1797, one of the captured leaders of a *palenque* near Jaruco was reported to be Huachinango Pablo, a Yucatecan Indian.

When the *apalencados* were not able to get the goods they lacked by way of their illegal trade, they would round up several bands of maroons, and with great agility would cross hills and wilderness for up to twenty to forty miles in order to raid an estate, a sugar mill, or a coffee plantation, taking with them whatever they needed . . . especially bags, clothing, guns, and so forth. By using violence, they would force Negro slaves on these plantations to follow them. This happened in 1815, in the east, when sixty Negroes from a *palenque* on the San Andrés mountain attacked and sacked several coffee plantations at night and took with them slaves and provisions.

The fight against the *palenques* of maroon Negroes was intensified during the first half of the nineteenth century. Bands of *rancheadores* [slave hunters], equipped with dogs trained to pursue maroons, were formed, and prizes of money or promotions were awarded to those who succeeded in capturing or destroying a *palenque*. The merciless persecution of which they were the object, the growth and the development of the sugar industry, the clearing of the forests, and finally the wars of independence led to the end of the old *palenques*. Some were transformed into nuclei of houses, where their peaceful inhabitants continued to lead a primitive and isolated life in the same place where they had built their original cabins. Some *apalencados* became unsociable, rejecting all contact with the neighboring populations, to the extent that we still use *"coger monte"* [to take to the bush] to express extreme bashfulness.

This indolent, scattered peasant population, which had no roots, was a neutral and passive element in our wars of independence. When dislodged by gunfire, they joined the liberating armies in which they served in the "supply trains," and when located in towns or in the capital, they obeyed the orders given by Valmaseda and Weyler, dying of hunger without showing any signs of rebelliousness.

The 1868 decree of the liberators that abolished slavery recognized the existence of the *palenques* and decreed that:

> the slaves inhabiting *palenques* who present themselves to the Cuban authorities shall, of course, be declared free and will have the right to live amongst us or continue living in their mountain towns, as they wish, recognizing and respecting the Government of the Republic.

Having justly obtained their freedom, most of the *apalencados* did not move away from their *palenques*. The birth of a nation did not mean very much to them, and there was no significant difference in their miserable existence. Their towns were renovated and enlarged with the influx of white peasants who sought refuge in them, mostly because they would be out of the reach of the authorities, of legal stipulations, and of the hindrances of the law. The land abandoned by absent owners very often became living sites for those who lacked everything and were satisfied with little. The *conucos* [horticultural plots] and other cultivated lands occupied an extensive geographical territory, but were fairly isolated from each other. The feeling of uncertainty increased since they could not count on economic resources. This led to their bitter fight against the owners of large farms, in which they ranged themselves solidly against the agricultural development of the island.

Because of their geographical location and the new means

of communication, some of these old *palenques* gave rise to towns or rural neighborhoods, which later grew so much that they lost all trace or influence of the primitive *palenque*, except for the African origin of their names, such as Palenque; Barrio de Ato Songo; Palenque in Santiago de Cuba; the "barrio" [neighborhood] of Consolación del Sur in Piñar del Río; Bamba, now called Jovellanos; and so forth.

Once the *palenques* had ceased to exist, or had at least lost their importance and their image as something to be feared, many of their inhabitants established themselves on small farms scattered throughout the countryside, where many traditions of the *palenque* still prevail.

CHAPTER THREE

Hunting the Maroons
with Dogs in Cuba

DEMOTICUS PHILALETHES

I think you would like to read the account of a *rancheria* which I witnessed. It is a regular hunt of those negros who run away from the plantations and assemble in the interior of woods, building very imperfectly a *rancho* (hut), which only serves to keep off the rain. Sometimes several *ranchos* are seen together according to the number of runaways; and when they secure places of difficult access, they rapidly increase and form *palenques*, or villages, where they cultivate roots and bananas for their food, which together with the animals they catch with traps, or steal from neighboring plantations, afford them sufficient nourishment. There are permanent *palenques* in the mountains of *El Cobre* and *El Cuzco*, which the government has not been able to break up, notwithstanding their having been many years in existence, and troops having been repeatedly sent to dislodge them.

Rancherias are regular palenques, though on a smaller scale, of from ten to twenty negros. They live on the vegetables, pigs, and poultry which they steal during the night; they are almost entirely naked; their arms are the spades or cutlasses with which they work, and they carry commonly with them *chuzos*, or long sticks of hard wood sharpened and scorched at the end, to render them still harder. They seldom make use of arrows, and more seldom yet secure the services of a gun.

From Demoticus Philalethes, *Yankee Travels Through the Island of Cuba*. New York: D. Appleton and Co., 1856, pp. 38–42.

I was in a sugar plantation in the *"Vuelta de Abajo,"* called "La Tumba," and one evening the party of the famous *ranchador* "Pepe Torres" arrived. It comprised three men and five dogs. Their object was to make a descent on a *rancheria,* about three miles from the plantation, of from twelve to fifteen negros, headed by a native *chino* (light-colored negro), who it was known had a sword, and had obtained the renown of *guapo* (courageous). The *ranchadores* carried swords, and a knife in its case, tied in a belt.

I did not wish to lose this opportunity of witnessing a hunting party of this description, and though I took with me my sword and gun, I made up my mind not to take any active part, but remain neutral as long as possible. My companions agreed that I should accompany them on those terms, and we started an hour before sunrise (Ave Maria). The dogs were tied in pairs with a rope, both ends of which were in the hands of the *ranchador,* and passed through the rings of their collars, so that by loosening one end only they were liberated. Pepe Torres had only one, which besides being tied, was muzzled. On entering the woods it was difficult to restrain the dogs; they had already scented the runaways, and pulled the strings vigorously.

I was behind the other *ranchadores.* Presently I observed two huts, in one of which a fire was brightly blazing: by its light I espied a naked negro with a coal in his hand in the act of lighting his pipe. His back was turned towards us.

At this moment (the morning's dawn), we heard the barking of a small dog, and four or five negros rushed suddenly from the huts evidently alarmed. On seeing them, one of our dogs barked, and they shouted and began to run. Shortly afterwards, others issued from both huts, stumbling as if they had been sleeping, and commenced also flying in all directions. Our three men rushed to the huts, and the dogs which pulled most strenuously, increased their velocity. Pepe Torres, with sword in hand, entered the first hut; the other two the second, and I slowly approached the door where the first named was, and saw two negros on their knees, and one lying on the ground, struggling with the dog, which in spite of the muzzle, bit him very often. Pepe Torres gave one of them a rope to tie the other in such a manner as to make the elbows come close together on the back; and this done, he tied himself with the other end of the rope, the arms of that one who had done the same to the first; he then called the dog and

bade him to go to a corner, kicking him at the same time; the
animal growled and obeyed; the third was also tied, and he
helped the three to lay on the ground face downwards. The
two *ranchadores,* who had found nobody in the other hut,
followed the others. As Pepe was hurrying out of the second
hut, I saw a *chuzo* passing about three inches from my eyes,
and heard soon after the dog howling, as the instrument had
scratched one of his legs, and blood was trickling from the
wound. Pepe Torres commenced swearing, and said that he
would revenge the wound of his dog, and taking him by the
collar went in the direction marked by the *chuzo* so swiftly
that I could hardly follow him. The dog readily found the
track, and notwithstanding his lameness, we lost sight of him.
We went on, and after a short interval, heard him barking.
Pepe ran, and also disappeared; but I heard the dog's voice
and it served me as a guide.

The sun was already shining, and I had just emerged
from the wood: a thick row of *cañas bravas* (reeds) was before me; I was about to pass through them, when I saw on
the other side a pond, in the center of which a mulatto was
standing with the water rising to his waist, without any hat,
but a handkerchief tied round the head, and a long sword in
his hand. He had his back turned towards me, and on the opposite border Torres was standing, so that I remained unperceived. The runaway defied the guajiro, making a proposal that he should tie the dog, and he would then meet
him in single combat. He did it quickly and the other began to emerge from the pond. The resolute *ranchador* was
waiting at the top of the height unconcerned, so that the
other had to ascend in order to attack him. This he was doing
most undauntedly, notwithstanding the disadvantage, when
the dog, which had been jumping and barking, and which
was not (perhaps purposely) well tied, got loose and rushed
towards him, when only six or eight paces from Torres. On
turning round to defend himself against the dog, Pepe
jumped and struck him with the sword, which entering the
right shoulder almost split the body in two, as the sword
would have cut the left hip if it had descended with a little
more force. I was touched at the treacherous murder of the
courageous mulatto, and hid myself from the sight of the
murderer. I, then, went back to the huts, where I found that
the number of prisoners had increased by three, which the
other *ranchadores,* whose names I do not recollect, had cap-

tured. Torres arrived shortly afterwards, bringing, as a trophy, the sword of his victim, and overflowing with joy at his exploit. He related the story in such a manner as to make me almost doubt the evidence of my own eyes; so highly colored was the sanguinary scene. They had been fighting over a quarter of an hour; he had been struck by the mulatto, two or three times with the back of the sword, and finally had split him in two. Neither the dog, which could claim an equal share of the triumph, nor I, who knew that all was false, denied his assertions. He, nevertheless, ought to have known, by my countenance, that I had seen everything. He recalled to my mind that inimitable creation of Shakespeare, "Swaggering *Jack Falstaff*," who with "hack'd sword," maintained mortal combat with his foes, "full seven hours by Shrewsbury clock."

Of the six runaways taken, only one belonged to the plantation "La Tumba": the others were from neighboring estates, where they were taken in order to collect four dollars *captura* (seizure) for each. I was requested to take to the plantation the one belonging to it; I accepted, and intended to loosen the rope with which he was tied, but thought that he could escape. I was very much annoyed; but the evil was caused by my promise. I concluded, then, to be at least his *padrino* (protector), and obtained the relinquishment of flogging, but could not prevent his being shackled, in order to avoid a second escape.

CHAPTER FOUR

Life in a Venezuelan Cumbe

MIGUEL ACOSTA SAIGNES

I would like next to discuss the *cumbe* [maroon village] of Ocoyta, which was destroyed in 1771 and whose lifestyle was described by its survivors.[1]

On October 25, 1771, Colonel Francisco de Arce, captain general of the province, commissioned Germán de Aguilera "to pursue and capture the Negro Guillermo and his companions, that is, the other fugitives, using as large a military force as he thought sufficient and the people whom he considered trustworthy." They were referring to Guillermo Ribas, a Negro slave owned by Magistrate Marcos de Ribas, who had been a runaway for a long time, and who had been the leader of many maroons in several *cumbes* from Panaquire to the coast. The captain general considered a concerted effort to eliminate him indispensable, for Guillermo had "taken possession of the Arboleda estate, a cocoa plantation owned by the Alayones in Panaquire, had evicted its overseer, caused the field hands to flee, and taken the cocoa from the barn. . . ."

On November 23, 1771, Juan Antonio Rodríguez and Bartolomé Núñez Villavicencio, on behalf of themselves and the other estate owners in Panaquire, Caucagua, Taguaza,

From Miguel Acosta Saignes, *Vida de los esclavos negros en Venezuela.* Caracas: Editorial Hesperides, 1961. Translated from pp. 285–95, and reprinted with the permission of the author and Editorial Hesperides.
[1] This information is in a document entitled "Criminal proceedings against the Negro Guillermo and his followers (also runaway slaves) for having settled on one of the mountains of Ocoyta in

and Capaya, offered the governor monetary support to help pursue Guillermo. However, such cooperation was not necessary. On the same day, the governor was notified that some of the inhabitants of Ocoyta had been killed and that others had been captured. Immediately, he ordered an investigation of the events. The declarations made by those who participated in the destruction of the *cumbe* provide information that can be used to reconstruct some of the characteristics of life there. José Alejandro Medina, a soldier under the command of the commissioned Germán de Aguilera, gave the following description:

> They [the troops] were situated near the maroons' cabins on a hill called Ocoyta in the ravine by the name of Perdenal in the Panaquire district . . . on Sunday, November 10. Guillermo left his hut and, with a short carbine pointed towards his people, called his companions and said: "boys, they're coming to get us." He took a powder-flask and with his carbine and his sabre ran out with the others—some of whom had no visible weapons. . . . They fired at them in closed formation killing Guillermo and Mina, another Negro. The rest then ran away, so that the Spaniards were only able to capture 8 adults (6 men and 2 women) and 4 children. Juan Isidro, one of the captives, was later wounded in Guarenas. . . . By the trail they left, we know some of those who escaped were wounded . . . but we do not know how many there actually were. . . . The one who was wounded in Guarenas worked for Guillermo as his executioner, and it was with his own hands that Corporal Pedro Casañas was beaten up that time when the maroons attacked this town.

Germán de Aguilera, head of the expedition, took with him to Panaquire Guillermo's head and one of his hands, and destroyed the fourteen cabins that constituted the *cumbe*. They claimed to have found in them eight firearms, a barrel of gunpowder, sabers, many spears, and arrows. Aguilera stated that

> Guillermo had been a fugitive for many years. One night, he had approached his master, knocked him down, killed a

the district of Panaquire and killing, stealing, and committing other crimes, 1771." It can be found in the Archivo General de la Nación, Sección Diversos: Tomo 43, 93.

slave, cruelly punished another, stole from his master and threatened to kill him. Since then, he has been a fugitive in the wilderness attracting slaves, punishing, stealing, and committing other atrocities. . . . On one occasion he killed a slave in Chuspa after robbing him, and on another, he went to the town of Panaquire with 18 armed men, tied up Corporal Pedro Casañas and putting him in the center of the town square, stuck a rod between his legs, and had his executioner, Isidro Rengifo, give him a cruel beating. . . . This happened also on another occasion, according to one of the prosecutors. . . . Despite having been captured in the *cumbe* of Chuspa, Guillermo managed to escape but only after first wounding 8 of the men under the command of Nicolás de la Rosa, a lieutenant from Caucagua. . . . This time he ended up in Picacho de Ocumare, where he robbed and beat up a merchant who had happened to walk by, and who was lucky enough to die on the spot. For, while on the same road, Guillermo came across a man, his wife, and a daughter, tying up the man and beating him, and then raping the women. . . . He had such perverted tendencies that, according to his own companions, he used to say he would behead himself rather than let himself be captured alive if he ever found himself in great difficulty and with no possibility of escape. . . .

A soldier from Aguilera, Asencio Antonio Herrero, said Guillermo "used to come and go from Barcelona."

We can learn quite a bit from those reports. The Ocoyta *cumbe* consisted of fourteen cabins. They used to store weapons there that must have been stolen while raiding Panaquire and other towns, as well as by robbing merchants on the road. The place also functioned as a headquarters for Guillermo and his men. This was not at all a peaceful community devoted to tasks of production designed to free them from their masters. This was an active center of resistance and attack. Guillermo used to go from Ocoyta to Chuspa and from Ocumare to Barcelona in what must have been an incessant journey from *cumbe* to *cumbe*, to maintain close contact among them, to trade cocoa (which was a common activity of the maroons), and to plan raids on the estates and towns where their masters or representatives resided.

Let us see what other information is available in these reports: Juan de la Cruz Muñoz, a soldier from Curiepe, reported they had captured a female Negro slave (the property of Bernardo Llanos), who was said to be the concubine of Guillermo, and a free *zamba* [the progeny of a mixed Indian/Negro union], who was that of Francisco Mina.

According to what the corporal told Guerra of Panaquire, Guillermo had been a runaway for three years. He had spent the last two years in a *cumbe* in the "Marrones" region. He had succeeded in getting the keys to the barn on the estate also called "Marrones," and had taken all their cocoa.

Lately . . . with a large number of armed men—a few of his own as well as some disguised ones who claimed to be Indians—he assaulted the town of Panaquire. . . . He was urged to do this by a young man of British extraction whose name was Ubaldo and who was the overseer at the Alayones estate, and by Juan José Oviedo, a free *zambo*. It is equally well-known that this Englishman corresponded with Guillermo, ate and drank with him, and gave him news of what was going on. It was also public knowledge that Guillermo, though leader of all these people, had a deputy called Vicente Sojo and an executioner, Isidro Rengifo, who inflicted the punishments prescribed by Guillermo. The slaves of the estates in those valleys had so much freedom that neither the owners nor the overseers dared to point a finger at them since they would always threaten to join their Captain Guillermo. . . .

The estate owners frequently gave each other news of Guillermo. José González Miranda, for instance, wrote to his brother Francisco Miranda on December 12, 1771, all the way from Caucagua to inform him that Guillermo had been in that area and had attacked his brother-in-law Casañas in Panaquire. These dispatches are included in the official proceedings in the Archives.

Pedro José, "a creole Negro slave owned by Pedro Peñalver of Barcelona," was one of Guillermo's captured companions. In an interrogation, he explained that he had fled with his wife in September 1771, from his master's large estate in Cupira, with the idea of going to Panaquire to see if Baltasar de León, who lived there, would buy them. Though they were tired when they reached the Alayones estate, Ubaldo told them he could not help them. He thought it best for them to stay in the wilderness until Sunday, when he could talk to some people in Panaquire. Guillermo got there and with some anxiety "persuaded him to leave." Vicente Sojo took him to the *cumbe*. Ubaldo later notified him that Baltasar de León had agreed to buy him, but when he tried to return to Panaquire, Guillermo stopped him and forbade him to go. He did not immediately flee, because his wife was pregnant. Because of this, he ran away at the first sound of shots, and found two slaves from the Sojos and another one from the Ibarras in the wilderness. They banded together with six other men and two women (one of whom was still nursing a child). Most of them went to the Guapo, but he, his wife, and Eleno Sojo decided to move to Panaquire to live with Baltasar de León. However, he was seized there by Corporal Casañas. He also declared that Guillermo had confiscated in the Truy River a canoe from Barcelona carrying clothing, spirits [aguardiente], and machetes. He explained that in the *cumbe* only those who were close to Guillermo had arms. The attack on Panaquire—as had been suspected—had been suggested to Guillermo by Ubaldo the Englishman, and by others from his group . . . a total of twenty-six men.

Another inhabitant of the *cumbe* of Ocoyta was Andrés Domingo Pardo, who is referred to as Andrés Hermoso in the official document, since he was Francisco Hermoso's slave. He had escaped from his owner's estate in Capaya in October 1771. In Aramina he met Guillermo who invited him to move to his refuge. They left in the company of Joaquín Nieves and his wife, Marucha Algarín. Julián and Francisco Tostado also joined them. Juan Isidro, and José Antonio Rengifo, who had just escaped on that very day, joined them in Capaya. Santiago Machado had also left Aramina. Vicente Sojo, Francisco Mina, Acacio, Eleno Sojo (who later took his wife and his three children with him), José Luis Blanco, and Juana Francisca and her small son were waiting for them in Ocoyta. (Juana Francisca was Bernardo Llanos' slave as well as Guillermo's wife; while in the *cumbe* she gave birth to another son.) Francisco Mina and his wife María Valentina, a free *zamba,* joined them later on. He asserted that they sustained themselves by hunting, and mentioned the following individuals as Guillermo's confidants: Vicente Sojo, his deputy; Francisco Mina; Eleno Sojo; José Antonio Rengifo, his messenger; and Juan Isidro Rengifo, who executed the sentences imparted by Guillermo. As far as they knew, there were eight firearms stored in their huts, a barrel of gunpowder, and a bag of ammunition, which they stole from the corporal in Panaquire.

Juana Francisca Morena, also referred to in the document by her owner's last name (Bernardo Llanos), stated that she had fled with her two children in June of that year from the estate in Caucagua where she lived. She gave birth to a third child in the *cumbe*. According to her, the men did not take the women with them on their forays, and did not relate to them the events of the excursions. Before she left for Panaquire at the time of the attack on the *cumbe*, she saw an Indian arrive there whom she did not know. She added that, prior to her move to this *cumbe*, she had already been a runaway once for a period of two months.

We can gather the following interesting information from these declarations: The *cumbe* was built with the influx of individuals recruited by Guillermo, but in reality not only did it attract those he had persuaded to escape but also others who were anxious to escape from the authority of their masters. Unfortunately, the document does not explain why Guillermo decided to assemble all these people in Ocoyta, since he had been a fugitive for three years, during which he seems to have ambled aimlessly from one region to another. The information supplied by Andrés Hermoso regarding their sustenance and survival is surprising. According to him, they lived by hunting. Surely, this must have been due to the fact that the *cumbe* was destroyed shortly after being founded, for they practiced horticulture in other *cumbes*. The fact that the women ran away with their small children reveals the intention of the maroon slaves to found stable communities. We have also met Ubaldo, the Englishman, who must have been an agent for the merchants who bought cocoa from the maroons. We have seen an Indian arrive furtively at the *cumbe* on one occasion. Note also that not all the inhabitants of the *cumbe* had been slaves.

Juan Isidro Rengifo, the slave of Doña María de la Concepción Arrechedera, said he had escaped six months earlier. He reported that the *cumbe* had twenty men, each armed with a spear and a machete. They also had two sabers, seven firearms, half a barrel of gunpowder, and a knapsack of ammunition and slugs of lead. He was wounded when the *cumbe* was attacked, along with José Acacio and Antonio Caravallo. He related the story of the attack on Panaquire, which was carried out by fifteen of the twenty men of Ocoyta. They took soap, candles, lengths of cloth, and liquor from the town. He said he was twenty-nine years old.

The lot of the inhabitants of the *cumbe* of Ocoyta after its destruction is part of the history of this community, and tells us something of the destiny of captured maroons. Isidro Rengifo was sentenced to the gallows

> where he will irremediably suffer. His right hand shall later be cut off so that this punishment will be imprinted on the minds of those in the town. The other prisoners (except for the children) shall be taken out to see the execution of Isidro Rengifo. (The children shall be returned to their owners, once the capturers receive their compensation.) These prisoners, who shall each receive 200 lashes, have been sentenced by His Royal Highness as follows: the Negress Juana Francisca Llanos, adulterer, Guillermo's concubine, and a maroon for the second time, shall be locked up for eight years in the poor house of "la Caridad" in this city, where she will be engaged in domestic chores; the free *zamba* María Valentina will be imprisoned for 5 years . . . ; the rest of the slaves shall be put to work in public and royal works which His Highness shall prescribe. Later, they will be banished forever from the Kingdom of Nueva España, with the owners deciding their destinations. But they will never be allowed to return to this Province, under penalty of life imprisonment. . . .

They were informed of their sentences, but nothing was said about the punishment to be inflicted on those who had escaped (if they were ever found) or on the Englishman Ubaldo.

Rengifo was executed at ten o'clock on the morning of December 19, 1771. And Pedro José Peñalver, Andrés Hermoso, J. A. Rengifo, and Eleno Sojo each received their two hundred lashes.

Shortly afterward, they caught Ubaldo. He testified on February 12, 1772, and said his name was José Eduardo de la Luz Perera, that he was an Englishman, single, a farmer, and twenty-five years old. He left London at a tender age to work for the captain of a ship en route to the Canary Islands. He made several voyages and was captured by one of the ships of the Compañía Guipuzcoana, which brought him to

La Guaira. He was set free, decided to stay, and was baptized. His godfather was Estéban Perera. He denied all the charges, and while he affirmed that he had hidden Juan Muchinga from Guillermo (since the latter wanted to kill the former), he claimed that he had never been friendly with Guillermo. The interview was suspended. On March 7, 1772, in a letter written from jail, he complained of having spent months suffering "intolerable work and misfortunes." He was asking for his freedom, since there was no evidence against him, for he was only being accused of having given bananas to the maroons. Shortly after, he was declared free. He had to move to Spain, after paying a fine of one hundred pesos. On March 16, Tomás Pellicer put up this money for him.

In order to get an idea of what usually happened when maroons were caught and sentenced, let us briefly glance at the claims presented by the owners of the various slaves who were sentenced. On May 12, 1772, Second Lieutenant Bernardo de Llanos y Castillo Cabeza de Vaca asked to have his slave Juana Francisca returned to him based on

> What is prescribed by laws 21, 22, 23, 24, 26 in the 5th section of the 7th Book of the Digest. . . . The suppressed slaves who have committed no thefts, assaults, murders, or any other serious crimes, which is the case with my slave, should be returned to their owners. . . .

According to the second lieutenant's summary, he was the one who was really being punished "by being denied her services." This petition was dismissed as "irrelevant." But the owner was not cowed by this, and on May 20 he proposed that she simply be sent to his home or his estate as a prisoner, or that he be given another female slave. This was also rejected.

On May 17, 1772, Mateo Blanco of Ponte protested against the order to sell to José Luis Blanco in Veracruz. According to his argument, such a procedure went against the provisions of the Laws of the Indies. In his opinion, his slave had committed no crime other than that of escaping, and the owner himself had contributed money to the project of exterminating the *cumbe*. He therefore thought he had a perfect right to ask for the return of his slave. Governor José Carlos de Aguero, who wanted to appear merciful, noted that José Luis had not been captured during the attack on Guillermo. In sentencing José Luis Blanco and Vicente Sojo, he argued:

> I must sentence them, so I sentence each to a punishment of 50 lashes . . . after which they shall be taken to the pillory for two hours to be publicly humiliated. Their crime is to be publicized and once the sentence has been executed, they are to be returned to their masters, who shall pay the costs of their capture and who shall keep a chain on their feet for six months. This will serve as a punishment for them and as a warning to the rest. . . .

At the beginning of 1773, the governor found out, through Juan Fernando Palacios (governor of Veracruz), that the slaves sentenced to exile from Nueva España had been returned. The viceroy had not admitted the four men, who had been taken there by the ship *La Santísima Trinidad*. The captain of the ship, Luis de Jáuregui, demanded 176 pesos for the round trip plus a corresponding commission. They were being returned "because their owners had not submitted the papers authorizing their sale." Governor Agüero forced the respective owners to pay the debt, accept their slaves, and use them "keeping an iron chain attached to their feet for two years. In a manifestation of his kindness, His Highness substitutes this sentence for the original one, being aware of the fact that their owners could make use of their services. . . ."

Having witnessed this case of official generosity, Second Lieutenant Bernardo de Llanos y Castillo Cabeza de Vaca again pressed for the return of his slave Juana Francisca. This time, His Highness revealed his magnanimity in choosing to please the second lieutenant, providing that Juana Francisca be forced to bear an iron chain on her foot for two years.

José Antonio Rengifo's owner, Doña Concepción Arrechedera, also paid the expenses of the capture and put the chain on his foot. Doña Catalina Xerez de Aristiguieta did the same to Eleno Sojo.

From the sixteenth century on, there were numerous settlements of maroons throughout what was to become Venezuela. This was the consequence of historical circumstances, which did not offer slaves who longed for their freedom any way out except definitive flight and the establishment of communities in deserted areas or in places appropriate for the smuggling traffic. The large number of *cumbes* that were in existence at any one time indicates an untiring rebelliousness, expressed not in the form of organized wars but rather in the founding of communities that became centers of liberation for the most ill-treated slaves, and that also became nuclei of clandestine trade. Ocoyta is the case of a very active *cumbe*, but it does not seem appropriate to class its activities among true *rebellions*. To call Guillermo's activities guerrilla warfare would be to place them within an inappropriate historical framework. This is not, of course, to belittle the meaning of the maroons' activities. On the contrary, our intention in studying maroons is to show the lack of truth in the view that portrays the colony as a haven of peace. This study has brought together historical materials that had traditionally been presented as simple anecdotes, and tried to show their historical significance: that the slaves used every available means to attain their freedom; that the only practical possibility was the establishment of isolated communities in inaccessible places, since the idea of organized cooperation leading to simultaneous uprising of sufficient scope to gain control was inconceivable, that the experience of these maroons and their distinctive methods of resistance should be considered a factor of great importance in trying to understand the behavior of the masses during the War for Independence in 1810. . . . After April 19, when the maroons were given arms and organized militarily under leaders who promised them all sorts of riches, they abandoned the *cumbes* and hurled themselves into combat. It was the beginning of a new historical era, as the oppressed masses of slaves took over these new means of combat in the midst of this struggle headed by the Creoles, who had attained (with the ultimate support of the dispossessed) sufficient class consciousness as well as theoretical and practical know-how to guide the process of national liberation.

CHAPTER FIVE

Palenques *in Colombia*

AQUILES ESCALANTE

Throughout the Americas, the Negro responded to exploitation in several ways—by malingering, by poorly carrying out his tasks, by revolting, or by escaping individually or collectively to form *palenques*, where groups of maroon slaves sought refuge in the thick, tropical forests and formed communities where they could keep their original cultures alive.

During the final decade of the sixteenth century, the authorities of Cartagena officially ordered individuals harboring runaway slaves to report this fact to the government. An order issued at a later time prescribed that a formal report had to be filed within six days of a slave's flight.

> Furthermore, it was agreed and decided that: no slave, male or female, shall run off and leave the service of his master under penalty—should his absence be for as long as 15 days—of receiving 100 lashes as follows: he shall be tied up at the city pillory in the morning, decorated with strings of bells around his body, whipped 100 times, and left in that position all day long for the other slaves to see. And whosoever dares to remove him from the pillory during that day shall have to pay a fine of 20 pesetas, which will go to the judge, the accuser, and the Council in equal shares.

From Aquiles Escalante, "Notas sobre el palenque de San Basilio, una communidad negra en Colombia," *Divulgaciones Ethnologicas* 3 (5):207–359 (1954). Translated from pp. 225–31, and reprinted with the permission of the author and publisher.

Furthermore, a captured runaway who has been absent from the service of his master for more than one month shall have his genitals cut off in public and displayed at the city pillory, so that other slaves may come to realize the consequences.

Furthermore, captured slaves who have been runaways for over a year shall be sentenced to death.

Furthermore, female slaves who have been runaways for more than 15 days shall receive 200 lashes in the same manner as male slaves who are caught 15 or more days after having run away.

Furthermore, whoever captures and keeps a slave who has been away from his master for more than 15 days and does not return him to his rightful owner shall have to pay a fine of 5 pesetas, plus a contribution of 10 pesetas to encourage others to pursue runaways.

Also, a large enough force is to be formed to go on expeditions against the maroons, who live in the wilderness, and to bring them back to the city. Since some of these Negroes are going around and defending themselves with weapons (like those used by the authorities), the Government has decreed that individuals who foresee a threat of danger from maroons shall have permission to kill them, if and when they cannot be captured alive. Such permission has been granted especially since it would be advantageous to clean up the territory where these Negroes are based and from where they raid the neighboring roads. Therefore, those individuals who kill Negroes for these reasons shall not be subject to any form of legal prosecution.

Furthermore, settlers of neighboring areas shall be obliged to help pursue and capture maroons, whenever the commissioned authorities call upon them to do so. They shall be reminded on such occasions of the material benefits which will accrue from the elimination of maroon raids on their own property.

Furthermore, if an Indian or a Spaniard captures a runaway slave in this way, the slave's owner shall have to pay him 10 pesetas per captured slave. If either the runaway's corpse or his head (which would confirm his death) are returned to the owner, the payment shall be 5 pesetas, which shall come from the same source as above [Urueta 1890, I:219].

The maroons sowed unrest in various parts of the country. In the district of Santa Marta, a group of runaway Negroes from the area of La Ramada set fire to the city of Santa Marta, during the last days of the administration of García de Lerma.

In the district of Popayán, the *palenque* of Castillo on the westernmost side of the valley of the Patía River was famous for the frequency of its raids and depredations on the surrounding area. The authorities tried to subjugate them on repeated occasions but always failed. The Audiencia de Quito tried, in 1732, to bring them under control peacefully by authorizing Andrés Fajardo to offer them peace, freedom, and the right to live unmolested, providing that they agreed to reject new runaways—a condition that they would never honor. Governor José Francisco Carreño decided to subjugate them once and for all, and so prepared an expedition consisting of one hundred well-armed men under the leadership of Juan Alvarez Uría and Tomás Hurtado. The insurgents were led by the Negro Jerónimo. On Corpus Christi day in June 1745, they were definitively defeated. To a significant degree, this was the work of the Franciscan father, José Joaquín de Barrutieta, who, by means of persuasion, managed to get the fugitives to surrender (Aragon 1939:82).

Viceroy Pedro Mendinueta's account of the pacified Negro community [*reducción negrera*] at the Mocoa Mission reads as follows:

The existence of this community can be attributed to the zeal of Father Francisco Javier de la Paz, an Augustine priest from the Pasto convent, who founded it in 1793, assembling (with the aid of the Governor of Popayán) over 200 Indians and a few Negro runaways in his two settlements.

Realizing that certain ornaments and sacred vessels were necessary to the welfare of Father Paz's two settlements, and in order to insure the happiness of the Negro runaways of his *palenque*, I decided, at the Junta de Hacienda [a meeting of the financial commission of the state] to give them the necessary aid [Posada and Ibáñez 1910, VIII:437].

Don Pedro Zapata assumed the position of governor of Cartagena de Indias on January 10, 1654. He was very concerned with the fortification and defense of the city, and during the first three years of his administration,

> undertook an important task: to exterminate a Negro community located near the Magdalena River. Over 50 years earlier, runaways from Cartagena had founded a settlement called Palenque, located on the banks of this river and surrounded by a very thick forest. Since this Palenque was equidistant from Cartagena and Santa Marta, it is not surprising that the Governor of Santa Marta (who believed Palenque to be within his jurisdiction) objected to don Pedro's projected expedition against it. Nevertheless, it was carried out, and while Ramón de Cagarriga, then Governor of Santa Marta, protested against Pedro's intrusion, the maroons were finally subjugated and baptized. When Counselor Gabriel de Mencos (former Governor of Santa Marta) had asked don Ramón whether it would be more advantageous to have the Governor of Santa Marta or the Governor of Cartagena bring them into submission, he replied that the *palenque* was located within the jurisdiction of Santa Marta and that it would therefore be better if he did it, especially since he could rely on a group of bellicose highland Indians, who would be needed for such an undertaking [de Escariche 1948:60].

The most vigorous insurrectionist movement on the Caribbean coast of Colombia occurred in Cartagena de Indias at the beginning of the seventeenth century during the administration of Jerónimo de Sauzo Casarola (who became governor about 1600). The fiery and daring Domingo Bioho was the first slave to revolt publicly. Claiming to have been king of an African state, he plunged himself with thirty Negro men and women into the forests and the marshy areas of Matuna (south of the town of Tolú). There, without difficulty, he defeated a group of nearly twenty slave owners who had been on their track and who had apparently thought that their former "possessions" would magically surrender to them when discovered. Frightened, the slave owners turned back after the ambush, and immediately approached the governor to urge him to organize troops to fight the rebels. The maroons had been rapidly growing in numbers thanks to the influence of Domingo, now known as "King Benkos," who put an end to the period of colonial tranquillity in Cartagena, Tolú, Mompós, Tenerife, and so forth, by assaulting and robbing plantations, cattle ranches, cultivated farms . . . even canoes carrying fellow Negroes who had been sent to fell large trees for lumber.

On one of his incursions into the south, Benkos Bioho found a site marvelously suited to the founding of a settlement where he could consolidate his strength. Stockades were built to fortify the new town, which later gave rise to the *palenque* of San Basilio.

The defeat and death of Juan Gómez, head of the first expedition sent against these maroons, forced the governor to appoint a second group, more carefully organized and led by Diego Hernández Calvo, Alcalde de la Hermandad. Francisco de Campos was named second-in-command.

Benkos was well organized, having numerous spies situated at strategic points. Having been notified far in advance of this second attack, he was able to stop the advance of the Spanish forces at some distance from the *palenque* at a place of his choosing. The Spanish forces had taken with them a group of submissive slaves. Francisco de Campos, who had merely been watching the battle, fell to the ground with a wounded foot. The Africans captured him and took him to the *palenque* as hostage.

There he found Princess Orika, daughter of Bioho, who had been his lover in Cartagena at a time when her mother, Queen Wiwa, and her brother, Prince Sando, were slaves of Captain Alonso de Campo. Her father, Domingo Bioho, had been bought by the merchant, Juan de Palacios.

The lovers' encounter renewed the amorous relationship. Queen Wiwa and Princess Orika visited and diligently cared for the wounded prisoner. But love overcame family ties, and one night Orika unexpectedly and, at her own risk, offered to give Captain Francisco de Campos his liberty.

The couple prepared to escape, but a bullet killed Francisco de Campos, despite the fact that he was already at some distance from the town. Princess Orika was tried and sentenced to death (Mogollón:IV).

Don Diego Fernández de Velasco, who was Jerónimo de Suazo's successor, considered the 36,612 pesos and 3 reales that had already been spent to persecute the maroons an exorbitant sum and, therefore, decided to make a treaty with them. Juan Polo was placed in charge of the negotiations, and was authorized to grant the rebels a few prerogatives.

Benkos would not be allowed to use the title "King of the Arcabuco," but would be permitted to wear his favored Spanish-style clothes (including a sword and golden dagger). Governor García Girón, however, uncovered a new plot by Benkos and captured him, and finally had him hanged.

Although this 1619 rebellion is the most famous involving San Basilio, there was another movement in 1696, which was finally suppressed by Sancho Jimeno, acting governor of Cartagena at that time (Dr. Alberto Miramón: personal communication).

The final suppression of these maroons (1713–17) was the work of the Most Illustrious [Bishop] Don Antonio María Casiani, a member of the Congregation of San Basilio. It was carried out with the agreement and support of the governor of the Province of Cartagena, don Francisco Baloco Leigrave.

In 1772, San Basilio was included within the Mahates district.

San Basilio. Community of Negroes in the interior of the country. It originated as a settlement of runaway slaves, protected by the ruggedness of the Maria Mountain, which stood between the marshy lands of the area and their own site in Mahates. They were not pacified until the early part of this century, despite several armed and bloody expeditions which were sent against them. The Most Illustrious Bishop and then Governor Antonio María Casiani, with the consent of the governor of the province, finally made a treaty with them, which included a general pardon and the conferral of freedom on them, providing they agreed to refuse to let new runaway slaves live among them. They have not intermingled with other people and they have a distinctive language which they teach their children (though they more often use a kind of pidgin Spanish). Their government consists of a political leader, a military captain, and a mayor. These are subordinate to and approved by the governor of the province, who is responsible for the whole parish including its outlying farms and ranches. The priest takes care of 178 families—396 communicants and 90 slaves [Urueta 1890, III:328].

Currently, the police inspector is democratically elected and his appointment is ratified by the mayor of Mahates.

During the second half of the eighteenth century, the state considered among its principal duties to help to increase the size of the population and to make available the necessary means for the development of different aspects of the economy. In line with this philosophy, on August 12, 1774, Lieutenant Antonio de la Torre, adviser of the Negro militias in Cartagena, was commissioned to found a series of towns in what is now the Department of Bolívar. In his account of the fulfillment of the mission he brings us news of the *palenque:*

> With strength and perseverance, I was able to overcome the many horrors and difficulties stemming from encounters with the Negroes of the Palenque de San Basilio, as well as from the thickness of the jungle which made it difficult to see sunlight. One must also add to the sum of our problems a number of cliffs, precipices, and swamps which we had to overcome. I took advantage, however, of the fact that the Negroes of the Palenque of San Basilio respected me. These Negroes are the descendants of others who, protected by those rugged mountains, defended their freedom by killing many individuals—including a few of their former masters who intermittently attempted to recapture them. These expeditions finally ended in a treaty mediated by the Most Illustrious [Bishop] Casiani, which allowed the maroons to remain at their original site on the slope of the María Mountain at three leagues from the Gambote pass. They were also granted the right to name a political leader and to exclude all white men (except for the priest) from the town, and the maroons agreed in return to forbid future runaways to live among them. There were a few other provisions and conditions in the treaty, which were all observed to the letter [Urueta 1890, IV:51].

The founder of the towns on the María la Alta mountain, with the authorization of Governor Juan de Torrezar Díaz y Pimienta, gave the *palenqueros* in 1774 the title of "the community of San Basilio."

The *palenqueros* remained totally isolated from our civilization until the latter part of the nineteenth century. Consequently, they were able to develop a closed type of economy: rudimentary agriculture based on rice, corn, manioc, banana, and peanut; cattle raising in the Bajo Grande de Palenque, where they harvested corn in January and grazed cows until September. Occasionally, they left the town to exchange their produce, and during the days prior to the traditional district festival, they usually commissioned someone to buy general supplies in Cartagena. It was sugar cane agriculture that finally incorporated them into the national life of Colombia. In 1907, the sugar mill of Sincerín was established, followed by the refinery of Santa Cruz, located in the same Department of Bolívar. The presence of the sugar plantations led to a very substantial growth of the area of Malagana. The inhabitants of San Basilio for the first time received high salaries by working in the sugar cane industry, and this gave them a new outlook on life. The sudden break from the lifestyle of the first *palenqueros* was deeply regretted by the kinsmen of those who went off. Some even wept as one does for a funeral, particularly for those who were going off to work on the construction of the Panama Canal or on the banana plantations of the Department of Magdalena.

REFERENCES NOT CITED IN GENERAL BIBLIOGRAPHY

Aragón, Arcesio
  1939 *Fastos payaneses*. Bogotá: Imprente Nacional.
de Escariche, Julia Herráez
  1948 *Don Pedro Zapata de Mendoza, Governador de Cartagena de Indias*. Sevilla: Consego Superior de Investigaciones Cientificas.
Mogollón, J. V. (ed.)
  Historia, Leyenda y tradiciones de Cartagena. Cartagena.
Posada, Eduard and Ibañez, P. M.
  1910 *Relaciones de Mando*. Biblioteca de Historia Nacional.
Urueta, José P.
  1890 *Documentos para la historia de Cartagena*. Cartagena: Tipografia de Araújo L.

CHAPTER SIX

Negro Slave Control
and Resistance in
Colonial Mexico, 1519–1650[1]

DAVID M. DAVIDSON

Negro resistance to enslavement was an integral feature of the history of African slavery in the Americas. Studies in the past few decades in the United States and Latin America have successfully refuted if not entirely erased the once accepted notions of Negro docility and acquiescence in slavery. These works have provided a most convincing panorama of slave mutinies, insurrections, clandestine conspiracies, and individual escapes. Repeated evidence of more subtle forms of resistance—for example, suicide and voluntary abortion and infanticide—reveals further the determined refusal of many slaves to accept their position, and their reluctance to bear children in slavery. Such resistance occurred in varying degrees wherever Europeans established Negro slavery in the New World, primarily in the southern United States, the Antilles, the Pacific and Caribbean coasts of Central and South America, and northeastern Brazil. Although most studies have been restricted to these regions, there is a considerable body of evidence to indicate that Negro slave resistance was also present in colonial Mexico.

Recently, and primarily through the efforts of Gonzalo Aguirre Beltrán, we have gained substantial information con-

Reprinted with the permission of the author and the publisher from *The Hispanic American Historical Review* 46 (3): 235–53 (1966).
[1] Financial assistance from the Committee on Comparative Tropical History of the University of Wisconsin helped make possible the research for this article.

cerning the number and role of Africans in Mexico (see in particular his 1946, but also Pi-Sunyer 1957, and Toro 1920–21). It is now fairly certain that in the period 1519–1650 the area received at least 120,000 slaves, or two thirds of all the Africans imported into the Spanish possessions in America (Aguirre Beltrán 1946:199–222). The early development of Negro slavery in colonial Mexico was a direct response to the serious labor shortage resulting from the startling decline of the Indian population (cf. Borah 1951). Demographic studies suggest that the indigenous population of central Mexico alone, which may have been as high as 25,000,000 in 1519, had decreased to around 1,075,000 by 1605 (Borah and Cook 1963:4, 88; cf. also Cook and Simpson 1948; Cook and Borah 1960; Kubler 1942; and Gibson 1964:5–6, 136–47, 448–51, 460–62). The spread of European diseases, wars, relocations, and the ecological changes wrought by Spanish settlement and control all contributed to the decline. The advance of Spanish mining and, particularly, ranching and agriculture (which spread quickly in the sixteenth century to provision Mexico when decreasing indigenous food production threatened starvation) produced a demand for labor that the declining Indian population could not fulfill (Simpson 1952; Chevalier 1963; Sandoval 1951; Dusenberry 1963; Morrissey 1951).

Although the crown soon made concessions to the colonists' demands for workers by sanctioning forced wage labor (the *repartimiento*), and by failing or refusing to thwart the spread of debt peonage, it hoped to fill the need with African slaves (cf. Simpson 1934–40; Gibson 1964:220–56; Chevalier 1963: 277–88; Wolf 1959: 202–32). Royal decrees throughout the late sixteenth century prohibited the use of Indians in certain industries considered detrimental to their health, especially sugar processing and cloth production, and ordered their replacement by Negro slaves. African labor was also encouraged for the mines.[2]

The response to these conditions was a constant demand for Negroes, a flourishing slave trade, and a rising Negro

[2] See, for example, the Empress' instructions to Viceroy Antonio de Mendoza, April 25, 1535 (*Colección* 1864–84:XXIII, 532); decree of Philip III, November 24, 1601 (ibid., XIX, 164); Archivo General de la Nación, Mexico City (cited hereinafter as AGN), Ordenanzas, Vol. 2, fols. 129–32v, 313–16v; Tierras, Vol. 2769, exp. 10.

population throughout the sixteenth and early seventeenth centuries. As a result, by 1570 Mexico contained over twenty thousand Negroes, and by 1650 there were more than thirty-five thousand Negroes and over one hundred thousand Afromestizos (mulattoes and zambos).[3] Slaves were found throughout the colony, serving in the mines, plantations, and ranches, as well as in the urban areas as peddlers, muleteers, craftsmen, day laborers, and domestics.

Concentrations of Negro population appeared in four distinct areas.[4] In the eastern region, from the coastal lowlands between Veracruz and Pánuco to the slopes of the Sierra Madre Oriental, there were some eight thousand to ten thousand Africans. The port of Veracruz alone contained about five thousand Negroes and Afromestizos in 1646, most of whom served as carriers and dock hands, while in the rural areas over three thousand slaves worked on the sugar plantations and cattle ranches that spread inland to the mountains. In the region north and west of Mexico City were at least fifteen thousand slaves in silver mines and on cattle, sheep, and mule ranches. In the broad belt extending south-westward from Puebla to the Pacific coast were another three thousand to five thousand slaves on sugar plantations and ranches, in mines, and on the docks of Acapulco. Finally, the largest Negro concentration of all was in Mexico City and the Valley of Mexico, where twenty thousand to fifty thousand Africans, slave and free, were employed in urban occupations.

Spanish officials sought to incorporate this large, culturally distinct labor force into the neomedieval structure of the American colonies. Legislation spanning the 1530s to 1550s, intended for the most part for general application to the

---

[3] Gonzalo de Salazar and others to Charles V, November 10, 1525 (Paso y Troncoso 1939–42, I:87); Audiencia of Mexico to Charles V, August 5, 1533 (ibid., III:112); cf. also *Actas* 1889–1911, VI: 227–28, 491; VII:36, 122, 330–31; XII:45; Conde de Coruña to Philip II, *Cartas* 1877:340; Aguirre Beltrán 1944:412–31; Aguirre Beltrán 1946:3–50, 210–21. Internal slave sales are preserved in AGN, Historia, Vol. 407 (1554–1646) and Vol. 408 (1647–1749), and in Archivo de Notarías, Mexico City (cited hereinafter as AN), Protocolos, Vols. 1–3, Escribanos Martín de Castro and Diego de Ayala.

[4] The following figures are based on the estimates in Aguirre Beltrán 1946:210–21, my re-examination of the sources cited there, and further archival research.

Indies, stipulated the privileges and limitations pertaining to the slaves' place within society. Royal intentions derived in general from the profound hispano-Catholic faith in the organic structure of a divinely imposed social unity, in which each person or group found its privileges and limitations defined according to its role in the hierarchy of inequality (cf. McAlister 1963). More specifically, as Frank Tannenbaum has noted, this policy was rooted in the Iberian heritage, which had long allowed slaves a legal and moral personality (1963:45–53 and passim; cf. also Elkins 1963:52–80).

Yet the current of realism that accompanied and at times contradicted much of Spain's early idealism in America emerged forcefully in the regulation of slavery. The royal concern for slaves as Spanish subjects and Catholic souls was tempered by the need to create a stable and dependable labor force, maintained by consent in a situation where physical control was difficult. Much of the legislation concerning slavery assumed a conciliatory tone in which certain privileges granted to slaves were intended to reduce or eliminate causes of slave discontent.

Thus royal decrees and Church proclamations provided legal release from bondage by allowing slaves to purchase their freedom and by encouraging voluntary manumission. Such declarations served equally to give substance to the Spanish belief in the essentially transitory nature of slavery and in the humanity of the slave. Some of them, such as the royal cedula of 1536 to Mexico, also suggested that slaves would work with more spirit and be less inclined to revolt (Puga 1878: 32–33; *Recopilación* 1943, VII, Título V, Leyes 6–8). In seeking to make slave life more palatable by guaranteeing family solidarity and marital privileges, the King observed that a protected marital life was not only a Christian obligation, but also an essential means of insuring slave tranquillity and stability (Konetzke 1953, I:450; cf. also ibid. I:99, 210, 318; Galván Rivera 1859:347). Both Church and Crown were adamant in restricting the disciplinary authority of masters and in encouraging good treatment, for, as Juan de Solórzano commented, such conditions would protect the slaves as well as preserve an important labor base (Royal ordinance, ca. 1545, Konetzke 1953, I:237; Solórzano y Pereyra 1948, Libro II, Capítulo vii, Número 13). Finally there was the desire to hispanize Africans in order to bring them into a community of spiritual and cultural brotherhood with their masters (Konetzke 1953, I:237–38; Galván Rivera 1859:193–94, 197; Lorenzana 1769:72–73, 138). Slaves would receive the benefits of hispanic culture and religion, and their masters might rest assured that such fraternal bonds would temper resentment. In these respects the dictates of self-interest and religion went hand in hand.

The conciliatory measures appear to have had only a limited effect. Slaves did not achieve much success in purchasing their freedom or in being manumitted, if the few recorded instances of these are true indications.[5] Such extralegal channels to freedom as intermarriage and miscegenation were relatively more successful. Master-slave marriages provided one source of slave freedom, especially in the seventeenth century, when the Church pressed many masters to legalize their illicit unions with slave women (Aguirre Beltrán 1946:248–54). Although the Crown generally disapproved of Negro-white unions, they flourished and contributed to the rise of the free mulatto population (Konetzke 1953, I:347; cf. also *Advertimientos* 1956:33–34; *Cartas* 1877:299–300; *Instrucciones* 1867:259). Many children were freed who might otherwise have been slaves.

Slaves also tried to gain freedom by marrying into the free Indian population. Bartolomé de Zarate complained to the Emperor in 1537 that Negroes were marrying Indians and declaring themselves freed (Konetzke 1953, I:185). Although the *Siete Partidas,* Spain's ancient legal code, had granted liberty to some slaves who married free persons (*Las Siete,* IV, xxii, 5), Charles V nullified this provision, thus emphasizing that if the authorities would condone a trickle of free Negroes, they would not tolerate a substantial loss of their slave labor (Konetzke 1953, I:185; *Actas* 1889–1911, IV:245). Despite the royal desires, slaves continued to marry Indians in order that their children might be free. "Indian women are very weak and succumb to Negroes," wrote Viceroy Martín Enríquez in 1574. "Thus Indian women would rather marry Negroes than Indians; and neither more nor less, Negroes prefer to marry Indian women

---

[5] Examples of manumission are in AN, Protocolos, Escribano Diego de Ayala, Vol. 2, fols. 109–9v, and Escribano Martin de Castro, fols. 198v–200, 493–95v, 606–10v. Examples of slaves purchasing their freedom are found in AN, Protocolos, Vol. 3, fols. 352v–53; AGN, Historia, Vol. 408, fol. 51.

rather than Negresses, so that their children will be born free" (*Cartas* 1877:299). Spanish law and custom respected these marriages, which, with common law unions, produced the free zambo population of Mexico (cf. Aguirre Beltrán 1946:260–68).

Legislation that sought to cure some of the worst abuses in slave life provided only minimal protection. Whereas both Crown and Church hoped to protect the familial stability of slave life, many masters seemed bent on its disruption (cf. ibid.:247 ff.). Juan de la Peña informed Philip II in 1569 that masters were separating slave families by selling male slaves, "from which results great harm to their wives and children, because they remain in this land with no aid" (Konetzke 1953, I:450). The Archivo General de la Nación has many examples of masters forcing slaves to marry against their will, separating slave families, and violating wives and daughters. Both Crown and Church did on occasion protect slave families, but in general Aguirre Beltrán seems accurate in stating that slave family life was highly unstable and vulnerable to the masters' whims (1946:258).[6]

The regulation of slave treatment and discipline did not fare much better. Under Spanish law mistreated slaves had access to courts for redress of grievances, and at least a few took advantage of this protection (AGN, Inquisición, Vol. 75, exp. 38; Vol. 353, fols. 22–32). There are also some notable instances when local officials, priests, and even sympathetic neighbors intervened on behalf of mistreated slaves (AGN, Inquisición, Vol. 292, fols. 2–4, 12–18, 172–73; Vol. 309, fols. 583–86; Zavala and Castelo 1939–45, III:38). At other times royal inspectors would investigate cases of brutality and correct the grievances, as in the *visita* of the cloth mills of Coyoacán in the 1660s (AGN, Historia, Vol. 117, fols. 15–59).[7] Yet the rarity of such intervention suggests

[6] Examples may be found in AGN, Historia, Vol. 117, fols. 15–59; Inquisición, Vol. 29, fols. 63–65; Vol. 31, fol. 1; Vol. 259, fol. 60; Vol. 292, fols. 2–4. AGN, Inquisición, Vol. 77, exp. 45; Vol. 101, exp. 7; Vol. 339, fols. 583–86; Vol. 808, exp. 2; General de Parte, Vol. 2, fol. 209v. See the detailed case of Church intervention in *Un matrimonio* 1935.

[7] AGN, Historia, Vol. 117, fols. 15–59. For a brief discussion of this inspection see Gibson 1964: 533–34. Other cases of intervention are in AGN, Inquisición, Vol. 253, fols. 287–90; Vol. 322, fol. 178; Vol. 431, fols. 265–79.

that the legal buffers between masters and slaves remained essentially on paper.

Furthermore, neither Crown nor Church intervened in situations that modern opinion would consider brutal. In the many cases of Negroes tried by the Inquisition for blasphemy, it usually came out that slaves cursed upon being beaten by their masters.[8] The slaves were tried for their crimes, while the violence that provoked them was ignored. Indeed, both Crown and Church sanctioned severe penalties for slaves who disobeyed the law. The Inquisition viewed whipping as an acceptable punishment and gave "some lashes very piously and without cruelty" (rarely exceeding two hundred) to Negroes found guilty in court.

That many Negroes were tried and punished in courts and not by their masters seems to have made little difference regarding slave treatment. Repeated evidence reveals that cruelty and mistreatment were as much a part of slavery in colonial Mexico as they were in most slave regimes in the New World. As the King frankly stated on more than one occasion, slaves in Mexico and the Spanish Indies in general were subject to "scandalous abuses," and mistreated "to such an extreme that some die without confession." "The poor slaves are molested and badly cared for" (Konetzke 1953, II:754 ff., III:113; for a discussion of the discrepancy between royal law and slave treatment in Spanish America in general, cf. Harris 1964:65–78).

The hispanization of Mexico's African population sought to ease the transition into slavery. While conversion was certainly one facet of the broader evangelical mission of Spanish expansion, in regard to slave control the policy served three possible functions: It would influence the development of a society where shared religious and cultural values produced a slave regime based on consent; it would provide certain outlets for slave tensions and discontent through religious ritual and social activities; and it sought to offer slaves spiritual equality in the City of God in return for deference and obedience to their masters in this world.[9] Iberian Cathol-

---

[8] See, for example, AGN, Inquisición, Vol. 145, exp. 7; Vol. 256, exp. 15; Vol. 271, exps. 14, 18; Vol. 273, exp. 6; Vol. 274, exp. 3; Vol. 276, exp. 1; Vol. 282, exp. 10; Vol. 291, exp. 1; Vol. 298, exps. 1, 9, 12; Vol. 306, exp. 4.

[9] As Cuevas notes, the Church tacitly tolerated if it did not openly encourage Negro slavery, and it held a dim view of

icism was ideally suited to these ends with its many saints' days and fiestas, auxiliary social organizations, and ingrained sense of hierarchy.

Hispanization of Africans was relatively successful, judging from the countless references to creole Negroes in the archives. True religious conversion was somewhat more difficult, although missionaries apparently made notable gains (cf. García Pimental 1897:172, 255, and passim; AGN, Historia, Vol. 31, fols. 17v–18). Evidence of Negro brotherhoods (*cofradías*) in the urban and mining districts suggests that some slaves benefited from the social outlets and religious balm of Christianity (García Pimental 1897:45–46; *Cartas* 1877:283; AGN, Ordenanzas, Vol. 1, fols. 146, 149v–50; Vol. 3, fol. 77; Vol. 4, fol. 60; Muriel de la Torre 1956–60, I:145, 253–55). The Church also established hospitals to serve the Negro population, although the charitable intentions and social functions of these institutions probably outweighed their medical efficacy (Muriel de la Torre 1956–60, I:210–11, 253–55).

That many slaves did adopt the forms and receive the benefits of hispanic culture and religion did not make them contented with their servile life. Christian slaves were just as likely to resist or revolt as any others. In fact, in 1523, the first slaves to revolt in the colony erected crosses to celebrate their freedom "and to let it be known that they were Christians" (Herrera y Tordesillas 1934–57, Década III, Libro V, Capítulo 8).

Unfortunately, conciliatory legislation and hispanization failed to eliminate the general causes of slave resistance in Mexico. Unstable familial and marital life, mistreatment, overwork, and the scarcity of effective channels to freedom undoubtedly contributed heavily to slave discontent (cf. Corro 1951:8; Martin 1957:120–21). Although these conditions certainly varied from one region, master, and economic activity to another, the worst treatment and the most brutal revolts occurred in the mines and sugar plantations of the colony. Here the deplorable circumstances intensified that common factor behind all slave resistance, the wholly human desire for freedom. "The love of liberty is natural," wrote

Negroes and mulattoes (1921–28, II:43). Of the few notable exceptions in which clergy spoke out openly against Negro slavery, see particularly Archbishop Montúfar to the King, June 30, 1560 (Paso y Troncoso 1939–42, IX:53–55).

Padre Alonso de Sandoval in 1627, "and in exchange for receiving it, [slaves] would join and give their lives for it" (de Sandoval 1956, I, Capítulo XXVIII). The frequent slave revolts throughout the first century and a half of Mexico's colonial history substantiate Padre Alonso's judgment.

Although individual Negroes fled in the early years, the first alleged effort by slaves to organize a large-scale uprising occurred in 1537 (AN, Protocolos, Vol. 3, fols. 87–87v, 46o–6ov; Herrera y Tordesillas 1934–57, Década III, Libro V, Capítulo 8). On December 10, 1537, Viceroy Antonio de Mendoza informed the Emperor of a plot intended to free the slave population of the young colony. "On the twenty-fourth of the month of November past," wrote Mendoza, "I was warned that the Negroes had chosen a king, and had agreed amongst themselves to kill all the Spaniards and rise up to take the land, and that the Indians were also with them (*Colección* 1864–84, II:198–99). Mendoza sent an agent to corroborate the rumor and soon received the reply that a plot existed, which included the capital city and the outlying mines. He swiftly arrested the "king" and his principal lieutenants, and, after eliciting confessions, had the leading conspirators drawn and quartered. There is a good possibility that the alleged plot, although it never materialized, was not a figment of the viceroy's imagination, since an independent sixteenth-century source also records the plot and subsequent events (Muñoz Camargo 1892:264).

Whether reality or fantasy, however, the conspiracy struck fear into the Spanish population and created a serious concern for Negro slave activity. In the months following the plot, Mendoza, the cabildo of Mexico City, and the commander of the fort guarding the city all expressed their fears of future slave retaliation and called for defensive measures to protect the city (*Colección* 1864–84, II:199–201; *Colección* 1932, I:85–87; *Actas* 1889–1911, IV:98–99).

Continued tension in Mexico City and the occurrence of at least two more revolts in the 1540s prompted Spanish officials to issue a number of decrees restricting Mexico's Negro population (Lopez Cogolludo 1957, Libro V, Capítulo XI; Bancroft 1883–86, II:537). Mendoza's ordinances of 1548 prohibited the sale of arms to Negroes and forbade public gatherings of three or more Negroes when not with their masters (cf. González Obregón 1951: 334–35). The viceroy also declared a night curfew on Negroes in the capital city. Mendoza's warnings to Luis de Velasco apparently alarmed the new viceroy, for he repeated Mendoza's restrictions in 1551 and wrote in 1553: "This land is so full of Negroes and mestizos who exceed the Spaniards in great quantity, and all desire to purchase their liberty with the lives of their masters" (*Colección* 1864–84, IV:494, cited in González Obregón 1951:335; *Cartas* 1877:263–64). In the same year Velasco also established a civil militia (the *Santa Hermandad*) in the colony, in part to cope with slave uprisings (Cuevas 1921–28, II:42).

With restrictive measures barely under way, Mexico experienced its first widespread wave of slave insurrections in the period 1560–80 as a result of the increased use of Negroes in mines and estates (cf. Aguirre Beltrán 1946:210, and Martin 1957:120–24). By the 1560s fugitive slaves from the mines of the north were terrorizing the regions from Guadalajara to Zacatecas, allying with the Indians and raiding ranches. In one case maroons from the mines of Guanajuato joined with unpacified Chichimec Indians in a brutal war with the settlers. The viceroy was informed that they were attacking travelers, burning ranches, and committing similar "misdeeds" (AGN, Mercedes, Vol. 5, fols. 65–70, 158, 232–33, 359; Powell 1952:62). To the east, slaves from the Pachuca mines took refuge in an inaccessible cave from which they sallied forth periodically to harass the countryside. Negroes from the Atotonilco and Tonavista mines joined them with arms, and created an impregnable *palenque* (AGN, Mercedes, Vol. 5, fols. 69–70). Local reports revealed that the uprisings were spreading eastward, and that much of the area in the quadrangle between Mexico City, Zacatecas, Pánuco, and Veracruz faced similar revolts (AGN, Mercedes, Vol. 5, fols. 201, 232–33, 459–60, 564).

The futile stream of instructions from the viceroy to local officials indicates that the bureaucracy and slave owners, outnumbered by slaves in the mining regions, were helpless in the face of such anarchy. Spanish control of Mexico had never been weaker, and, as the secret report of a Mexico City councilman in 1569 stated, almost everyone was in revolt against the conquerors (Paso y Troncoso 1905–48, III suplemento:73–74). Viceroy Martín Enríquez noted in 1572 and 1574 that the cooperation between Negroes and Indians made repression all the more difficult and requested aid from Spain (*Cartas* 1877:283, 299–300).

A series of royal decrees from 1571 to 1574, forming a fugitive slave code, consolidated previous restrictive legislation and articulated a complex system of slave control and surveillance (*Recopilación* 1943, Libro VII, Título V, leyes 21–22). Slaves absent from their masters for more than four days were to receive fifty lashes; those absent for more than eight days were to receive one hundred lashes "with iron fetters tied to their feet with rope, which they shall wear for two months and shall not take off under pain of two hundred lashes." The death sentence was to be applied to all those missing for six months, although this penalty was reduced at times to castration (AGN, Ordenanzas, Vol. 1, fols. 34–34v). In other circumstances the leaders of revolts were condemned to summary hanging, while the other maroons were to be returned to slavery. Local governments aided by rural police units were to provide a vigilance system in the countryside, and overseers were to make nightly checks on plantations and ranches. The decrees established rewards for the capture of runaways and encouraged fellow slaves and returned fugitives to join or aid the posses. The Crown hoped to prevent any assistance for fugitives by placing heavy fines on those caught aiding slaves (*Recopilación* 1943, Libro VII, Título V, Ley 22).

The insurrections continued into the 1570s as Martín Enríquez attempted to implement the royal ordinances. Yet neither the code of 1571–74 nor the issuance of restrictive legislation in the 1570s and 1580s was of any avail (AGN, Ordenanzas, Vol 1, fols. 78–80v, 86v, 102–3). A viceregal order of 1579 revealed that the contagion of revolt nearly covered the entire settled area of the colony outside of Mexico City, in particular the provinces of Veracruz and Pánuco, the area between Oaxaca and Gualtuco on the Pacific coast, and almost the whole of the Gran Chichimeca (AGN, Ordenanzas, Vol. 1, fols. 34–34v; Vol. 2, fols. 232–32v; Zavala 1947:126–27; and for other revolts in this period see AGN, General de Parte, Vols. 4–6). Only emergency repressive measures and the continued importation of Africans maintained Mexico's slave labor supply.

During the last decades of the sixteenth century the focus of slave revolts shifted to the eastern sugar regions of the viceroyalty. Isolated uprisings had occurred there since the 1560s, but by the turn of the century the slopes and lowlands between Mount Orizaba and Veracruz teemed with small maroon settlements and roaming bands of slaves who raided the many plantations and towns in the area (cf. AGN, Historia, Vol. 31, fols. 31–48; Pérez de Ribas 1896, I:282–84; Corro 1951).

The geography of the region so favored maroon guerrilla activities that local authorities proved incapable of thwarting their raids or pursuing them to the *palenques*. Andrés Pérez de Ribas noted: "And although some justices of these districts had sallied out a few times, accompanied by other Spaniards, to castigate and apprehend the fugitive rabble, they failed to achieve their goal because the site chosen by the Negroes for their dwelling was extremely rugged and difficult [to approach]" (1896, I:283). The viceroy appointed two Spanish captains, Pedro de Bahena and Antón de Parada, to pacify the area in 1606, but they were equally powerless to prevent the raids, which destroyed property and freed increasing numbers of slaves. In that year the viceroy wrote to Bahena with dismay: "I understand that the number of Negro maroons who are gathered in revolt within the jurisdiction of Vieja and Nueva Veracruz, Río Blanco, and Punta de Antón Lizardo is very large and their liberty and daring much greater, and that they have begun to enter the town of Tlalixcoyán to rob and sack the homes and seize Negro domestics, taking them from the homes of their masters and threatening the Spaniards, setting fire to their houses" (Corro 1951:17). Maroon activity was so successful that, as Pérez de Ribas observed, the *camino real* between Mexico City and Veracruz was unsafe for travelers and commerce. In one attack of 1609 "the Negro maroons robbed and destroyed some wagons which carry from Veracruz to Mexico City the clothing that comes from Spain, routing the carriers and breaking to pieces the Spaniard who led them" (1896, I:283–84). In 1609 such activities prompted Viceroy Luis de Velasco to commission Captain Pedro Gonzalo de Herrera to lead a pacifying force to the distraught area. The story of this expedition is perhaps the only surviving detailed account of an armed encounter between Spanish troops and ex-slaves in the colony. It takes the form of a long letter written in 1609 by the Jesuit Juan Laurencio, who accompanied Herrera's expedition.[10] An ex-

10 Although the original letter, addressed to one Padre Rodrigo de Cabredo, is apparently no longer extant, a copy was printed in full by Pérez de Ribas in 1654 in his 1896, I:284–92. A slightly

amination of this encounter should reveal the general nature of maroon activity and life in colonial Mexico and the difficulties experienced by the ruling authorities in suppressing fugitives.

Herrera, a "man of valor, wealth, experience, and prudence," traveled to the coast where he assembled an army in January 1609. While stationed at Veracruz he added 150 Indian archers and another 100 or so irregulars to his original nucleus of 100 Spanish troops in the King's pay. On January 26 the full expeditionary force left the city in search of the maroons. The Negroes knew of Herrera's departure but continued their raiding in the hinterland. In one attack they captured a Spaniard and brought him to their main settlement at the Cofre de Perote in the mountains near Mount Orizaba (Pérez de Ribas 1896, I:284–85).

The ruler of the Negro settlement was an aging first-generation African referred to as Ñaga, Ñanga, or Yanga. Padre Juan wrote: "This Yanga was a Negro of the Bron [sic] nation, of whom it is said that if they had not captured him, he would have been king in his own land. . . . He had been the first maroon to flee his master and for thirty years had gone free in the mountains, and he has united others who held him as chief, who are called Yanguicos" (ibid.).[11] In Yanga's settlement were some sixty huts housing about eighty adult males, twenty-four Negro and Indian women, and an undetermined number of children. Although the settlement had existed in that location for only nine months, "they had already planted many seedlings and other trees, cotton, sweet potatoes, chile, tobacco, squash, corn, beans, sugar cane, and other vegetables" (Pérez de Ribas 1896, I:290). The settlement was by necessity a war camp, with its internal structure oriented to the needs of self-defense and retaliation. Padre Juan noted a distinct division of labor within the *palenque*,

---

paraphrased version is preserved in the eighteenth-century manuscript copy of Pérez de Ribas' narrative in AGN, Historia, Vol. 31, fols. 48–56. Pérez de Ribas' original account, including the letter, was printed by the eighteenth-century Jesuit historian Francisco Javier Alegre in his 1956–60, II:175–83. See the notes in Alegre for more recent works utilizing the letter.

11 "Bron" probably refers to Brong or Abron, a subgroup of Akan culture living to the northwest of Ashanti in present-day Ghana (Murdock 1959:254). Aguirre Beltrán (1946:126, 244) notes that many Africans of this subgroup were imported into Mexico.

with half the population tending the crops and cattle and the remaining men comprising a constant military guard and forming the guerrilla troops, which periodically raided the countryside. The command of the army was in the hands of a Negro from Angola, while Yanga reserved to himself the civil administration. Most of the Negroes had received some religious instruction before escaping, and, like many other maroons in the Americas, they retained at least a limited form of Catholicism. The town had a small chapel with an altar, candles, and images (ibid., I:285, 288–90).

The captive Spaniard was brought before Yanga, who supposedly assured him: "Do not fear, Spaniard, for you have seen my face, and so you cannot die." Yanga then ordered the captive to write a letter to Herrera, "full of notable arrogance," in which Yanga dared the Spaniards to defeat him. The Spaniard delivered the letter to Herrera, who had made camp unaware of the *palenque's* location and thus learned the whereabouts of the Negroes.

On February 24, 1609, Herrera and two companies left on a reconnaissance mission, and they had their first encounter with the maroons (ibid., I:285–86). Yanga, soon regretting his burst of pride, had sent a flying squadron to raid a neighboring sugar mill to acquire reinforcements. Halfway through the raid the Negroes fled upon seeing Herrera's troops and returned to the settlement, where they sounded a general alarm. Herrera did not pursue, but remained in the area and established a permanent camp protected by a palisade. From the new site he could see the *palenque,* some two leagues away, securely nestled in an imposing and rugged mountain range. Herrera sent out two scouting parties to check possible approaches to the *palenque,* and on the next day the Spaniards held Mass and marched to attack. They soon came across a water hole used by the maroons. "We arrived at a fountain placed between two rocks," said Padre Juan, "from whose water the Negroes take sustenance, for although it is far from their town, they have nothing else to drink. Next to the fountain was a large field of tobacco, squash, and corn, which [we] desolated and destroyed to deprive our enemy of provisions" (ibid., I:286–87). Then Herrera, apparently experienced in guerrilla tactics, sent his nephew up the trail with a dog to check for sites conducive to ambush. The dog soon began to bark and revealed a troop of Negroes hidden in the bush. The Spanish army advanced, and the first battle began.

There was a brief exchange before the Negroes fled up the mountain to their settlement, with the soldiers in pursuit. Although the army had harquebuses and the Negroes mainly bows and arrows and a few firearms, the Spaniards advanced only with great difficulty. The maroons had thrown up numerous barricades, which blocked the narrow passages up the precipitous slope. Many in the army fell wounded in the attempt to scale the obstacles, Padre Juan receiving an arrow in the leg.

Upon reaching the top, Herrera found the *palenque* deserted. Earlier Yanga had sent his people to another location, and he and the remaining inhabitants fled just before the army arrived, leaving most of their possessions behind. Padre Juan described what was left in the village: "The spoils that were found in the town and huts of these Negroes were considerable. A variety of clothing that they had gathered, cutlasses, swords, axes, some harquebuses and coins, salt, butter, corn, and other similar things without which, although the enemy was not left totally helpless, he was very much weakened." While the army remained in the settlement, Herrera received a second note from Yanga. Again he defied the Spaniards and refused to make peace. Herrera raised the white flag calling for a truce and negotiations, but he received no further reply from the maroons (ibid., I:287–90).

The Spanish commander than decided to pursue the slaves and left a few men to guard the village. He soon caught up with the main body of the maroons who, upon seeing the Spaniards, climbed a rocky and thickly wooded mountain from which they poured a hail of arrows. After a brief exchange in which both sides suffered severe casualties, Herrera again called for negotiations. Yanga refused and led his people farther into the interior. Herrera could find no trace of him and returned to the *palenque*, where he waited.

Padre Juan's narrative ends here, but Pérez de Ribas reported that Yanga and Herrera soon came to terms, although he did not explain the circumstances (ibid., I:290–93). Judging from the terms of the negotiation, however, the two leaders arrived at a mutual accommodation, which was not a surrender for the slaves. The terms of the truce, as preserved in the archives, included eleven conditions stipulated by Yanga upon which he and his people would cease their raiding.[12] The African demanded that all of his people who had fled before September of the past year (1608) be freed and promised that those who had escaped slavery after that date would be returned to their masters. He further stipulated that the *palenque* be given the status of a free town and that it have its own cabildo and a *justicia mayor*, who was to be a Spanish layman. No other Spaniards were to live in the town, although they could visit on market days. Yanga asked that he be named governor of the town and that his descendants succeed him in office. He also required that only Franciscan friars minister to his people and that the Crown finance the ornamentation of the church. In return Yanga promised that for a fee the town would aid the viceroy in capturing fugitive slaves. The Negroes, he said, would aid the Crown in case of an external attack on Mexico.

As Pérez de Ribas noted, the viceroy accepted these terms (1896, I:293). Besides being unable to conquer Yanga, the authorities needed the aid of his guerrillas to capture other fugitive slaves in the area. Thus, shortly after the negotiations, the new town of San Lorenzo de los Negros was established as a free Negro settlement not far from the old *palenque*. How long it existed is unknown, but the Italian traveler Gemelli Careri, who traversed the region in 1698, testified to its prosperity and industry (1745, IV:520–21).

Yanga's maroon movement is a notable incident in the history of Negroes in Mexico—the only known example of a fully successful attempt by slaves to secure their freedom en masse by revolt and negotiation and to have it sanctioned and guaranteed in law. This experience demonstrates that, under capable leadership, slaves could maintain an active guerrilla campaign, negotiate a truce, and win recognition of their freedom. In view of the tenacity displayed by other

[12] The terms of the truce, entitled *Las condiciones que piden los negros Simarrones de esta Comarca*, are contained in a manuscript copy of a letter from the Commissary of Veracruz to the Inquisition in Mexico City, in AGN, Inquisición, Vol. 283, fols. 186–87. The letter is dated March 8, 1608, received in Mexico City on March 24, 1608. The discrepancy in the year (Pérez de Ribas states that the negotiations took place in 1609) is probably due to a mistake by either the scribe, the letter writer, Pérez de Ribas, or Padre Juan Laurencio. The document refers directly to Yanga and undoubtedly includes the terms to which Pérez de Ribas refers.

maroons as well, it is likely that similar incidents occurred
that have not been recorded.

The violence of slave insurrections in the eastern slopes and
northern mining regions kept Mexico City in a prolonged
state of anxiety. By the first decade of the seventeenth
century the Negro population of the capital had grown enor-
mously, and there was a general fear that the urban slaves
would unite to take the city.[13] The tensions in the metropolis
exploded in 1609 and 1612 when rumors circulated that the
Negroes had chosen leaders and planned massive uprisings.[14]
In both cases elaborate defensive preparations followed brief
periods of panic and confusion. Negroes were apprehended
and punished, and the plots, if indeed they existed at all,
never materialized. Yet whether or not these conspiracies
actually existed, the terror that they caused was a reflection
of the tensions inherent in multiracial Mexico, where insecurity plagued the Spanish and creole population well
into the seventeenth century (cf. Leonard 1959:37–52).

A violent Negro-Indian uprising in Durango in 1616 and a
rash of retaliatory raids in the following years by the maroons
of Veracruz province prompted further restrictive decrees but
little effective action by the authorities (Priestly 1929:45–47;
AGN, Historia, Vol. 31, fols. 31v–32; AGN, Ordenanzas,
Vol. 3, fol. 77; Vol. 2, fol. 13v; Vol. 4, fols. 26v–27v, 40v–
41v, 60, 82, and passim). Countless minor revolts and escapes occurred in the sheep ranching regions of the north in
the 1620s and 1630s. As Viceroy Rodrigo Pacheco Ossorio
observed in 1626, it was so easy to flee the ranches that it
was almost a daily happening. In fact, he noted that some
ranchers were near bankruptcy, not merely because of the
loss of their slaves, but also because of the exorbitant fees
charged by local officials for capturing fugitives (AGN, Ordenanzas, Vol. 4, fols. 78v–79v; Zavala 1947:130–32). Con-
stables and *corregidores* held a monopoly of slave-captur-
ing in the ranching regions and made lucrative profits by

[13] For travelers' estimates of the Negro population of Mexico
City in the early seventeenth century see Champlain 1859:25;
Ordóñez de Ceballos 1905, II:332; Vázquez de Espinosa 1948:
146.
[14] Reports of these incidents are in Torquemada 1943, I, Libro
v, Capítulo 70; Vetancurt 1960–61, II:217. AGN, Ordenanzas, Vol.
1, fols. 146–50, contains the hurried restrictive legislation.

reselling runaways, not always to their original owners. The frequent complaints of ranchers and viceroys indicate that slaves continued to flee, local officials continued to capture them and charge high fees, and ranchers continued to suffer throughout the first half of the seventeenth century (AGN, Ordenanzas, Vol. 2, fols. 13v, 41–43; Vol. 4, fols. 104, 110, 117, 121–24v, 138, 140–53v; Zavala 1947:125, 129).

It is apparent that officials and slave owners found it extremely difficult to prevent or contain slave resistance. Few in numbers, they were forced to rely on the scarce royal troops in Mexico aided by untrained and undisciplined bands of mestizos and Indians. These haphazard military operations faced serious strategic and tactical problems, especially in campaigns against distant hideaways in the frontier regions. Mexico's rugged terrain compounded the difficulties, for fugitives could establish settlements in the mountains and isolated *barrancas,* which afforded excellent defensive sites. Moreover, Indian cooperation seems to have been instrumental to the success of various revolts and made the job of repression all the more difficult. With such a weak system of control, the flight and insurrection of slaves continued into the eighteenth century, and it was only the abolition of slavery in the early nineteenth century that put an end to slave resistance in Mexico.

In conclusion, some implications of slave control and resistance in colonial Mexico are evident. In the first place, it appears that flight and revolt constituted the most effective avenue to liberty for the slave population, despite the existence of an elaborate (if often ineffective) machinery of control and conciliation. Thus a major consequence of resistance was the development of the free Negro and Afromestizo population of the colony. Second, slave resistance, real or imagined, had a notably disturbing effect on the society of the conquerors. In this respect the anxiety of colonial society differed more in degree than in kind from that of the fear-ridden slavocracies of the Caribbean and southern United States. The same restrictive and precautionary measures, the same false alarms, and similar bands of roaming vigilantes characterized Mexico as well. Moreover, preventive legislation and Spanish fears extended to the free Negro population, and the status of freedmen in the colony suffered regardless of their role in slave resistance (cf. Dusenberry

1948). Finally, the study of Negro slave activity reveals an area of social life barely perceived by many students of colonial Mexico—the relations within the nonwhite and mixed peoples in the multiracial societies that developed throughout tropical America. Of particular importance here are Indian-Negro relations, where miscegenation, marital and common law unions, cooperation in resistance, and also mutual antagonisms provide a rewarding field of study of social history. Slave resistance in Mexico is more than just another chapter in the Negroes' long struggle for freedom and justice. In the context of Mexican social history it illustrates the interplay of diverse races and cultures that makes that history one of the most complex and fascinating in the New World.

REFERENCES NOT CITED IN GENERAL BIBLIOGRAPHY

Actas de Cabildo de la Ciudad de México.
  1889–1911 (47 vols.). Mexico.
Advertimientos generales que los virreyes
  dejaron a sus sucesores para el gobierno de Nueva España,
  1590–1604.
  1956 Mexico.
Aguirre Beltrán, Gonzalo
  1944 "The Slave Trade in Mexico." *Hispanic American Historical Review* 24:412–31.
Alegre, Francisco Javier
  1956–60 *Historia de la Provincia de la Compañia de Jesús en la Nueva España.* Roma.
Bancroft, Hubert Howe
  1883–86 *History of Mexico.* San Francisco.
Borah, Woodrow
  1951 *New Spain's Century of Depression.* Berkeley: University of California Press.
——— and Cook, Sherburne F.
  1963 *The Aboriginal Population of Central Mexico on the Eve of the Spanish Conquest.* Berkeley: University of California Press.
Cartas de Indias. Madrid.
  1877
Champlain, Samuel
  1859 *Narrative of a Voyage to the West Indies and Mexico in the Years 1599–1602.* London.
Chevalier, François
  1963 *Land and Society in Colonial Mexico.* Berkeley: University of California Press.
Colección de documentos inéditos para la historia de Hispano-America.
  1932 (14 vols.). Madrid.

Colección de documentos inéditos relativos al descubrimiento, conquista y colonización de las posesiones españolas en América y Oceania, sacados en su mayor parte del Real Archivo de Indias.
1864–84 (42 vols.). Madrid.

Cook, Sherburne F. and Borah, Woodrow
1960 *The Indian Population of Central Mexico, 1531–1610.* Berkeley: University of California Press.

Cook, Sherburne F. and Simpson, Lesley Byrd
1948 *The Population of Central Mexico in the Sixteenth Century.* Berkeley: University of California Press.

Corro, Octaviano
1951 *Los cimarrones en Veracruz y la fundación de Amapa.* Mexico.

Cuevas, Mariano
1921–28 *Historia de la Iglesia en Mexico.* El Paso and Mexico.

Dusenberry, William H.
1948 "Discriminatory Aspects of Legislation in Colonial Mexico." *Journal of Negro History* 33:284–302.
1963 *The Mexican mesta.* Urbana: University of Illinois Press.

Galván Rivera, Mariano
1859 *Concilio III provincial mexicano, celebrado en México el año de 1585.* Mexico.

García Pimental, Luis (ed.)
1897 *Descripción del Arzobispado de México hecha en 1570 y otros documentos.* Mexico.

Gemelli Careri, John Francis
1745 "A voyage round the world." *In* Churchill, Awnsham (ed.), *A Collection of Voyages and Travels.* London.

Gibson, Charles
1964 *The Aztecs Under Spanish rule.* Stanford: Stanford University Press.

González Obregon, Luis
1951 *Rebeliones indígenas y precursores de la independencia mexicana en los siglos XVI, XVII y XVIII* (2nd ed.). Mexico.

Harris, Marvin
1964 *Patterns of Race in the Americas.* New York.

Herrera y Tordesillas, Antonio de
1934–57 *Historia general de los hechos de los castellanos en las islas y tierra firme del mar océano.* Madrid.

Instrucciones que los virreyes de Nueva España dejaron a sus sucesores.
1867 Mexico.

Konetzke, Richard (ed.)
1953 *Colección de documentos para la historia de la formacción social de Hispanoamérica, 1493–1810.* Madrid.

Kubler, George
1942 "Population Movements in Mexico, 1520–1600." *Hispanic American Historical Review* 22:606–43.

Las Siete Partidas.
   1931 New York.
Leonard, Irving A.
   1959 *Baroque Times in old Mexico*. Ann Arbor: University of Michigan Press.
López Cogolludo, Diego
   1957 *Historia de Yucatán*. Mexico.
Lorenzana, Francisco Antonio
   1769 *Consilios provinciales primero y segundo, celebrados en la muy noble y muy leal ciudad de México . . . en los años de 1555, y 1565*. Mexico.
Martin, Norman F.
   1957 *Los vagabundos en la Nueva España, siglo XVI*. Mexico.
McAlister, Lyle N.
   1963 "Social Structure and Social Change in New Spain." *Hispanic American Historical Review* 43:349–70.
Morissey, Richard J.
   1951 "The Northward Advance of Cattle Ranching in New Spain, 1550–1600." *Agricultural History* 25:115–21.
Muñoz Camargo, Diego
   1892 *Historia de Tlaxcala*. Mexico.
Murdock, George Peter
   1959 *Africa: Its Peoples and Their Culture History*. New York.
Muriel de la Torre, Josefina
   1956–60 *Hospitales de la Nueva España*. Mexico.
Ordóñez de Ceballos, Pedro
   1905 "Viaje del mundo." *In* M. Serrano y Sanz (ed.), *Nueva biblioteca de autores Españoles*. Madrid.
Paso y Troncoso, Francisco del (ed.)
   1905–48 *Papeles de Nueva España*. Madrid.
   1939–42 *Epistolario de la Nueva España. Biblioteca histórica mexicana de obras inéditas, secunda serie* (16 vols.). Mexico.
Pi-Sunyer, Oriol
   1957 "The Historical Background to the Negro in Mexico." *Journal of Negro History* 42:237–46.
Powell, Philip Wayne
   1952 *Soldiers, Indians and Silver: The Northward Advance of New Spain, 1550–1600*. Berkeley: University of California Press.
Priestly, Herbert Ingram
   1929 *The Coming of the White Man*. New York.
Puga, Vasgo de|
   1878 *Provisiones, cédulas, instrucciones de su majestad, ordenanças de difuntos y Audiencia para la buena expedición de los negocios y administración de Justicia y Governación de esta Nueva España . . .* Mexico.
Recopilación de leyes de los reynos de las Indias.
   1943 Madrid.

Sandoval, Alonso de
1956 *De instaurada Aethiopium salute*. Bogotá.
Sandoval, Fernando B.
1951 *La industria del azúcar en Nueva España*. Mexico.
Simpson, Lesley Byrd
1934–40 *Studies in the Administration of the Indians of New Spain*. Berkeley: University of California Press.
1952 *Exploitation of Land in Central Mexico in the Sixteenth Century*. Berkeley: University of California Press.
Solórzano y Pereyra, Juan de
1948 *Política indiana*. Madrid.
Tannenbaum, Frank
1963 *Slave and Citizen: The Negro in the Americas*. New York: Vintage.
Toro, Alfonso
1920–21 "Influencia de la raza negra en la formación del pueblo mexicano." *Ethnos* 1:215–19.
Torquenmada, Juan de
1943 *Monarquía indiana*. Mexico.
"Un matrimonio de esclavos."
1935 *Boletín del Archivo General de la Nación* 6:541–56.
Vázquez de Espinosa, Antonio
1948 *Compendio y descripción de las Indias Occidentales*. Smithsonian Miscellaneous Collections, 108. Washington, D.C.
Vetancurt, Augustín de
1960–61 *Teatro mexicano*. Madrid.
Wolf, Eric R.
1959 *Sons of the Shaking Earth*. Chicago: University of Chicago Press.
Zavala, Silvio (ed.)
1947 *Ordenanzas del trabajo, siglos XVI y XVII*. Mexico.
——— and María Castelo (eds.)
1939–45 *Fuentes para la historia del trabajo en Nueva España*. Mexico.

PART TWO

The French Caribbean

In the French territories, marronage was a particularly visible and integral part of the slave system since, except in thinly populated French Guiana or in the rugged hill country of Saint-Domingue, the relatively compact size of the islands prevented the formation of large-scale communities. In the French Caribbean, *petit marronage* was especially prevalent, a constant thorn in the side of the plantation enterprise; it was Frenchmen who labeled marronage the "plague" or the "gangrene" of colonial society. The maroon heritage is deeply woven into the fabric of French Antillean history. Today, throughout these islands, one comes upon out-of-the-way rural settlements that trace their ancestry back to maroon pioneers. In Haiti, modern historians are busy glorifying the role that they now believe the maroons played in their own national revolution. And, in a not unrelated political act charged with ideological implications, the late President-for-life François Duvalier unveiled shortly before his death what must be the most imposing memorial to maroons anywhere, the magnificent statue by sculptor-architect Albert Mangonès of "Le Marron Inconnu de Saint-Domingue"—The Unknown Maroon (see the cover of this book).

The selections that follow include a general survey and two case studies. First, Gabriel Debien, a prolific French historian of slavery, presents an overview of marronage in the French Caribbean that goes beyond documentary history to seek the underlying causes of the phenomenon. (For a more detailed analysis of "causes," see Fouchard 1972, which appeared after this book was already in press.) Then, the most famous of French maroon communities, that of le Maniel, which straddled the border between French and Spanish Hispaniola, is examined from two perspectives—that of the contemporary historian M. L. E. Moreau de Saint-Méry and that of the modern French scholar Yvan Debbasch, in an extract from his "essay on the desertion of Antillean slaves"—one of the most comprehensive of all works to date on marronage.

Suggestions for further readings on maroons in the French Caribbean are found in the bibliographical note for Part Two.

CHAPTER SEVEN

Marronage in the French Caribbean

GABRIEL DEBIEN

. . . Planters distinguished two types of marronage: *grand marronage* and *petit marronage*. *Grand marronage* was, in the true sense, flight from the plantation with no intention of ever returning (de Culion 1803, I:240). Usually, such fugitives fled alone, sometimes in twos or threes. Some lived for long periods in isolation, but others more or less quickly formed bands under the direction of a chief, or joined a band that was already established. These bands lived in the hills, in the most remote, least-traveled districts. There was a scattering of women among them. These fugitives had settled into a way of life that was almost "collective."

Pillaging was far from being their main activity; but they nonetheless terrorized certain areas, or at least created an atmosphere of anxiety, for whoever said "band," presupposed armed band and hostile intentions. As a result, the mounted police were sent out against them, and sometimes the militia, or even professional troops if the situation called for it. Whenever the maroons had raided the supplies of a plantation, or stolen horses or cattle, such an expedition was organized, though never too hastily . . . since they could never

Translated, with considerable editing, from Gabriel Debien, "Le marronage aux Antilles Françaises au XVIIIe siècle," *Caribbean Studies* 6(3):3–44 (1966). Translated and reprinted by permission of the author and the Institute of Caribbean Studies. Copyright 1966 by the Institute of Caribbean Studies, University of Puerto Rico.

really hope to destroy all the maroons, but only to capture a few and punish them.

It is these well-established maroons who are most often spoken of in administrative correspondence and in the reports of militia commandants or of colonists writing to the minister or the governor. Although there were many such bands in existence, they caused serious trouble only in certain districts and particular circumstances. They posed a real danger to the crops, but rare was the colonist who really believed his personal safety threatened.

The first band of any numerical significance known to us is a group of four to five hundred maroons in Martinique who, in 1665, were under the direction of a maroon named Francisque Fabulé, who had taken the name of his master. This band wreaked such havoc that the Sovereign Council was forced to negotiate with it, and through the mediation of a slave of Lord Renaudot, it agreed to grant Fabulé his freedom and one thousand pounds of tobacco. In addition, no maroon in the band was to be punished. Fabulé remained peaceful for a while, serving—probably as a domestic—in the house of Clodoré, the governor. But he seduced a young Negress, induced her to steal, and convinced her to stab her master. Whipped for this "crime," he once again took flight. Recaptured, he was condemned to the galleys for life since . . . he had recently taken up to fifty Negroes to the forest "and with them had committed robberies, thefts, and even a few murders and assassinations" (Arrêt du Conseil Supérieur du 10 mai 1671; Moreau de Saint-Méry 1784–90, I:136; Dutertre 1667, I:201; Peytraud 1897:34).

Houel, governor of Guadeloupe, sent word to the King on the thirteenth of March, 1668, that more than thirty maroons were living in Grande-Terre, which was otherwise uninhabited at the time. He asked that an example be set by beheading those who could be captured during the night (Archives Nationales, Section Colonies, C⁸/A19).

The decree of the thirteenth of October, 1671, from the Supreme Council of Martinique, deplored the fact that fugitive slaves were living together in the forest, where they had cleared land, constructed dwellings, and planted crops; they stole and committed all sorts of disorderly acts (Moreau de Saint-Méry 1784–90, I:248).

Lefebvre d'Albon, inspector of the navy at Cayenne, reported on the twenty-fifth of May, 1707, that a troop of maroons led by a certain Gabriel, who preferred to be called M. le Gouverneur, included some Indians. One of them informed on the band, and one Indian man and five Indian women were captured, including two of the informer's wives. They were sentenced to various punishments (Archives Nationales, Section Colonies, F³/91).

These bands were especially daring. Fear inflated the estimates of their numbers. The pillage of a few fields of provisions or of sugar cane, the theft of a few cattle inspired desperate fear of mass nocturnal attacks, of whole towns in flames. Therefore, however harsh the punishments meted out to maroons, they never seemed to be sufficient. . . .

In point of fact, the most frequent crime was the abduction of Negresses. Very rarely did the bands number more than one hundred (for example, there were sixty in Grenada on the fifteenth of June, 1725 [Archives Nationales, Section Colonies, B⁸/321]). The six hundred maroons in Guadeloupe (mentioned by the minister to the administrators of Martinique on the nineteenth of March, 1726) were divided into four bands, and groups of more than sixty to eighty slaves were never sighted. According to Moyencourt, they numbered no more than two hundred in all (ibid., B 48:322).

Again on Guadeloupe, the twenty-first of May, 1737, forty-eight maroons were put on trial, eighteen of them in absentia. Their leader was a certain Bordebois; eight were condemned to be broken alive: They had kidnapped a child, then killed and eaten him (ibid., F³/22b, fᵒ 133:321). . . .

In Saint-Domingue, there were few peaceable and industrious bands; those that were known had become so because of their raids on plantations. During the first half of the eighteenth century, almost all these raids focused in the Sud du Cap region. Since 1719, bands of maroons had been devastating the crops. Chastenoye, during his interim term of office, began pursuing them in 1724. He met with a great deal of difficulty in trying to rally against them the "coloreds" whom they called their allies. These were eventually persuaded by an ordinance that threatened severe penalties unless they participated in pursuing the maroons. The maroon chief was taken at Montègre, above the village of Tannerie, between Grande-Rivière and Limonade. He was Colas-Jambes-Coupées, who was executed at Bois-de-Lance. . . .

[*Editor's note:* Debien next discusses the maroons of Baho-

ruco or "le Maniel," treated in more detail in the selections
by Moreau de Saint-Méry and Debbasch, below.]

In the Grande-Anse region, on the southern peninsula, the
leader of the band was Plymouth, a maroon who had come
from the English islands. This band operated around Nippes.
The first counterattack of the colonists, aided by soldiers,
was successful. The mission they made in 1730 in the hills of
Anse-du-Clerc produced twenty-three prisoners and a good
many more maroons killed, among them Plymouth.

The settlements in the region surrounding le Cap were
spared after 1740. The bands had either been dispersed or
lacked leaders. The vulnerable areas were Trou and Fort-
Dauphin, between le Cap and the Spanish frontier. In 1734,
Polydor terrorized the Trou region. The planters, joined by
the mounted police, went in pursuit of him. A slave, who
was subsequently granted his freedom in recognition, was
responsible for his capture, and Polydor was killed in the
savanna that bears his name. In 1774 and 1775, it was Noël's
band that inspired terror up until the day he was captured.
After him, other leaders, Télémaque Conga and Isaac and
Pyrrhus Candide, continued to devastate fields of crops
and abduct Negro women at Ecrevisses and Trou. Conga
was soon taken and condemned to death by the Council of
le Cap. It was never found out whether he had led the same
band as Noël. At any rate, after his death, the entire northeast remained peaceful.

But let it be noted that all of these disturbances were
nothing in comparison with the trouble the maroons caused
in Grenada in 1725, Antigua in 1729, and Saint John in
1734. The Danes managed to control the rebel fugitives only
with the assistance of the governor of Martinique. Never had
the bands at Saint-Domingue made depredations equal to
those of the Jamaican rebels or those of Surinam, who
even succeeded in subduing European troops. In general, the
maroons of Saint-Domingue, even when organized in bands,
remained fairly peaceful, and in Martinique and Guadeloupe
there were hardly any troops of maroons worthy of the
name. . . .

The term "marronage" was also used, "but improperly,"
in speaking of absences of two or three days, or even of a
week, which slaves made "out of laziness and libertinage
rather than with the aim of desertion" (de Culion 1803, I:
240). We will call this *petit marronage* or *marronage léger*,

which was an act of individuals or at most of very small groups.

These maroons did not go very far from the plantation from which they fled, but remained on its edges, or hid in the house of a relative or a friend from the neighboring plantation. They subsisted not by systematically pillaging crops, but by stealing small amounts of food and committing minor thefts, in a kind of symbiosis with the plantation. These maroons exchanged fish, game, and stolen objects with the slaves for manioc, peas, and vegetables. Sometimes they worked in towns as freemen. This form of escape might be termed absenteeism, which could have been a result of the temperament of the slave, the nature of the work assigned, or the conditions of that work. In the case of those who lacked a particular skill, it was also due to the instability of their condition. With the exception of the maroons who had been town slaves, whether serving under a free artisan or as a domestic, hardly any skilled slaves became maroons. The field slaves were the ones who most often took flight.

Despite the prevalence of this sort of marronage, which affected almost every plantation, the colonists did not seem very concerned about it. Planters, including those who were residing in France, do not seem to have questioned their plantation managers on the subject, nor did the managers bring up the issue with the owners. One might imagine that they avoided doing so because the number of maroons could reflect badly on their handling of the slaves. However, among the managers as among the planters, there seems to have been a genuine casualness about it. The representatives of the planters only began to speak about maroons when they had deserted in groups, or when an unfriendly neighbor threatened to mention them to the master who was living in France. "This second sort [of marronage] is inconsequential, and the colonists pay little attention to it" (de Culion 1803, I:240); while in the settlers' eyes collective marronage, involving organized and supposedly armed bands, constituted sedition and a serious crime, individual marronage was only a minor infraction when it was short-lived, and was not yet "an inveterate vice." It was viewed simply as a shortage that had to be made up for, because there was never enough available manpower, especially during the seasons when cane was cut and coffee beans harvested.

The colonists' view of *petit marronage* is best seen at the time of the assessment or sale of plantations. It was then that a careful census of slaves was accomplished. One might think that the distinction between slaves who are actually on the premises and those who have fled would be crucial at this time. However, this distinction was not always carefully made. Usually maroons are simply included in the estimates along with those slaves who are present. And in the margin of the list of slaves it was simply noted who was a maroon and how long he had been gone, so that it would be clear what the chances are that he would return. Those slaves who had already been absent for a long time, however, were not included in the estimate, at least not always. . . .

Some buyers, protective of their own interests, asked that the maroons be grouped separately at the end of the list by name, and only provisionally included in the total. It was agreed that if these maroons did not return by the final transfer of title a few weeks hence, their market value would be deducted from the total; but this precaution was rather rare. It did not occur until the end of the eighteenth century, and then only in Martinique and Guadeloupe. This sort of marronage, therefore, was far from being considered out-of-the-ordinary. It was a special kind of coming-and-going, which was recognized by the experienced settlers as impossible to stop: The work groups were simply too numerous, and it was not worthwhile to survey them day and night in order to prevent a few slaves from escaping. Peytraud was exaggerating to a considerable extent when he said that marronage was "the chronic plague" or "open wound" of the Antilles (1897:343). He should have specified which type of marronage was in question. The word "wound" is much too tragic—at least in the French islands.

THE GOVERNMENT AND THE MAROONS

Peytraud was quite correct in stating that marronage was as old as slavery in the islands, indeed in all the colonies. It existed among white indentured servants as well as among black slaves. As early as 1639 on Saint-Christophe, the mother colony of our islands, Governor d'Olive ordered more than sixty fugitive slaves pursued, and many were severely punished (ibid., 37). Two years later, in Guadeloupe, the King pardoned a slave condemned to death for marronage (sixteenth of February, 1641) (Archives Nationales, Section

Colonies, F³/257, f⁰ 13). In July 1655, a Guadeloupean slave who had led a seditious movement was condemned to be hanged (Satineau:292 [No further citation given—Ed.]).

Whether it was because marronage was becoming more frequent and to encourage more captures or in order to avoid disputes over bounty prices, the Superior Council of Guadeloupe fixed the size of rewards that would be granted for returning a maroon to his master:

150 pounds of sugar when the maroon had been gone for less than two months;

300 pounds of sugar if he had been gone for six months;

600 pounds of sugar if a year had passed;

900 pounds of sugar if more than a year had gone by

(Moreau de Saint-Méry 1784–90, I:128).

The bounty for maroons who had been missing for more than three years was not fixed, which indicates that this must have been a highly unusual situation. As for habitual offenders, this decree allows them to be hamstrung; but this is a question of private justice. . . .

Père Labat, who was not one to belabor details, nonetheless remarks that these matters were carried out much more simply in Martinique:

Those who capture them [maroons] and return them to their masters, to prison officials, or to local officers, receive 500 pounds of sugar as a reward. If anyone surprises them either in the forest or in the practice of stealing, he is authorized to shoot if they do not surrender. If someone captures them after having wounded them, provided the wound is not mortal, he is entitled to the same reward. If one should kill them, he is cleared simply by making a declaration to the local officer or clerk of that juridiction, and in swearing to that declaration [1741, I:132].

. . . Article 38 of the *Code Noir* prescribes that

the fugitive slave who has been absent for one month, counting from the day that his master officially reported his flight, shall have his ears cut off and his shoulder branded with a fleur de lis; that if he repeats his crime for a period of one month, again counting from the day his master made it known to the authorities, he shall be hamstrung and branded with a fleur de lis on the other

shoulder; and that the third time his punishment shall be
death;

But in practice the colonists took into account the amount
of time the maroon had spent in the islands, and a recent
arrival would usually receive nothing but a few lashes. They
also considered the length of the slave's absence; the punishment differed according to whether the period had been
several days, less than two months, or longer. It was especially serious when the slave had been absent for more
than a year, or when he was a repeater. On the twentieth of
June, 1672, the Superior Council of Martinique condemned
a new slave to death, even though he had fled before the
end of his first year on the island, because he had remained
away for three years (Peytraud 1897:346). . . .

The treatment of maroons grew less harsh at the beginning
of the eighteenth century, at least from the administrative
perspective. On the ninth of February, 1713, the governor of
Martinique recommended to the colonel of the regiment of
the militia that he treat the maroons as humanely as possible,
avoiding the death penalty and refraining from shooting at
them except in cases of absolute necessity (Peytraud 1897:
351).

At Saint-Domingue, the ruling of the fourteenth of March,
1741, replaced the death penalty or galley sentence for repeated or long-standing marronage with forced labor in a
chain gang and branding on the cheek. . . .

This sentence was applied in fact only to maroons who
were armed. When the marronage was merely casual, the
punishments set down by law were not carried out in all
their severity. Offenders who were otherwise good slaves were
to be treated with some gentleness. . . . And a slave captured for the second time still only received a few lashes.

The Crown would have liked to prevent masters from
punishing their slaves too severely. To this end, a brief but
official letter was sent from the King. Thus the decree of the
Superior Council of Martinique on the ninth of January,
1727, punished Cartier, a surgeon convicted of having cut
off the leg of one of his slaves in order to prevent a repetition
of his escaping (Archives Nationales, Section Colonies,
C^8/13). But since the question of public reimbursement for
the maiming and killing of maroons led to so many financial

problems, and since these judicial interventions depended a great deal on the disposition of the individual magistrate, fixed guidelines were never really drawn.

Nevertheless, in order to check marronage, the mounted police was established, firm bounty prices set, and a list of escaped slaves officially kept.

A memo sent from Martinique in 1687 called for the establishment of a mounted police and the installment of a provost with special jurisdiction. As a result of the assembling of slaves in the north of Saint-Domingue, and at Cul-de-Sac and Maribaroux, not far from the Spanish colony, a joint ruling of the governor and intendant dated the twenty-seventh of March, 1721, created a special company of mounted police to pursue fugitives in the north. . . . At this date, it was estimated that there were about a thousand maroons at large in the French colony.

It must be presumed that the mounted police was not long in operation, for a ruling of the twentieth of January, 1733, once again called for its organization. In the jurisdiction of each of the two Councils—Cap and Petit Goave—there was a chief provost assisted by two lieutenants, three or four officers, and about forty bowmen, who must all have been free colored men. But from 1734 on, slaves who could expect to be freed were also admitted. This measure reveals a good deal about the administrators' views of marronage.

A decree of the Superior Council of Guadeloupe dated the sixth of April, 1682, required all settlers having maroon slaves to register them within the week at the nearest judicial office, either verbally or in writing (ibid., F³/236, f⁰ 665).

In addition, complaints involving marronage had to be written out and signed either by the landowner or the manager. Captured maroons were taken to the local jail, and there the following information was recorded: the name of the fugitive slaves; the brands they bore; their specific talents; their physical description; the name of their owner and his plantation; the place of capture; the length of absence, so that the bounty reward could be determined; and finally, the name of the person who captured them (Arrêt du Conseil Supérieur du Cap, 12 septembre 1740, Art. 35).

The captured maroons were considered to be "under the

guardianship and care of the jailers." In order to get them back, their masters were required to pay twelve livres bounty to their captors if they had been caught on the grounds of a plantation or six livres if they had been found inside a slave barracks or along a road. (Arrêt du Conseil Supérieur de la Guadeloupe, 9 juillet 1741; Satineau:294). The jailer was paid fifteen sols for officially registering the maroon, thirty sols entry fee, and thirty sols exit fee, and finally fifteen sols a day for feeding him—in principle, cassava and meat (Moreau de Saint-Méry 1784–90, III:625). . . .

At first, unclaimed slaves were offered for sale at the local court within three months, although their masters retained, for a year and a day, the right either to reclaim them or to receive their full value. But, on the fifth of January, 1731, the district collector of Fort-Dauphin was authorized by the Conseil du Cap to sell unclaimed slaves after forty days; and on the sixth of April, 1733, a royal ordinance reduced the delay to a month for Saint-Domingue (ibid., III:296, 355, and Archives Nationales, Section Colonies, B 125, f⁰ 187). This measure was extended to apply to Martinique by a ruling of the intendant Clugny on the thirty-first of July, 1743. If, at the end of a month spent in jail, the maroons remained unclaimed, they were either sold or put into chain gangs to work on royal projects (ibid., IV:717). Peytraud cites a ruling of the twenty-sixth of October, 1746, that allowed them to be sent to chain gangs as soon as they were captured (ibid., IV:367). Up until the middle of the eighteenth century, then, no consistent practice had been established in this matter, and treatment differed from one island to the next.

The decrease in the length of the prison stay and the suppression of the sale of maroons were intended to prevent or reduce speculation by the jailers on the sale of captured slaves. By conspiring with the sheriffs, they were able to obtain the unclaimed maroons for themselves at an extremely low price, and they even set some slaves free for the price of a bribe.

With the appearance of the first newspapers, the intendants had notices published of escaped slaves as well as notices of maroons who had been captured. Nothing was more likely—in principle—to facilitate the reclamation of slaves and reduce the time they spent in jail (Moreau de Saint-

Méry 1784–90, IV:706; *Lettre de l'intendant aux officiers de la juridiction du Cap;* Peytraud 1897:367). There were, then, lists of escaped slaves, giving their names, trades, ages, tribal origins, and branding, and the conditions and date of their escape. There were also lists of recaptured slaves, which gave their physical descriptions, a description of their clothes, their wounds, and their scars and information on their fluency in communicating. . . .

Toward the end of the eighteenth century, no doubt because the progress of the struggle against the maroons was still unsatisfactory, particular attention was given to the surveillance of freed slaves who were offering refuge to the maroons and receiving the goods they had stolen; their cooperation with the fugitives was punished by stiff fines, by prison terms, and even by the revocation of their freedom. It would seem, nonetheless, that the authorities were never successful in reducing this particular infraction to any appreciable extent. . . .

PUNISHMENTS

[While] slaves who ran away during their first year in the colony were not severely punished . . . the first marronage of an American-born slave, a Creole, was punished by thirty, forty, or even fifty lashes. Taken into account were the slave's skills, previous record, relationship with the driver, and so forth. Whenever a maroon, after an absence of a few days or a few weeks, returned of his own accord, he received only mild punishment, or perhaps none at all. Announcement of escapes published in the newspapers often promised that if the maroon returned, he would not be harmed. This seems to have depended on the temperament of the master and the manager, and the circumstances of flight. More than one colonist was of the opinion that to give no punishment was to encourage recidivism.

Regarding the return of the maroons, one procedure in particular was quite often followed. Maroons were aware that it was to their advantage to make their reappearance around the time of the big celebrations at Christmas and New Year's. In these circumstances, they would receive only light punishment. They would enlist the aid of a "protector." The oldest woman in the master's family usually performed this role; or sometimes it was the parish priest who pleaded their cause. It was common practice not to deny the pardon that was thus solicited. The important role the clergy played in the surrender of maroons, and the negotiations they carried out in order to bring smaller bands back, led to the colonists' accusation in 1791 that they were in connivance with the refractory maroons, that they were protecting them no matter what, that they were, indeed, "accomplices of the rebels."

At times, the fugitive would ask a neighbor to intercede and would be led back to the plantation under his protection. The colonists usually rendered each other this service, and it was considered somehow a matter of honor. The settler called upon would leave his home in order to reconcile the slave with his master. And if he could not come in person, he would send a letter in his own hand. . . . This sort of mediation was usually quite effective, but it should be remembered that the colonist-advocate would only intervene in cases where there was a chance of complete pardon. Even when the master could not totally dismiss the crime, he often reduced the punishment.

In the case of a repeated offense, the most common punishment was a few days' detention "at the bar." Here, the legs of the offender were held fast between two small beams fixed to the foot of the plank on which he slept at the plantation "hospital" [which often doubled as prison]. The only suffering caused in this way was a good deal of discomfort; it was not unlike being in a sort of makeshift detention room. Nonetheless, the slaves dreaded it because it deprived them of communication with their fellows.

In the case of a third or fourth escape, each one of a few months' duration, more severe punishment was inflicted. Then the whip would be the prelude to such measures as the chain, the collar, and the *nabot*.

The chain, or *empêtre*, as it was sometimes called in Saint-Domingue, made the maroon into a convict, at least for a while. It consisted of shackles about three feet in length, to which were fastened two rings, which were closed by means of either a padlock or hinges. The lower part of the legs was put in these rings and protected by a piece of cloth in order to prevent abrasions. The chain was light enough not to prevent the slave from walking, but it slowed him down considerably. If the slave was so strong that the rings failed to impede movement, a weight was added to the chain.

The collar was a different sort of punishment, a moral punishment, a stigma, which tended to isolate the erstwhile maroon. It consisted of a flat circular piece of iron from which projected three or four spikes, each four or five inches long. It was fixed to the neck of repeated offenders by means of a padlock. The colonists intended it to be a sign of humiliation, and in fact the slaves dreaded the collar itself as well as the results of wearing it. The punishment was inflicted on women as well as on men. For a woman wearing the collar, no more *dombaults* [suitors], no more dancing, no more singing. She was universally rejected. Even if some women were thick-skinned enough to wait out the duration of their sentence without too much bother, the great majority of them did not take at all well to being made into an object of repulsion. Men as well as women fled, collar and all, and did not easily manage to free themselves of it without a blacksmith's tool.

The *nabot* (a large, iron, circular device weighing six, eight, or even ten pounds) was the severest punishment of all. It was cold-riveted to the foot. Still it did not prevent further escapes, for there were some maroons who were captured with the *nabot* still attached to their foot. It would seem that it was virtually impossible for them to remove it. The *nabot* appears to have been an invention of the last decades of the eighteenth century, and we have found instances of it only in Saint-Domingue.

The *cachots effrayants* were also an invention of the last twenty years before the Revolution. As their name indicates, they were tiny maximum-security cells, which were probably totally without light. The correspondence of various managers reveals that they were constructed on just about every plantation having more than 150 slaves. But it appears that they were especially reserved for slaves accused of poisoning, or for maroons who had been captured armed.

Nabots and these private dungeons became much more prevalent as the colonists began to rely less and less on the tribunals for dealing with maroon Negroes. These punishments were then substituted for judicial sentences. However, when the colonists felt that they could not control marronage themselves, they had recourse—always with a great deal of reticence—to the magistrates in order to punish the guilty parties. This process was long and costly. The judge would send the maroon to the pillory, have his ears cut off, or sentence him to death. . . .

TESTIMONIES

The letters written by plantation managers contain descriptions of the punishment of maroons, and the account books of plantations permit us a closer look at the fugitives. . . .

At Léogane, in the west of Saint-Domingue, Parison, manager of the Galbaud du Fort sugar estate, was a man who spoke quite openly about maroons. He had no fear of being reproached by the owner, Madame Galbaud du Fort, a Creole, living in Nantes, who insisted on hearing the complete truth (The Papers of Galbaud du Fort, at the home of Mme. la comtesse du Fort, at Angers).

March 6, 1768 . . . We are left with a Creole Negress named Zabeth whom I am despairing of. . . . From her earliest infancy she has been a thief and a maroon. These qualities have only become more prominent with age. Seeing that she was about to die because she had been chained for so long, I had the chain removed without her having requested it. The next day under the pretext of illness, I sent her to the "hospital" [so that she would not interfere with the work of others but still be under surveillance]. On the following day she asked the surgeon's permission to go into the garden. Permission was granted. The same evening, at eight o'clock, she stole the belongings of another Negress. . . . [She was] captured in the act. . . . I held myself to threatening her that if she once again attempted flight, I would have her chained for the remainder of her days. She did not hesitate to make all the right promises, and in the same breath was off to the Lemaire residence [the neighboring plantation] to commit a similar theft. At ten o'clock, she was brought back to me along with the stolen objects. . . . Since she was in no condition to be punished, I sent her to the Place Brouillet where a few sick Negroes are kept in relatively free circumstances. Two days later, I sent along to her some material and a change of clothing. But as soon as she received these provisions, she was off again. . . . Caught once more, she was sent to the mill and chained. About a month ago, before daybreak, she saw that the mules were tired and [in order to wound herself slightly] she slipped her hand between the rollers. She was stopped on the spot. She had three broken fingers, and humanity demanded that she be placed in the hospital, without, however, removing the large chain. Think of it! A week ago, this same Negress lifted up part of the palisade surrounding the hospital and ran away carrying two shirts belonging to other Negresses. . . . She is now restrained at the bar.

April 11, 1768 . . . Seeing that she was about to die in chains, I arranged for others to ask my pardon so that I would have nothing with which to reproach myself. At the request of several people with whom I had spoken beforehand, I had the chain removed, after having had her own grave dug before her eyes, with her even removing a few shovelfuls of dirt. Despite this spectacle, which should have intimidated her for good, she fled once again . . . after having stolen the clothes of two Negroes, even though almost no work had been asked of her and she had been treated like a free woman. Seeing that she is near death, I have had her chained in a mill, a better place for her to die than a hospital. Perhaps the example will have some effect, for I see that the gentle treatment accorded her has inspired two other slaves to become maroons.

April 23, 1768. That bad fellow La Tripe—who was a maroon for two years—broke his leg in trying to extricate it from the bar. The only solution was to cut his leg off. He almost died an hour later, by undoing the bandages. Since that time his hands have remained bound, and I have kept him guarded night and day so that he won't die, but will be able to serve as a living example for the others.

September 29, 1768 . . . La Tripe . . . seeing that a wooden leg had been fashioned for him so that he might be made useful killed himself during the night.

In May 1774, Madame du Fort decided to send a group of slaves from her sugar plantation at Léogane to her coffee plantation in Abricots on the southern cape. She hoped that they would work better under a new driver. On the fifteenth of October, the manager of the coffee plantation wrote to Parison:

Among the group of Negroes you sent me is an old Negro named Jasmin Barbe-Blanche, a Congo, who, without having any motive to my knowledge, escaped on the 17th of the same August. He took with him his wife, an old woman named Nanette. Marquis joined them. The three of them, with Jasmin leading, went to Cayemittes [in the south]. I had the entire region searched until I was sure they couldn't possibly be there. Then I made a declaration of escape at Jérémie and Tiburon. Finally, Monsieur le Chevalier . . . the notary at Jérémie, wrote me on the 15th of September that all three of them were in the jail at Jérémie. . . . I sent for them right away. They were returned to me along with the attached bill which I was obliged to pay:

for capture, at 30 livres per head	90 livres
for the jailer	96 livres
for the surgeon	60 livres
	246 livres

The three maroon Negroes arrived at midnight. Since I didn't have any "bar" [see above], I gave them to the driver to be kept under guard. Jasmin found a way of escaping again. I captured him on the 22nd of September, but he had suffered a great deal in the forest because of inclement weather and lack of food. He had eaten only green corn and raw yams. . . . He had constant diarrhea, and his feet were swollen; he died on the 24th of September. Old Nanette has been sent back to me from jail, covered with ulcers.

Old Jasmin confessed to me before dying that as soon as he realized that he was being taken from Léogane to be brought here, he planned to return there, that he knew Grande Anse [on the southern peninsula, between Abricots and Léogane], and that knowing that there was a river that had to be crossed by ferry, he had kept a silver cuff link with which to pay the Negro who took him across. Marronage is almost suicidal for the Negroes of this region. . . .

Marquis escaped again a few days ago. Would you send along either a chain or collars to restrain him? He is one fellow upon whom I've bent every effort in an attempt to make him behave. But he has stolen all of the Negroes' chickens, and every belonging of theirs that he could, and I fear to even whip him once for fear of killing him, because he's so frail. . . .

Other letters written from Léogane reveal that the maroons had no greater enemies than the free Negroes and mulattoes who owned little gardens or pastures in the hills. The fugitives, driven to hunger, would settle within striking distance of these fields, and raid them during the night, taking away sheep or goats (Labat 1741, I:132). Freemen organized pursuits of the thieves, and it was they who brought the greatest number of maroons back to jail. But it should be mentioned that other freemen, and even mulattoes, helped the maroons avoid being caught by pursuers and their fierce dogs.

Often, the plantation slaves would participate in the search for their comrades. This should not cause much surprise, since in everyday speech, "maroon" implied thief.

From Parison, the 8th of December, 1769. I always have reason to be generally satisfied with your Negroes. Recently they proved me right. . . . After a new arrival had fled in the company of one of the longtime slaves, they all went in search of them the following Sunday without being asked, and demanded that the latter slave be given a good thrashing. I didn't believe it to be a good idea to allow the new slave to be punished at all, for he was more in need of reassurance than of punishment because of the scare he had received in seeing all those men armed and after him [Papiers Galbaud du Fort].

. . . There are good slaves and bad slaves, and the latter are always punished more severely. . . . Because Tom'tom had hurt himself the very night he had escaped, he was soon recaptured, but he had to remain a month without working. "The punishment I have decided on for him is only twenty-five lashes of the whip and the prohibition from going out at all for six months, under penalty of a hundred lashes if he should secretly attempt it" (Parison, April 21, 1787). "Tom'tom is really a rather good fellow, and he was gone for only a few days; it was, moreover, his first escapade."

Claude's story is more tragic. He had been bought as a young boy, along with his two sisters. He first ran away in 1743, after some twenty peaceful years. This escapade followed upon a major theft. He was caught almost right away, and sentenced by the local court at Léogane to be hamstrung. The sentence was carried out forthwith, as can be seen by the plantation accounts, which include seventy livres paid to the jailer for this operation. Nine years later, in November 1752, Claude was once again a maroon, after having stolen a neighbor's horse. His theft was accompanied by threats and acts of violence, and as a result Claude was hanged. In compensation, the plantation was allotted six hundred livres from the indemnity account for executed slaves, only about half of Claude's real value.

From the accounts of the La Barre sugar plantation [in the Vases district in the valley of Arcahaye, in the western part of Saint-Domingue], which have of course come down to us in an incomplete state, it is possible to grasp the seriousness of marronage by examining the cost outlay in relation to the number of maroons captured. . . . The accounts for the years 1786–90, kept by the owner himself, are detailed. They reveal that it was practically always the same slaves who became maroons—and who were caught again.

September 7, 1786. Recovery of Jolicoeur from jail, 24 livres 15 sols.

January 3, 1787. Recovery of Jolicoeur and La Ramée, caught in the Spanish colony, 64 livres 17 sols. Expenses for Chanlate, who went to fetch these Negroes from the Port-au-Prince jail, traveling costs and food, 30 livres.

July 3, 1788. Cost for printing a notice in the newspaper, [*les Affiches Américaines*] for Jolicoeur, 6 livres.

July 15, 1788. Recovery of Jolicoeur, caught on the Guilhem plantation, 8 livres 5 sols.

Jolicoeur was a young Hausa, twenty-three years of age, and La Ramée was of the same age and tribe. Jolicoeur was in the habit of running off and getting into fights on every holiday. The first time he fled was on the fifteenth of August, and the second, Christmas. He had been recaptured less than three weeks later. These escapes were apparently motivated by quarrels, fights among his friends, and drinking bouts. Jolicoeur was chained at the plantation. This shows that a distinction was made between *grand marronage*, which lasted for several months or even longer, and absences of a week or two. In 1790 Jolicoeur was assessed at 2,500 livres, and La Ramée at 3,000; these prices show they were no mere "garden slaves," and that their escapades did not cause them to be considered "inveterate maroons," whose price often depreciated. Jolicoeur and La Ramée had, indeed, not run away since 1778.

Between 1786 and 1790, three other recoveries are listed in the accounts—one in 1786, and the others in 1787 and 1789. The first two are so insignificant that they probably represent arrests of slaves picked up in town without a pass. But the return of Charles, a young Nago, twenty-nine years old, from a group that had just been bought by a slave trader, required a real chase, probably on a Sunday, in which all the slaves took part: "March 19, 1789—to the Negroes for the recovery of Charles, 82 livres 10 sols." The plantation owned at that time 170 slaves (Debien 1945:32). . . .

[*Editor's note:* Debien next offers additional documentation drawn from plantation correspondence, and then discusses in some detail the special case of marronage by slave drivers.]

MAROON LIFE

The "new" slaves who escaped during the first days or weeks after they were bought from the slave traders were both the most numerous and least dangerous of all maroons, since they knew neither the countryside nor the creole language. Sometimes they fled even before receiving an outfit of clothes from their new master, and before being branded. They knew neither the name of their master nor of the plantation from which they escaped, and they could not be made to state either their own name or that of their tribe. They wandered around in rags and were rather easily caught. Very few of the new women slaves escaped in this way.

Creole maroons were not as rare as one might think, but this was perhaps less because they were Creoles than because they lived in the cities, where more slaves fled than on the plantations. It was much easier for them to escape than for the others, because they had almost unlimited freedom of movement as domestics, artisans' helpers, or skilled laborers hired by the week or month. They managed better than any of the others to pass themselves off as freemen.

Creole maroons . . . did not take to the rough life of the forest. The life of the Creole fugitive was not very different from the one he led under his master. He was a "skilled slave," and could work at his trade, but in passing himself off as free. If he came from one town, he moved to another, and sometimes even changed trades. He lived near the ports, taking advantage of the anonymity of transient workers. For him, marronage was an immediate entrance into a world of freedom. His work, and the complicity of his new boss, who had failed to inquire into the origins of his worker, provided a better hiding place for him than all the thickets and all the hills, or embarkation to another island.

There were few women who escaped, and when they were captured they were not found to have established housekeeping with another maroon. When they did escape, it was usually in twos.

There were not one or several ethnic groups that showed a particular tendency to marronage; if the Congos or the Aradas appeared most frequently on the lists of those captured, it was not because they had a deeper yearning for freedom but simply because they were much more numerous [in the slave population].

All ages were represented, even the elderly. But the very young slaves were few, perhaps because the great majority of them were Creoles, and marronage was not the spontaneous reaction of the young slave born in that country. . . .

The escape of a whole band was not a common occurrence, probably because there were few strong leaders, or because these were well surveyed. Maroons who left in groups were not the ones who formed bands. It would seem rather that the "troops of brigands" were formed by maroons who had left individually and who formed groups and armed themselves later.

Whenever the slaves' gardens were pillaged, it was the plantation slaves themselves who pursued the maroons, and they did so spontaneously. They knew that a capture would bring a reward for the whole slave group and that those of them who had remained on the plantation to work suffered because of the absence of the others; the grinding took longer, and the whole work load was heavier. On the other hand, when it was merely a question of minor thefts, the plantation slaves often cooperated with the maroons; then it was only the manager who did not know where they were. They remained very near the plantation and its food supply, and even slept in its houses. . . .

[*Editor's note:* The remainder of this section deals with the economic adaptations of maroons, covered in large part elsewhere in this book; Debien's next two sections, which discuss flight across national borders and the role of maroons during the Haitian Revolution, have been eliminated here.]

THE CAUSES OF MARRONAGE

The causes of marronage were many and complex, but there was nothing mysterious about them, and it appears that they remained fairly constant throughout the history of colonial slavery.

As early as 1670, Père Dutertre summarized them very neatly in two perceptive pages. He understood the first essential distinction to be made: separating escapes of "new" slaves from those of the "seasoned" slaves. His observations are those of a thoughtful, intelligent onlooker (1667, II:498). As fundamental causes behind the marronage of acclimated slaves, he cites "mistreatment by their masters and drivers, or the lack of food." And in point of fact, the colonists' severity, their overly harsh punishments, or the mere threat of such punishments are the reasons that are most often cited in available documents. These punishments provoked vengeance, blows, and sometimes even murder: Flight was a natural consequence.

Père Dutertre wrote on the twenty-ninth of August, 1657, that some slaves in Martinique, exasperated by the harsh treatment they had received from M. La Planche, killed both him and his wife and then fled:

> These fugitives . . . when they have tasted that wretched, miserable way of life, are not easily brought around; they debauch the others, and in Martinique colonists were reduced to the point where they did not dare utter an unpleasant word to a Negro, nor try to correct him, for fear that he would run off to the forest. Even Negresses started imitating them, fleeing with tiny infants seven or eight days old [ibid.].

"The fear of punishment often makes them flee to the woods and become maroons," repeats Père Labat (1741, II: 50).

The majority of maroons were forced into fleeing through the injustice, greed, and severity of their masters, admits the governor of Martinique himself (in his instructions to the colonel of the militia, ninth of February, 1731). The cruel

and unnatural conduct of several masters to their slaves
caused frequent desertions (Archives Nationales, Section Colonies, F³/250, f⁰ 857; F³/90, 18 mars 1755).

Group desertions were much more common when the representative of an absentee owner [rather than the planter him-
self] was in charge of the slaves. Disputes easily arose in
these circumstances, and refusals to obey tended to lead to
acts of violence, or even to collective murder.

On the twenty-seventh of April, 1744, judicial proceedings
were initiated against sixty-six maroons accused of having
killed the bookkeeper. They had been considered the "elite of
the plantation." They would return to their houses every evening saying that they would not give themselves up as long
as the bookkeeper remained on the plantation. Then one day,
the bookkeeper surprised a pregnant maroon woman while
she was bathing and stabbed her to death. Two months later,
the maroons carried him off and killed him. A number of
them were condemned, but the King pardoned them (Archives Nationales, Section Colonies, F³/226, f⁰ 133). Extenuating circumstances—an unjust bookkeeper—clearly existed
for this crime, and this particular marronage resembled a
work strike. By fleeing, the slaves simply wished to rid themselves of an unbearable bookkeeper.

On the Bréda sugar estate at Haut-du-Cap, the attorney
Villevaleix delivered a like complaint against the plantation
manager.

31st of July 1790. The Negro Francisque has died at
Haut-du-Cap as a result of punishment, merited or not, suffered at the hands of the manager. His condition at the
hospital moved me to pity; and I realized that there are
nine maroon Negroes who persist in refusing to give themselves up in spite of my formal promise that nothing will be
done to them. Their obstinance made me suspect the truth,
and I decided to probe discreetly into what was going on
without, however, upsetting the order of things. I discovered that the manager treats them with great severity, and
that he neglects many things that should be done for them,
especially at the hospital. I decided to get a new manager,
replacing M. Valsemey by M. Labertonnière who was persuaded to give up a very pleasant situation only through
friendship to me. A better replacement could not have
been found, and I hope that all will go well now. . . .

We have corrected numerous abuses that had continued for a long time. . . . The nine maroons returned two days after their tyrant left, and they all appeared quite content [Debien:167–68]. . . .

In addition, there was a constant, close connection between marronage and poor or insufficient food. It was not that all farmland and manpower were involved in monocrop farming. The local sugar cane, coffee, and indigo plantations left room for some diversity. . . . Nonetheless, crops for commercial export were the planters' principal concern, to the detriment of raising food supplies, and there is ample testimony to this fact in both official and private correspondence.

From the vantage point of fifteen years in the King's service in the islands, one officer-colonist stated that many instances of marronage could be explained by "the scarcity and high cost of salt beef" [*Discours sur l'estat passé et présent (après 1685*). Archives Nationales, Section Colonies, C⁸/B¹]. In answer to the questions asked by Versailles for the preparation of the *Code Noir*, the administrators of Martinique had stated the same thing a few years before: "There is reason to require the large land-owners to feed their slaves adequately; if they do not, they take to stealing . . . and end up maroons" (Archives Nationales, Section Colonies, F³/248, f⁰ 681).

In Guadeloupe in 1704: "The owners of the large sugar estates will lose the island because they feed their slaves badly, forcing them to work night and day while they themselves sleep with their women . . . they furnish them with none of the necessities of life, and think about nothing but making sugar, which drives the Negroes to flee to the forest" (ibid., F³/226, f⁰ 559. Peytraud, f⁰ 371). . . .

At Fort-Dauphin, in Saint-Domingue, near the Spanish border, the Cottineau sugar plantation, employing 120 slaves, was managed by the son and nephew of the proprietors, who lived in France. The results of not enough food and of too much work and discipline were very much in evidence there, as was the effect of the proximity of the border. . . .

Lory de la Bernadière, père, to Delisle, Nantes, the 20th of February 1767. I am not able, Sir, to conceal from you that it has occurred to our ladies [Mmes. Lory and de la Fonchais, heirs of the Cottineau sugar plantation] that the frequent marronage afflicting the plantation is in part due to excessive discipline and lack of provisions. There are many men who curry favor at others' expense. It would be inhuman to refuse food and innocent satisfactions to the poor devils whose labors make our fortune. The ladies were assured that you had as many as a score of maroons to contend with at a time. It is easier for you than for us to discover the reasons for it, but our concern is that the slaves be provided with what justice would require they have.

For the masters who were living in France, then, who were kept informed not only by the monthly reports of their managers but also by information told them in confidence by colonial neighbors in France for a visit, there is no doubt that insufficient food, overwork, and harsh discipline were the basic causes of marronage. The slaves' only food supply consisted of what they harvested from their own gardens, and these gardens were never able to assure a sufficient diet by themselves. . . .

The most important holidays—the feast of St. John, the feast of St. Louis, Christmas, and New Year's—were also prime occasions for escapes. The log books list the numerous maroons who ran away at the beginning of January, and the account books record the expenses incurred in reclaiming them throughout the course of the month. The week between Christmas and New Year's was always a time of carousals, games, fights, and the greatest freedom. Fugitives were caught inside the district, even within their own parish. These were obviously the escapades of youths on a spree; a good half of them returned of their own accord. In punishing these "escapes," tact had always to be employed.

There was less hesitancy to deal with escapes that followed upon a theft, since the crime in question was no longer a matter of accidental occurrence, of good slaves led astray by bad companions, but of ingrained habit. Flight was very often preceded by a theft. . . .

Transfers of slaves from one plantation to another, always a swift affair, were dreaded by good managers, since they went hand in hand with marronage. The slaves knew that they would have to accept different working conditions. Special consideration had therefore to be given to collective marronage resulting from fear, apprehension, or general dissatisfaction arising upon the transfer of slaves or the sale of the

plantation. The slaves had a real apprehension of being up-
rooted, of working under a new manager or bookkeeper
whom they did not know. Their reaction was to run away,
the easiest form of nonsubmission. Experience must have told
them that it was the most effective means of expressing their
opposition. This particular kind of insubordination could also
be combined with a reaction against an excessively harsh
manager, or insufficient food—as illustrated by the situation at
the Deshaies sugar plantation in Guadeloupe:

> Upon arriving at Deshaies (writes the new manager
> Poullavec to the proprietress Mme. Lagarde on the 22nd
> of February 1763) I found the plantation deserted except
> for five or six Negresses whom I saw in the garden. All the
> other slaves had run away in October. The land was prac-
> tically barren, producing nothing but a few new plants
> which would not provide anything to eat for another year.
> These women told me that the Negroes had deserted be-
> cause of the bad treatment they had received, and the
> neglect they suffered both in regard to their ordinary needs
> and in the case of sickness—despite the sizable doctor's fees
> still left to be paid. Anyway, all of these had come back by
> the 1st of this month, but in such a state of illness or ex-
> haustion from their stay in the forest that more money had
> to be spent to get them back into shape. My arrival has
> flattered them; they call me M. Lagarde [Du Halgouët
> 1933:170].

A few months later, another problem: more marronage.
The plantation had been sold. The slaves knew that they had
no power over the imposition of a new master, but they did
not want to move to another district.

> They are disturbed that I cannot remain their master for
> much longer, and they know that I intend to sell them. In
> order not to be transferred away, they hid when the in-
> ventory was being taken.
> As soon as we arrived, all the Negroes, big and small,
> young and old alike, went into hiding, letting it be known
> to us that they were unwilling to be moved to M. Dur-
> brois' plantation at Capestaire, but that they would consent
> to be sold on the grounds that the land be included in the
> same transaction. They were absolutely unmovable in their

resolution, ran off in protest, and have been impossible to find.

But since slaves belonged "to whoever bought them," and were not supposed to have "a will of their own," these were setting a particularly bad example and were preventing Mme. Lagarde from finding a buyer. She finally found one, but with the condition that all the slaves be recovered before the end of a month. An example was going to be set.

Given these circumstances and our intended goal, I returned to Deshaies, arriving an hour after midnight in the hope of surprising and apprehending some of the leaders of the last sedition. But even though they were not expecting me, the watchmen saw me coming in the dark and the Negroes broke camp immediately. When daylight came, I found only a few old men and old women who are incapable of lifting hand or foot to go anywhere. I therefore decided that in order to be successful in this mission I would have to burn down all their houses and carry off everything that belongs to them [20 mai 1763, ibid., p. 172].

The nearby settlers were in connivance with the slaves, who failed to offer Poullavec any help, and who must have helped at least some of the runaways. Poullavec discovered nine children "seeking shelter" at neighboring estates, and left for Basse-Terre with his paltry find to lodge a complaint with the governor.

M. Dalrymphe ordered the district commissioners to organize search parties made up of all nearby settlers. But these were to no avail. "The searches are carried out, but uncooperative settlers warn the maroons, so that they are in effect only complying formally with the orders. This stratagem has, therefore, not yet yielded any results."

Since the maroons had not returned at the end of a month, the sale was canceled.

Another slave exodus in Guadeloupe to avoid a similar change of plantation indicates that this was not an isolated case. The Huelbourg sugar estate in the Petit-Cul-de-Sac district had been inherited by Mme. d'Aoust at the death of her mother and brother. It was managed by Léonard Villers-au-Tertre, Mme. d'Aoust's brother. Mme. d'Aoust was eager

to have her slaves sent to another plantation in order to reduce general maintenance costs. François Fillion was given
the job of overseeing the transfer. When the appointed day
arrived, not a single slave was to be found at Huelbourg.
They had apparently fled. Upon instituting a search, Fillion
managed to find one of them. He was named Janot Frison
and gave the impression of being a very sensible fellow.
Fillion tried to reason with him. Frison answered that since
he had a wife and two children who belonged to Lord Villers, he wanted Mme. d'Aoust's legal representative either to
sell him to Villers or to buy his wife and children from the
said master, for he would not leave without them (ibid.,
175).

Granted, this is Guadeloupe where the institution of slavery
was less severe than in Saint-Domingue, and where there
were many more instances of marriage among slaves. [But it
seems that more generally] slaves remained attached to the
plantation where they had been born, or where they had
lived for many years, or where they had their own families.
. . . It seems that slaves had a fear of falling into harsher
hands, and that they had formed a network of habit that
was difficult to break.

Wars did more than bring plantation slaves various sorts
of difficulties and disruptions; it also caused whole groups of
them to run away. In Saint-Domingue there were escapes of
maroons into the Spanish colony during the war with the
British.

In Martinique and Guadeloupe, which had been occupied
by the British during the Seven Years' War and which were
harassed by Spanish raids, slaves gained an increasing sense
of freedom. The bookkeeper at Deshaies had to build
ajoupas [shelters] in the forest as protection for himself, the
Negroes, and all their belongings, and to keep watch night
and day with the other colonists in the district. Slaves took
advantage of this atmosphere of alarm by refusing to work.
They even threatened to go off to the Spaniards if they were
mistreated. . . .

It is rather easy to sum up the principal causes of marronage. There are two dominant ones: 1. the harsh treatment received at the hand of bookkeepers and managers,
and the fear of punishment, and 2. an inadequate diet,
which is often related to the first cause since it brings on
exhaustion, which in turn provokes harsh punishment. The

other major causes of marronage are much less important: the desire to escape after committing theft or assault, drunken celebrations on prolonged holidays, and the transfer of slaves from one plantation to another.

REFERENCES NOT CITED IN GENERAL BIBLIOGRAPHY

Culion, Valentin de
    1803 *Examen de l'esclavage et particulièrement de l'esclavage des nègres dans les colonies de l'Amérique.* Paris.
Debien, Gabriel
    Études antillaises, XVIIIe siècle. *Cahiers des Annales,* No. 11.
Dutertre, R. P. Jean-Baptiste
    1667 *Histoire générale des Antilles habitées par les François.* Paris: Thomas Iolli.
Du Halgouët
    1933 *La Guadeloupe.* B^in. Sté. Arch. Nantes.
Labat, R. P. Jean-Baptiste
    1741 *Nouveau voyage aux îles d'Amérique.* Paris: T. Le Gras.
Moreau de Saint-Méry, M. L. E.
    1784–90 *Loix et constitutions des colonies françoises de l'Amériques sous le vent.* Paris: *chez l'auteur.*

CHAPTER EIGHT

The Border Maroons
of Saint-Domingue:
Le Maniel

M. L. E. MOREAU DE SAINT-MÉRY

For over eighty-five years, maroon Negroes lived in the mountains of Bahoruco or Béate and the surrounding areas, which they regarded as their own territory and which formed the theater for their terrible brigandage.

In March 1702, M. de Galiffet ordered these Negroes pursued by fifteen men, who spent sixty-eight days in the forest and who sometimes went four or five days without finding water. They killed three Negroes and captured eleven; about thirty others escaped; they destroyed their food supply and their crops. On the twenty-fifth of October, 1715, it once again became necessary to order them to be driven off, which was achieved in 1717 by M. Dubois, commanding officer of Cul-de-Sac. He found in their settlement a well forty feet deep. They reappeared in 1719, in the same period when their leader, who was named Michel, was captured. In 1728, M. Charles Baudouin, who has since then been commanding officer of the militia at Jacmel, went after them with a detachment of settlers, and took forty-six prisoners. In 1733, thirty-two prisoners were taken. In 1740, they repaired to the Forest of Mirebalais, where M. Marillet, provost marshal of the mounted police at Cul-de-Sac, at-

From M. L. E. Moreau de Saint-Méry, *Description . . . de la partie française de l'isle Saint-Domingue* (1797–98). Philadelphie: chez l'auteur. Translated from Vol. 2, pp. 497–503.

tacked them along with twenty-two bowmen. Seven were killed, and fourteen, all of whom had been born in the forest, were captured, and from these it was learned that twenty-three had escaped. They turned up again in 1742, at Anses-à-Pitre. The Jacmel settlers advanced in 1746, killing several of them. The Negroes, at that point, went elsewhere; when they had found enough recruits, they resumed their incursions, committing acts of war and abducting the Negroes. M. Baudouin Desmarattes, the son-in-law of the above-mentioned Baudouin, went against them in 1757 and captured twelve.

New expedition in December 1761. Protected by an epaulement [a kind of earthen parapet], the Negroes defied their adversaries by dancing. These latter became infuriated and rushed right into ditches, the bottom of which had been filled with pointed stakes of pine wood and then covered with lianas and creeping plants; fourteen mulattoes, or about half the attackers, were maimed. Many Negroes were killed; others were captured with their arrows and their firearms. Under the generalcy of M. de Belzunce, the leader of the Negroes gained a certain reputation and renewed the disorders, which had appeared to be tapering off; so that in 1776 M. d'Ennery was obliged to establish one outpost at Boucan-Patate, which the Negroes attacked while the guardhouse was being built, and another at the dry branch of the river at Anses-à-Pitre. In spite of that, they pillaged, killed, and abducted Negroes from the Grands-Bois and Fond-Parisien areas up to Sale-Trou. (On the seventeenth of August, they also assassinated the agent at Bellevue.)

For this reason, the leaders of the two colonies [French and Spanish, respectively] joined forces in order to pursue them. M. de Saint-Vilmé, the [French] King's representative at Mirebalais, arrived on the twenty-seventh of December, 1776, at Croix des Bouquets with a detachment of 20 grenadiers and 20 riflemen from the regiment of Port-au-Prince. Men from the colored militia of the parishes of Cul-de-Sac and Port-au-Prince assembled there also, thus making, along with the men from Mirebalais camped in Grands-Bois and the ones marching from Jacmel, some 180 men in all.

M. de Saint-Vilmé located the Negro colony at Bahoruco and attacked it on the sixth of January, 1777, but since their dogs had barked during the whole preceding night, they had fled to the forest, which was so thickly wooded that the troops were unable to penetrate it. Because the soldiers were overwhelmed with fatigue, and had even been reduced to drinking their own urine, the detachment was forced to withdraw to get provisions. More than thirty mulattoes left the ranks, and it was necessary to wait for a replacement of fifteen grenadiers or riflemen. Provisions for a month were dispatched. Then M. de Saint-Vilmé took up the march once again, but no maroon Negroes could be found.

A Spaniard offered to guide M. de Saint-Vilmé to the caves where the Negroes were presumed to have taken refuge. Since he had advised them that it would be impossible to obtain water during five or six days, they sent to Port-au-Prince for tin cans holding about six liters of water; in addition, twenty-five men from the Port-au-Prince regiment joined their ranks. At Cayes, they loaded a boat with provisions for a hundred men for one month, and sent it toward Béate. When they believed that the boat had arrived, the troops began their advance once again; it was the sixth of March. They arrived at the caves, but the Negroes had apparently just abandoned them. So they went on to the Spanish border, and thence the detachment, which consisted now of only eighty men from the regiment, returned to Port-au-Prince on the twenty-sixth of March. This expedition cost eighty thousand *livres,* and the settlers from Cul-de-Sac and Port-au-Prince had supplied, for three months, fifty Negroes and forty mules for the transport of provisions.

Beginning in the month of April, the maroon Negroes led attacks on Fond-Parisien. Thirty riflemen from the Port-au-Prince regiment were sent under the direction of M. de Coderc. On the sixth of May, 1777, they began ravaging Boucan-Greffin. They returned there on the twenty-ninth of November, 1778, and pillaged M. Coupé's home, carrying off his housekeeper.

This Negress, who was named Anne, had refused to follow the maroon Negroes and so was tied up and pulled along by force. After two days' march, they arrived at their destination. The leader of the band, Kébinda, who had been born in the forest, gave Anne to his valet as a concubine. Since Anne resisted, the leader took her for himself; but she still resisted. She tried to run away, but was recaptured and condemned to death by the entire troop; the leader opposed this decision. Finally subjugated by a passion that had been fired by her refusals, the leader let himself be persuaded by

Anne after some four months' time that she would become his wife, provided that he marry her *at church*. He left with her one night, and when they arrived at the guardhouse at the Spanish frontier, Anne began to scream, thus causing him to be captured. Anne was brought to M. Coupé, and was given her freedom under the name "Anne Fidèle" [Faithful]. Kébinda, although he was released by the Spaniards, died a short while later, from sadness over his betrayed love.

The Negroes continued their disorders in 1779, 1780, and 1781. A detachment from Jacmel was even sent out against them at the end of March 1781, but unsuccessfully, for it had to return for lack of water at Anses-à-Pitre. In the month of October, new crimes caused a sergeant and ten men to be sent from Port-au-Prince to Grands-Bois, and as many men again to Fond-Verrettes, and finally twenty cooperative colored men, paid thirty sous a day, to land belonging to Mme. de Lilancour.

Finally, in 1782, M. de Saint-Larry, a former surveyor and lieutenant of the militia, who since 1779 had been living at Anses-à-Pitre, where he was constantly required to be on his guard, being far from any French settlement and near the badly policed Spaniards, made an attempt to get to know those Spaniards who were in contact with the maroon Negroes. He succeeded in winning their allegiance, and confided to Diego Félis, a free Spanish quadroon, his plan to convince the Negroes to surrender and form a community sanctioned by the government. He also spoke about his plan to Antonio Félis, another free quadroon, and to Juan Lopez and Simon Silvère, who were all Spaniards living near the border.

The Negroes gave a favorable response, and M. de Saint-Larry informed M. Darcé, representative to the King at Jacmel, and M. de Vincent, second in command at Port-au-Prince. He was told to maintain communications. M. de Saint-Larry had Diego Félis deliver them some gifts, and ask that a dozen of them present themselves on the plain of Trou-Jacob, which was five leagues from his home; he himself intended to go alone, by sea.

On the appointed day, fourteen Negroes, covered only by a *tanga*, wearing a leather pouch at the waist and sporting firearms and machetes, came from one direction, accompanied by Diego Félis; M. de Saint-Larry, attired in uniform, came from the other, along with Messieurs Lopez and Silvère. The maroon leaders were Santiago, a Spanish Creole Negro captured by the maroons forty-five years earlier, and Philippe, who had been born in the forest. They announced that they were willing to withdraw to the parish of Neybes, where they would be governed by three or four Spaniards, and to be baptised there a year later, and that they would go after that to the place assigned them. Santiago gave 137 grains of corn to demonstrate the number of Negroes involved; and M. de Saint-Larry, after distributing some gifts of cloth and handkerchiefs among them, promised to return in two months' time.

The administrators, to whom M. de Saint-Larry gave an account of these happenings, sent his report along to the Chamber of Agriculture at Port-au-Prince.

At the same time, Diego Félis came to inform M. Baudouin Desmarattes that the Negroes who were willing to cooperate wished to see his son. This latter left on the eighth of April and arrived at Cape Mongon on the fifteenth; guided by Diego Félis across the forest, he arrived at the tip of Nisao on the seventeenth at 3 P.M. Diego fired a shot from his rifle, and two hours thence thirty-two armed Negroes came to meet them. They spent until the nineteenth together, and then the Negroes led the young Desmarattes back to his canoe. The administrators, informed of the Negroes' request for liberty and for a place of refuge, wrote back, acceding to their wishes.

The Chamber of Agriculture of Port-au-Prince, being thus consulted, as I said above, decided, on the third of May, 1783, that these Negroes should be granted their freedom and made welcome, on condition that they settle in the French colony.

However, this negotiation was not completed, and a leader and two Negroes came to M. Desmarattes in November 1784 to express their impatience. In February 1785, M. de Bellecombe sent word to Diego Félis to bring two of the leaders to see M. Desmarattes, and he in turn sent them to Port-au-Prince, accompanied by his son.

The government then consulted with the president of the Spanish colony, and appointed M. Jean-Marie Desmarattes *fils* to conclude the arrangement to be adopted. On the fourth of May, Don Isidro de Peralta granted freedom to those fugitives who were Spanish and who would agree to live in an area to be designated later, and he appointed Don Luis de Chavez y Mendosa, dean of the royal court at Santo-Domingo, in charge of these matters. The two commissaries went to the mountains of Bahoruco, made all the arrangements, and filed a report at Neybes on the twenty-eighth of May.

The Negroes numbered 130, of whom 125 were either French or the descendants of French Negroes. It was agreed that Santiago, their leader, even though he was Spanish, would settle with the 125 in French territory, and that all the [former] homes of these Negroes would be demolished. The Negroes promised to pursue and capture all [future] maroon Negroes of the two nations for a bounty of twelve gourdes, as agreed by the treaty of the third of June, 1777, between France and Spain.

On the twelfth of June, the two administrators of the colony approved in common all that had been arranged, pardoned and freed these Negroes by official decree, and allowed them enough provisions for eight months, until the land that they were given would be sufficiently productive.

On the eleventh of December, 1785, a letter from the minister approved the entire operation, commenting at the same time that the affair seemed a bit rushed. But in February 1786, the Negroes announced to the French and Spanish commissaries their refusal to go where they were expected, and it is believed that the insinuations of some Spaniards who . . . [found considerable advantage in their trade with the maroons] were the true cause. Several of them had already been baptised at Neybes.

Since then, the Negroes have strictly made good their promise not to make any more incursions; but their proximity still keeps settlers away, and the mounted-police posts have been re-established.

Such is the true information on these individuals who sometimes devastated great expanses of land, and among whom may be found men sixty years old who never lived anywhere but in these forests where they were born. The particular characteristic of these latter men is disquiet, and it is painted all over their faces; fear works on them all. One could fill a whole volume with all that has been said about their numbers and their way of life. Fear has counted up to eighteen hundred of them. Their real abode is near Nisao, in the mountains that are north of Azua, and this was their place of retreat when they were forced to flee from the mountains of Bahoruco, where they plotted their raids and found a ready sustenance from wild animals. As outposts, they use huts manned by two watchmen who retreat to another post, and so on from post to post until all have rejoined the main body of troops. Their sentries are dogs, of which they have a great many, and the Spaniards buy for them, even in the French sector, arms and munitions.

When they pillaged they would set out and await, for a long time if necessary, the propitious moment. Cruel if they wanted to intimidate or get revenge, they abducted other Negroes and made them their slaves. They only accepted those who came to them voluntarily, and only after making sure that they were not spies; on the least suspicion, they would put them to death. The only example of someone escaping from their colony is the mulatto woman belonging to M. Fouquet, a settler in the mountains at Cul-de-Sac.

These Negroes, after the expedition of M. de Saint-Vilmé, wandered about for fear of being surprised, and were sometimes obliged to live off of tree leaves and wild fruits. The acute dysentery that resulted, and the smallpox that struck them after that, killed off a great number of them. They even contemplated surrender, but Santiago, who had been living among them for some fifty years, dissuaded them from this course. Taking advantage of their superstitiousness, he leads them by exercising among them the role of priest. He taught them how to pray in Spanish, and a tiny cross and a rosary are, in his hands, two weapons with which he soon overwhelms their feeble powers of reason.

Who could assure that this influence will not continue to be exercised, as it has been for so long? Who would dare affirm that whoever Santiago's successor might be will not be even more formidable than he? In that eventuality, the governor should resolve to destroy this community forever. But in that case, it will be necessary to recall that their numbers have increased, during the period that they have been free from pursuit. But a troop whose supplies and munitions are renewed, pursuing another that lacks these advantages and whose wounded are as much as condemned to death by the climate, is sure to triumph if confidence does not abandon it.

Scarcely had the treaty on boundaries been signed in 1776 when seven or eight people settled near the guardhouse at the bank of the river at Anses-à-Pitre; but several murders, including that of M. Cambon, a mounted police officer whose quarrels with M. Gallard, one of the oldest inhabitants of Anses-à-Pitre, had caused great confusion, caused these people to leave the district, where M. de Saint-Larry remained alone.

CHAPTER NINE

Le Maniel: Further Notes

YVAN DEBBASCH

On the southern flank of the colony [of Saint-Domingue] was the most famous of the maroon communities that the French settlers ever had to contend with: le Maniel.[1] First reported at the end of the seventeenth century, it survived a century of pursuits which, if they were not continuous, were at least relatively frequent; when civil war unleashed its horrors, the blacks of le Maniel were too fond of their independence simply to join the ranks of the insurgents; much of the time, they remained aloof from the conflict, or, when they joined it, they always stayed somewhat on the fringes; at the beginning of the nineteenth century, in an independent Haiti, their descendants were still grouped, if not in a little state of their own, then at least in a society with strong links to its past. The community of le Maniel, to be sure, benefited from a propitious terrain; but the factor that worked most in its favor was the propinquity of the Spanish:

From Yvan Debbasch, *"Le marronnage: essai sur la désertion de l'esclave antillais,"* L'Année Sociologique 1961:1–112; 1962:117–95. This translation includes portions of pp. 74–77, 186–91. The extensive footnotes of the original text have been omitted here for want of space. Translated and reprinted with the permission of the author and Presses Universitaires de France.

[1] In fact, two separate bands existed at a very early date [1717], and there is no indication that they were allied. . . . And the same state of affairs existed at the end of the eighteenth century. Those wishing to study this maroon bastion should keep in mind this heretofore unacknowledged coexistence of two communities in the same region. On the other hand, from our point of view in this essay, there is no danger in speaking of le Maniel as a bloc.

the tolerance of the authorities allowed it to escape annihilation; the complicity of Spanish frontiersmen allowed it to resolve without difficulty the problem of getting the supplies of arms and tools that so preoccupied all maroon societies and led certain of them to commit the worst sort of imprudences.

The attitude of the Spanish authorities should not evoke surprise; the eastern colony suffered much less from marronage than did its neighbor; le Maniel was therefore a magnet that attracted almost exclusively slaves from the French sector; in 1784, a survey of the band reveals the presence of only three Spanish deserters—three out of 137. Moreover, the existence of a group of French maroons at the frontier served the interests of the Spanish colony; according to an ancient statute of the court of Santo Domingo, a slave's crossing into le Maniel forever nullified the rights of his master and made the slave a *res nullius;* captured in the eastern part of the island, a maroon of this type became the property of the Crown. Finally, how would it be possible not to take into account the sentiment of francophobia, which was widespread among the masses as well as among the rulers? Anything that could harm the French settlements merited by that very fact the greatest indulgence.

Now, nothing was more necessary to the unqualified success of the French pursuits than an understanding with the Spaniards. When attacked, the whole community of le Maniel slipped away by crossing the border; at the very worst its gardens and shelters were destroyed—but not the band itself. Which amounts to saying that in order to accomplish their goal, the French needed either the cooperation of their neighbors, or, at the very minimum, the recognition of their right of pursuit into Spanish territory. Often promised, the participation of Spanish troops in a joint military effort proved itself on the battlefield to be merely symbolic, maladroit, and willfully ineffective; and as for the right of pursuit, the Catholic kings were never willing to grant it.

The indirect aid of the Spanish authorities was bolstered by the support of the frontier populations, of which the town of Neybes was the center. To le Maniel's advantage, these people acted as both spies and receivers of stolen goods. Whenever there was clear danger of attack, they were able to warn the maroons; and they probably did this less out of sympathy with them than to protect the commercial exchange that had been set up at Neybes for small tradesmen, both among the settlers of the region and in the maroon community. There is no doubt that these people exercised a great deal of influence on le Maniel: It is they who, at the end of the eighteenth century, precipitated the breakdown of the negotiations that were designed to obtain the dissolution, or at least the displacement of the band, in exchange for its freedom.

At Saint-Domingue, as has been mentioned, the frontier was truly "the seat of evil." Potential escapees passed through in that direction, and many maroons settled down there. For the French colony, it was a chronically open wound.

. . . The reason why the maroon society of le Maniel received special attention was not at all a matter of numbers, either real or imagined, even though it is true that numerical estimates of the population were exaggerated; but what band had not been swelled by public rumor? All things considered, the figures that were proposed for le Maniel were about as large as those rumored about the other bands that were devastating the countryside and inspiring fear in the Saint-Domingue settlers at the end of the eighteenth century. Moreover, once an accurate census had been made and the "thousands" of le Maniel maroons suddenly dwindled to 137, the desire to negotiate with this handful of descendants of the original maroons was not diminished. Nor was it solely le Maniel's talent for prolonged resistance that inspired in those who were conscious of it the will to negotiate; this talent could have easily been recognized without a concomitant realization as to the uselessness of pursuit and the necessity of negotiation. The reason that a political solution was considered at the very end of the eighteenth century was simply that the problem posed by le Maniel had been modified by a brand-new factor: the interest on the part of French settlers for the territory controlled by the maroon community. Until 1775 or thereabouts, the latter had no permanent contact with the belt of land under cultivation. The disagreement between the French and the Spanish over the frontiers, which was most acute in the south, had blocked, in fact, all real progress in the interior colonization of the disputed sector. Le Maniel was most certainly a disturbing phenomenon, especially because it was both an asylum for the maroons of the nearby work groups and a home base for raids on the settled plains; pursuit was sufficient remedy as long as that state of affairs lasted. But a 1776 boundary treaty changed the status quo; scarcely had the treaty been signed when some whites and mulattoes settled near the new border; right after that, a classic struggle between settlers and maroons broke out, since the peaceful habitation of the former would have eventually brought about the disappearance of the maroon community. Le Maniel retaliated by means of surprise attack, crop destruction, and the kidnaping of slaves; as for the settlers, many of them left, and those who remained performed their labors in an atmosphere of war, with firearms in hand. The land could be further cultivated only at the price of an agreement with the band, since it was realized that the settlers could never be rid of them. It is significant that the initiative came from that settler who was most firmly established in the dangerous area, and the most committed to remaining on his concession.

A militia lieutenant of the Jacmel battalion, Saint-Larry was living "twelve hours away from the nearest Frenchman, without any access by road, and was surrounded by badly disciplined neighbors" (Arch. Col. F³/132, p. 325). This hazardous position allowed him to see where the solution to his problem lay, and this was also the solution of those who, at that time, were looking in the direction of the southern part of the French colony (Moreau de Saint-Méry 1958, III:1166). With the endorsement of the regional authorities and the cooperation of some Spanish mulattoes, a skillful maneuver toward rapprochement was begun, and this helped dissipate the quite understandable mistrust of the maroons; when, in 1782, a meeting was finally arranged—in Spanish territory, to the reassurance of both parties—a dialogue on the fate of the community was begun, a dialogue that continued until 1786.

Concerning the initial demands of the community leaders, the attorney general of La Mardelle said quite rightly that they were "exactly the same as those of the Negro maroons of Jamaica"—in addition to which he could have mentioned those of the Surinam maroons: in the first place, the recognition of the freedom of all the members of the band, the fundamental clause in an agreement of this sort; next, the continuation of tribal life, on its own territory, and under a vague sort of sovereignty granted by the colonial authorities. In exchange for these two concessions, the Negroes of le Maniel offered to pursue maroons themselves. In short, what they were asking for was the approval of a de facto state in exchange for peace.

The proposition could only be coolly received by a colonial opinion that was informed by the discouraging experience of the British [in Jamaica] and for which the question of le Maniel, crucial in a frontier district, nevertheless offered no risk to the future of the French colony as a whole. Jamaica and Surinam had been forced to put up with the whims of the maroon leaders; but Saint-Domingue was far from that extreme point. Everyone agreed that the question of le Maniel should be settled peacefully, but not by paying the full price; everyone was more or less ready to forget the past but unwilling to mortgage the future by sanctioning the establishment of a black society at the very gates of the colony. This was the reason for the counterpropositions of the administrators of the Chamber of Agriculture at Port-au-Prince: the maroons would be granted their freedom and given land, either in family units or, if necessary, as a group, in return for the pursuit of fugitives; the plots of land would be situated in the French colony in a district surrounded by cultivated land and thus less favorable to the revival of a hostile community.

Attracted by the possibility of a less arduous existence, and weakened by a recent epidemic, the Negroes of le Maniel finally accepted what little was offered them. But when the time came for emigrating, they retracted; the negotiations had been drawn out, thus allowing Spanish propaganda to work its influence on the band. The frontier settlers, anxious to maintain their commercial activities with the maroon community, led them to believe there was a trap involved. For their part, the authorities of the eastern region were hoping, in accordance with precedents that their neighbors regarded as unfortunate, to have the descendants of the fugitives settle, as citizens, in the very area in which they were then living. For other reasons too, it seemed expedient to break the agreement: Though in the colony the French administrators believed it necessary to grant freedom to all the maroons, at Versailles the officials were very wary of establishing such a precedent; the French were therefore looking for a way out of this awkward situation when the maroons themselves, in reaching a decision on their own, solved their predicament for them.

But for having attempted a reconciliation, the French won

a promise that the leaders of le Maniel made on the very day of the breach—and kept: "They promised that they would make no incursion into the French colony, and that the fugitive Negroes who would come to them from that time on would be returned for a bounty of fifty *écus* each" (Lettre La Luzerne au ministre, 6 février 1786, Arch. Col. C^{8B}/38); upon the announcement of this news, the requests for land grants in the frontier sector of Sale-Trou multiplied to the point where Governor La Luzerne predicted, in 1786, that it would very soon be "one of the best barriers against the fugitives" (Lettre des administrateurs, 30 avril 1786, ibid.). Without having to undergo the humiliation of a formal treaty, the colony had, in the last analysis, won the match.

PART THREE

The United States

As in so many colonies, among the very first group of slaves to be landed in what is now the United States were the first maroons-to-be.

A Spanish colonizer, Lucas Vasquez de Ayllon, founded, in the summer of 1526, a community whose probable location was at or near the mouth of the Pedee River in what is now South Carolina. The settlement consisted of about five hundred Spaniards and one hundred Negro slaves. Trouble soon beset it. Illness caused numerous deaths, carrying off, in October, Ayllon himself. Internal dissension arose, and the Indians grew increasingly suspicious and hostile. Finally, probably in November, several of the slaves rebelled, and fled to the Indians. The next month what was left of the adventurers, some one hundred and fifty souls, returned to Haiti, leaving the rebel Negroes with their Indian friends —as the first permanent inhabitants, other than the Indians, in what was to be the United States [Aptheker 1969:163].

There is considerable irony, but certainly little accident, in the fact that the study of North American maroons has been so largely neglected. It had long been known that periodic slave truancy, *petit marronage,* was an everyday feature of Southern plantation life. But Aptheker's pioneering 1939 paper, reprinted here, documented a staggering number of actual maroon settlements, scattered over much of the United States, and showed that many of them lasted for periods of years. As the bibliographical note to this section suggests, there has been a good deal of work on American slave revolts and, more recently, on more subtle forms of resistance. But few scholars have attempted research on North American marronage or maroon communities (Mullin [1972] is the outstanding exception). Today, from the backlands of New Jersey through Appalachia, southwestward into Texas and even across the Mexican border, the descendants of many of those maroons who chose to cast their lot with Indians can still be found, largely forgotten, and often desperately poor. It seems quite likely that some maroon traditions are kept alive by these people. One enterprising student recently found a highly developed, innovative technology for "losing the hounds," which apparently originated among maroons from Georgia rice plantations, vividly remembered and discussed by local poor whites (Hodges 1971). The United States, then, still presents challenging opportunities of both an ethnographic and historical nature for the study of maroons, ones that should flesh out our understanding of North American slavery more generally. Though Aptheker's paper is little more than a bare survey, it has not yet been superseded.

Suggestions for further readings are found in the bibliographical note to Part Three.

CHAPTER TEN

Maroons Within
the Present Limits of
the United States

HERBERT APTHEKER

An ever-present feature of antebellum southern life was the existence of camps of runaway Negro slaves, often called maroons, when they all but established themselves independently on the frontier. These were seriously annoying, for they were sources of insubordination. They offered havens for fugitives, served as bases for marauding expeditions against nearby plantations and, at times, supplied the nucleus of leadership for planned uprisings. Some contemporary writers and a few later historians have noticed, in a general and meager way, the existence of this feature of American slavery.[1] It merits, however, detailed treatment.

It appears that notice of these maroon communities was taken only when they were accidentally uncovered or when their activities became so obnoxious or dangerous to the slavocracy that their destruction was felt to be necessary. Evidence of the existence of at least fifty such communities

Reprinted with the permission of the author and publisher from *Journal of Negro History* 24:167–84 (1939). Copyright by the Association for the Study of Negro Life and History, Inc. This essay appeared also in Herbert Aptheker *To Be Free: Studies in American Negro history.* New York: International Publishers (1948), pp. 11–30.
[1] See, for example, Janson 1807:328–30; Russell 1863:88–89; Olmsted 1904, II:177–78 and 1860:30, 55; Higginson 1870:248; Parton 1860, II:397–98; Siebert 1899:25; Ellis 1927:169; Moody 1924:224–25; Taylor 1928:23–24; Phillips 1909b:229.

in various places and at various times, from 1672 to 1864, has been found. The mountainous, forested, or swampy regions of South Carolina, North Carolina, Virginia, Louisiana, Florida, Georgia, Mississippi, and Alabama (in order of importance) appear to have been the favorite haunts for these black Robin Hoods. At times a settled life, rather than a pugnacious and migratory one, was aimed at, as is evidenced by the fact that these maroons built homes, maintained families, raised cattle, and pursued agriculture, but this all but settled life appears to have been exceptional.

The most noted of such communities was that located in the Dismal Swamp between Virginia and North Carolina.[2] It seems likely that about two thousand Negroes, fugitives, or the descendants of fugitives, lived in this area. They carried on a regular, if illegal, trade with white people living on the borders of the swamp. Such settlements may have been more numerous than available evidence would indicate, for their occupants aroused less excitement and less resentment than the guerrilla outlaws.

The activities of maroons in Virginia in 1672 approached a point of rebellion so that a law was passed urging and rewarding the hunting down and killing of these outlaws (Hening n.d., II:299; Bruce 1896, II:115). An item of November 9, 1691, notices the depredations caused by a slave, Mingoe, from Middlesex County, Virginia, and his unspecified number of followers in Rappahannock County (*Order Book*, Middlesex County, 1680–94:526–27 [Virginia State Library]; Bruce 1896, II:116). These Negroes not only took cattle and hogs, but, what was more important, they had recently stolen "two guns, a Carbyne & other things."

In June 1711, the inhabitants of the colony of South Carolina were kept "in great fear and terror" by the activities of "several Negroes [who] keep out, armed, and robbing and plundering houses and plantations" (Holland 1823:63; Wallace 1934, I:372). These men were led by a slave named Sebastian, who was finally tracked down and killed by an Indian hunter. Lieutenant Governor Gooch of Virginia wrote to the Lords of Trade, June 29, 1729, "of some runaway Negroes beginning a settlement in the Mountains & of their

2 See references in Note 1, as well as Stowe 1856 and articles by Edmund Jackson in the Pennsylvania *Freeman*, January 1, 1852, and Margaret Davis in *South Atlantic Quarterly* 33:171–84 (1934).

being reclaimed by their Master" (Virginia Manuscripts from British Record Office, Sainsbury, IX:462, Virginia State Library). He assured the Lords that the militia was being trained to "prevent this for the future."

In September 1733, the governor of South Carolina offered a reward of £20 alive and £10 dead for "Several Run away Negroes who are near the Congerees, & have robbed several of the Inhabitants thereabouts." The Notchee Indians offered, in April 1744, to aid the government of South Carolina in maintaining the subordination of its slave population. Three months later, on July 5, 1744, Governor James Glen applied "for the assistance of some Notchee Indians in order to apprehend some runaway Negroes, who had sheltered themselves in the Woods, and being armed, had committed disorders. . . ." (*Council Journal* [MS.] V:487, 494; XI:187, 383, South Carolina Historical Commission, Columbia, S.C.).

The number of runaways in South Carolina in 1765 was exceedingly large. This led to fears of a general rebellion (Wallace 1934, I:373). At least one considerable camp of maroons was destroyed that year by military force. A letter from Charleston of August 16, 1768, told of a battle with a body of maroons, "a numerous collection of outcast mullattoes, mustees, and free negroes" (Boston *Chronicle*, October 3-10, 1768).

Governor James Habersham of Georgia learned in December 1771 "that a great number of fugitive Negroes had Committed many Robberies and insults between this town [Savannah] and Ebenezer and that their Numbers (which) were now Considerable might be expected to increase daily" (Candler 1907, XII:146-47, 325-26). Indian hunters and militiamen were employed to blot out this menace. Yet the same danger was present in Georgia in the summer of 1772. Depredations, piracy, and arson were frequent, and again the militia saw service. A letter from Edmund Randolph to James Madison of August 30, 1782, discloses somewhat similar trouble in Virginia (Conway 1888:50-51). At this time it appears that "a notorious robber," a white man, had gathered together a group of about fifty men, Negro and white, and was terrorizing the community.

The British had combated the revolutionists' siege of Savannah with the aid of a numerous body of Negro slaves, who served under the inspiration of a promised freedom. The defeat of the British crushed the hopes of these Negroes.

They fled, with their arms, called themselves soldiers of the King of England, and carried on a guerrilla warfare for years along the Savannah River. Militia from Georgia and South Carolina, together with Indian allies, successfully attacked the Negro settlement in May 1786, with resulting heavy casualties (Stevens 1859, II:376–78; Woodson 1928:123; Historical Manuscripts Commission, Report on American Manuscripts, London 1904, II:544). Governor Thomas Pinckney of South Carolina referred in his legislative message of 1787 to the serious depredations of a group of armed fugitive slaves in the southern part of the state (Pinckney 1895: 95; Wallace 1934, II:415).

Chesterfield and Charles City Counties, Virginia, were troubled by maroons in November 1792 (letter dated Richmond, November 19 in Boston *Gazette*, December 17, 1792). At least one white man was killed while tracking them down. Ten of the runaways were finally captured, with the aid of dogs. The neighborhood of Wilmington, North Carolina, was harassed in June and July 1795 by "a number of runaway Negroes, who in the daytime secrete themselves in the swamps and woods . . . at night committed various depredations on the neighbouring plantations" (Wilmington *Chronicle* [photostat, Library of Congress], July 3, 10, 17, 1795; Charleston *City Gazette*, July 18, 23, 1795; Taylor 1928, V:23–24). They killed at least one white man, an overseer, and severely wounded another. About five of these maroons, including the leader, known as the General of the Swamps, were killed by hunting parties. It was hoped that "these well-timed severities" would "totally break up this nest of miscreants—At all events, this town has nothing to apprehend as the citizens keep a strong and vigilant night guard." Within two weeks of this first report, of July 3, the capture and execution of four more runaways was reported. On July 17 it was believed that only one leader and a "few deluded followers" were still at large.

The existence of a maroon camp in the neighborhood of Elizabeth City, North Carolina, in May 1802 is indicated by the fact that the plots and insubordination uncovered among the servile population at that time were attributed to the agitation of an outlawed Negro, Tom Copper, who "has got a camp in one of the swamps" (Raleigh *Register* [State Library, Raleigh], June 1, 1802; New York *Herald*, June 2, 1802). In March 1811, a runaway community in a swamp in

Cabarrus County, North Carolina, was wiped out. These maroons "had bid defiance to any force whatever, and were resolved to stand their ground" (Edenton *Gazette*, March 22, 1811; Johnson 1937:514). In the attack two Negro women were captured, two Negro men killed, and another wounded.

The close proximity of the weakly governed Spanish territory of East Florida persistently disturbed the equanimity of American slaveholders. Many of the settlers in that region, moreover, were Americans, and they, aided by volunteers from the United States, raised the standard of revolt in 1810, the aim being American annexation (Pratt 1925:92, 116, 192–95, 212). In the correspondence of Lieutenant Colonel Thomas Smith and Major Flournoy, both of the United States Army and both actively on the side of the rebels or "patriots" in the Florida fighting, and of Governor Mitchell of Georgia, there are frequent references to the fleeing of American slaves into Florida, where they helped the Indians in their struggle against the Americans and the "patriots." A few examples may be cited.

Smith told General Pinckney, on July 30, 1812, of fresh Indian depredations in Georgia and of the escape of about eighty slaves. He planned to send troops against them, for "The safety of our frontier I conceive requires this course. They have, I am informed, several hundred fugitive slaves from the Carolinas and Georgia at present in their Towns & unless they are checked soon they will be so strengthened by desertions from Georgia & Florida that it will be found troublesome to reduce them." And it was troublesome. In a letter to Governor Mitchell of August 21, 1812, Smith declared, "The blacks assisted by the Indians have become very daring." In September further slave escapes were reported from Georgia. On September 11, a baggage train under Captain Williams and twenty men, going to the support of Colonel Smith, was attacked and routed, Williams himself being killed by Indians and maroons. In January 1813, further escapes were reported, and in February, Smith wrote of battles with Negroes and Indians and the destruction of a Negro fort. One Georgian participant in this fighting, Colonel Daniel Newman, declared the maroon allies of the Indians were "their best soldiers" (Davis 1930–31:106–7, 111, 138; *Niles' Weekly Register*, December 12, 1812, III:235–37).

The refusal of the Senate of the United States, at the moment, to sanction occupation of East Florida finally led to a lull in the fighting. By 1816, however, the annoyance and danger from runaway slaves again served as justification for American intervention. With southern complaints ringing in its ears (see, for example, Richmond *Enquirer,* July 10, 1816), the administration dispatched, in July, United States troops with Indian allies under Colonel Duncan Clinch against the main stronghold of the maroons, the well-stocked Negro fort on Appalachicola Bay. After a siege of ten days a lucky cannon shot totally destroyed the fort and annihilated 270 men, women, and children. But 40 souls survived (Connecticut *Courant,* September 10, 24, 1816; *State Papers,* 15th Cong., 2d sess., Vol. IV; McMaster n.d., IV:431; McMaster's account is practically copied by Fuller 1906: 228).

Another major expedition against a maroon community was carried out in 1816. This occurred near Ashepoo, South Carolina. Governor David R. Williams' remarks concerning this in his message of December 1816 merit quotation (Cook 1916:130):

A few runaway negroes, concealing themselves in the swamps and marshes contiguous to Combahee and Ashepoo rivers, not having been interrupted in their petty plunderings for a long time, formed the nucleus, round which all the ill-disposed and audacious near them gathered, until at length their robberies became too serious to be suffered with impunity. Attempts were then made to disperse them, which either from insufficiency of numbers or bad arrangement, served by their failure only to encourage a wanton destruction of property. Their forces now became alarming, not less from its numbers than from its arms and ammunition with which it was supplied. The peculiar situation of the whole of that portion of our coast, rendered access to them difficult, while the numerous creeks and water courses through the marshes around the islands, furnished them easy opportunities to plunder, not only the planters in open day, but the inland coasting trade also without leaving a trace of their movements by which they could be pursued. . . . I therefore ordered Major-General Youngblood to take the necessary measures for suppressing them, and authorized him to incur the necessary expenses of such an expedition. This was immediately executed. By a judicious employment of the militia under his command, he either captured or destroyed the whole body.

The Norfolk *Herald* of June 29, 1818, referred to the serious damages occasioned by a group of some thirty runaway slaves, acting together with white men, in Princess Anne County, Virginia (quoted in New York *Evening Post*, July 7, 1818). It reported, too, the recent capture of a leader and "an old woman" member of the outlaws. In November of that year maroon activities in Wake County, North Carolina, became serious enough to evoke notice from the local press, which advised "the patrol to keep a strict look out" (Raleigh *Register*, November 13, 27, 1818). Later an attack upon a store "by a maroon banditti of negroes" led by "the noted Andey, alias Billy James, better known here by the name of Abaellino," was repulsed by armed citizens. The paper believed that the death of at least one white man, if not more, might accurately be placed at their hands. The Raleigh *Register* of December 18, 1818, printed Governor Branch's proclamation offering $250 reward for the capture of seven specified outlaws and $100 for Billy James alone. There is evidence that, in this same year, maroons were active in Johnston County, in that state, and one expedition against them resulted in the killing of at least one Negro (Johnson 1937:514).

Expeditions against maroons took place in Williamsburg County, South Carolina, in the summer of 1819 (Phillips 1909a, II:91). Three slaves were killed, several captured, and one white was wounded. Similar activities occurred in May 1820 in Gates County, North Carolina. A slave outlaw, Harry, whose head had been assessed at $200, was killed by four armed whites. "It is expected that the balance of Harry's company [which had killed at least one white man] will very soon be taken" (Edenton *Gazette*, May 12, 1820, quoted by New York *Evening Post*, May 17, 1820).

Twelve months later there was similar difficulty near Georgetown, South Carolina, resulting in the death of one slaveholder and the capture of three outlaws (New York *Evening Post*, June 11, 1821). The activities of considerable maroon groups in Onslow, Carteret, and Bladen Counties, North Carolina, aided by some free Negroes, assumed the proportions of rebellion in the summer of 1821. There were plans for joint action between these outlaws and the field slaves against the slaveholders. Approximately three hundred members of the militia of the three counties saw service for about twenty-five days in August and September. About twelve of these men were wounded when two companies of militia accidentally fired upon each other. The situation was under control by the middle of September, although the militia men "did not succeed in apprehending all the runaways & fugitives, [still] they did good by arresting some, and driving others off, and suppressing the spirit of insurrection."[3] A newspaper item of 1824 discloses that the "prime mover" of the trouble mentioned above, Isam, "alias General Jackson," was among those who escaped at the time, for he is there reported as dying from lashes publicly inflicted at Cape Fear, North Carolina (New York *Evening Post,* May 11, 1824).

In the summer of 1822 activity among armed runaway slaves was reported from Jacksonborough (now Jacksonboro), South Carolina (Washington *National Intelligencer,* July 23, August 24, 1822). Three were executed on July 19. In August Governor Bennett offered a reward of two hundred dollars for the capture of about twenty maroons in the same region. It is possible that these Negroes had been enlisted in the far-flung conspiracy of Denmark Vesey, uncovered and crushed in June 1822.

The Norfolk *Herald* of May 12, 1823, contains an unusually full account of maroons under the heading "A Serious Subject." It declares that the citizens of the southern part of Norfolk County, Virginia,

have for some time been kept in a state of mind peculiarly harrassing and painful, from the too apparent fact that their lives are at the mercy of a band of lurking assassins, against whose fell designs neither the power of the law, or vigilance, or personal strength and intrepidity, can avail. These desperadoes are runaway negroes, (commonly called outlyers). . . . Their first object is to obtain a gun and ammunition, as well to procure game for subsistence as to defend themselves from attack, or accomplish objects of

[3] See petition of John H. Hill, colonel commandant of the Carteret Militia, dated December 1825, and accompanying memoranda in Legislative Papers, 1824–25 (No. 366), North Carolina Historical Commission, Raleigh; R. H. Taylor 1928, V:24; G. G. Johnson 1937:514.

vengeance [Quoted in New York *Evening Post*, May 15, 1823].

Several men had already been killed by these former slaves, one, a Mr. William Walker, very recently. This aroused great fear. "No individual after this can consider his life safe from the murdering aim of these monsters in human shape. Every one who has haply rendered himself obnoxious to their vengeance, must, indeed, calculate on sooner or later falling a victim" to them. Indeed, one slave-holder had received a note from these amazing fellows suggesting it would be healthier for him to remain indoors at night—and he did.

A large body of militia was ordered out to exterminate these outcasts and "thus relieve the neighbouring inhabitants from a state of perpetual anxiety and apprehension, than which nothing can be more painful." During the next few weeks there were occasional reports of the killing or capturing of outlaws, culminating June 25 in the capture of the leader himself, Bob Ferebee, who, it was declared, had been an outlaw for six years (ibid., May 29, June 5, June 30, 1823). He was executed July 25. In October of this year runaway Negroes near Pineville, South Carolina, were attacked. Several were captured, and at least two, a woman and a child, were killed. One of the maroons was decapitated, and his head stuck on a pole and publicly exposed as "a warning to vicious slaves" (Charleston *City Gazette* quoted in New York *Evening Post*, October 24, 1823; *Niles' Weekly Register*, October 18, 1823, XXV, p. 112; Kirkland and Kennedy 1926, Part Two:190).

A maroon community consisting of men, women, and children was broken up by a three-day attack made by armed slaveholders of Mobile County, Alabama, in June 1827. The Negroes had been outlaws for years and lived entirely by plundering neighboring plantations. At the time of the attacks the Negroes were constructing a stockade fort. Had this been finished it was believed that field slaves thus informed would have joined them. Cannon would then have been necessary for their destruction. The maroons made a desperate resistance, "fighting like Spartans." Three were killed, others wounded, and several escaped. Because of the poor arms of the Negroes but one white was slightly wounded

(Mobile *Register*, June 20, 21, 1827, quoted in New York *Evening Post*, July 11, 12, 1827; Phillips 1909b: 229).

In November 1827 a Negro woman returned to her master in New Orleans after an absence of sixteen years. She told of a maroon settlement some eight miles north of the city containing about sixty people. A drought prevailed at the moment so it was felt that "the uncommon dryness . . . has made those retreats attainable . . . and we are told there is another camp about the head of the bayou Bienvenu. Policy imperiously calls for a thorough search, and the destruction of all such repairs, wherever found to exist" (New York *Evening Post*, December 4, 1827).

In the summer of 1829 "a large gang of runaway negroes, who have infested the Parishes of Christ Church and St. James [South Carolina], for several months, and committed serious depredations on the properties of the planters" was accidentally discovered by a party of deer hunters (ibid., August 10, 1829). One of the Negroes was wounded and four others were captured. Several others escaped, but the Charleston *Mercury* hoped the citizens would "not cease their exertions until the evil shall be effectually removed."

Maroons were important factors in causing slave insubordination in Sampson, Bladen, Onslow, Jones, New Hanover, and Dublin Counties, North Carolina, from September through December 1830. Citizens complained that their "slaves are become almost uncontrollable. They go and come and when and where they please, and if an attempt is made to correct them they immediately fly to the woods and there continue for months and years Committing grievous depredations on our Cattle, hogs and Sheep" (Johnson 1937:515, 517; Taylor 1928, V:31). One of these fugitive slaves, Moses, who had been out for two years, was captured in November. From him one elicited the information that an uprising was imminent, that the conspirators "had arms & ammunition secreted, that they had runners or messengers to go between Wilmington, Newbern & Elizabeth City to 'carry word' & report to them, that there was a camp in Dover Swamp of 30 or 40—another about Gastons Island, on Price's Creek, several on Newport River, several near Wilmington." Arms were found in the place named by Moses

in possession of a white woman living in a very retired situation—also some meat, hid away & could not be accounted for—a child whom the party [of citizens] found a little way from the house, said that his mamy dressed victuals every day for 4 or 5 runaways, & shewed the spot . . . where the meat was then hid & where it was found—the place or camp in Dover was found, a party of neighbours discovered the camp, burnt 11 houses, and made such discoveries, as convinced them it was a place of rendezvous for numbers (it is supposed they killed several of the negroes).[4]

Newspaper accounts referred to the wholesale shooting of fugitives. In 1830 the Roanoke *Advertiser* stated: "The inhabitants of Newbern being advised of the assemblage of sixty armed slaves in a swamp in their vicinity, the military were called out, and surrounding the swamp, killed the whole party" (quoted in *The Liberator* [Boston], January 8, 1831). A later item dated Wilmington, January 7, 1831, declared, "There has been much shooting of negroes in this neighborhood recently, in consequence of symptoms of liberty having been discovered among them" (New York *Sentinel*, quoted in *The Liberator*, March 19, 1831). It is of interest to note that Richmond papers, on receiving the first reports of Nat Turner's revolt of August 1831, asked concerning the rebels, "Were they connected with the desperadoes who harrassed (sic) N. Carolina last year?" (Richmond *Enquirer*, August 30, 1831).

In June 1836 there is mention that "a band of runaway negroes in the Cypress Swamp" near New Orleans "had been committing depredations" (Louisiana *Advertiser*, June 8, 1836, quoted by *The Liberator*, July 2, 1836). The next year, in July, was reported the killing of an outlaw slave leader, Squire, near New Orleans, whose band, it was felt, was responsible for the deaths of several white men (New Orleans *Picayune*, July 19, 1837). Squire's career had lasted for three years. A guard of soldiers was sent to the swamp for his body, which was exhibited for several days in the public square of the city.

The year 1837 also saw the start of the Florida or Semi-

4 See letter dated November 15, 1830, Newbern, from J. Turgwyn to Governor John Owen in Governor's *Letter Book* XXVIII:247–49, and letter from J. I. Pasteur to Governor Owen also dated Newbern, November 15, 1830, in Governor's Papers No. 60, Historical Commission, Raleigh.

nole War, which was destined to drag on until 1843. This war, "conducted largely as a slave catching enterprise for the benefit of the citizens of Georgia and Florida," was, before its termination, to take an unknown number of Indian and Negro lives together with the lives of 1,500 white soldiers and the expenditure of $20 million (Foreman 1932:366, 383; see also *The Liberator*, March 18, 1837). The Indians had, at the beginning of hostilities, about 1,650 warriors and 250 Negro fighters. The latter were "the most formidable foe, more blood-thirsty, active, and revengeful, than the Indian" (Sprague 1848:309; Giddings 1858:121, 139).

Armed runaways repulsed an attack near Wilmington, North Carolina, in January 1841, after killing one of the whites. A posse captured three of the Negroes and lodged them in the city jail. One escaped, but two were taken from the prison by some twenty-five whites and lynched (Wilmington *Chronicle*, January 6, 1841, in *The Liberator*, January 22, 1841). Late in September two companies of militia were dispatched in search of a body of maroons some forty-five miles north of Mobile, Alabama (New Orleans *Bee*, October 4, 1841). "It is believed that these fellows have for a long time been in the practice of theft and arson, both in town and country. . . . A force from above was scouring down, with bloodhounds, &c to meet the Mobile party." A month later frequent attacks upon white men by runaway Negroes were reported from Terrebonne Parish, Louisiana (Lafourche [La.] *Patriot* in *The Liberator*, November 12, 1841).

Several armed planters near Hanesville, Mississippi, in February 1844, set an ambush for maroons who had been exceedingly troublesome. Six Negroes, "part of the gang," were trapped, but three escaped. Two were wounded, and one was killed (Hanesville *Free Press*, March 1, 1844, cited by *The Liberator*, April 5, 1844). In November 1846, about a dozen armed slaveholders surprised "a considerable gang of runaway negroes" in St. Landry Parish, Louisiana. The maroons refused to surrender and fled. Two Negroes, a man and woman, were killed, and two Negro women were "badly wounded." The others escaped (New Orleans *Picayune*, quoted in *The Liberator*, December 4, 1846).

Joshua R. Giddings referred to the flight in September 1850 of some three hundred former Florida maroons from

their abode in present Oklahoma to Mexico (1858:316, 334, 337). This was accomplished after driving off Creek Indians sent to oppose their exodus. The Pennsylvania *Freeman* of October 30, 1851, citing the Houston *Telegraph* (n.d.), states that fifteen hundred former American slaves were aiding the Comanchee Indians of Mexico in their fighting. Five hundred of these Negroes were from Texas. Giddings also referred to unsuccessful expeditions by slaveholders of Texas in 1853 into Mexico to recover fugitive Negroes, and declared that at the time he was writing (1858), maroons in southern Florida were again causing trouble. F. L. Olmsted gave evidence of maroon troubles in the 1850s in Virginia, Louisiana, and northern Alabama (1904:177; 1860:30, 55).

A letter of August 25, 1856, to Governor Thomas Bragg of North Carolina, signed by Richard A. Lewis and twenty-one other citizens, informed him of a "very secure retreat for runaway negroes" in a large swamp between Bladen and Robeson counties (Governor's *Letter Book,* No. 43, pp. 514–15, Historical Commission, Raleigh). There "for many years past, and at this time, there are several runaways of bad and daring character—destructive to all kinds of Stock and dangerous to all persons living by or near said swamp." Slaveholders attacked these Negroes on August 1, 1856, but accomplished nothing and saw one of their own number killed. "The negroes ran off cursing and swearing and telling them to come on, they were ready for them again." The Wilmington *Journal* of August 14 mentioned that these runaways "had cleared a place for a garden, had cows, &c in the swamp." Mr. Lewis and his friends were "unable to offer sufficient inducement for negro hunters to come with their dogs unless aided from other sources." The governor suggested that magistrates be requested to call for the militia, but whether this was done or not is unknown.

A runaway camp was destroyed, and four Negroes, including a woman, were captured near Bovina, Mississippi, in March 1857 (Vicksburg *Whig,* cited by *The Liberator,* April 3, 1857). A similar event, resulting in the wounding of three maroons, occurred in October 1859 in Nash County, North Carolina (*The Day Book,* Norfolk, October 13, 1859). An "organized camp of white men and negroes" was held responsible for a servile conspiracy, involving whites, which was uncovered in Talladega County, Alabama, in August

1860 (cf. Laura White, in *Journal of Southern History*, 1 [1935], p. 47).

The years of the Civil War witnessed a considerable accentuation in the struggle of the Negro people against enslavement. This was as true of maroon activity as it was generally. There were reports of depredations committed by "a gang of runaway slaves" acting together with two whites along the Comite River, Louisiana, early in 1861 (New York *Daily Tribune*, March 11, 1861). An expedition was set "on foot to capture the whole party." A runaway community near Marion, South Carolina, was attacked in June 1861 (Henry 1914:121). There were no casualties, however, the slave hunters capturing but two Negro children, twelve guns, and one ax.

Confederate Brigadier General R. F. Floyd asked Governor Milton of Florida on April 11, 1862, to declare martial law in Nassau, Duvar, Clay, Putnam, St. John's, and Volusia counties "as a measure of absolute necessity, as they contain a nest of traitors and lawless negroes" (*Official Records of the Rebellion*, Ser. I, Vol. LIII, p. 233). In October 1862, a scouting party of three armed whites, investigating a maroon camp containing one hundred men, women, and children in Surry County, Virginia, were killed by these fugitives (*Calendar of Virginia State Papers*, XI, pp. 233–36). Governor Shorter of Alabama commissioned J. H. Clayton in January 1863 to destroy the nests in the southeastern part of the state of "deserters, traitors, and runaway Negroes" (*Official Records of the Rebellion*, Ser. I, Vol. XV, p. 947; Tatum 1934:63).

Colonel Hatch of the Union Army reported in August 1864, that "500 Union men, deserters, and negroes were . . . raiding towards Gainesville," Florida (Tatum 1934:88). The same month a Confederate officer, John K. Jackson, declared that

> Many deserters . . . are collected in the swamps and fastnesses of Taylor, La Fayette, Levy and other counties [in Florida], and have organized, with runaway negroes, bands for the purpose of committing depredations upon the plantations and crops of loyal citizens and running off their slaves. These depredatory bands have even threatened the cities of Tallahassee, Madison,

and Marianna [*Official Records of the Rebellion*, Ser. I, Vol. XXV, Part II, p. 607].

A Confederate newspaper noticed similar activities in North Carolina in 1864 (Richmond *Daily Examiner*, January 14, 1864). It reported it

> difficult to find words of description . . . of the wild and terrible consequences of the negro raids in this obscure . . . theatre of the war. . . . In the two counties of Currituck and Camden, there are said to be from five to six hundred negroes, who are not in the regular military organization of the Yankees, but who, outlawed and disowned by their masters, lead the lives of banditti, roving the country with fire and committing all sorts of horrible crimes upon the inhabitants.
>
> This present theatre of guerrilla warfare has, at this time, a most important interest for our authorities. It is described as a rich country, . . . and one of the most important sources of meat supplies that is now accessible to our armies. . . .

The account ends with a broad hint that white deserters from the Confederate Army were fighting shoulder to shoulder with the self-emancipated Negroes.

The story of the American maroons is of interest not only because it forms a fairly important part of the history of the South and of the Negro, but also because of the evidence it affords to show that the conventional picture of slavery as a more or less delightful, patriarchal system is fallacious. The corollary of this fallacious picture—docile, contented slaves— is also, of course, seriously questioned. Indeed, taking this material on maroons in conjunction with that recently presented on servile revolts, leads one to assert that American slavery was a horrid form of tyrannical rule, which often found it necessary to suppress ruthlessly the desperate expressions of discontent on the part of its outraged victims.

REFERENCES NOT CITED IN GENERAL BIBLIOGRAPHY

Bruce, P. A.
    1896 *Economic history of Virginia in 17th century*. New York.
Candler, A. D. (ed.)
    1907 *The colonial records of Georgia*. Atlanta.

Conway, M. D.
    1888 *Omitted chapters in history disclosed in the life and papers of Edmund Randolph.* New York.
Cook, H. T.
    1916 *Life and legacy of David R. Williams.* New York.
Davis, T. F.
    1930–31 "United States Troops in Spanish East Florida, 1812–13." *The Florida Historical Society Quarterly* 9:3–42.
Ellis, S. M.
    1927 *The solitary horseman.* Kensington.
Foreman, Grant
    1932 *Indian removal.* Norman.
Fuller, H. B.
    1906 *The purchase of Florida.* Cleveland.
Giddings, J. R.
    1858 *The exiles of Florida.* Columbus.
Hening, W.
    n.d. *Statutes at large of Virginia.*
Henry, H. M.
    1914 *Police control of the slave in South Carolina.* Emory.
Higginson, T. W.
    1870 *Army life in a black regiment.* Boston.
Holland, E. C.
    1823 *A refutation of the calumnies.* Charleston.
Janson, Charles W.
    1807 *The Stranger in America.* London.
Johnson, G. G.
    1937 *Ante-bellum North Carolina.* Chapel Hill.
Kirkland, T. J. and Kennedy, R. M.
    1926 *Historic Camden.* Columbia.
McMaster, J. B.
    n.d. *History.*
Moody, V. A.
    1924 "Slavery on Louisiana Sugar Plantations." *The Louisiana Historical Quarterly* 7:191–301.
Olmsted, Frederick L.
    1860 *Journey in the back country.* London.
    1904 *Journey in seaboard slave states.* London.
Parton, James
    1860 *Life of Andrew Jackson.* Boston.
Phillips, U. B.
    1909a *Plantation and frontier documents.* Cleveland.
    1909b "Racial problems, adjustments and disturbances in the Ante-Bellum South." In *The South in the Building of the Nation,* Vol. 4. Richmond, pp. 194–241.
Pinckney, C. C.
    1895 *Life of General Thomas Pinckney.* Boston.

Pratt, J. W.
  1925 *Expansionists of 1812.* New York.
Russell, William H.
  1863 *My diary North and South.* Boston.
Siebert, W. H.
  1899 *The underground railroad.* New York.
Sprague, John T.
  1848 *The origin, progress, and conclusion of the Florida War.*
  New York.
Stevens, W. B.
  1859 *A history of Georgia.* Philadelphia.
Stowe, Harriet B.
  1856 *Dred, a tale of the Great Dismal Swamp.* Boston.
Tatum, Georgia Lee
  1934 *Disloyalty in the Confederacy.* Chapel Hill.
Taylor, R. H.
  1928 "Slave Conspiracies in North Carolina." *North Carolina
  Historical Review* 5:20–34.
Wallace, D. D.
  1934 *The history of South Carolina.* New York.
Woodson, C. G.
  1928 *The Negro in our history,* Washington.

PART FOUR

Brazil

Maroon settlements dotted the vast map of Brazil, from the forests of the interior, where they were often merged with bands of Indians, to the outskirts of major urban centers. The selections that follow offer a broad overview of Brazilian maroon communities. First, the historian R. K. Kent discusses the political organization of the most famous of all *quilombos*, Palmares, showing in what sense it was indeed "an African state in Brazil." Roger Bastide, perhaps the dean of Afro-Brazilian studies, then presents a survey of the many other maroon communities in Brazil, offering as well some incisive comments on the meaning of marronage as a form of cultural resistance. Finally, Stuart B. Schwartz, an historian whose current research continues to focus on maroons, examines in detail the communities that surrounded the city of Bahia, demonstrating the kind of sophisticated work that might be done by working closely with documents for other regions of Brazil as well.

Additional readings on Brazilian maroons are found in the bibliographical note to Part Four.

CHAPTER ELEVEN

Palmares: An African State in Brazil[1]

R. K. KENT

Without slaves from Africa, reported an early Portuguese source, "it is impossible to do anything in Brazil" (Breve discurso . . . n.d.). Although prior arrivals are suspected, the first known landing of slaves from Africa on Brazilian soil took place in 1552 (Neiva 1949, IV:491–92). In 1580, five years after the founding of Loanda and on the eve of Brazil's sugar boom, there were no fewer than 10,000 Africans in Brazil (Calmon 1959, II:347). Fifty years later, Pernambuco alone imported 4,400 slaves annually from Africa (Boxer 1952:225). It also contained 150 *engenhos,* or a third of the total sugar mill and plantation complex in Brazil (Mauro 1960:193 [Table]). In 1630, the Dutch West India Company (WIC) captured Pernambuco, and within a decade Portugal had abandoned Brazil to the Dutch. It was ultimately the decision of local settlers, the *moradores,* to fight the West India Company that led to restoration of Portuguese control in 1654. The Dutch retreat from Brazil, however,

Reprinted with the permission of the author and Cambridge University Press from *The Journal of African History* 6:161–75 (1965).

[1] An earlier paper on Palmares was read at the University of Wisconsin's seminar in Latin-American History, under Dr. John Phelan. I am indebted to the editors of the Journal of African History and to Dr. Jan Vansina for suggestions that made the revision easier. I am also grateful to the Foreign Area Program for its 1963–64 Fellowship at the University of Wisconsin. There is no connection between the program and the views expressed herein.

was secured through a joint Afro-Portuguese effort, which gave the Black Regiment of Henrique Dias its colonial fame. If early settlement and a sugar-based economy could not have been sustained without the African laborer, neither could the Portuguese continue to hold Brazil without the African soldier. The subsequent evolution of Brazil is no less a story of Euro-African enterprise. Exploitation of gold and diamonds in the eighteenth century, pioneering shifts of population from the coast to the interior, dilution of monoculture, formation of mining states, or advent of an abolitionist movement in the nineteenth century were all dependent on the same combination (cf. Boxer 1961, Freyre 1956, Ramos 1939). The blend of race, language, and culture in contemporary Brazil confirms this evolution.

Africa's impact on Brazil and, more generally, the role of the Negro[2] in Brazilian history and society are subjects of an extensive literature (cf., for example, Rodrigues 1962). Its principal stress is on assimilation rather than divergence, and frequently the early colonial society has been postulated from descriptions left by European and North American travelers who visited Brazil much later (cf. Codman 1867; Couty 1881; Dent 1886; Gardner 1849; Kidder 1845; Koster 1817; Saint-Hilaire 1852; and von Spix and von Martius 1824). It is hence not surprising that active Negro resistance to slavery in Brazil has not received comparable attention and is consequently less known.

According to one working definition, there were three basic forms of active resistance; fugitive slave settlements called *quilombos;* attempts at seizure of power; and armed insurrections, which sought neither escape nor control but amelioration (Carneiro 1947:13). The latter two prevailed in the first half of the nineteenth century, a period of political transition in Brazil and of accelerated slave trade with Africa (Gomes 1950, V:56 [Tables I and II]). They encompass, for example, nine Bahian revolts between 1807 and 1835, which involved a number of Hausa, Yoruba, and Kwa-speak-

---

2 "Negro," as a term used in colonial Brazil, did not apply to *pretos* ("blacks") alone. It included sometimes *pardos* or *gente do cor,* people "of color" not easily accepted as either *pretos* or *brancos* ("whites"). It also applied to *crioulos* or those born in Brazil of African or mixed parentage, to *ladinos* or those who spoke Portuguese and usually espoused the Catholic faith, and to the *Africanos* or those who were neither Portuguese-speaking nor native to Brazil.

ing groups, as well as the Ogboni Society, Muslim *alufas*, and even a back-to-Africa movement (cf. Brasil 1909; Caldas Britto 1903; Nina Rodrigues 1935). The *quilombos* constitute a pre-nineteenth-century phenomenon and are of considerable interest to the African historian. They came closest to the idea of re-creating African societies in a new environment and against consistently heavier odds. Once formed, the *quilombos* were regarded as a threat to the Portuguese plantation, an inducement for escape from the slave hut. They were rarely, therefore, allowed to last a long time. Of the ten major *quilombos* in colonial Brazil, seven were destroyed within two years of being formed. Four fell in the state of Bahia in 1632, 1636, 1646, and 1796. The other three met the same fate in Rio in 1650, Parahyba in 1731, and Piumhy in 1758. One *quilombo*, in Minas Gerais, lasted from 1712 to 1719. Another, the "Carlota" of Mato Grosso, was wiped out after existing for twenty-five years, from 1770 to 1795.

Nothing, however, compares in the annals of Brazilian history with the "Negro Republic" of Palmares in Pernambuco. It spanned almost the entire seventeenth century. Between 1672 and 1694, it withstood, on the average, one Portuguese expedition every fifteen months. In the last *entrada* against Palmares, a force of six thousand took part in forty-two days of siege (Pitta 1880, VIII:239; Southey 1819, III:27; Ennes 1948:209–10). The Portuguese Crown sustained a cumulative loss of four hundred thousand cruzados (Ennes 1938: 113), or roughly three times the total revenue lease of eight Brazilian captaincies in 1612.[3] As Brazil's classic *quilombo*, Palmares gained two more distinctions. It opened the study of Negro history in modern Brazil. Minutes of the Brazilian Historical Institute reveal that Palmares caused lively discussions in 1840, and that search for written materials relative to it began in 1851 (cf. *Revista do Instituto Historico e Geographico Brasileiro (RIHGB)* (1841, III:151–54; 1851, XIV:491). Important gaps in knowledge persist, but enough primary sources have been found and published to trace the development of Palmares, to examine it as a society and

[3] See Engel Sluiter in preface to the "Report on the State of Brazil, 1612," *Hispanic American Historical Review* (1949), XXIX/4, 521; full Portuguese text reproduced, 521–62. It is generally accepted that Diogo de Campos Moreno, aide to governor Diogo de Meneses (1608–12), penned the "Rezão do Estado do Brasil."

government, and to suggest its significance to both Brazilian
and African history.[4]

I

Early writers attributed the birth of Palmares to Portuguese-Dutch struggles for Pernambuco, from which slaves
profited by escaping in groups (cf. Pitta 1880, VIII:235;
Southey 1819, III:23; Loreto Couto 1757, VIII:Ch. 4; and
Varnhagen 1930, III:319). They made no reference to Palmares as a *quilombo*. Southey came across the term in a
Minas Gerais decree of 1722 (1819, III:248 and 248n.). An
official letter, sent from Pernambuco to Lisbon in 1692, contains the first and only definition of Palmares as a *quilombo*
in primary sources (cf. Ennes 1938:243). The point is worth
stressing. The accepted definition of a *quilombo* as a fugitive
slave settlement has been continuously applied to Palmares
since the turn of this century, and the problem of interpretation has been more difficult as a result. An early nineteenth-
century historian, for example, could easily classify Palmares
as the "unusual exception, a real government of escaped
Blacks on Brazilian soil" (Denis 1825:147). But subsequent
identification of the state, which was a major historical event
with a mere colony of escaped slaves, could not provide a

[4] Firsthand descriptions (1645), "Diario da Viagem do Capitão
João Blaer aos Palmares," actually written by Jürgens Reijmbach
(extract from the *Brieven en Papieren uit Brasilien*, translated
into Portuguese by Alfredo de Carvalho for the *Revista do Instituto Arqueológico Pernambucano* (1902), X:87–96; (1675–78).
"Relação das Guerras feitas aos Palmares de Pernambuco no tempo
do Governador d. Pedro de Almeida," *RIHGB* (1859), XXII:303–
29. Material from the Municipality of Alagoas: (1668–80) 22
"Documentos" from the *Segundo Livro de Veracões* (n.d.). Material from the Arquivo Historico Colonial in Lisbon: (1671–
97) 95 *"Documentos"* collected and published by Ernesto Ennes
(1938), 133–484. Firsthand descriptions and materials from Municipality of Alagoas have been printed together in the document
appendix to Edison Carneiro's *O Quilombo dos Palmares*, 2nd ed.
(1958), 201–68, and will be quoted from that volume. Material
of dubious value: "Memoria dos feitos que se deram durante os
primeiros anos da Guerra com os Negros quilombolas, dos Palmares," *RIHGB* (1876), XXXIX:293–322. This would-be "Memoria dos feitos" has been discredited as a doctored copy of the
"Relação das Guerras," published in the same review seventeen
years earlier.

framework to fit the problem. *Ki-lombo*, according to Cavazzi (1687:207; 1690:163, 165 [Chi-Lambo Plan]), was a Jaga war camp, and there is no lack of sources that have translated it correctly as "arrayal" (Souza 1939:267; Capello and Ivens 1881:130). Could a historico-linguistic link between a Palmares in a formative stage and the Jaga *ki-lombo* perhaps be assumed, *faute de mieux?*

Slaves who freed themselves by escaping into the bush became something of a problem several decades before the Dutch took Pernambuco. In 1597, a Jesuit Father, Pero Rodrigues, was able to write that the "foremost enemies of the colonizer are revolted Negroes from Guiné in some mountain areas, from where they raid and give much trouble, and the time may come when they will dare to attack and destroy farms as their relatives do on the island of São Thomé" (quoted in Ribeiro 1958:458). Shortly after his arrival from Portugal, Governor Diogo Botelho (1602–8) learned from an Amerindian chief named Zorobabé that there was a "*mocambo* . . . of Negroes from Guiné . . . in the *palmares* of river Itapicuru" (Do Salvador 1961:315). Zorobabé was asked to destroy the *mocambo* and return with slaves, but "few were brought back since the Indians killed many and Zorobabé sold some along the way" (ibid.). If the Itapicuru *mocambo* went almost unnoticed by Portuguese authorities, this was not the case with a similar manifestation farther north. In the captaincy of Pernambuco, reported a high official in 1612, "some 30 leagues inland, there is a site between mountains called Palmares which harbours runaway slaves . . . whose attacks and raids force the whites into armed pursuits which amount to little for they return to raid again. . . . This makes it impossible to . . . end the transgressions which gave Palmares its reputation" ("Report on the State of Brazil," *Hispanic American Historical Review* [*HAHR*], XXIX/4, 553; Carneiro 1958:90; Carneiro worked with an earlier copy). Diogo Botelho, before he left Brazil, sent a punitive expedition to Palmares ("Correspondencia do Diogo Botelho, Governador do Estado do Brazil [1602–28]," *RIHGB* [1910], LXXIII/1, 86 and 151).

Clearly, *quilombo* does not appear in the vocabulary of early seventeenth-century Brazil. Instead, the fugitive slave settlement is known as *mocambo*, an appropriate description since *mu-kambo* in Ambundu means a hideout (Malheiro 1867, III:21; Mendonça 1935:220). Around 1603, *palmares* was simply any area covered by palm trees. There was no connection between the Itapicuru *mocambo* south of Sergipe and the Palmares of Pernambuco. Palmares was not regarded as an ordinary *mocambo*. By 1612, it had a considerable reputation. It was an organization with which the *moradores* could not cope alone. The foundation of Palmares thus appears to have taken place in 1605–6, possibly earlier, but certainly not later. As the report of 1612 indicates, the first Portuguese expedition against Palmares attained little by way of military victory. Nothing else, however, is heard of Palmares until the mid-1630s. Do Salvador's history of Brazil, written in 1629, and recently published official documents for the years 1607–33 are equally silent on Palmares (Biblioteca Nacional, *Livro Primeiro do Governo do Brasil*, 1607–33 [1958]). In 1634, a Pernambucan *morador* described Palmares as a "great calamity" (Brito Freire 1675, VII:525n; cf. also *RIHGB* [1841], III:153n.). The Dutch viewed it as a "serious danger" in 1640.[5] Increasing *palmarista* militancy after 1630 can safely be associated with slaves who took advantage of the Dutch presence to escape and who eventually found their way into Palmares. It is also certain that Palmares antedates the Dutch in Brazil by at least a quarter of a century. Given an earlier origin, and the absence of *quilombo* from the contemporary vocabulary, it is even less probable that Jagas were the founders of Palmares. It would be tempting to accept a recent claim that the Jagas gave Palmares its ruling dynasty, after being sent to Brazil in 1616 by the Angolan governor, Luis Mendes de Vascocellos, who assumed office in August 1617 and fought against the Ngola *with* Jaga auxiliaries (Vansina 1963:370; Freitas 1954, I:266, 278). A large contingent of Jagas was sold into slavery after a punitive expedition against Kasanje in 1624 and may have reached Brazil along with other prisoners from the *guerra preta* (cf. E. G. Ravenstein's "A Sketch of the History of Angola," published together with *The Strange Adventures of Andrew Battell of Leigh* [1901], 167–68). But the account of Andrew Battell, who was with the Jagas until 1603, shows nothing to indicate that any of them could have landed in Pernambuco by 1605 (ibid.). There remains the alternative of "Negroes from Guiné."

"Negroes from Guiné" were mentioned long before 1597 in

[5] See "A Situacão do Negro sob o Dominio Hollandes" in *Novos Estudos Afro-Brasileiros* (1937), II: 217.

connection with attempted rebellion (Da Nobrega to Tome de Sousa [July 5, 1559], lines 831–55 [Leite 1954, III: 101]). Rocha Pitta, a contemporary of Palmarés, held that it was founded by "forty Negroes from Guiné" who had abandoned plantations around Porto Calvo (1880, VIII:235). But the "Guiné" of early Portuguese sources is not a fruitful geographical expression. It stood for nearly anything between a limited section of West Africa and the entire continent. "Slaves from Guiné," according to the 1612 report, "are bought dearly because of the gifts and duties which must be paid for them in Angola" ("Report," *HAHR* [1949]:523). Henrique Dias wrote a letter—most likely in 1648—which stated that the Black Regiment was composed mainly of "Angolas" and *crioulos* with a sprinkling of "Minas" and "Ardras" (Freye 1956: 301; Mauro 1960:153).[6] With Loanda as the undisputed slave funnel from the 1580s until well into the seventeenth century, it is quite unlikely that more than a handful of *palmaristas* originated outside the Angola-Congo perimeter (cf. Rinchon 1929:59–80; Vianna Filho 1946). *Crioulos*—in Pernambuco of 1605—could not have been numerous either. All of this leads to the only plausible hypothesis about the founders of Palmares. They must have been Bantu-speaking and could not have belonged exclusively to any subgroup. Palmares was a reaction to a slave-holding society entirely out of step with forms of bondage familiar to Africa. As such, it had to cut across ethnic lines and draw upon all those who managed to excape from various plantations and at different times. The Palmares that emerged out of this amalgam may be glimpsed in a little more detail during the second half of the seventeenth century.

II

Dutch activities concerning Palmares, from 1640 until the Reijmbach expedition of 1645, are known mainly through Barleus (1923) and Nieuhof (1704).[7] They begin with a reconnaissance mission by Bartholomeus Lintz, a Dutch scout

[6] Affonso de E. Taunay dates the letter to 1648 in Vol. VIII (1946) of his *Historia Geral das Bandeiras Paulistas*, with pp. 37–169 devoted to Palmares.

[7] Taunay 1946, VIII:55, implies heavy borrowing by Nieuhof from Barleus (1647) *Rerum per octenium in Brasilia*. I am indebted to Mr. Bruce Fetter of the University of Wisconsin for his translation of the Dutch text of Barleus pertinent to Palmares.

who brought back the first rudimentary information about Palmares. Lintz discovered that Palmares was not a single enclave, but a combination of many *kleine* and two *groote* units. The smaller ones were clustered on the left bank of the Gurungumba, six leagues from its confluence with the larger Paraiba and twenty leagues from Alagoas. They contained "about 6,000 Negroes living in numerous huts" (Barleus 1923:315). The two large *palamars* were deeper inland, thirty leagues from Santo Amaro, in the mountain region of Barriga, and "harboured some 5,000 Negroes" (ibid.). In January 1643, the West India Company sent its Amerindian interpreter, Roelox Baro, with a force of Tapuyas and several Dutch regulars to "put the large Palmares through 'fire and sword,' devastate and plunder the small Palmares" (Barleus 1923:370). Baro seems to have returned without his men to report that "100 Negroes of Palmares were killed as against one killed and four wounded Dutchmen, our force having captured 31 defenders, including 7 Indians and some mulatto children" (ibid.).[8] The four Dutchmen and a handful of Tapuyas were found two months later. There was no one with them.

A second Dutch expedition left Selgado for Palmares on February 26, 1645. It was headed by Jürgens Reijmbach, an army lieutenant who kept a diary for thirty-six consecutive days (cf. Carneiro 1958:255–58). His task was to destroy the two *groote* Palmares. On March 18 Reijmbach reached the first and found that it had been abandoned months earlier. "When we arrived the bush growth was so thick that it took much doing to cut a path through." Three days later, his men located the second one. "Our Brasilenses managed to kill two or three Negroes in the bush but most of the people had vanished. Their kin—the few captives told Reijmbach— "knew of the expedition for some time because he had been forewarned from Alagoas." This Palmares, reads the entry of March 21,

is equally half a mile long, its street six feet wide and running along a large swamp, tall trees alongside. . . . There are 220 *casas*, amid them a church, four smithies and a huge *casa de conselho;* all kinds of artifacts are to be

[8] Baro left a subsequent *Relation du Voyage . . . au Pays des Tapuies* (April 3–July 14, 1647), translated from the Dutch by P. Moreau (Paris, 1651).

seen. . . . (The) king rules . . . with iron justice, without
permitting any *feticeiros* among the inhabitants; when
some Negroes attempt to flee, he sends *crioulos* after them
and once retaken their death is swift and of the kind to in-
still fear, especially among the Angolan Negroes; the king
also has another *casa*, some two miles away, with its own
rich fields. . . . We asked the Negroes how many of them
live (here) and were told some 500, and from what we
saw around us as well we presumed that there were 1,500
inhabitants all told. . . . This is the Palmares *grandes* of
which so much is heard in Brazil, with its well-kept lands,
all kinds of cereals, beautifully irrigated with streamlets.

In military terms, Reijmbach fared no better than his two
predecessors, Bartolomeu Bezzerra and Roelox Baro. An un-
destroyed Palmares, of which "so much is heard in Brazil,"
remained free of further interference by Pernambucan authorities until 1672. The ensuing two decades can best be
described as a period of sustained war, which ended in the
complete destruction of Palmares in 1694. As is often the
case, warfare and more intimate knowledge of the enemy
went together, and the growing information about Palmares
in the 1670s threw light on its evolution during the twenty-
seven years of relative peace.

"Our campaigns," complained a group of Pernambucan
moradores in 1681, "have not had the slightest effect on the
Negroes of Palmares . . . who seem invincible" (cf. Ennes
1938:136). The claim was not altogether true. Of the eight
expeditions between 1672 and 1680, two did hurt Palmares.
They were led by *capitão-mor* Fernão Carrilho, who had
distinguished "himself in the destruction of *mocambos* in the
Captaincy of Sergipe del Rey" (cf. Ennes 1938:135). The
Carrilho *entradas* of 1676–77 produced the most extensive
firsthand report ever found. The Palmares of 1677 encompassed over sixty leagues:

In the northeast, *mocambo* of *Zambi*, located 16 leagues
from Porto Calvo; north of it, at 5 leagues' distance, mocambo of *Arotirene*; along it two others called *Tabocas*;
northeast of these, at 14 leagues, the one of *Dombabanga*;
8 leagues north another, called *Subupuira*; another 6
leagues north, the royal enclave of *Macoco*; west of it, at 5
leagues, the mocambo of *Osenga*; at 9 leagues from our

Serinhaem, northwest, the enclave of *Amaro;* at 25 leagues
from Alagoas, northwest, the palamar of *Andalaquituche,*
brother of *Zambi;* and between all these, which are the
largest and most fortified, there are others of lesser importance and with less people in them [*Relacão* in Carneiro
1958:202].

There was no doubt, went the report, that Palmares maintained its "real strength" by providing "food as well as security" for the inhabitants—largely tillers of land who planted
"every kind of vegetables" and knew how to store them
against "wartime and winter." All the inhabitants of Palmares
considered themselves:

> subjects of a king who is called *Ganga-Zumba,* which
> means Great Lord, and he is recognized as such both by
> those born in Palmares and by those who join them from
> outside; he has a palatial residence, *casas* for members of
> his family, and is assisted by guards and officials who have,
> by custom, *casas* which approach those of royalty. He is
> treated with all respect due a Monarch and all the honours
> due a Lord. Those who are in his presence kneel on the
> ground and strike palm leaves with their hands as sign of
> appreciation of His excellence. They address him as Maj-
> esty and obey him with reverence. He lives in the royal en-
> clave, called *Macoco,* a name which was begotten from the
> death of an animal on the site. This is the capital of Pal-
> mares; it is fortified with parapets full of caltrops, a big
> danger even when detected. The enclave itself consists of
> some 1,500 *casas.* There are keepers of law (and) their of-
> fice is duplicated elsewhere. And although these barbarians
> have all but forgotten their subjugation, they have not com-
> pletely lost allegiance to the Church. There is a *capela,* to
> which they flock whenever time allows, and *imagens* to
> which they direct their worship. . . . One of the most
> crafty, whom they venerate as *paroco,* baptizes and marries
> them. Baptismals are, however, not identical with the form
> determined by the Church and the marriage is singularly
> close to laws of nature. . . . The king has three (women),
> a *mulata* and two *crioulas.* The first has given him many
> sons, the other two none. All the foregoing applies to the
> *cidade principal* of Palmares and it is the king who rules
> it directly; other *cidades* are in the charge of potentates

and major chiefs who govern in his name. The second *cidade* in importance is called *Subupuira* and is ruled by king's brother (Gana) *Zona*. . . . It has 800 *casas* and occupies a site one square league in size, right along the river *Cachingi*. It is here that Negroes are trained to fight our assaults (and weapons are forged there) [*Relacão* in Carneiro 1958:203–4].

Nearly three decades of peace had a number of important results in the internal evolution of Palmares.

Instead of the two major *palmars* of 1645, there were now ten. There was a very substantial element in the Macoco of those native to Palmares, people unfamiliar with *engenho* slavery. Afro-Brazilians continued to enjoy preferential status, but the distinction between *crioulos* and Angolas does not appear to have been as sharp as it was in 1645. There was a greater degree of religious acculturation. The reference to a population composed mainly of those born in Palmares and those who joined from outside suggests that slaves had become less numerous than free commoners. According to Pitta, the only slaves in Palmares were those captured in razzias (1880, VIII:236). But they had the option of going out on raids to secure freedom by returning with a substitute. This is confirmed by Nieuhof, who wrote that the main "business" of *palmaristas* "is to rob the Portuguese of their slaves, who remain in slavery among them, until they have redeemed themselves by stealing another; but such slaves as run over to them, are as free as the rest" (1704, II:8).

Although slim and often corrupted, the linguistic evidence leads to two unavoidable conclusions. The king and most of the hierarchy at the head of individual *mocambos* were not *crioulos*. Macoco/Makoko points to Loango[9a]; Tabocas/Taboka to Ambundu[b]; Andalaquituche/Ndala Kafuche to Kisama[c]; Osenga/Osanga/Hosanga to Kwango[d]; Subupuira/Subusupu hara vura and Zumba to Zande[e]; Dombabanga/Ndombetbanga to a Benguella-Yombe composite.[f] Arotirene

[9a-f] A. de O. de Cadornega, *Historia Geral das Guerras Angolanas* (1942 ed.), III:235, 249, 172, 186, and 240–41 and Furtado map of 1790/16°–17° Lat.; L. M. J. Visconde de Paiva Manso, *Historia do Congo—Documentos* (1877), 176–77 and 283–85; Jan Vansina, Personal Communication (January 30, 1964); C. R. Lagae, *La Langue des Azande*, III (1925):145–75 (*Zumba*=one of the group and consensus; elected ruler; *Subusupu hara vura*=forged

appears to be Amerindian.[g] Zambi/Nzambi and Ganga/ Nganga, respectively "divinity" and "lord," are too widely used in Central Africa to be traced further. Given as "brother," Zona may be an extreme corruption of Mona, an equally common term. Amaro/Amargo derives from a very bitter kind of wild-growing tea shrub, chimarrão,[h] which is close enough to *cimarrones*, as marooned slaves were called in the West Indies. The principle of *cujus regio ejus religio*, slightly bent to accommodate ethnic subgroups, cannot be deduced from this evidence. What it does affirm, however, is that Palmares did not spring from a single social structure. It was, rather, an African political system that came to govern a plural society and thus give continuity to what could have been at best a group of scattered hideouts.

The almost equally long years of peace and war between 1645 and 1694 point to Palmares as a fluctuating "peril." While not necessarily unfair to the merits of a particular event, the Portuguese took it for an article of faith that Palmares was an aggressor state. No written document originating within Palmares has come to light. It probably does not exist. The late Arthur Ramos made a search for oral traditions in the 1930s. It yielded only an annual stage play he was able to attend in the township of Pilar (Ramos 1939: 109–16; Pilar, in the district of Alagoas, was formerly Aloea or Cariri):

> The sensation of security (in Palmares) diminished after the first attacks of the colonists. The Palmares Negroes reacted by increasing their defences . . . to maintain their little republic, the Negroes were forced to make sorties to the neighboring Indian villages and the towns of nearby valleys. This brought about (more) reprisals. . . . The play recalls this sequence of events as it persists in the memory of the people.

However blurred by the passage of time, the play at least allows for aggression on each side. There is no need to depend, in this case, on collective memory to look for evidence with which both the specific and broad nature of the "peril" can be illustrated.

---

weapon of war). [g] Probably Araticum of the Arapua mountains in Pernambuco. [h] James L. Taylor, *A Portuguese-English Dictionary* (1958), 40.

Pernambucan authorities did not view Palmares from th[e] perspective of the *moradores* who were in contact with it. They were too far removed from the general area of Palmares. Reijmbach, for example, had to march at a fast clip for twenty days to reach it from the coast, which the Pernambucan governors—Dutch or Portuguese—seldom left. The governors did, however, respond to *morador* pressure. "*Moradores* of this Captaincy, Your Majesty, are not capable of doing much by themselves in this war. . . . At all hours they complain to me of tyrannies they must suffer from [the Negroes of Palmares]" (cf. Ennes 1938:142). Among the complaints most frequently heard were loss of field hands and domestic servants, loss of settler lives, kidnaping and rape of white women. Two of the common grievances do not stand up too well. Women were a rarity in Palmares and were actively sought during razzias. But female relatives of the *morador* did not constitute the main target, and those occasionally taken were returned unmolested for ransom (Southey 1819, III:24). Checking the "rape of Sabines" tales, Edison Carneiro discovered one exception to the ransom rule, reported by a Pernambucan soldier in 1682 (1958:62). Equally, close examination of documents in the Ennes and Camara de Alagoas collections—117 in all—failed to reveal a single substantiated case of a *morador* killed in *palmarista* raids. Settler lives appear to have been lost in the numerous and forever unrecorded "little" *entradas* into Palmares. They were carried out by small, private armies of plantation owners who sought to recapture lost hands or to acquire new ones without paying for them. Some of the *moradores* had secret commercial compacts with Palmares, usually exchanging firearms for gold and silver taken in the razzias (Pitta 1880:237). Evidence of this is not lacking. A gubernatorial proclamation of November 26, 1670 bitterly denounced "those who possess firearms" and pass them on to *palmaristas* "in disregard of God and local laws" (cf. Carneiro 1958:227–28). In 1687, the state of Pernambuco empowered a Paulista Colonel-of-Foot to imprison *moradores* merely suspected of relations with Palmares, "irrespective of their station" (Ennes 1938:24). Town merchants are also known to have carried on an active trade with Palmares, bartering utensils for agricultural produce (Ramos 1939:64). More than that, they "were most useful to the Negroes . . . by supplying advance information on expeditions

prepared against them (and) for which the Negroes paid dearly" (Freitas 1954, I:291). And Reijmbach's entry of March 21, 1645 makes it clear that this relationship was an old one.

Loss of plantation slaves, through raids as well as escape, emerges as the one solid reason behind the *morador-palmarista* conflict. The price of slaves is known to have increased considerably by the late 1660s. The very growth of Palmares served to increase its fame among the plantation slaves. "More and more Negroes from Angola," wrote a governor in 1671, "have now for some years fled on their own from the *rigor de cativeiro* in mills and plantations of this Captaincy (Ennes 1938:133). But this growth was not one-sided. Salients in the *morador* frontier, which had protruded from the littoral by the early 1640s, contracted between 1645 and 1654, a decade of Portuguese-Dutch struggle for Pernambuco. Contacts with Palmares were thus minimized until new bulges began to form. In a painstaking study of territorial expansion in Brazil, Felisbello Freire has shown that this movement away from the coast began in the late 1650s from Bahia, Sergipe, and Espirito Santo (1906:6–106). It was retarded by no more than a few years for southern Pernambuco. The northern section merely took a little longer. "The Negroes," writes Carneiro, "had good relations with *moradores*, as long as the latter kept kept their slave huts and plantations away from the free lands of Palmares" (1958:76). But what looked like free lands to the Portuguese were not regarded in the same light by rulers of Palmares, and neither party understood the problem. There were, to be sure, no "great frontier" proportions in the inland movement of the concluding seventeenth-century decades. According to Basilio Magalhães, it was an *"expansão pequena,"* at fifty or so leagues inland (1935:17–171). Palmares was, however, well within it. Toward the end of the seventeenth century, its territorial domain was estimated at about eleven hundred square leagues (Ennes 1948:212). "Those who live in a state of constant danger," reads another proclamation, "are people in the vicinity of the *mocambos* belonging to Palmares" (cf. Carneiro 1958:231).

The hard-hitting Carrilho *entradas* of 1676–77 evoked at least one response familiar to Palmares besides warfare. As he had done earlier, whenever a new governor came to Pernambuco, Ganga-Zumba sued for peace. The terms, however, were new and rather surprising. On June 18, 1678:

> The junior lieutenants whom don Pedro (de Almeida) had sent to Palmares returned with three of the king's sons and 12 more Negroes who prostrated themselves at the feet of don Pedro. . . . They brought the king's request for fealty, asking for peace which was desired, stating that only peace could end the difficulties of Palmares, peace which so many governors and leaders had proferred but never stuck to; that they have come to ask for his good offices; that they have never desired war; that they only fought to save their own lives; that they were being left without *cidades,* without supplies, without wives. . . . The king had sent them to seek peace with no other desires but to trade with *moradores,* to have a treaty, to serve his Highness in whatever capacity; it is only the liberty of those born in Palmares that is now being sought while those who fled from our people will be returned; Palmares will be no more as long as a site is provided where they will be able to live, at his grace [*Relação* in Carneiro 1958:219].

Three days after the embassy's arrival, the new governor, Aires de Souza Castro—replacing Almeida—called a council of state. He proposed that a draft treaty be sent to Ganga-Zumba extending peace, the requested liberties, and the release of *palmarista* women, who seem to have constituted by far the largest group of captives. The council agreed, and a *sargento-mor* who had served in the Black Regiment and knew how to read and write, was sent to the Macoco, *"para que lesse e declarasse ao rei e aos mais o tratado de paz"* (ibid., 221). Ganga-Zumba was confirmed as supreme ruler over his people. The question of Palmares' territorial limits was not settled in any precise way. "The solemnity which surrounded all these acts," wrote Nina Rodrigues, "gave a real importance to the Negro State which now the Colony treated as one nation would another, (for) this was no mere pact of a strong party concluded with disorganized bands of fugitive Negroes" (1935:132).

On paper, the treaty seemed conclusive. But there were peculiarities in the immediate situation. A strong detachment, which had been attacking Palmares since 1677 or early 1678, vas not demobilized, and a group of Alagoar *moradores*, ed by a spokesman named João da Fonesca, made certain hat it would remain there (cf. Carneiro 1958:244–45). The nk was hardly dry when Aires de Souza Castro began to listribute some 192 leagues of land to sixteen individuals who iad taken part in wars against Palmares, Carrilho alone ob- aining a twenty-league *sesmaria* (cf. Ennes 1938:153). By 679, a *palmarista* "captain named Zambi (whose uncle is Gana-Zona) was in revolt (with João mulato, Canhonga, Gaspar [and] Amaro, having done the person of Ganga- Zumba to death" (cf. Carneiro 1958:247). By March 1680, Zambi was being called upon to surrender, without success (ibid.). The war was on once more.

Reactions to the treaty, on both sides, are revealing. Ganga- Zumba's peace proposal contained two clauses that could not be fulfilled. To allow a sovereign, if vassal, state to exist in Pernambuco would have meant reversing a 150-year-old policy of exclusive Portuguese claim to Brazil. The Almeida- le Souza move was, therefore, a tactical one. It was, as Ennes stated after careful study, "an easy way of postponing that question which already had, without any positive accomplish- ment, consumed infinite time" (Ennes 1948:202). Con- versely, to hand over to the Portuguese half or more of some fifteen thousand to twenty thousand *palmaristas*—a difficult logistical problem in its own right—would have required the kind of obedience that only a modern totalitarian state can secure (cf. Carneiro 1958:206).

The native-newcomer ratio was not identical in every *mocambo* of Palmares. The Macoco, at forty-five leagues from Porto Calvo, must have had a far greater number of the native-born than did the *mocambos* of Zumbi, at sixteen leagues from Porto Calvo, and Amaro, at nine leagues from Serinhaem. Sociocultural differences, moreover, between *crioulos* and recent arrivals from Africa were not sufficiently great to challenge the unity of Palmares, which stood against the Portuguese economic and political order. The diplomacy of Ganga-Zumba, an elected ruler, might have worked had the promise to return those who found refuge in Palmares been observed. It might have worked if Palmares had been contiguous to other similar states facing an intrusive minor- ity. Again, it might have worked if Palmares had been a homogeneous society with hereditary rulers. None of these conditions were present. In its time and place, Palmares had

only two choices. It could continue to hold its ground as a
independent state or suffer complete extinction. Zambi's pa
ace revolt finally brought the unyielding *palmarista* and m
rador elements to full agreement.

Six expeditions went into Palmares between 1680 an
1686. Their total cost must have been large. In 1694, th
Overseas Council in Lisbon was advised that Palmares cause
a cumulative loss of not less than 1,000,000 cruzados to th
"people of Pernambuco" (Ennes 1938:195). The estima
appears exaggerated unless the 400,000 cruzados contribute
directly by the Crown were included. A single municipali
did, however, spend 3,000 cruzados (109,800 reis) in th
fiscal year 1679–80 to cover the running cost of Palmare
wars (cf. Carneiro 1958:248), and a tenfold figure for th
local and state treasuries would seem modest for the s
years. Casualties aside, the results did not justify the cos
Palmares stood undefeated at the end of 1686. It was a
parent that the state of Pernambuco could not deal wi
Palmares out of its own resources. In March 1687, the ne
governor, Sotto-Maior, informed Lisbon that he had accepte
the services of *bandeirantes* from São Paulo, "at small e
pense to the treasury of Your Majesty" (cf. Ennes 1948:205
The Paulistas of the time were Portuguese-Amerindian *met*
and transfrontiersmen, renowned in Brazil for special ski
in jungle warfare. Their leader, Domingos Jorge Velho, ha
written to Sotto-Maior in 1685 asking "for commissions a
commander-in-chief and captains in order to subdue . .
(Palmares) (cf. Ennes 1948:204; his translation). Large
because Lisbon could not be convinced that their service
would come cheap, the Paulistas did not reach Pernambuc
until 1692. In crossing so great a distance, 192 lives wer
lost in the backlands of Brazil, and 200 men deserted th
Paulista ranks, unable to face "hunger, thirst, and agony."

The story of Palmares' final destruction has been told i
great detail. Two thirds of the secondary works discuss th
Paulistas and the 1690s, some sixty of the ninety-five docu
ments in the Ennes collection refer to little else, and Enne
has published a useful summary in English (1948). Th
Paulistas had to fight for two years to reduce Palmares to
single fortified site. After twenty days of siege by the Pau
istas, the state of Pernambuco had to provide an addition
three thousand men to keep it going for another twenty-tw
days. The breakthrough occurred during the night of Fel

uary 5–6, 1694. Some two hundred *palmaristas* fell or
urled themselves—the point has been long debated—"from a
ock so high that they were broken to pieces." Hand-to-hand
ombat took another two hundred *palmarista* lives, and over
ve hundred "of both sexes and all ages" were captured and
old outside Pernambuco. Zambi, taken alive and wounded,
vas decapitated on November 20, 1695. The head was ex-
ibited in public "to kill the legend of his immortality."

III

The service rendered by the destruction of Palmares, wrote
ne of Brazil's early Africanists, is beyond discussion. It re-
noved the "greatest threat to future evolution of the Brazilian
eople and civilization—a threat which this new Haiti, if
ictorious, would have planted (forever) in the heart of
razil" (Nina Rodrigues 1935:124). Indeed, Palmares came
uite close to altering the subsequent history of Brazil. Had
hey not experienced the threat of Palmares in the seven-
eenth century, the Portuguese might well have found them-
elves hugging the littoral and facing not one, but a number
f independent African states dominating the backlands of
ighteenth-century Brazil. In spite of hundreds of *mocambos*
hat tried to come together, Palmares was never duplicated
n Brazilian soil. This is ample testimony of its impact on the
'ortuguese settler and official. They organized special units,
nder *capitães-do-mato* or bush captains, to hunt for *mocam-
os* and nip them in the bud. And they sought to prevent,
t ports of entry, an overconcentration of African slaves from
he same ethnic group or ship. This policy was abandoned
n the wake of the Napoleonic wars, and the immediate
epercussion came by way of the nine Bahian revolts after
807. The well-established thesis that uninhibited miscegena-
ion and the corporate nature of the Portuguese society in
razil produced a successful example of social engineering
nust also take into account the historical role of Palmares.

Palmares was a centralized kingdom with an elected ruler.
;anga-Zumba delegated territorial power and appointed to
ffice. The most important ones went to his relatives. His
ephew, Zambi, was the war chief. Ganga-Zona, the king's
rother, was in charge of the arsenal. Interregnum problems
o not seem to have troubled Palmares, the history of which
pans about five generations of rulers. Zambi's palace revolt

did not displace the ruling family. Assuming that Loanda was the main embarkation point for Pernambucan slaves which is confirmed by the linguistic evidence, the model for Palmares could have come from nowhere else but Central Africa. Can it be pinpointed? Internal attitude toward slavery prostrations before the king, site initiation with animal blood the placing of the *casa de conselho* in the "main square," or the use of a high rock as part of man-made fortress lead in no particular direction. The names of *mocambo* chiefs suggest a number of possible candidates. The most likely answer is that the political system did not derive from a particular Central African model, but from several. Only a far more detailed study of Palmares through additional sources in the archives of Angola and Torre do Tombo could refine the answer. Nonetheless, the most apparent significance of Palmares to African history is that an African political system could be transferred to a different continent; that it could come to govern not only individuals from a variety of ethnic groups in Africa but also those born in Brazil, pitch black or almost white, latinized or close to Amerindian roots; and that it could endure for almost a full century against two European powers, Holland and Portugal. And this is no small tribute to the vitality of the traditional African art in governing men.

REFERENCES NOT CITED IN GENERAL BIBLIOGRAPHY

Barleus, Caspar
   1923 *Nederlandsch Brazil onder het bewind van Graaf Johan Mauritz.* (Translated from Latin by S. P. L'Honore Naber.)
Boxer, Charles R.
   1952 *Salvador de Sá and the struggle for Brazil and Angola 1602–1686.* London: Athlone Press.
   1961 *The Golden Age of Brazil.* Berkeley: University of California Press.
Brasil, Etienne Ignace
   1909 "La secte musulmane des Malês et leur révolte en 1835." *Anthropos* 4:99–105, 405–15.
*Breve discurso sobre o estado das
   quatras capitanias conquistadas.* [Quoted by J. A. G. de Neto Mello in *Novos Estudos Afro-Brasileiros,* 1937, II:205.]
Brito Freire, Francisco de
   1675 *Nova Lusitania, Historia de guerra Brasilica.*
Caldas Britto, A. E. de
   1903 "Levantos de Pretos na Bahia." *RIHGB* (Bahia) 29:69–90

Salmon, Pedro
1959 *História do Brasil*. Rio de Janeiro: Livraría José Olímpio Editôra.

Capello, H. and Ivens, R.
1881 *De Benguella a Terras de Iacca*.

Cavazzi da Montecuccolo, Giovanni Antonio
1687–90 *Istorica descrittione de' tre regni Congo, Matamba e Angola*. Bologna.

Codman, J.
1867 *Ten Months in Brazil*. Boston.

Couty, L.
1881 *L'esclavage au Brésil*. Paris.

Denis, Ferdinand
1825 *Résumé de l'histoire du Brésil*. Paris: Lecointe et Durey.

Dent, C. H.
1886 *A Year in Brazil*. London.

Freire, F. F. de Oliveira
1906 *História territorial do Brasil*. Rio de Janeiro.

Freitas, Mario Martins de
1954 *Reino negro de Palmares*. Rio de Janeiro: Biblioteca do Exército Editôra.

Freyre, Gilberto
1956 *The Masters and the Slaves: a Study in the Development of Brazilian Civilization*. New York: Knopf.

Gardner, G.
1849 *Travels in the Interior of Brazil, 1836–1841*. London.

Gomes, Alfredo
1950 *Achegas para a historia do trafico africano no Brasil*. Anais, Instituto Historico e Geographico Brasileiro.

Kidder, D. P.
1845 *Sketches of Residence and Travels in Brazil*. London.

Koster, H.
1817 *Travels in Brazil, 1809–1815*. Philadelphia.

Leite, Serafim (ed.)
1954 *Cartas dos primeiros Jesuitas do Brasil*.

Loreto Couto, Domincos Do
1757 *Desaggravos do Brasil e glorias do Pernambuco*.

Magalhães, Basilio
1935 *Expansão geographica do Brasil colonial*. São Paulo: Companhia Editora Nacional.

Malherio, A. M. Perdigão
1867 *A escrividão no Brasil*. Rio de Janeiro.

Mauro, Frédéric
1960 *Le Portugal et l'Atlantique, 1570–1670*. Paris.

Mendonça, Renato
1935 *A influencia africana no Português do Brasil*. São Paulo: Companhia Editora Nacional.

Neiva, Artur Hehl
1949 *Provenencia das primeiras levas dos escravos african*
Anais, Instituto Historico e Geographico Brasileiro.
Nieuhof, Johan
1704 "Voyage and Travels into Brazil and the East Indies."
A. and J. Churchill (eds.), *Collection of Voyages and Trave*
II:1–369. London.
Pitta, Sebastião da Rocha
1880 *História da América Portuguêza* (1st ed., 1730). Lisbo
F. A. da Silva
Ribeiro, René
1958 "Relations of the Negro with Christianity in Portugue
America." *The Americas* 14 (4).
Rinchon, Dieudonné
1929 *La traite et l'esclavage des Congolais par les Européer*
Brussels.
Rodrigues, José Honório
1962 "The Influence of Africa on Brazil and of Brazil on Africa
Journal of African History 3:49–67.
Saint-Hilaire, A. de
1852 *Voyages dans l'intérieur du Brésil*. Paris.
Do Salvador, Frei Vicente
1961 *História do Brasil, 1560–1627*. São Paulo.
Souza, B. J. de
1939 *Dicionario da terra e da gente do Brasil*. São Paulo: Cor
panhia Editora Nacional.
von Spix, J. B. and von Martius, C. F. P.
1824 *Travels in Brazil 1817–1820*. London.
Vansina, Jan
1963 "The Foundation of the Kingdom of Kasanje." *Journal*
African History 4 (3).
Varnhagen, F. A. de
1930 *História geral do Brasil*. São Paulo: Edições Melhor
mentos.
Vianna Filho, Luis
1946 *O negro na Bahia*. Rio de Janeiro: Livraría José Olímp
Editôra.

CHAPTER TWELVE

The Other Quilombos

ROGER BASTIDE

If Palmares was the most famous and certainly the largest of all the *quilombos*, it was far from being the only one; the history of Brazil attests to the importance of collective flight and of resistance both to slavery and to the assimilation of white culture (as does its geography—many places are still named *Quilombo*, in memory of the Negro fugitives who settled there). . . .[1]

The first *quilombo* dates back almost to the beginning of the slave trade in 1575, at Bahia, and was later destroyed by Luis Brito de Almeida (Handelmann:Chapter 8). A letter from Père Rodrigues in 1597 states that "the colonists' principal enemies are the rebellious Guinea Negroes who live in

From Roger Bastide, *Les religions Africaines au Brésil*, Paris: Presses Universitaires de France, 1960. Translated from pp. 126–35, and reprinted with the permission of the author and Presses Universitaires de France.

1 See, for example, Malheiros:37. Even in the south of the country, where the population of African descent is less numerous, as at Santa Catarina, there are many such place names, including Aix in the municipalities of Florianopolis, Tijucas, Imaruhy, and Chapoco (Boiteux). There are considerably more in the central and northern regions. The *Guia Postal do Brasil* for 1930 lists some 101 post offices with this name—including 35 in Minas, 22 in São Paulo, 19 in Rio—and under the name *mucambo*, 28 in Bahia, 10 in Piauí, 8 in Sergipe, and 5 in Pernambuco. And one could add some 50 names of mountains and rivers (M. Pinto; cf. also Taunay [2]: 51–52). The oldest historical documents date from the beginning of the seventeenth century, and can be found in the *Documentos Historicos do Arquivo Municipal do Salvador*, Vol. I.

the mountains from which they make periodic raids" (cited in Leite II:358). A letter written in 1607 by the governor, the Count of Ponde, to the King reports an uprising of the Hausa Negroes in Bahia, and in 1601 a *quilombo* cut the road from Bahia to Alagôas at Itapicum (Bezerra:154). In 1650, Captain Mancel Jourdan da Silva had difficulty destroying some *quilombos* near Rio de Janeiro (Ramos 1938: 15). In 1671, another *quilombo* made its appearance in the state of Alagôas (Bezerra:178). In 1704, Dias da Costa was summoned to "annihilate the *mocambos* (of Bahia), take the Negroes prisoner, and to destroy the Maracaz and Cucuriù Indians as well as the *caboclos* they had subjugated." In 1707, Domingos Netto Pinheiro was given the responsibility for destroying the *mocambos* in the region extending from the Jacobina and Carinhanha mountains to Rio São Francisco (Vianna:65). In the vicinity of São Paulo, along the "river of treason," there was another *quilombo* in existence from at least 1737 to 1787.[2]

But it was the Minas region that would soon become the favored location for this type of resistance, for reasons that are easily understood. The discovery of gold and precious stones had caused a dislocation of the population, and slaves were taken from the fields and put to the arduous labor of mineral extraction; the discovery of new veins and of new streams rich in nuggets increased the influx of Africans who were thrown, soon after their arrival, into this new area; the fear of thefts prompted the severest sort of surveillance. The traveler passing through the ancient towns of Minas Gérais was struck by the omnipresence of prisons with fortress-thick walls, which had become their architectural centers. These prisons were testimony to the brutal repression of fugitive slaves (Barros Latif:169).

This repression only aggravated feelings of hatred. The white population began to live in perpetual fear of colored revolts. And it was believed that those revolts were organized by outsiders, specifically by the fugitives from the *quilombos*. In 1719, it was rumored that the Negroes were plotting to massacre the whites while they were all assembled in church on Good Friday. Hearsay had it that the *quilombolas* from

[2] Nuto Santana, in a newspaper article entitled "O Ribeirão da traição," cites a certain number of documents on this *quilombo*: Actas XI:79; XII:17–484; XVIII:116, 455. See also Taunay (1), I:123.

Rio das Mortes had already elected the king, princes, and chief officials of the new state. At first the governor was skeptical, but he finally decided to take precautions. At Rio das Mortes, the lieutenant general, Jean Ferreira Tavares, ordered the arrest of the kings of the Minas and Angola nations along with all those who were suspected of having been designated as future magistrates of the black republic. In 1756, another panic spread among the whites, and the scenario of another novel much like the first captured the public imagination. The Negroes were planning to take advantage of the white custom of going to church on Holy Thursday by descending upon them and killing the white and mulatto men, but sparing the women. An officer was reputed to have uncovered this plot, and the Africans, seeing their plan ruined, were said to have fled to the woods (Vasconcelos [1]:326). There is no hard evidence that these plots actually existed (Vasconcelos [2]:164–75; Veiga:77). But the existence of such rumors is certainly a fair reflection of what must have been the atmosphere of alarm that prevailed throughout the territory.

The entire region of Campo Grande and São Francisco was overrun with fugitive Negroes, who posed a constant problem to the settlers. In 1741, Jean Ferreira had organized an expedition against them, but they managed to escape, regroup, and begin to ambush people traveling along the Goyas road in search of gold. In 1746, there was another and more successful expedition: 120 Negroes were taken and their land given to white pioneers. But in 1752, an expedition led by Père Marcos was attacked and 40 men, including 19 slaves, were killed; this proved that the danger was still very much present (Nina Rodrigues:148).

The *quilombos* at Minas were well organized and were certainly the largest except for Palmares. They had a population of about twenty thousand Negroes, who had flocked from every corner of Brazil, from São Paulo and from Bahia; these were joined by a number of mulattoes, criminals, and brigands; the inhabitants were divided among dozens of different villages, four of these being larger than the rest and fortified: Ambrosio, Zundu, Gareca, and Calaboca, all located near Sapucahy. Each of these had its king, officers, and ministers, who reigned with bloody despotism. The attitude toward the whites was ambivalent; on the one hand, the *quilombolas* mistrusted them, and had spies stationed along the trails and even inside the villages of the whites; on the other hand, they made their living through trading, and their secret agents exchanged gold, animal skins, and forest edibles for arms and food. It was deemed necessary to send out a large expeditionary force against the *quilombos,* under the command of Captain Bartholomeu Bueno de Prado, who returned bearing as trophies three thousand pairs of ears![3]

The *quilombos* seemed indestructible. In 1769, again in Minas, there was the annihilation of more of them at Sabambaia (Vasconcelos [2]:168). In 1770, there was the destruction of the *quilombo* of Carlotta in Mato Grosso. In 1772, a group of Negro fugitives and Indians attacked the village of San José de Maranhao (Resende Silva:707). In 1778, two *quilombos,* composed of pagan Negroes from thirty to sixty years of age, were destroyed in the state of São Paulo, on the shores of the Tieté (Nina Rodrigues:149). Another instance of Negroes and Indians coming together is found in 1795 at Piolho, in Mato Grosso. Many slaves had taken refuge there some twenty-five years earlier; they had fought against the Indians in that territory, the Cabixés, in order to steal their women, and from the resulting unions were born children of mixed Indian and Negro blood, called Caborés. An expedition led by Francisco Pedro de Mello was to come upon six descendants of these former slaves who functioned as leaders, priests, and doctors; besides these old Negroes, the *quilombo* was composed of Caborés and Indians. They obtained their food by fishing and hunting, and cultivated corn, various types of beans, manioc, sweet potatoes, pineapple, tobacco, cotton, and bananas; they raised chickens and made their clothes from cotton.

At São Vicente, the first *quilombo* taken (which included six Negroes, eight Indian men, nineteen Indian women, and ten male and eleven female Caborés), the Indians and Caborés turned out to be familiar with Christian doctrine and were able to speak Portuguese, having been taught both by the former slaves. Farther on, a larger *quilombo* was found, consisting of two sections some fifty paces apart, one containing ten houses and the other, eleven. The *quilombolas* had

[3] On the *quilombos* of Minas, see Resende Silva:707; Dornas: 70–109; Vasconcelos (2):164; Carneiro, n.d.; Mata Machado filho 1939:277; Eugenio do Assis 1948; Falconi 1949:8–9. The *quilombos* of Minas lasted well into the nineteenth century, as can be seen from Rezende:43 and Guimaraes.

abandoned it in order to build one deeper in the bush, and the new one was again divided in two sections, this time some three leagues apart; the first, consisting of fourteen Negroes and five slaves, was headed by Antoine Brandão, himself a Negro, and the second, made up of thirteen Negro men and seven Negresses, was commanded by Joaquim Felix, a former slave. It is possible that this division into two quarters represents an acceptance of the dualistic division of the exogamous clans of the Indians (Pinto:31–45). The impulse to form *quilombos* did not disappear during the nineteenth century. In 1810, a *quilombo* was discovered at Linhares in the state of São Paulo (*Documentos Interessantes* LIX:319). Around 1820, J. E. Pohl came upon a *quilombo* in the region of Minas, which was made up of fugitives from the state of São Paulo. Pohl adds: "They also had among them a minister who performed religious services" (II:307–8). Another one was discovered in 1828, at the very gates of Recife, at Cahuca; this was governed by a chief named Malunguinho, and was surrounded by ditches and palisades, from which the inhabitants made periodic sorties to make raids. It appears that a communal way of life was practiced in the *quilombo*, which would seem to indicate a return to African traditions (da Costa). In 1829, a group of Indians was sent to destroy another one at Corcovado, near Rio.[4] In 1855, the Maravilha *quilombo* in Amazonia was destroyed (Protasio Frikel 1955:227–29). And in 1866, Negroes from Para were still fleeing into the Indian villages of French Guiana (Magalhaes:Chapter II).

As can be seen, there is not much sociological data available for the study of *quilombos*, since contemporary commentators were of course not interested in the internal organization or customs of these Negro fugitives, but rather in the military techniques that could be employed to destroy them. Nonetheless, it would seem that in most cases, as in Palmares, we are dealing with "tribal regression," a kind of return to Africa. And that religion played a role in this cultural resistance is proved by the *quilombo* of Rio Tieté, where all the inhabitants were "pagans." Again in the early years of the nineteenth century, the Englishman Burton found among the *quilombeiros* living near Diamantina some African "survivals,"

[4] See Debret:512–13; Dabadie:34; Walsch:342. In this last work, one finds evidence of the survival of various elements of African religion: for example, the use of cowries.

such as the use of certain charms and of poison (strazon inum) (II:97). But as white civilization spread from the coast and began to penetrate the interior, the Negro fugitives found themselves coming into ever-increasing contact with the Indians who had been driven back previously. It has often been said that the Africans and the Indians were enemies, and it is perfectly true that they often found themselves, due to circumstance, pitted against each other. But their common hatred for the white masters brought them to sympathize with each other and to join together.

It should be noted that each time such a fusion took place, it was the Negroes who took charge of the new community, whether by reducing the Indians to slavery, as in Bahia in 1704, or by becoming the military or religious leader of the community, as in Mato Grosso in 1795. As late as 1867, d'Assier exclaimed: "How many times mulattoes fleeing from slavery or deserting military service, have been proclaimed captains of tribes of Indians with whom they had taken refuge" (80).

Even more curiously, we may observe two separate instances where a black woman was elevated to this role, and solely for religious reasons: Women were thought to have special magical powers, such as being more susceptible to ritual trance. There must have been a religious syncretism, with the dominant influence coming from African civilization, which supplied both the liturgy and the mythology for the Negro priest and the procedures for magical cures for the Negro "doctor." But even more interesting, this syncretism encompassed elements of white culture as well, and the Negro became an instrument for the diffusion of Portuguese Catholicism, albeit in a modified and corrupt form, among the Indians. The Indian, of course, also contributed his share to this strange civilization forged in the middle of the Brazilian sertão. The tribal organization of the Negroes had been completely destroyed by the institution of slavery, and there remained nothing more than the memory of the ancient African divine kingdoms. In contrast, the Indians had preserved their old social structure. Thus there was created, or so we might infer from the documents cited, a social system that combined the dual organization of the Indian tribes (the two sections or camps of the *quilombos* of Mato Grosso) with the African tribal federation under the rule of a monarch-priest.

All of that, of course, is ancient history. But the past did

not die without leaving its mark on the present. It is not
known how far inland the fugitive slaves penetrated nor how
significant was the diffusion of their cultures. Martius suggests
that it was a rare Amerindian tribe that did not come into
contact with the Africans (cited in Pinto:32). Roquette
Pinto traces the origins of Nambicuara agriculture to the
quilombos of the Caborés (38). Traces of *mocambos* of
Negro fugitives have been discovered as far away as Amazonia, as for example in the Trombetas region at Alcobaça,
where one was headed by a Negress, Filippa Maria Aranha,
who was so powerful that the Portuguese had to form an
alliance with her instead of fighting her; descendants of this
group have become guides for travelers wanting to descend
the rapids of the Tocantins (Moraes:135–49; Pereira 1952:
178). When the Portuguese arrived at Passanha (state of
Minas), the land was settled by Malali Indians, among
whom were living some Negro fugitives, and these Indians
had accepted as their chief another Negress (Saint-Hilaire
[2], I:413). Saint-Hilaire, who visited the Malali in 1817,
found that they looked more like mulattoes than Indians, and
the captain of the Malalis claimed that his grandmother had
been a Negress [2], I:424).

When Saint-Hilaire visited the Caribocas of Minas in 1819,
a tribe that was then disappearing (only eighteen villages
were left), mulattoes and creole Negroes would come there to
marry Indian women and thus share the privileged position
enjoyed by Brazilian Indians at that time; he witnessed there
a strange combination of beliefs, in which Catholicism could
have played only an indirect role, since no priest was willing
to come to the village. Tupi was the language of these people; God was invoked under the name Nhandinhan ([I],
II:253–71). Elsewhere, the native religion seemed to dominate, as in the village of Haut-des-Bois (Minas), where
Macuni women married Negroes; Saint-Hilaire observed that
whenever the wind blew violently, the women would smoke
in front of their houses in order to chase the storm. All of
that, it goes without saying, existed under the veneer of official Christianity (Saint-Hilaire [2], II:49).

Besides these remote *quilombos,* there were—because of the
nature of the environment, where the wilderness often came
right to the edge of large cities—small *quilombos* made up
solely of Negroes, without any admixture of Indians. This
was the case, for example, with Marcel Congo's *quilombo* in

the forest of Santa Catarina near Petropolis, which was de
stroyed by Caxias in 1839 (Lacerda Marcos 1935).

We have little information on the role of religion in thi
quilombo. But we can attempt to get some idea from th
identity of its constituent ethnic groups, which can be in
ferred from the names of some of its members: Marce
Congo, Justino Benguela, Antonio Nagô, Canuto Maçam
bique, Afonse Angola, Miguel Crioulo, and Maria Crioula
The common denominator of these diverse peoples coul
only be a Catholicism more or less tinged with native "fe
tishism."

Moreover, this *quilombo* was involved in a whole series o
murders, assassinations, individual and collective flights, and
revolts where religion must have constantly come into play
along with physical and moral hardships. Perhaps it wa
even Freemasonry that gave colored men the idea of a gen
eral rebellion in the period following Caxias' destruction o
this *quilombo;* a revolt was in fact planned by a secret
society divided into "circles" of five members each who did
not know each other but who were united through a president to the supreme leader, a free mulatto blacksmith, Es-
tevão Pimentel (1847). But the blacks had not yet adopted
Masonic traditions; they had a Negro patroness, Klbanda, in
whose supernatural intervention they had more confidence
than in formal organization and political action. It was this
trusting and semipagan Catholicism that led to their down-
fall and sabotaged their conspiracy. Although this attempted
revolt dates from a time when the *quilombo* was no longer in
existence, it still gives some insight into it, and supports the
preceding hypothesis that during the earlier period, the religious element that supported the faith of these humble be-
lievers was less ancestral "fetishism" than a popular form of
Christianity.

But these are later happenings, dating from the Empire.
For the colonial period, it seems safe to say that the phenomenon of *quilombos* represents the resistance of a civilization
that refused to die (a struggle in which African religion
played a key role) as much as a direct protest against the
institution of slavery. This viewpoint is confirmed by the
transformation that the *quilombos* underwent through the
medium of Negro folklore, and just as the bards of old had
sung the exploits of Charlemagne and his brave men in the
chansons de geste, so too black folklore made Palmares into a

popular drama, complete with songs and dances; in this folk-
loric form, it survived in Alagôas until the beginning of the
twentieth century. These *quilombos* of the poor colored folk
always maintained something of the tone of racial protest:

> Enjoy yourself, Negro
> The white man doesn't come here
> And if he does
> The devil will carry him off [Brandão (2):95–98; (1):
> 89–90].

Sociologists studying contact between heterogeneous civilizations are obliged to organize phenomena into conceptual
frameworks, so that they can interpret them better and distinguish, for example, instances of "counteracculturation" [re-
sistance to assimilation] from instances of "syncretism," that
is, accommodation to the dominant civilization. But in fact,
these concepts are relevant only at a certain degree of ab-
straction. Syncretism is always more or less "counteracccultura-
tive" and acculturation is always more or less "syncretic."

Marronage involved more a nostalgia for Africa than an
exact reconstitution of it (in Brazil, this meant in particular
Bantu Africa, with its large kingdoms); for new geographical, demographic, and political conditions obtained, and
these had to be dealt with. Most important, marronage cannot
be separated from the total social context in which it arose,
which is that of the struggle of an exploited group against
the ruling class. The *quilombo* or *mocambo* was always ready
for war; but one can only fight by adapting oneself to the
adversary. War, then, along with peaceful exchange, is one
of the processes by which civilizations interpenetrate even as
they engage each other in combat. Of course, the *quilombos*
were the work of pure Africans who had not yet had the time
to forget the realities of their own countries, more than of
Creole Negroes; but that does not mean that they were not
yet marked by the institution of slavery and by catechization,
albeit in a superficial and external form: The Palmares sanctuary sheltered Catholic saints; and the maroon Negro
brought to the Indians of Mato Grosso, in areas not yet
reached by Christian missions, the rudiments of Catholicism.

All the African religious phenomena of the colonial era, or
almost all, must be understood in the context of this climate
of cultural resistance. But resistance is not a normal phenom-

enon; it produces distortions, it creates pathological states, it hardens minds and institutions. A certain Marxist interpretation of marronage does not seem to me to be plausible; for the resistance involved here was not only or primarily an economic resistance against a certain form of labor, but a resistance of the whole of African civilization, whose memory was only intensified by the harsh regime of slavery. And the proof of this is that religion there was not separated, as it is today, from the rest of social life, but rather, as in the land of their ancestors, remained closely integrated with it. On the other hand, it is through the Marxist concept of class struggle that one can best grasp the nature of marronage, provided that "class" is defined in all its complexity, not solely in relation to production, but in terms of its own culture. From this viewpoint, marronage may be seen as the first step of that struggle: the segregation of the common people on Mount Avantin. The second step is that of armed revolution; if *quilombos* best define forms of resistance prevalent in Brazil during the seventeenth and eighteenth centuries, then revolts constitute the form proper to the nineteenth century.

REFERENCES NOT CITED IN GENERAL BIBLIOGRAPHY*

d'Assier, A. *Le Brésil contemporain.*
Barros Latif, M. M. de *As Minas Gerais.*
Bezerra, Felte *Etnies Sergipanas.*
Boiteux *Dicionario historico e geografico do Estado de Santa Catarina.*
Brandão, Alfredo (1) "Os negros na história do Alagoas." *Estudos afro-brasileiros.* (2) "Viçosa de Alagoas." *Estudos afro-brasileiros.*
Burton, R. E. *Explorations of the Highlands of the Brazil.*
Carneiro, Edison *O Quilombo de Carlota,* Ms.
Costa, Pereira da "Folklore pernambucano." *RIHGB* 40.
Dabadie *Récits.*
Debret, J. B. "Voyage pittoresque." *RIHGB* 90 (144).
Dornas filho, J. "Povoamento do alto S. Francisco." *Sociologia* 27:70–109.

* *Editor's note:* Bastide's bibliographical citations in *Les religions africaines* . . . are incomplete and often inconsistent; dates, publishers, and places of publication are rarely given, and an author's name may be spelled several different ways in the course of a few pages. With apologies to the reader, I have nevertheless had to leave citations as in the original.

Eugenio do Assis, J. *Levante de escravos no distrito de S. José des Queimades, Estado de Espirito Santo*. Museu Paulista. 1948.

Falconi, Ivaldo "Um quilombo esquecido." Correio das Artes, João Pessoa, 25-9-1949.

Guimaraes, B. *Lendas e romances: una historia de quilombola*.

Handelmann *Historia do Brasil*.

Lacerda Marcos, Carlos *O Quilombo de Mancel Congo*, Rio, R. A., 1935.

Leite, P. Serafim *História da Cia. Do Jesus*.

Magalhaes, Perdigão *A escravidão no Brasil*.

Malheiros, Perdigâo *A escravidão no Brasil*.

Mata Machado filho, Aires de "O negro e o garimpo em Minas Gerais." *R.A.M. de S.P.* 51, 1939.

Moraes, R. *Amfiteatro Amazônicô*.

Nina Rodrigues *Os africanos no Brasil*.

Pereira, Nunes "Negros escravos na Amazônia." *In Anais X⁰ Congresso Brasileiro de Geografia* III:1952.

Pinto, Moreira *Apontamentos para o Dicionârio geografico do Brasil*.

Pinto, Roquette *Rondonia*.

Pohl, J. E. *Reise in innern von Brasilien*.

Protasio Frikel, Fr. "Tradiçoes historico-lendárias dos Kachuyana e Kahyana." *Revista do Museu Paulista*, n.s., 1955.

Ramos, A. [Article in] *Boletin da Sociedade Luso-Americana* 24 (December 1938).

Resende Silva, J. "A formaçao territorial de Minas Gerais." *In Anais do III⁰ Congresso Sul-Riograndense de História e Geografia* III.

Rezende *Recordacôes*.

Saint-Hilaire, A. de (1) *Voyage aux sources du Rio San Francisco*. (2) *Voyage dans les provinces de Rio de Janeiro et de Minas Gerais*.

Taunay, A. de E. (1) *Historia da cidade de S. Paulo no seculo XVIII*. (2) *Subsidios para a historia do trafico africano no Brasil*.

Vasconcelos, Diogo de (1) *História antiga de Minas Gerais*. (2) *História media de Minas Gerais*.

Veiga, Xavier da *Efemeridades Mineiras*.

Vianna, U. *Bandeiras e Sertanistas baianos*.

Walsh, R. *Notices of Brazil*.

CHAPTER THIRTEEN

The Mocambo: *Slave Resistance in Colonial Bahia*[1]

STUART B. SCHWARTZ

The social and economic pattern of colonial Brazil, based upon the coerced labor of Africans and Indians, was continually threatened by various forms of resistance to the fundamental institution of slavery. Far from having the placid, well-adjusted society of dormant nineteenth-century plantations that Gilberto Freyre and others have imposed on the colonial past, Brazil through much of its early history was beset by the chronic instability of slave society and the threat of slave recalcitrance or resistance (cf. for example Freyre 1933, 1956). Throughout the New World, wherever slavery was a basic institution, the fear of slave revolt and the problem of fugitive slaves plagued colonists and colonial officials. Brazil was no exception. Through the first three centuries of Brazilian history runs a thread of slave resistance and colonist fear.

Most analyses of this resistance have concentrated either on the great slave revolts of the early nineteenth century or on the actions of the "Black Republic" of Palmares, a community of over five thousand escaped slaves in Alagoas (1630–97).[2] This concentration of effort, although under-

Reprinted from *Journal of Social History* 3:313–33 (1970), with the permission of the author and editor.

[1] I wish to express my thanks to Jan Vansina of the University of Wisconsin for his suggestion. Parts of this article were presented to the thirty-eighth International Congress of Americanists, Stuttgart, 1968.

[2] There is still, however, no adequate monograph dealing with the slave revolts of the early nineteenth century (1807–35), which are

Eugenio do Assis, J. *Levante de escravos no distrito de S. José des Queimades, Estado de Espirito Santo.* Museu Paulista. 1948.

Falconi, Ivaldo "Um quilombo esquecido." Correio das Artes, João Pessoa, 25-9-1949.

Guimaraes, B. *Lendas e romances: una historia de quilombola.*

Handelmann *Historia do Brasil.*

Lacerda Marcos, Carlos *O Quilombo de Mancel Congo,* Rio, R. A., 1935.

Leite, P. Serafim *História da Cia. Do Jesus.*

Magalhaes, Perdigâo *A escravidão no Brasil.*

Malheiros, Perdigâo *A escravidão no Brasil.*

Mata Machado filho, Aires de "O negro e o garimpo em Minas Gerais." *R.A.M. de S.P.* 51, 1939.

Moraes, R. *Amfiteatro Amazônicô.*

Nina Rodrigues *Os africanos no Brasil.*

Pereira, Nunes "Negros escravos na Amazônia." *In Anais X⁰ Congresso Brasileiro de Geografia* III:1952.

Pinto, Moreira *Apontamentos para o Dicionârio geografico do Brasil.*

Pinto, Roquette *Rondonia.*

Pohl, J. E. *Reise in innern von Brasilien.*

Protasio Frikel, Fr. "Tradiçoes historico-lendârias dos Kachuyana e Kahyana." *Revista do Museu Paulista,* n.s., 1955.

Ramos, A. [Article in] *Boletin da Sociedade Luso-Americana* 24 (December 1938).

Resende Silva, J. "A formaçao territorial de Minas Gerais." *In Anais do III⁰ Congresso Sul-Riograndense de História e Geografia* III.

Rezende *Recordacôes.*

Saint-Hilaire, A. de (1) *Voyage aux sources du Rio San Francisco.* (2) *Voyage dans les provinces de Rio de Janeiro et de Minas Gerais.*

Taunay, A. de E. (1) *Historia da cidade de S. Paulo no seculo XVIII.* (2) *Subsidios para a historia do trafico africano no Brasil.*

Vasconcelos, Diogo de (1) *História antiga de Minas Gerais.* (2) *História media de Minas Gerais.*

Veiga, Xavier da *Efemeridades Mineiras.*

Vianna, U. *Bandeiras e Sertanistas baianos.*

Walsh, R. *Notices of Brazil.*

CHAPTER THIRTEEN

The Mocambo: *Slave Resistance in Colonial Bahia*[1]

STUART B. SCHWARTZ

The social and economic pattern of colonial Brazil, based upon the coerced labor of Africans and Indians, was continually threatened by various forms of resistance to the fundamental institution of slavery. Far from having the placid, well-adjusted society of dormant nineteenth-century plantations that Gilberto Freyre and others have imposed on the colonial past, Brazil through much of its early history was beset by the chronic instability of slave society and the threat of slave recalcitrance or resistance (cf. for example Freyre 1933, 1956). Throughout the New World, wherever slavery was a basic institution, the fear of slave revolt and the problem of fugitive slaves plagued colonists and colonial officials. Brazil was no exception. Through the first three centuries of Brazilian history runs a thread of slave resistance and colonist fear.

Most analyses of this resistance have concentrated either on the great slave revolts of the early nineteenth century or on the actions of the "Black Republic" of Palmares, a community of over five thousand escaped slaves in Alagoas (1630–97).[2] This concentration of effort, although under-

Reprinted from *Journal of Social History* 3:313–33 (1970), with the permission of the author and editor.
[1] I wish to express my thanks to Jan Vansina of the University of Wisconsin for his suggestion. Parts of this article were presented to the thirty-eighth International Congress of Americanists, Stuttgart, 1968.
[2] There is still, however, no adequate monograph dealing with the slave revolts of the early nineteenth century (1807–35), which are

standable because of the dramatic nature of these episodes, has left unstudied a large body of scattered material on Afro-Brazilian resistance to slavery and the responses of Brazilian colonial society to it. The following is an examination of some of the material relating to slave escape and escapee communities in the captaincy of Bahia.

Salvador da Bahia de Todos os Santos was the colonial capital of Brazil until 1763 and an important urban center thereafter.[3] Its importance derived not only from its administrative functions but also from its role after 1550 as the center of a thriving area of sugar production. The rich lands surrounding the Bay of All Saints (*Recôncavo*) became between 1570 and 1680 a major area of large-scale sugar production oriented toward export to Europe. Although by the eighteenth century Brazilian sugar had lost its dominant place in the world market, and other crops in Bahia such as tobacco had begun to rival it in importance, the patterns of sugar production and the resultant social relations continued to dominate the political and social life of the region. Slavery, born and nurtured to a large extent by the requirements of sugar production, persisted even after those demands had decreased. The necessities of sugar agriculture, however, together with the failure of the early colonists to develop a free wage-labor market among the Indians and increasingly stringent royal opposition to Indian enslavement on moral and theological grounds, meant that slavery in Brazil still had to be predicated on the importation of Africans.[4]

Figures on the African slave trade to Brazil are extremely tenuous. Import began in earnest after 1550, and by 1600 there were between 13,000 and 15,000 slaves of African origin in Brazil (de Goulart 1950:106).[5] By the latter date the

generally thought to have been religious in nature, since they were led by Muslims. On Palmares there is an extensive but uneven literature; the best is Carneiro 1966. Important documents are published in Ennes 1938.

[3] The city of Salvador was established in 1549 as the capital of Brazil and of the captaincy of Bahia. Brazilians traditionally refer to the city as Bahia. I try to avoid confusion by referring to the city as Salvador, the captaincy as Bahia, and the bay as the Bay of All Saints.

[4] On Portuguese-Indian relations in Brazil, the central works are Marchant 1942 and Kieman 1954. A more recent monograph is Thomas 1968.

[5] This is a judicious argument on slave importation. Mauro (1956)

importance and value of these laborers were fully recognized; as one royal councilor stated, "It is a well-known and certain fact that the major part of the production of Brazil depends on and is sustained by the Negroes from Angola [Africa]."[6] By 1798 there were 1,500,000 slaves in Brazil, and the majority were of African or Afro-Brazilian origin (Poppino 1968:160).[7] Statistics on the slave population of Bahia are even more difficult to establish, but a survey of some of the parishes of the captaincy in 1724 indicated that slaves constituted 50 to 65 percent of the total population (Soares de França 1724).[8]

Although interpretations of the nature of slavery in Brazil vary widely, it is generally recognized that despite various integrative mechanisms, substantial recalcitrance and resistance to the slave regime persisted.[9] This resistance took a number of forms, from individual violent acts of vengeance to attempts at abortion and suicide.[10] Prior to the nineteenth-

---

calculates that 400,000 African slaves were imported to Brazil between 1570 and 1670.

[6] Consulta of the Conselho da Fazenda, British Museum (hereafter abbr. BM), Additional Ms. 20.786, fols. 123–123ᵛ, rpt. in Brásio 1954, 4:130.

[7] Alden's analysis of late colonial population statistics (1963) does not indicate slave numbers in Bahia, nor does the standard eighteenth-century source, Caldas 1951. The difficulty in establishing the precedence of African slaves in Brazil is at present insurmountable, since Portuguese records usually indicate only the port of embarkation and not the tribal or regional origins. Verger (1964:3–7) divides the trade into four cycles: Guiné, 1550–1600; Angola, 1600–1700; Coast of Mina, 1700–70; and Bight of Benin, 1770–1851.

[8] For example, the parish of Matoim had 1220 slaves out of 1727 inhabitants (71 percent); Pirajá, 381 out of 678 (56 percent); Pitanga, 2568 out of 5051 (51 percent); and Conceição in Salvador, 2820 out of 4938 (57 percent). The French traveler A. Frézier states that there seemed to be 20 blacks to every white in Salvador in 1716, but this is probably an exaggeration (1716:301).

[9] Frederickson and Lasch (1967) point out the pitfalls of equating all noncooperative acts by slaves as resistance in a political or collective sense.

[10] Individual acts of violence were not common but did exist; for example, Gregorio, a mulatto slave, slew his master Francisco Mendes de Burgos in 1670 (Arquivo Público do Estado da Bahia [hereafter abbr. APB], Livro das alvaras de fiança e perdão, No. 459, fol. 69ᵛ). On suicide among Bahian slaves, see Antonil 1967: 163–64, and Arquivo Nacional da Torre do Tombo (hereafter

century slave revolts, however, the most successful form of overt resistance was flight and the establishment of runaway communities called variously *ladeiras, mocambos,* or *quilombos.*[11]

Conditions on the great sugar plantations of the *Recôncavo* during the period of the sugar boom (1570–1670) and throughout most of the eighteenth century were simply "hellish," an adjective that contemporaries often used to describe these plantations.[12] Despite the admonitions of the Crown and various clerics, a number of factors contributed to the unpleasantness of the slave regime. The nature of the labor itself called for great physical exertion, especially during the *safra* ("harvest"), which lasted in Bahia from late July to November. During this season the cane was cut and brought to mills, which began grinding at four in the afternoon and operated continuously until ten o'clock the following morning; then the kettles and machinery were cleaned and readied for the next day's operations (da Costa, n.d.). During this period the slave could expect four hours of sleep. As one overseer put it, "the work is great and many die . . ."[13] Even under the best conditions, this sort of labor could exact a heavy toll, but in seventeenth- and eighteenth-century Brazil the prevailing theory of slave management was to extract as much labor at as little cost as possible. Thus conditions of housing, clothing, and food often left much to be desired.

---

abbr. ANTT), Cartório dos Jesuitas, Maço 9, doc. 1. A letter of Antonio Serrão, superintendent of the *engenho* of Sergipe do Conde, to D. Fernando de Noronha, Count of Linhares, also notes suicide, especially by eating dirt (September 8, 1575); apparently this was a favorite form of self-destruction among slaves in the New World (Russell 1946:433). Orlando Patterson (1967: 264–65) deals with this phenomenon in Jamaica.

[11] *Mocambo* was by far the most popular term applied to these communities, although *quilombo* came into common usage in the eighteenth century. *Mu-Kambo* (*mocambo*) is an Ambundu word meaning "hideout." See the discussion of etymology in Kent 1965: 163–64. I use these terms interchangeably.

[12] C. R. Boxer often cites this image, for example, 1963:103. The expression was in common usage in colonial Brazil (Antonil 1967: 159). A mid-seventeenth-century manuscript states, "the work is so great that one of these *engenhos* is called ínferno" (da Costa, n.d.). I wish to thank José Antônio Gonçalves de Mello, who provided me with a copy of this manuscript.

[13] ANTT, Cartório dos Jesuitas, Maço 8, doc. 152 (Bernardo Ribeiro to the Countess of Linhares [September 27, 1605]).

Nutrition was especially poor; manioc flour, fish, and whale meat were staples, while raw brandy was used primarily as a stimulant to increase work capacity.[14] The diet was not only poorly balanced, but it was also often insufficient. On at least two occasions a century apart, 1604 and 1701, the Crown intervened to force plantation owners to provide adequate food to their slaves.[15]

Added to the rigors inherent in the system of sugar production and to occasional acts of individual cruelty, slaves also suffered from a planned policy of punishment and terror as a means of control. Plantation owners believed that only by severity could work be accomplished and discipline maintained, especially when the ratio in the fields was often forty slaves to one white sharecropper or overseer (da Costa, n.d.). This sort of institutionalized brutality, when coupled with arduous labor, poor working conditions, and simple cruelty, contributed to the motivations for escape.

There were, of course, institutions such as marriage, religious brotherhoods, and manumission that alleviated the burden of bondage in Brazil, but these institutions can also be viewed functionally as mechanisms that reinforced slavery by making the slave docile, patient, and cooperative.[16] It is also

[14] Some idea of the diet of plantation slaves in Bahia can be acquired from the entries in the account books of the *engenho* of Sergipe do Conde (1622–53), published as Vol. 2 of *Documentos para a historia do acucar* (hereafter abbr. *DHA*) (Rio de Janeiro, 1956). On the use of brandy as a stimulant, see Costa Filho 1963:174.

[15] Biblioteca da Ajuda (BA), 51-V-48, fol. 88. Philip III to Conselho da India (April 30, 1606) noted that slaves serving on the *engenhos* were obliged to steal continually because of the ill treatment given them by their masters, who did not provide necessary sustenance. A royal order to Governor D. João de Lancastre (Lisbon, January 31, 1701) ordered plantation owners to set aside one day a week for slaves to grow their own food (APB, Ordens Régias 6 [1700–1], No. 103). The testimonies of Antonil (1711 [1967]) and Viceroy D. Marcos de Noronha (1756) indicate that this abuse continued (Boxer 1963:111).

[16] The Church, for example, although it mitigated the rigors of slavery in Brazil, also reinforced the institution. Christianization was often imposed, and at one point in the eighteenth century the Crown had to command the Bishop of Bahia to halt his practice of fining slaves for not attending Mass and forcing them to join religious brotherhoods (Biblioteca Geral da Universidade da Coimbra [hereafter abbr. BGUC], Cod. 711, *Livro de Registro da Relação*

true that royal authorities in Brazil did on occasion attempt to keep the treatment of slaves within bounds. A royal order of 1688 stated that excessively cruel treatment could be denounced, even by the slave himself, and that the masters implicated could be forced to sell the slave in question (BGUC, Cod. 711, fol. 73). This law led to a rather famous case in 1690 when D. Anna Cavalcanti was forced to sell her Congolese slave Ursula because of excessive cruelty.[17] Although there are other instances of judicial proceedings against cruel masters, these cases are rare and are greatly outweighed by the many references to the circumvention of the protective legislation.[18] Moreover, justice diminished in a direct ratio to the distance from major towns. When in the eighteenth century rural oligarchs established dominance over vast areas, they often controlled all aspects of life, including the treatment of slaves, with little fear of either statutes or royal authorities.[19]

Since no work equal in scope or excellence to Richard Wade's *Slavery in the Cities* (1964) has yet been done on the colonial cities of northeastern Brazil, very little is known about the conditions of servitude in urban centers like Salva-

---

da Bahia, fol. 29). Statements such as the famous sermon preached by Father Antônio Vieira to plantation slaves in Bahia in 1633 emphasize patience and martyrdom, an emphasis certainly appreciated by the slave owners (Ribeiro 1958 and Koster 1816:411). Clerics in the colony who had deviant ideas on slavery were not appreciated; two Jesuit Fathers, Miguel Garcia and Gonçalo Leite, who stated in the sixteenth century that "no African or Indian slave was justly captured," were crying in the wilderness, and a like-minded Franciscan was run out of Bahia in 1794 through colonist pressure on the archdiocese (Leite 1965b:353 and Prado 1967:428).

[17] See BGUC, Cod. 706, *Livro de Registro da Relação da Bahia*, fol. 25, and APB, Ordens Régias 1 (1648–90) No. 56.

[18] Arquivo Historico Ultramarino (Lisbon) (hereafter abbr. AHU), Consulta of the Conselho Ultramarino, Cod. 593, fols. 27–28, reports the arrest of two cruel masters in Maranhão. APB, *Livro de Perdão da Relação*, No. 495, fol. 75ᵛ, notes the arrest of Francisco Jorge for killing his African slave by excessive flogging; he was pardoned on April 21, 1678. On the common disregard of these statutes see Koster 1816:408; Frézier 1716:301; and Boxer 1964.

[19] Statements on the lawlessness of the interior are legion; for example, see AHU, Bahia, *papeis avulsos, caixa* 8 (2d noncatalogued ser.), February 21, 1663.

dor. Physical mobility and the opportunity to acquire enough
wealth to enable self-purchase probably mitigated the strain
of slavery in the cities, but here too there were numerous examples of cruelty and double-dealing.[20] Slaves who had
purchased their freedom were liable to find the contract broken and their slavery continued or were, as in the case of
Luiz Marinho Lima, a freedman, illegally enslaved again.[21]

Even those who succeeded in achieving freedom in the
cities found a number of discriminatory laws that limited
their dress, occupation, and political power and prevented
their full integration in society. A law of 1621 prohibited any
Negro, Indian, or mulatto from exercising the craft of gold-
smith, while a statute of 1726 prohibited mulattoes or those
married to mulattoes from service in the town council of Bahia.[22] Conditions such as these in both city and plantation
partially explain why freedmen and those slaves still in captivity were willing to aid the inhabitants of the *mocambos*.
This aid was not constant and should be considered along
with the activities of the mulatto bush captains and the black
militia units used in antifugitive activities.[23] Nevertheless,

[20] A case in point is that of the black slave Marcelina Dias Syl-
vestre, whose owner, a prostitute, set a price for her freedom and
then refused to set her free (APB, Ordens Régias 6 [1700–1], No.
139A). For other instances see APB, Ordens Régias 3 (1694–95),
No. 59 (January 25, 1695), and APB, *relação* 495 *alvará* of
perdão (April 17, 1677).

[21] See APB, Ordens Régias 14 (1719–20), No. 12, King to Count
of Vimioso, Governor of Brazil (February 4, 1719).

[22] The ordinance of 1621 is cited in Mariela Alves, *Mestres ourives
de Ouro e prata da Bahia* (Salvador) 1962:7, and that of 1726 is
recorded in BGUC, Cod. 71, fol. 130. Negroes were prohibited
from carrying arms in Salvador by an ordinance of April 4, 1626
(*Documentos historicos do Arquivo Municipal*: Atas da camara
[of Bahia], 6 vols. [Salvador: 1949], 1:33, 106 [hereafter abbr.
ACB], and Biblioteca Nacional do Rio de Janeiro [hereafter
abbr. BNR], 2:33; 23; 15, n. 14). Russell-Wood 1967 develops
this theme using primary source materials.

[23] The "Henrique Dias" regiments were named after the Afro-
Brazilian leader of a black regiment against the Dutch; his loyalty
and valor became legendary. The loyal black militia units were
highly valued by colonial officials because as some said: "The repugnance which the natives of Brasil [colonials] have toward sol-
diering is incredible" (APB, Ordens Régias 20 [1723–26], No. 37,
King to Governor Vasco Fernandes Cezar de Meneses [March 18,
1726]). The best biography of Henrique Dias is de Mello 1954.

there are occasional references to contact between the *mocambos* and Afro-Brazilians of the city, a contact that colonists and officials were anxious to eliminate.[24]

Runaway communities flourished in almost all areas of the captaincy of Bahia, although in some regions the problem was unusually acute (see Figure 1). The geography and

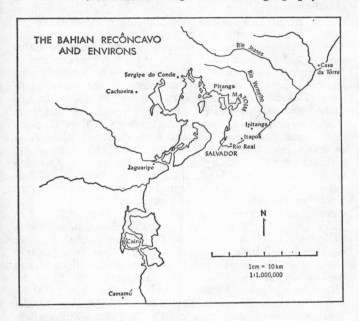

Figure 1: The Bahian *Recôncavo* and environs.

ecology of much of the Bahian littoral aided escape, and the result was a large number of fugitives and *mocambos*. The frequency of *mocambo* formation and the extent of their geographical distribution within the captaincy is underscored by the following list, which spans two centuries: There are references to *mocambos* in Jaguaripe (1591), Rio Ver-

[24] In 1646 the *Câmara* (town council) of Salvador moved to eliminate certain taverns that were "hideouts of thieves to which Negroes from the *mocambos* came to contact and to carry many slaves from within the city" (ACB, 2:312).

melho (1629), Itapicurú (1636), Rio Real (1640), Cairú (1663), Camamú (1723), Santo Amaro (1741), Itapoã (1763), and Cachoeira (1797).[25]

One region that had a particularly high incidence of runaways and *quilombo* formation was the southern district of Cairú and Camamú. The farm lands centering on these towns were devoted to manioc production, and the labor requirements did not call for the back-breaking work of the sugar plantations. The ratio of slaves to the free population was high—46 percent slave in Camamú and 55 percent in Cairú —but not overwhelming. Relatively good conditions and a large proportion of slaves in the population have been postulated in other situations as factors that stimulate slave resistance (Kilson 1964; cf. also Patterson 1967:274–80). In this case, however, the most important contributing factor to slaves' successful escapes was the unstable military situation in the area. Cairú and Camamú were constantly threatened by attack from the hostile Aimoré Indians. This fact and the distance from the military aid of Salvador made suppression of slave *mocambos* difficult. Attacks by the "savage gentiles" (*gentio barbaro*) and the depredations of *mocambos* were linked in the minds of the colonists, and various measures were taken to suppress both. Expeditions were organized in 1663, 1692, 1697, and 1723, but the frequency of repetition indicates their lack of success. Freedmen, "tame" Indians, and black militiamen were all used in these expeditions,[26] but a major innovation was the use of Indian fighters and backwoodsmen from São Paulo. This tactic, initiated in the 1670s by Governor Afonso Furtado de Mendoça, was the same that brought about the eventual destruction of the great *quilombo* of Palmares in 1684–85 (Lopes Sierra 1676; Pitta 1724 [1880]:192–97).

The threat of *mocambos* in this region was serious. On occasion these communities reached large proportions, and

[25] This list could be greatly extended. I have intentionally chosen with two exceptions *quilombos* not mentioned by Pedreira (1962).
[26] APB, Cartas do Governo, No. 150, D. João de Lancastre to Camara of Cairú (Bahia, December 10, 1697), notes the anti-*quilombo* services of Benito Maciel, a *crioulo forro*. In 1667 the governor of Brazil, Alexandre de Sousa Freire, asked the governor of Pernambuco for forty black militiamen to be used along with Bahian Negroes and Indians against *quilombos* in Cairú and Camamú (AHU, Bahia *papeis avulsos, caixa* 10 [1st noncatalogued ser.], August 15, 1667).

one was reported in 1723 to have had over four hundred inhabitants.[27] Size, however, was not the sole determinant of the *mocambo* danger in Southern Bahia. In 1692 a group of fugitive slaves began to sack farmlands around Camamú and threatened to seize the town itself. With five mulatto captains these runaways not only disrupted the south but also threw the *Recôncavo* into turmoil, since word of their depredations reached the slave quarters of the sugar estates, and the planters feared a similar outbreak. This *mocambo* finally fell to a Portuguese military expedition in 1692. During the final siege of their stockade, the battle cry of the *mocambo* warriors was, "Death to the whites and long live liberty."[28]

The fear that towns like Cairú and Camamú might actually be seized underlined a basic reality. The majority of the Bahian *mocambos* were located close to centers of population or the surrounding plantations. Whereas Palmares flourished far in the interior of Alagoas, the Bahian runaway communities remained close to towns and farms, although often in inaccessible locations. In fact, some of the towns within the present urban network of Salvador originated as runaway communities.[29] The reasons for this pattern of fugitive settlement are varied. Certainly until the eighteenth century the interior remained effectively closed to black as well as white settlement, and for the same reason: hostile Indians. More importantly, however, the internal economy of the *mocambos* made such proximity a prerequisite for success. Rather than a return to African pastoral or agricultural pursuits, *mocambo* economy was parasitic, based on highway theft, cattle rustling, raiding, and extortion.

[27] See AHU, Conselho Ultramarino, Cod. 247, King to Vasco Fernandes Cezar de Meneses (February 12, 1723), fols. 339ᵛ–340.

[28] Consulta of the Conselho Ultramarino (Lisbon, November 9, 1692), Documentos Historicos da Biblioteca Nacional de Rio de Janeiro 89 (1950):206, describes the *mocambo* activity of 1692. The threat to Camamú is made clear in BA, 51-IX-30, letter of Governor Antônio Luiz Goncalves Câmara Coutinho to Secretary of the Conselho Ultramarino Andre Lopes de Laura (Bahia, 23-VI-1692), where the governor states, *"em Camamú se levantarem huns mulatos e convocarem asi grande quantidade de Negros querendose fazerse senhores daquella villa."*

[29] Pierson (1967:49) indicates that around Salvador the present towns of Matta Escura, Estrada da Liberdade, Armação, Pirajá, Itapoã, and Cabula originated as *quilombos*.

Such activities often led colonial officials to consider *mocambo* fugitives along with mulatto highwaymen as common criminals and thus subject to regular civil penalties. In a very real sense, *mocambo* depredations foreshadowed the social banditry or *cangaço* of postcolonial Brazil. Obviously in a slave society the ideological basis of social banditry varied from its classic form of archaic peasant protest. Nevertheless, the reactions of Brazilian slaves and Brazilian peasants against an oppressive social and economic order were strikingly similar. On at least one occasion—the Balaiada Revolt (Maranhão, 1837–40)—*mocambo* bands, bandits, and political dissidents joined forces against the state and national governments.

Colonists and royal officials used a number of measures to deal with *mocambo* formation and activity.[30] One tactic was to eliminate slave escape and to apprehend fugitives before they could join in bands. As early as 1612 Alexandre de Moura, captain of Pernambuco, petitioned for the creation of a *capitão do campo* (bush captain) in each of the eight parishes of Pernambuco; with the aid of twenty Indians, the *capitão* would hunt down escaped slaves.[31] When these officers were introduced into Bahia is uncertain, but by 1625 the town council of Salvador was setting the reward prices for these slave hunters.[32] The *capitão do campo* worked on a commission basis, receiving a reward for each slave captured. The *Câmara* of Salvador exercised its prerogatives by fixing the price of the reward in accordance with the distance involved. Thus for a fugitive captured between the Recôncavo and the Rio Real, the *capitão do campo* could expect eight hundred reis from the master, while the price for a slave captured at the Tôrre da Ávila was three thousand reis.[33] By 1637 these remunerations were extended to anyone

[30] See Biblioteca Nacional de Lisboa, *coleção pombalina*, Gov. de Pernambuco, 1690–93, fol. 85.

[31] Biblioteca do Ministerio das Relações Exteriores da Itamaraty [hereafter abbrev. BI], Correspondência de Alvaro e Gaspar de Sousa, King to Gaspar de Sousa (Lisbon, August 17, 1612), fol. 81. A similar office was created in Spanish America under Philip II (Acosta Saignes 1967:252).

[32] ACB, 1:4. The term *capitão do mato* eventually replaced *capitão do campo* in common usage, but in Bahia they were used interchangeably.

[33] Ibid. The prices were revised on January 24, 1629 so that bush captains in the Recôncavo could charge eight hundred reis for slaves apprehended less than three leagues from the plantation and three thousand reis for those taken beyond.

capturing a fugitive, not just to the *capitão do campo*.³⁴ This
system was not without difficulty, since overzealous bush captains were not above capturing slaves who were merely on
errands and then claiming the prescribed rewards.³⁵ On
the other hand, slave owners showed a marked reluctance to
pay the fee for old or infirm slaves who were no longer useful. On a number of occasions a back log of old slaves in the
municipal jail of Salvador moved the *Câmara* to auction them
publicly for expenses.³⁶ The bush captains were a relatively
effective means of apprehending individual runaways, but
they were unable to cope with such problems as either slave
revolt or already existing *quilombos*.

A second and still very much unstudied method of slave
control and capture was the calculated use of Indians as
slave catchers and as a counterforce to *mocambos* and possible slave revolts.³⁷ Absentee sugar barons like the Count of
Linhares and donataries like the Duke of Aveiro sought and
received permission to bring Indians from the *sertão* to serve
as a defense against African slave uprisings as well as a buffer
against still unreduced Indian tribes of the backlands.³⁸
Colonists in Bahia, especially in Jaguaripe, tried unsuccess-

³⁴ ACB, 1:326 (January 27, 1637). The *engenho* of Sergipe do
Conde rewarded bush captains, Indians, and other slaves for the
return of fugitives (see *DHA*, 2:83, 131, 144, 145, 157, 174, 222,
323, 367, 486, 488).
³⁵ AHU, Conselho Ultramarino, Cod. 247, King to Viceroy Marquis de Angreja (Lisbon, November 20, 1714).
³⁶ BGUC, Cod. 706 (March 7, 1703); Cod. 709 (May 5, 1703),
fol. 140; Cod. 711 (March 5, 1703), fol. 123; and ACB, 1 (February 13, 1637):328–29.
³⁷ Estimates of available military forces usually included the numbers of available Indian auxiliaries; see, for example, BM Additional Ms. 28461, publ. in *Documentos Ultramarino Portugueses*,
4 vols. to date (Lisbon: 1960), 1:17–19.
³⁸ The Duke of Aveiro, donatary of Porto Seguro, received permission to bring in Indians "necessary for the defense" of the
towns in his captaincy (Archivo General de Simancas [hereafter
abbr. AGS], *secretarias provinciales*, Libro 1487 [October 7,
1603]). Earlier, the Count of Linhares, acting on the advice of his
plantation factor, asked for and received permission to bring Indians to his *engenho* for defense and labor (ANTT, Cartório dos
Jesuitas, Maço 8, doc. 9, Gaspar da Cunha to Count of Linhares
[Bahia, August 28, 1685], and Maço 16, Provisão 1586).

fully in the seventeenth century to have Indian villages relocated near their farms.[39] The Jesuits opposed such reloca-
tion, fearing colonist control of Indian labor, but the Fathers
of the Company also recognized that Indian allies were the
"walls and bulwarks" of the colony.[40] Probably the most
explicit statement on the usefulness of these Indian allies
against a restive slave population was made in 1633 by Duarte Gomes da Silveira, a colonist in Parahiba. He writes:

> There is no doubt that without Indians in Brazil there can
> be no Negroes of Guiné, or better said, there can be no
> Brazil, for without them [Negroes] nothing can be done
> and they are ten times more numerous than the whites, and
> if today it is costly to dominate them with the Indians
> whom they greatly fear, . . . what will happen without
> Indians? The next day they will revolt and it is a great
> task to resist domestic enemies.[41]

Indian irregulars led by Portuguese officers or captains were
consistently and successfully employed against *mocambos*
from the sixteenth to the eighteenth centuries. The destruction of virtually every *mocambo* from Palmares to the much
smaller hideouts of Bahia and Rio de Janeiro depended to a
large extent on Indian troops or auxiliaries.

Paradoxically, there are also many references to the in-
corporation of escaped African and Afro-Brazilian slaves into
Indian villages and tribal units. Portuguese authorities were
especially concerned with this phenomenon and feared its
disruptive consequences, since these groups raided colonist
farms and cut lines of communication.[42] In 1706 the Crown
ordered that "blacks, mixed bloods, and slaves" be prevented
from penetrating the backlands, where they might join with

---

[39] See *Livro Primeiro do Governo do Brasil* 1607–33 (Rio de
Janeiro, 1958), pp. 307–10; BI, King to Gaspar de Sousa (Lisbon,
May 24, 1613), fols. 218–218ᵛ.

[40] ANTT, *manuscritos da Livraria*, No. 1116, fol. 629, memorial
on slavery, notes, "*os Brazis que são os mueros e baluartes daguelle
estado segundo dizem os portugueses que la vivem.*"

[41] AGS, Secretarias Provinciales, Libro 1583, fols. 382–89: "*Infor-
mación q. hize por mandado de VMg. sobre unos capitulos q.
Duarte Gomez de Silveira Vezino de Parahiba embió a la Mesa da
Consciencia.*"

[42] *Livro Primeiro* (see note 39), p. 529.

hostile Indians.[43] Despite such measures, however, Afro-Indian cooperation against the Europeans and slavery was common in both Portuguese and Dutch Brazil.[44]

A most interesting case in point were the communities of Tupinambá Indians and escaped slaves, which existed in Jaguaripe for over forty years. These communities originated as Indian villages in which a syncretic messianic religion called *Santidade* developed as a reaction to forced acculturation and probably to coerced labor.[45] The sect was concentrated in the area around Jaguaripe, and first references made between 1588 and 1591 note only Indian participants. By 1613 escaped Afro-Brazilian slaves had joined the Santidade villages and were raiding nearby farms and even stealing (or freeing) slaves in the city of Salvador.[46] As late as 1627, despite punitive expeditions, colonists in Jaguaripe were still suffering from attacks of the Santidade villages.[47]

This leads us to the still very much ignored problem of Afro-Indian social relations in colonial Brazil.[48] Despite Portuguese attempts to turn the Indian into an ally against African resistance, a number of factors drew Africans and Indians toward shared behavior and common goals. For the runaways and the unreduced tribes there was a common ground of opposition to the European-imposed system and slavery, which led naturally to cooperation. Such cooperation was no simple task, however, since tribal social organization of both the Tupi speakers and the Gê tribes was a highly complex combination of locale, consanguinity, and age groupings.[49] The mechanisms for the socialization of an outsider,

[43] Instituto Historico e Geografico Brasileiro (hereafter abbr. IHGB), 1, 2.25 (Lisbon: June 6, 1706).

[44] The best modern account of slavery in Dutch Brazil is de Mello 1951.

[45] For brief analyses see Pereira de Queiroz 1965, Ribeiro 1962, and Ricard 1948. I was unable to use Calazans 1952.

[46] BI, King to Gaspar de Sousa (Lisbon: May 24, 1613), fol. 218, and (Lisbon: January 19, 1613) fols. 185–185ᵛ.

[47] Arquivo Municipal da Câmara do Salvador, Livro de Provisões e Portarias 1624–42, Provisão de Diogo Luis de Oliveira, fols. 24–26.

[48] A beginning is made by Roger Bastide (1967), esp. chap. 4: "La recontre du Noir et de l'Indien."

[49] The bibliography of Brazilian Indian ethnology is enormous, as is evidenced by Baldus 1954–68. By far the best historical analysis is Fernandes 1963.

such as an escaped slave, remain unknown, although in the Santidade cult the religion itself was probably an integrative force.

Within captivity a number of factors brought Indians and blacks into intimate and common contact. Until 1640, and especially in the sixteenth century, there were still many Indian slaves on the Bahian plantations. Extant account books and other records indicate that intermarriage between Indian and African slaves was not uncommon. An inventory of the great *engenho* (plantation) of Sergipe do Conde made in 1571 indicates a number of Afro-Indian marriages, such as that of Domingos, a Guiné who fathered two children by his Indian wife Luiza.[50] These unions paralleled Portuguese-Indian sexual patterns in that they were usually between African men and Indian women.

To what extent Afro-Indian marriage, or simply marriage in general, was sponsored by plantation owners as a means of social control is still to be determined. Although the evidence is contradictory, there were those like Jesuit Father Belchoir Cordeiro who felt that African slaves became more tractable when brought into proximity with Christianized Indians (Leite 1965a; Koster 1816:411). Whatever the policy, considerable Afro-Indian contact took place, producing physically identifiable offspring (*cafusos*). This contact and the many instances of joint Afro-Indian resistance to the colonial situation give special poignancy to the fact that Indians remained throughout the colonial period the best weapons against slave resistance.

The primary colonial tactic against runaway communities was simply to destroy them and to kill or re-enslave their inhabitants. Portuguese opposition is easily explained. The raids and thefts of fugitive slaves endangered towns and plantations and often cut major lines of communication and travel.[51] Moreover, a *mocambo* either by theft or at-

[50] ANTT, Cartório dos Jesuitas, Maço 13, doc. 4. The *engenho* of Sergipe do Conde was the largest in Bahia. Initiated by Governor Mem de Sá and eventually owned by the Jesuits, it is the only *engenho* for which there are extant records for the sixteenth through the eighteenth centuries.

[51] One chapter of the instructions issued to proposed governor Francisco Giraldes in 1588 notes dangers caused by *mocambos* and orders their destruction (*DHA*, 1 [*Legislacão* (Rio de Janeiro, 1954)]:360). Governor Diogo de Meneses echoes similar senti-

traction drew other slaves from captivity. Both the soldier Diogo de Campos Moreno and the Jesuit Antonil, a century apart, refer to the attraction of *mocambos* to those slaves still in captivity, and one report of 1692 notes that "no settler will have his slave secure" so long as *mocambos* persisted.[52] In short, the *mocambo* posed a threat to the economic and social system of colonial Brazil, based as it was on coerced labor and on a structured series of corporations in which servile Afro-Brazilian slaves were the lowest group.

Accommodation with *mocambos* was for most colonials simply unthinkable. Unlike Jamaica, where a treaty was finally concluded with the runaway Maroons, similar tactics in Brazil were harshly rebuked (cf. Patterson 1967:270). In 1640 Viceroy D. Jorge de Mascarenhas, Marques of Montalvão, suggested as a wartime measure that a peace mission of a Jesuit linguist and Henrique Dias, leader of a pro-Portuguese black regiment, be sent to a certain *mocambo*. The mission was to offer freedom to the runaways if they would serve in the black regiment and if they promised to admit no other escapees. This suggestion met with a stern rebuff from the planter-dominated town council of Salvador, which said:

> Under no circumstances is it proper to attempt reconciliation nor to give way to the slaves who might be conciliated in this matter. That which is proper is only to extinguish them and conquer them so that those who are still domesticated will not join them and those who are in rebellion will not aspire to greater misdeeds. . . . [ACB, 1:477–78 (November 25, 1640)].

Such extermination was usually carried out by military expeditions conducted either by private individuals or government troops. Private contracts were sometimes made with skilled Indian fighters and backwoodsmen, who would carry out the expedition for a reward for each slave captured. The contractors were occasionally but not always given an appointment as captain of the expedition. Royal and local officials also planned military operations against *mocambos*, us-

---

ments in 1608 when he notes, "*os negros andão alevantados e ninguem pode com elles e podem creser de maneira g. custe muito trabalho o desbaratallos*" (*Anais da Biblioteca Nacional de Rio de Janeiro* 57 (1935):38.

[52] BA, 51-IX-30 (June 23, 1692), fol. 13ᵛ; Antonil 1967:164; Sluiter 1949.

ing forces of the official organizational structure such as government troops, militia, and Indian auxiliaries.

The varied and disparate documents that mention the activities of escaped slaves in Bahia tell us very little about the social and political organization of the *mocambos* or about the actual military operations against them. It is for this reason that the documents pertaining to the destruction of the *quilombo* known as the "Armadillo's Hole" (Buraco de Tatú) are of singular importance, for although by no means complete, they do provide a glimpse into what may have been the history of a typical Bahian *mocambo*.

In 1763 a Portuguese-led military expedition destroyed the Buraco de Tatú, located just east-northeast of the city of Salvador near the present-day bathing beaches of Itapoã. Responding to colonist complaints and disturbed by the actions of a number of runaway communities, D. Marcos de Noronha, Count of Arcos and Viceroy of Brazil, began in 1760 a concerted effort to destroy these irritating nodules of resistance. In that year he appointed Joaquim da Costa Cardozo captain-major of the conquest of "savage gentiles" and apparently entrusted him with the organization of a punitive expedition.[53] Although Costa Cardozo's title indicated that hostile Indians were the object of the operation, his activities were to center on Cairú, where the title was a traditional one and where, as we have seen, *mocambo* formation was common. Moreover, at the time of his appointment there was considerable interest in exterminating "various *quilombos* of Negroes that were in the outskirts of the city."[54] The number and exact location of these encampments is impossible to determine, but aside from Cairú and Itapoã there was at least one other, Santo Amaro, situated at Ipitanga.

Since 1743 the Buraco de Tatú had existed as a community of escaped slaves. Like most of the Bahian *mocambos*, its economy was basically parasitic, based on theft, extortion, and sporadic raiding of its immediate neighbors. The principal victims, however, were not white sugar-planters but rather the Negroes who "came every day to the city to sell the food-stuffs they grow on their plots."[55] Aside from being de-

---

[53] ANTT, Chancelaria de D. José I, Livro 70, fol. 257ᵛ (January 11, 1762).

[54] AHU, Bahia, *papeis avulsos*, No. 6451.

[55] Ibid., No. 6449. There is a copy of this document in IHGB, I:119, "Correspondência do Governador da Bahia 1751–82," fols.

spoiled of their produce and possessions, as was traditionally the case, the most appealing women were forced to return to the *quilombos*. Runaway communities seemed to suffer from a chronic lack of females, and escaped male slaves seemed to prefer black or mulatto women. Instances of the capture of European women are extremely rare, and in the case of the Buraco de Tatú, no such charge was made (cf. Kent 1965: 170).

Despite the exactions of the fugitives, there were freedmen and slaves who out of necessity or sympathy cooperated with the Buraco de Tatú. João Baptista, a mulatto farmer, worked with the runaways and supplied them with firewood.[56] He was apparently not alone in his practices. Blacks in the city of Salvador aided the *quilombo* by helping its inhabitants enter the city at night to steal powder and shot. Such contact was unsettling to colonists and officials who feared increased escapes or a general uprising. Here as in other instances, white settlers cooperated with the *quilombo* in order to avoid harm to life or property. This type of cooperation, although coerced, indicates that the fugitives of the Buraco de Tatú had no intention of a total war of liberation against the slave-owning segments of the population.

The *quilombo* itself was a well-organized village laid out in a rectilinear pattern of six rows of houses divided by a large central street [see Figure 2, which is redrawn from the original in Schwartz 1970]. There were thirty-two rectangular residential units (B), and since there were approximately sixty-five adults in the *quilombo*, we can assume that these units represent houses rather than compounds. The close correlation of two people to a house indicates a monogamous marital pattern. This assumption is tenuous, however, since the supporting documents curiously make no mention of children. But children born in the *mocambos* often became the property of the leader of the exterminating expedition, and this may explain their absence from the judicial records (ACB, 1:119 [January 24, 1629]). The monogamous marital pattern, the rectangular house shape, and the even rows of

163–65. It has also been printed in Castro de Almeida 1914, 2:44–45.
[56] AHU, Bahia, *papeis avulsos*, No. 6456, "Certidão da Sentença condemnatoria dos Negros do Quilombo denominado Buraco de Tatú" (January 12, 1764).

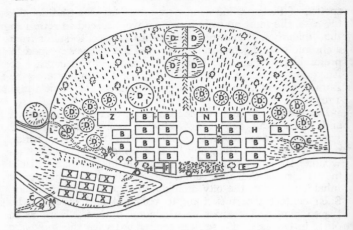

Figure 2: The Buraco de Tatú ("Armadillo's Hole").

houses may be a reproduction of a plantation's slave quarters rather than any specific African pattern. Conversely, the large central street equally dividing the houses of rectangular shape and the existence of what may have been a "palaver" house in front of a plaza (H) are all elements of villages of northwestern Bantu groups such as the Koko, Teke, and Mabea (Murdock 1959:276). The documents give almost no indication of the origin of the runaways in the "Armadillo's Hole." One, at least, was a *crioulo,* or Brazilian-born slave. Another was called a *mandingueiro,* a term that by the mid-eighteenth century simply meant "sorcerer" but that may also indicate Mandinga origins for at least this fugitive. The most reasonable conclusion is that no one African group lived in this *mocambo.*

Entry into the *mocambo* was made difficult by an extensive defensive network. The rear was protected by a swampy dike about the height of a man. Three sides of the village were protected by a maze of sharpened spikes (L) driven into the ground and covered to prevent detection by an unsuspecting intruder. This defense was augmented by a series of twenty-one pits (D) filled with sharp stakes and disguised by brush and grass. Leading into the *mocambo* was a false road especially well protected by the spikes and camouflaged traps.

Only when the watchman (N) placed planks (C, O, M) over some of the obstacles did entry and exit become possible. The Portuguese noted the effectiveness of this defensive system and took special pains to point out to the Crown the difficulties created by it. It was a defense quite unlike that of the palisaded Angolan *quilombo* described by Father Cavazzi in 1680 (see Fig. 3) (Cavazzi da Montecuccolo

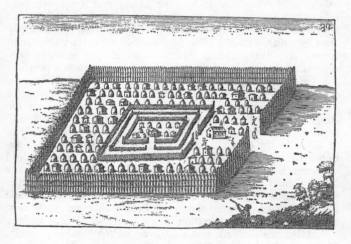

Figure 3: An Angolan palisaded *quilombo*.

1687:205–7). On the other hand, covered traps and sharpened stakes were used for village protection in Africa from Nigeria southward to the old kingdom of the Kongo and were also used to protect the Afro-Brazilian encampment of Palmares (Balandier 1964:114; van Wing 1921:148; Denam et al. 1826; and Kent 1965:168).

In the predatory economy of the Buraco de Tatú, agriculture does not appear to have been a major activity. This plan does show, however, a trellis of *maracujá* (Q) and a number of small gardens (F) perhaps equivalent to the dawn gardens of the Kongo. These seem to have been small and may have been devoted to herbs rather than staple crops. No *roças* or farmlands are indicated in the area surrounding the *mocambo*. The fugitives probably extracted agricultural produce as tribute from their neighbors and may have supplemented their diet with fish, since the village was located near the coast.[57]

A few aspects of the internal life of the *quilombo* can be ascertained. Politically the *mocambo* had two chieftains or captains. Antonio de Sousa was a war captain, and a second leader, Theodoro, controlled the *quilombo* itself (*"tive administração do quilombo"*). Each leader had a consort, who was called a queen. [On the original map from which Figure 2 was drawn, the structure labelled "Z" was said to be simply "the captain's house."] Nine houses (X) were separated from the main village. This separation may simply indicate latecomers or the divided political leadership. There is a possibility, however, that this may have distinguished a kin group unable to live in the large village or even an age group of young males required to live apart. If the latter were the case, however, the Portuguese probably would have found cause to mention it. Whether these fugitives practiced a form of Christianity or an African religion is unknown. Two individuals were mentioned as sorcerers, one of them an old woman (R). Women are traditionally the leaders of the Yoruba cults (*candomblé*) still practiced in Bahia, but the dates of this *mocambo* (1743–63) preceded the large-scale importation of Yoruba slaves in Brazil (Verger 1964:2–5; the most detailed examination of *candomblé* is Verger 1957).

The Buraco de Tatú was destroyed on September 2, 1763. Under the leadership of Joaquim da Costa Cardozo, a force of two hundred men, including a contingent of grenadiers, was enlisted for the anti-*quilombo* operations. The majority of the troops, however, consisted of an Indian auxiliary militia and Indians from the village of Giguriça in Jaguaripe. The battle orders issued to the expedition called for the troops to remain in the field without retreat until the *"quilombo* has been destroyed, the blacks captured, the resistors killed, the woods searched, the huts and defenses burned, and the trenches filled in"* (AHU, Bahia, *papeis avulsos*, No. 6649). Indian guides were used to scout the *quilombo*'s defenses before the final attack was launched. The assault probably came from the relatively unprotected coastal side of the village, and surprise seems to have been an important element in the attack's success. Although an old woman (T) sounded

[57] Some *mocambos* did farm for sustenance; see the document of 1796 in Pierson 1967:49.

the alarm, the greatly outnumbered defenders, some of whom were armed with bows (P), were overwhelmed. The hero of the defense was José Lopes, who fired two shots at the attackers and who shouted defiantly that it would take more than two hundred men to capture him. Unfortunately he was mistaken. Four inhabitants of the *mocambo* died in the attack, and sixty-one were taken prisoner. No casualties were reported among the expeditionary troops.

Upon their capture, the inhabitants of the Buraco de Tatú were incarcerated in the jail of Salvador. Thirty-one, whose only crime was to have escaped slavery, were, in accordance with a royal order of March 3, 1741, branded with the letter F (*fugido*) (BGUC, Cod. 707, Livro de Registro da Relação). Upon payment to the royal treasury by their masters, the slaves were returned to captivity. Certain of the slaves, however, were singled out for special punishment. Antonio de Sousa, war captain of the *quilombo*, was sentenced to a public flogging and life in the galleys. His friend Miguel Cosme, "reported to be a great thief," received a sentence of flogging and six years as a galley slave. Theodoro and José Lopes both were publicly whipped and sent to ten years in the galleys. José Piahuy, "a great backwoodsman and thief," received two hundred lashes and a four-year term at the oars, while the *crioulo* Leonardo received a like number of stripes. João Baptista, the mulatto farmer who was an accomplice of the fugitives, was sentenced to five years of penal exile and a stiff fine. The queens received relatively light sentences (AHU, Bahia, *papeis avulsos*, No. 6456).

So ended the Buraco de Tatú, but not the history of the resistance to slavery in Brazil. *Mocambos* remained a constant aspect of the Brazilian scene and the most important element of slave resistance. Unlike individual acts of violence or simple escape, *mocambos*, no matter what the ultimate goals or self-perceptions of their inhabitants, were joint acts against the existing social and economic order. In many ways the episode of the Buraco de Tatú represented the collective history of the Bahian *mocambos*. Rather small in size (less than a hundred individuals), located close to centers of population, and living off their neighbors, these communities developed syncretic traditions fusing African and Brazilian elements. The punitive military expedition and the use of Indians against the Buraco de Tatú represented the usual colonial response to the *mocambos*. Living by their wits and their daring, the Afro-Brazilian fugitives of the "Armadillo's Hole" maintained their independence for twenty years until their actions and the threat of their very existence caused the colonial authorities to exterminate their community. Overshadowed by more dramatic episodes, the Buraco de Tatú and similar communities were the basic form of slave resistance in colonial Brazil.

REFERENCES NOT CITED IN GENERAL BIBLIOGRAPHY

Alden, Dauril
  1963 "The Population of Brazil in the Late Eighteenth Century: A Preliminary Survey." *Hispanic American Historical Review* 43:173–205.
Antonil, André João
  1967 *Cultura e opulencia do Brasil* (*1711*), ed. A. P. Canabrava. São Paulo.
Balandier, Georges
  1964 *La vie quotidienne au Royaume de Kongo du xvi au xviii siècle*. Paris.
Baldus, Herbert
  1954–68 *Bibliografia crítica da ethnologia Brasileira*. Hamburg.
Boxer, C. R.
  1963 *Race Relations in the Portuguese Colonial Empire: 1415–1825*. Oxford.
  1964 "Nova e curiosa relação (1764)," ed. C. R. Boxer. *Race* 5:38–47.
Brásio, António
  1954 *Monumenta missionaria africana: Africa occidental*. Lisbon.
Calazans, José
  1952 *A santidade de Jaguaripe*. Salvador.
Caldas, José Antônio
  1951 *Noticia geral de toda esta capitania da Bahia desde o seu descobrimento ate o prezente anno de 1759* [fac. ed., Salvador].
Castro de Almeida, Eduardo (ed.)
  1914 *Inventário dos documentos relativas do Brasil*. Rio de Janeiro.
Cavazzi da Montecuccolo, Antonio
  1687 *Istoria descrizione de tre Regni Congo, Matamba, et Angola*. Bologna.
da Costa, Joseph Israel
  n.d. "The proposal of Joseph Israel da Costa to the Prince of Orange." Algemein Rijksarchief, Loketkas 6, Staten Generaal, West Indische Compagnie.
Costa Filho, Miguel
  1963 *A cana de-Açúcar en Minas Gerais*. Rio de Janeiro.

Denam, Major, Capt. Clapperton and Dr. Oudney
1826 *Narrative of travels and discoveries in Northern and Central Africa in the years 1822, 1823, and 1824.* London.

Fernandes, Florestan
1963 *Organização social dos Tupinamba.* São Paulo.

Freyre, Gilberto
1933 *Casa grande e senzala.* Rio de Janeiro.
1956 *The Masters and the Slaves.* (Trans. Samuel Putnam, 2nd rev. ed.). New York: Knopf.

Frézier, A.
1716 *A Voyage to the South Sea and Along the Coasts of Chili and Peru: 1712–1714.* London.

de Goulart, Mauricio
1950 *A escravidão africana no Brasil.* São Paulo.

Kieman, Mathias
1954 *The Indian Policy of Portugal in the Amazon Regions, 1614–1693.* Washington.

Koster, Henry
1816 *Travels in Brazil.* London.

Leite, Serafim
1965a "Enformação dalgumas cousas do Brasil por Belchior Cordeiro." *Anais da Academia Portuguesa da Historia,* 2nd. ser. 15:175–202.
1965b *Novas páginas de história do Brasil.* São Paulo.

Lopes Sierra, Juan
1676 Panegirico funebre al Senhor Alffonso Furtado de Castro del Rio de Mendonca. Bahia. BA, 50-IV-49.

Marchant, Alexander
1942 *From Barter to Slavery: the Economic Relations of Portuguese and Indians in the Settlement of Brazil, 1500–1580.* Baltimore.

Mauro, Frédéric
1956 "L'Atlantique portugaise et les esclaves (1570–1670)." *Revista da Facultude de Letras de Lisboa,* 2nd ser. 22:5–55.

de Mello, José Antônio Gonçalves
1951 *Tempo dos Flamengos: influência da ocupação holandesa na vida e cultura do norte do Brasil.* São Paulo.
1954 *Henrique Dias: governador dos pretos, crioulos, e mulatos.* Recife.

Murdock, George P.
1959 *Africa: its Peoples and their Culture History.* New York: McGraw-Hill.

Pedreira, Pedro Thomás
1962 "Os quilombos baianos." *Revista Brasileira de Geografia* 24:79–93.

Pereira de Queiroz, Maria Isaura
1965 *O messianismo no Brasil e no mundo.* São Paulo.

Pitta, Sebastião da Rocha
  1724 *Historia da America Portugueza.* Lisbon (1880).
Poppino, Rollie
  1968 *Brazil: the Land and People.* New York.
Prado, Jr. Caio
  1967 *The colonial Background of Modern Brazil.* Berkeley.
Ribeiro, René
  1958 "Relations of the Negro with Christianity in Portuguese America." *The Americas* 14:454–84.
  1962 "Brazilian Messianic Movements." In *Millenial Dreams in Action,* ed. Silvia L. Thrupp. The Hague, pp. 55–69.
Ricard, Robert
  1948 "Algunos enseñanzas de los documentos inquisitoriales del Brasil (1591–93)." *Anuario de Estudios Americanos* 5:705–15.
Russell, Marion J.
  1946 "American Slave Discontent in Records of the High Courts." *Journal of Negro History* 31.
Russell-Wood, A. J. R.
  1967 "Class, Creed and Colour in Colonial Bahia: a Study in Prejudice." *Race* 9:134–57.
Sluiter, Engel (ed.)
  1949 "Report on the State of Brazil, 1612." *Hispanic American Historical Review* 29:518–62.
Soares de França, Gonçalo
  1724 "Dissertações da história ecclesiastica de Brasil." Ms. in Sociedad de Geographia de Lisboa, res. 1-C-147.
Thomas, Georg
  1968 *Die portugiesische Indianerpolitiek in Brasilien: 1500–1640.* Berlin.
Verger, Pierre
  1957 *Notes sur la culte des orisa et vodun.* Dakar: IFAN.
  1964 *Bahia and the West African Trade.* Ibadan.
van Wing, J.
  1921 *Études Bakongo.* Louvain.

PART FIVE

Jamaica

With the "Bush Negroes" of Surinam, the Jamaican Maroons constitute the longest-surviving of all maroon groups. Materials for the study of their history are numerous and relatively accessible, yet only recently have sophisticated sociohistorical analyses been attempted (for example, Patterson 1970, Kopytoff 1972). The two selections here represent opposite poles of historical analysis—Bryan Edwards' leisurely, urbane account of Maroon history and character from the perspective of an eighteenth-century Jamaican planter, and the searching reinterpretation and explanation of these same events by the Jamaican-born professor of sociology at Harvard, Orlando Patterson.

Since these selections follow the Maroons only into the mid-eighteenth century, a word on the subsequent development of their society may be helpful. The end of the eighteenth century witnessed an improbable series of events, beginning with the Maroons of Trelawny Town taking offense at the lawful punishment of two of their number, administered in particularly humiliating circumstances—a whipping given by a black prison overseer in the presence of slave convicts. This led, after considerable mishandling of the situation by both sides, to armed skirmishes between these Maroons and the whites (who were aided by *chasseurs* and dogs imported from Cuba) and eventually to the forced deportation of the whole Trelawny Town population to Nova Scotia and thence, after many had died from the unfamiliar and severe climate, to Sierra Leone (see the bibliographical note to this section for readings on this period).

Turning to those Maroons who remained in Jamaica, it seems clear that the mid-eighteenth-century treaties with the whites altered their communities in many respects. In the general introduction, I discussed the apparent changes in self-image and political ideology that accompanied freedom. But the treaties had a debilitating effect on the internal organization of the Jamaican communities as well. One of their provisions was to reserve for whites the imposition of the death penalty (which had been a cornerstone of Maroon political control), greatly weakening the power of Maroon chiefs. Moreover, the chiefs, who could now be appointed only with the approval of the government, were granted life tenure, so that men long past their political prime, who in former times would have been replaced, began to come into frequent conflict with aspiring younger leaders. As a result, the eighteenth century witnessed a weakening of the mechanisms of social control in Maroon communities, an increase in factionalism, and the splitting up of a number of villages (Kopytoff 1972). A still more significant effect of the treaties was to bring the Maroons into increasing contact with the rest of Jamaican society. Land-hungry colonists competed fiercely for the areas adjacent to Maroon settlements (as happened also in Palmares [Kent 1965:171] and Saint-Domingue [Debbasch 1961/62:187–88]), forcing the Maroons to live shoulder-to-shoulder with other Jamaicans (Kopytoff 1972). Combined with the Maroons' increased participation in economic activities outside of their villages, in which they now dealt on a frequent basis with nonMaroons, this new physical proximity seems to have led to a relatively rapid creolization of Maroon culture. This gradual posttreaty trend toward homogenization, fostered by the small size of the island, Maroon economic activities, and the encroachment of settlers, received a further boost with the Maroon Lands Allotment Act of 1842, when the government instituted a program of integration of the Maroons into the national society (Kopytoff 1972). Today, there remains in these communities considerable consciousness of Maroon origins (increasingly encouraged by the tourist industry), and a good many African cultural "retentions" can be uncovered by the persistent researcher (see, for example, Dalby 1971). Yet a Maroon community today would look to the casual visitor much like "a typical rural village of the island; the people, the buildings and the daily activity resemble those of other country settlements" (Scott 1968:iii). Exactly how much of the Maroons' distinctive cultural heritage, and which particular aspects of it remain alive below the surface is a question that only sensitive in-depth field work, carried out in the immediate future, can answer.

Additional readings on the Jamaican Maroons are found in the bibliographical note to Part Five.

CHAPTER FOURTEEN

*Observations on the Disposition, Character,
Manners, and Habits of Life,
of the Maroon Negroes of the Island of Jamaica;
and a Detail of the Origin, Progress, and
Termination of the late War between those People
and the White Inhabitants*

BRYAN EDWARDS

Jamaica, as we have seen, was conquered from the Spaniards, during the protectorate of Cromwell, in the year 1655,
by an armament under the command of Admiral Penn and
General Venables. The Spanish inhabitants are said to have
possessed, before the attack, about fifteen hundred enslaved
Africans, most of whom, on the surrender of their masters,
retreated to the mountains, from whence they made frequent
excursions to harass the English. Major-general Sedgewick,
one of the British officers, in a letter to Secretary Thurloe
(1656) predicts, that these blacks would prove a thorn in
the sides of the English. He adds, that they gave no quarter
to his men, but destroyed them whenever they found opportunity; scarce a week passing without their murdering one
or more of them; and as the soldiers became more confident
and careless, the negroes grew more enterprising and bloody-
minded. "Having no moral sense," continues he, "and not understanding what the laws and customs of civil nations mean,

From Bryan Edwards, *The History . . . of the West Indies.* London: 1807, Vol. 1, Appendix 2, pp. 522–35, 537–45. (First published separately in 1796.) [Much of the historical portion of this
account is taken nearly verbatim from Long 1774.]

Cudjoe making peace with Guthrie. See Chapters 14 and 15. From Dallas, R. C., *The History of the Maroons*. London: T. N. Longman and O. Rees.

A Cuban hunting the maroons with dogs. See Chapters 3, 14 and 15. From Dallas, R. C., *The History of the Maroons*. London: T. N. Longman and O. Rees.

Surinam: Eighteenth-century war scenes. See Chapters 16 and 17. From Stedman, J. G., *Narrative of a five-years' expedition, against the revolted Negroes of Surinam ... from the year 1772, to 1777*. London: J. Johnson and J. Edwards (1796).

A maroon warrior.

A Coromantee ranger (antimaroon soldier).

European troops pursuing maroons through a swamp.

Amakti, chief of the Djuka from 1916 to 1931, flanked by village headmen. See Part Six. Courtesy of Silvia W. de Groot.

The four "Bush Negro" chiefs (in suits) visiting Chief Apétor II in Palimé, Togo, during their trip to West Africa. See Chapter 21. Courtesy of Silvia W. de Groot.

About the same time another party of the Maroons, having perceived that a body of the militia stationed at the barrack of Bagnel's thicket, in St. Mary's parish, under the command of Colonel Charlton strayed heedlessly from their quarters. and kept no order, formed a project to cut them off, and whilst the officers were at dinner, attended by a very few of their men, the Maroons rushed suddenly from the adjacent woods and attacked them. Several pieces were discharged, the report of which alarmed the militia, who immediately ran to their arms, and came up in time to rescue their officers from destruction. The Maroons were repulsed, and forced to take shelter in the woods, but the militia did not think fit to pursue them. Some rumours of this skirmish reached Spanish Town, which is distant from the spot about thirty miles; and, as all the circumstances were not known, the inhabitants were thrown into the most dreadful alarm, from apprehensions that the Maroons had defeated Charlton, and were in full march to attack the town. Ayscough, then commander in chief, participating in the general panick, ordered the trumpets to sound, the drums to beat, and in a few hours collected a body of horse and foot, who went to meet the enemy. On the second day after their departure, they came to a place where, by the fires which remained unextinguished, they supposed the Maroons had lodged the preceding night. They therefore followed the track, and soon after got sight of them. Captain Edmunds, who commanded the detachment, disposed his men for action; but the Maroons declined engaging, and fled different ways. Several of them, however, were slain in the pursuit, and others made prisoners. These two victories reduced their strength, and filled them with so much terror that they never afterwards appeared in any considerable body, nor dared to make any stand; indeed, from the commencement of the war till this period, they had not once ventured a pitched battle, but skulked about the skirts of remote plantations, surprising stragglers, and murdering the whites by two or three at a time, or when they were too few to make any resistance. By night they seized the favourable opportunity that darkness gave them, of stealing into the settlements, where they set fire to cane-fields and out-houses, killed all the cattle they could find, and carried the slaves into captivity. By this dastardly method of conducting the war, they did infinite mischief to the whites, without much exposing their own persons to danger, for

they always cautiously avoided fighting, except with a num
ber so disproportionally inferior to themselves, as to affor
them a pretty sure expectation of victory. They knew ever
secret avenue of the country; so that they could eithe
conceal themselves from pursuit, or shift their ravages fror
place to place, as circumstances required. Such were th
many disadvantages under which the English had to dea
with those desultory foes; who were not reducible by an
regular plan of attack; who possessed no plunder to allur
or reward the assailants; nor had any thing to lose, excep
life, and a wild and savage freedom.

Previous to the successes above mentioned, the distress int
which the planters were thrown, may be collected from th
sense which the legislature of Jamaica expressed in some o
their acts. In the year 1773, they set forth, that "the Maroon
had, within a few years, greatly increased, notwithstanding
all the measures that had been concerted, and made use o
for their suppression; in particular, that they had grown ver
formidable in the North East, North West, and South West
ern districts of the island, to the great terror of his Majesty'
subjects in those parts, who had greatly suffered by the
frequent robberies, murders, and depredations committed b
them; that in the parishes of Clarendon, St. Ann, St. Eliza
beth, Westmorland, Hanover, and St. James's, they were con
siderably multiplied, and had large settlements among the
mountains, and least accessible parts; whence they plundered
all around them, and caused several plantations to be thrown
up and abandoned, and prevented many valuable tracts of
land from being cultivated, to the great prejudice and dimi
nution of his Majesty's revenue, as well as of the trade,
navigation, and consumption of British manufactures; and to
the manifest weakening, and preventing the further increase
of the strength and inhabitants, in the island." We may learn
from hence, what extensive mischief may be perpetrated by
the most despicable and cowardly enemy. The Assembly,
perceiving that the employment of flying parties had proved
ineffectual, by the length of their marches, the difficulty of
subsisting them in the woods for so long a time as the
service required, and the facility with which the Maroons
eluded their pursuit, ordered several defensible houses, or
barracks, fortified with bastions, to be erected in different
parts, as near as possible to the enemy's most favourite
haunts: in each of these they placed a strong garrison, and

roads of communication were opened from one to the other. These garrisons were composed of white and black shot and baggage negroes, who were all duly trained. Every captain was allowed a pay of ten pounds, the lieutenants each five pounds, and serjeants four pounds, and privates two pounds per month. They were subjected to the rules and articles of war; and the whole body put under the Governor's immediate order, to be employed, conjunctly or separately, as he should see occasion. Their general plan of duty, as directed by the law, was to make excursions from the barracks, scour the woods and mountains, and destroy the provision gardens and haunts of the Maroons; and that they might not return without effecting some service, they were required to take twenty days provision with them on every such expedition. Every barrack *was also furnished with a pack of dogs, provided by the Churchwardens of the respective parishes;* it being foreseen that these animals would prove extremely serviceable, not only in guarding *against surprizes in the night,* but in tracking the enemy.

This arrangement was the most judicious hitherto contrived for their effectual reduction; for so many fortresses, stationed in the very centre of their usual retreats, well supplied with every necessary, gave the Maroons a constant and vigorous annoyance, and in short became the chief means of bringing on that treaty which afterwards put an end to this tiresome war.

About the year 1737 [1738?], the Assembly resolved on taking two hundred of the Mosquito Indians into their pay, to hasten the suppression of the Maroons. They passed an act for rendering free Negroes, Mulattoes, and Indians, more useful, and forming them into companies, with proper encouragement. Some sloops were dispatched to the Mosquito shore; and that number of Indians was brought into the island, formed into companies under their own officers, and allowed forty shillings a month for pay, besides shoes and other articles. White guides were assigned to conduct them to the enemy, and they gave proofs of great sagacity in this service. It was their practice to observe the most profound silence in marching to the enemy's quarters; and when they had once hit upon a track, they were sure to discover the haunt to which it led. They effected considerable service, and were, indeed, the most proper troops to be employed in that species of action, which is known in America by the name of

bush fighting. They were well rewarded for their good con
duct, and afterwards dismissed to their own country, whe
the pacification took place with the Maroons.

For in 1738, Governor Trelawney, by the advice of th
principal gentlemen of the island, proposed overtures o
peace with the Maroon chiefs. Both parties were now grow
heartily wearied out with this tedious conflict. The white in
habitants wished relief from the horrors of continual alarms
the hardship of military duty, and the intolerable burthen o
maintaining the army. The Maroons were not less anxiou
for an accommodation: they were hemmed in, and closel
beset on all sides; their provisions destroyed, and themselve
reduced to so miserable a condition, by famine and incessan
attacks, that Cudjoe afterwards declared, that if peace ha
not been offered to them, they had no choice left but eithe
to be starved, lay violent hands on themselves, or surrende
to the English at discretion [told directly to Long (1774:I
344)]. The extremity of their case, however, was not at tha
time known to the white inhabitants, and their number wa
supposed to be twice as great as it was afterwards found t
be. The articles of pacification (which I have subjoined
were therefore ratified with the Maroon chiefs, and fiftee
hundred acres of land assigned to one body of them[1], an
one thousand acres to another, which the legislature secure
to them and their posterity in perpetuity. The Assembly, b
subsequent laws, augmented the premium allowed the Ma
roons for apprehending fugitive slaves to three pounds pe
head; and they passed many other regulations for their bet
ter government and protection, for preventing their pur
chasing and harbouring negro slaves, and for directing i
what manner they should be tried in the case of felony, an
other crimes, committed against the whites,[2] and thus a

[1] This was the body that settled in Trelawney Town, and are th
ancestors of those who have lately taken up arms. The other Ma
roon negroes were those of Accompong Town, Crawford Town
and Nanny Town, to each of which lands were allotted. The ag
gregate number in 1795, was about sixteen hundred men, women
and children.
[2] On complaint made, on oath, to a justice of peace, of any felony
burglary, robbery, or other offence whatsoever, having been com
mitted by Maroon negroes, he is required to grant a warrant to ap
prehend the offenders, and to have all persons brought before him
or some other justice, that can give evidence; and if, upon exami
nation, it appears that there are grounds for publick trial, the jus

end was at length happily put to this tedious and ruinous contest; a contest which, while it lasted, seemed to portend nothing less than the ruin of the whole colony.

Articles of pacification with the Maroons of Trelawney Town, concluded March the first, 1738.

In the name of God, Amen. Whereas Captain Cudjoe, Captain Accompong, Captain Johnny, Captain Cuffee, Captain Quaco, and several other negroes, their dependents and adherents, have been in a state of war and hostility, for several years past, against our sovereign lord the King, and the inhabitants of this island; and whereas peace and friendship among mankind, and the preventing the effusion of blood, is agreeable to God, consonant to reason, and desired by every good man; and whereas his Majesty, King George the Second, King of Great Britain, France, and Ireland, of Jamaica Lord, Defender of the Faith, &c. has by his letters patent, dated February the twenty-fourth, one thousand seven hundred and thirty-eight, in the twelfth year of his reign, granted full power and authority to John Guthrie and Francis Sadler, Esquires, to negotiate and finally conclude a treaty of peace and friendship with the aforesaid Captain Cudjoe, and the rest of his captains, adherents, and others his men; they mutually, sincerely, and amicably have agreed to the following articles: First, That all hostility shall cease on both sides forever. Secondly, That the said Captain Cudjoe, the rest of his captains, adherents, and men, shall be for ever hereafter in a perfect state of freedom and liberty, excepting those who have been taken by them, or fled to them, within two years last past, if such are willing to return to their said masters and owners, with full pardon and indemnity from their said masters or owners for what is past; provided always, that if they are not willing to return, they shall remain in subjection to Captain Cudjoe and in friendship with us, according to the form and tenor of this treaty. Thirdly, That they shall enjoy and possess, for themselves and posterity for ever, all the lands situate and lying between Trelawney Town and the Cockpits, to the amount of

---

tice is to commit the accused, unless the offence be bailable, and bind over the witnesses. They are to be tried where the quarter sessions are held. . . .

fifteen hundred acres, bearing north-west from the said Trelawney Town. Fourthly, That they shall have liberty to plant the said lands with coffee, cocoa, ginger, tobacco, and cotton, and to breed cattle, hogs, goats, or any other stock, and dispose of the produce or increase of the said commodities to the inhabitants of this island; provided always, that when they bring the said commodities to market, they shall apply first to the custos, or any other magistrate of the respective parishes where they expose their goods to sale, for a licence to vend the same. Fifthly, That Captain Cudjoe, and all the Captain's adherents, and people now in subjection to him, shall all live together within bounds of Trelawney Town, and that they have liberty to hunt where they shall think fit, except within three miles of any settlement, crawl, or pen; provided always, that in case the hunters of Captain Cudjoe and those of other settlements meet, then the hogs to be equally divided between both parties. Sixthly, That the said Captain Cudjoe, and his successors, do use their best endeavours to take, kill, suppress, or destroy, either by themselves, or jointly with any other number of men, commanded on that service by his Excellency the Governor, or Commander in Chief for the time being, all rebels wheresoever they be, throughout this island, unless they submit to the same terms of accommodation granted to Captain Cudjoe, and his successors. Seventhly, That in case this island be invaded by any foreign enemy, the said Captain Cudjoe, and his successors hereinafter named or to be appointed, shall then, upon notice given, immediately repair to any place the Governor for the time being shall appoint, in order to repel the said invaders with his or their utmost force, and to submit to the orders of the Commander in Chief on that occasion. Eighthly, That if any white man shall do any manner of injury to Captain Cudjoe, his successors, or any of his or their people, they shall apply to any commanding officer or magistrate in the neighbourhood for justice; *and in case Captain Cudjoe, or any of his people, shall do any injury to any white person, he shall submit himself, or deliver up such offenders to justice.* Ninthly, That if any negro shall hereafter run away from their masters or owners, and fall into Captain Cudjoe's hands, they shall immediately be sent back to the chief magistrate of the next parish where they are taken; and those that bring them are to be satisfied for their trouble, as the legislature shall appoint.[3] Tenth, That all negroes taken, since the raising of this party by Captain Cudjoe's people, shall immediately be returned. Eleventh, That Captain Cudjoe, and his successors, shall wait on his Excellency, or the Commander in Chief for the time being, every year, if thereunto required. Twelfth, That Captain Cudjoe, during his life, and the captains succeeding him, shall have full power to inflict any punishment they think proper for crimes committed by their men among themselves, death only excepted; in which case, if the Captain thinks they deserve death, he shall be obliged to bring them before any justice of the peace, who shall order proceedings on their trial equal to those of other free negroes. Thirteenth, That Captain Cudjoe, with his people, shall cut, clear, and keep open, large and convenient roads from Trelawney Town to Westmorland and St. James's, and if possible to St. Elizabeth's. Fourteenth, That two white men, to be nominated by his Excellency, or the Commander in Chief for the time being, shall constantly live and reside with Captain Cudjoe and his successors, in order to maintain a friendly correspondence with the inhabitants of this island. Fifteenth, That Captain Cudjoe shall, during his life, be Chief Commander in Trelawney Town: after his decease the command to devolve on his brother Captain Accompong; and in case of his decease, on his next brother Captain Johnny; and, failing him, Captain Cuffee shall succeed; who is to be succeeded by Captain Quaco; and after all their demises, the Governor, or Commander in Chief for the time being, shall appoint, from time to time, whom he thinks fit for that command. In testimony, &c. &c. . . . .

Concerning the Maroons, they are in general ignorant of our language, and all of them attached to the gloomy superstitions of Africa (derived from their ancestors) with such enthusiastick zeal and reverential ardour, as I think can only be eradicated with their lives. The Gentoos of India are not, I conceive, more sincere in their faith than the negroes of Guinea in believing the prevalence of *Obi* (a species of pretended magick), and the supernatural power of their *Obeah* men. Obstacles like these, accompanied with the fierce and

---

[3] The Assembly granted a premium of thirty shillings for each fugitive slave returned to his owner by the Maroons, besides expences.

sordid manners which I shall presently describe, few clergymen would, I think, be pleased to encounter, lest they might experience all the sufferings, without acquiring the glory of martyrdom.

Under disadvantages of such magnitude was founded the first legal establishment of our Maroon allies in Jamaica. Inured, for a long series of years, to a life of warfare within the island, it is a matter of astonishment that they submitted, for any length of time, to any system of subordination or government whatever. It is probable they were chiefly induced to remain quiet by the great encouragement that was held out to them for the apprehending fugitive slaves, and being allowed to range over the uncultivated country without interruption, possessing an immense wilderness for their hunting grounds. These pursuits gave full employment to the restless and turbulent among them. Their game was the wild boar, which abounds in the interior parts of Jamaica; and the Maroons had a method of curing the flesh without salting it. This commodity they frequently brought to market in the towns; and, with the money arising from the sale, and the rewards which they received for the delivery to their owners of runaway slaves, they purchased salted beef, spirituous liquors, tobacco, fire-arms, and ammunition, setting little or no account on clothing of any kind, and regarding as superfluous and useless most of those things which every people, in the lowest degree of civilization, would consider as almost absolutely necessary to human existence.

Their language was a barbarous dissonance of the African dialects, with a mixture of Spanish and broken English; and their thoughts and attention seemed wholly engrossed by their present pursuits, and the objects immediately around them, without any reflections on the past, or solicitude for the future. In common with all the nations of Africa, they believed, however, as I have observed, in the prevalence of *Obi*, and the authority which such of their old men as had the reputation of wizards or *Obeah-men*, possessed over them, was sometimes very successfully employed in keeping them in subordination to their chiefs.

Having, in the resources that have been mentioned, the means of procuring food for their daily support, they had no inclination for the pursuits of sober industry. Their repugnance to the labour of tilling the earth was remarkable. In some of their villages I never could perceive any vestige of culture; but the situation of their towns, in such cases, was generally in the neighbourhood of plantations belonging to the whites, from the provision grounds of which they either purchased, or stole, yams, plantains, corn, and other esculents. When they had no supply of this kind, I have sometimes observed small patches of Indian corn and yams, and perhaps a few straggling plantain trees, near their habitations; but the ground was always in a shocking state of neglect and ruin.

The labours of the field, however, such as they were (as well as every other species of drudgery), were performed by the women, who had no other means of clearing the ground of the vast and heavy woods with which it is every where incumbered, than by placing fire round the trunks of the trees till they were consumed in the middle, and fell by their own weight. It was a service of danger; but the Maroons, like all other savage nations, regarded their wives as so many beasts of burthen; and felt no more concern at the loss of one of them, than a white planter would have felt at the loss of a bullock. Polygamy too, with their other African customs, prevailed among the Maroons universally. Some of their principal men claimed from two to six wives, and the miseries of their situation left these poor creatures neither leisure nor inclination to quarrel with each other.

This spirit of brutality which the Maroons always displayed towards their wives, extended in some degree to their children. The paternal authority was at all times most harshly exerted; but more especially towards the females. I have been assured, that it was not an uncommon circumstance for a father, in a fit of rage or drunkenness, to seize his own infant, which had offended him by crying, and dash it against a rock, with a degree of violence that often proved fatal. This he did without any apprehension of punishment; for the superintendant, on such occasions, generally found it prudent to keep his distance, or be silent. Nothing can more strikingly demonstrate the forlorn and abject condition of the young women among the Maroons, than the circumstances which every gentleman, who has visited them on festive occasions, or for the gratification of curiosity, knows to be true; the offering their own daughters, by the first men among them, to their visitors; and bringing the poor girls forward, with or without their consent, for the purpose of prostitution.

Visits of this kind were indeed but too acceptable both to the Maroons and their daughters: for they generally ended in drunkenness and riot. The visitors too were not only fleeced of their money, but were likewise obliged to *furnish the feast,* it being indispensably necessary, on such occasions, to send beforehand wine and provisions of all kinds; and if the guests expected to sleep on beds and in linen, they must provide those articles also for themselves. The Maroons, however, if the party consisted of persons of consequence, would consider themselves as highly honoured, and would supply wild-boar, land-crabs, pigeons, and fish, and entertain their guests with a hearty and boisterous kind of hospitality, which had at least the charms of novelty and singularity to recommend it.

On such occasions, a mock fight always constituted a part of the entertainment. Mr. Long has given the following description of a scene of this kind, which was exhibited by the Trelawney-Town Maroons, in the presence of the Governor, in 1764. "No sooner (he observes) did the horn sound the signal, than they all joined in a most hideous yell, or war-hoop, and bounded into action. With amazing agility they ran, or rather rolled, through their various firings and evolutions. This part of their exercise, indeed, more justly deserves to be styled *evolution* than any that is practised by the regular troops; for they fire stooping almost to the very ground; and no sooner are their muskets discharged, than they throw themselves into a thousand antick gestures, and tumble over and over, so as to be continually shifting their place; the intention of which is to elude the shot, as well as to deceive the aim of their adversaries, which their nimble and almost instantaneous change of position renders extremely uncertain. When this part of their exercise was over, they drew their swords; and winding their horn again, began, in wild and warlike gestures, to advance towards his Excellency, endeavouring to throw as much savage fury into their looks as possible. On approaching near him, some waved their rusty blades over his head, then gently laid them upon it; whilst others clashed their arms together in horrid concert. They next brought their muskets, and piled them up in heaps at his feet, &c.&c." . . .

In the year 1760, an occasion occurred of putting the courage, fidelity, and humanity of these people to the test. The Koromantyn slaves, in the parish of St. Mary, rose into rebellion, and the Maroons were called upon, according to treaty, to co-operate in their suppression. A party of them accordingly arrived at the scene of action, the second or third day after the rebellion had broken out. The whites had already defeated the insurgents, in a pitched battle, at *Heywood-Hall*, killed eight or nine of their number, and driven the remainder into the woods. The Maroons were ordered to pursue them, and were promised a certain reward for each rebel they might kill or take prisoner. They accordingly pushed into the woods, and after rambling about for a day or two returned with a collection of human ears, which they pretended to have cut off from the heads of rebels which they had slain in battle, the particulars of which they minutely related. Their report was believed, and they received the money stipulated to be paid them; yet it was afterwards found that they had not killed a man; that no engagement had taken place; and that the ears which they had produced, had been severed from the dead Negroes which had lain unburied at Heywood-Hall.

Some few days after this, as the Maroons and a detachment of the 74th regiment, were stationed at a solitary place, surrounded by deep woods, called Down's Cove, the detachment was suddenly attacked in the middle of the night by the rebels. The sentinels were shot, and the huts in which the soldiers were lodged, were set on fire. The light of the flames, while it exposed the troops, served to conceal the rebels, who poured in a shower of musquetry from all quarters, and many of the soldiers were slain. Major Forsyth who commanded the detachment, formed his men into a square, and by keeping up a brisk fire from all sides, at length compelled the enemy to retire. During the whole of this affair the Maroons were not to be found, and Forsyth, for some time, suspected that they were themselves the assailants. It was discovered, however, that, immediately on the attack, the whole body of them had thrown themselves flat on the ground, and continued in that position until the rebels retreated, without firing or receiving a shot.

A party of them, indeed, had afterwards the merit (a merit of which they loudly boasted) of killing the leader of the rebels. He was a young negro of the Koromantyn nation, named Tackey, and it was said had been of free condition, and even a chieftain, in Africa. This unfortunate man, having seen most of his companions slaughtered, was discovered wandering in the woods without arms or clothing, and was immediately pursued by the Maroons, *in full cry*. The chase was of no long duration; he was shot through the head; and, it is painful to relate, but unquestionably true, that his savage pursuers, having decollated the body, in order to preserve the head as the trophy of victory, *roasted and actually devoured the heart and entrails of the wretched victim*.[4]

The misconduct of these people in this rebellion, whether proceeding from cowardice or treachery, was, however, overlooked. Living secluded from the rest of the community, they were supposed to have no knowledge of the rules and restraints to which all other classes of the inhabitants were subject; and the vigilance of justice (notwithstanding what has recently happened) seldom pursued them, even for offences of the most atrocious nature.

In truth, it always seemed to me, that the whites in general entertained an opinion of the usefulness of the Maroons, which no part of their conduct, at any one period, confirmed. —Possibly their personal appearance contributed, in some degree, to preserve the delusion; for, savage as they were in manners and disposition, their mode of living and daily pursuits undoubtedly strengthened the frame, and served to exalt them to great bodily perfection. Such fine persons as are seldom beheld among any other class of African or native blacks. Their demeanour is lofty, their walk firm, and their persons erect. Every motion displays a combination of strength and agility. The muscles (neither hidden nor depressed by clothing) are very prominent, and strongly marked. Their sight withal is wonderfully acute, and their hearing remarkably quick. These characteristicks, however, are common, I believe, to all savage nations, in warm and temperate climates; and, like other savages, the Maroons have only those senses perfect which are kept in constant excercise. Their smell is obtuse, and their taste so depraved, that I have seen them drink new rum fresh from the still, in preference to wine which I offered them; and I remember, at

[4] The circumstances that I have related concerning the conduct of the Maroons, in the rebellion of 1760, are partly founded on my own knowledge and personal observation at the time (having been myself present) or from the testimony of eyewitnesses, men of character and probity. The shocking fact last mentioned was attested by several white people, and was not attempted to be denied or concealed by the Maroons themselves. They seemed indeed to make it the subject of boasting and triumph.

a great festival in one of their towns, which I attended, that their highest luxury, in point of food, was some rotten beef, which had been originally salted in Ireland, and which was probably presented to them, by some person who knew their taste, *because it was putrid.*

Such was the situation of the Maroon negroes of Jamaica, previous to their late revolt; and the picture which I have drawn of their character and manners, was delineated from the life, after long experience and observation.

CHAPTER FIFTEEN

Slavery and Slave Revolts:
A Sociohistorical Analysis of the
First Maroon War, 1665-1740[1]

ORLANDO PATTERSON

PART I

Few slave societies present a more impressive record of slave revolts than Jamaica. During the more than 180 years of its existence as a slave society, hardly a decade went by without a serious, large-scale revolt threatening the entire system. Between these larger efforts were numerous minor skirmishes, endless plots, individual acts of violence against the master, and other forms of resistance, all of which constantly pressed upon the white ruling class the fact that the system was a very precarious one, held together entirely by the exercise, or threat, of brute force.

The first eighty-five years of the English occupation of the island (1655-1740) were marked by one long series of revolts, which reached a dramatic climax during the last fifteen years of this period, at the end of which the whites, after coming close to disaster on several occasions, were forced to sue for peace and grant the rebels their freedom. It is customary to regard only these last fifteen climactic years as the First Maroon War. We hope to show, however, that almost all the revolts prior to 1740 were closely related and cannot meaningfully be separated from each other or from the events of the last decade and a half of the period.

Reprinted from *Social and Economic Studies* 19:289-325 (1970), with the permission of the author and the Institute of Social and Economic Studies.
[1] I would like to thank Professors Arnie Sio and Sid Mintz for their very useful criticisms of original drafts of this paper.

Jamaica, the largest British island in the Caribbean, was captured from the Spaniards in 1655 (as an afterthought following the failure to take San Domingue) as part of Cromwell's Grand Design on the Spanish possessions in the New World. During the more than 150 years of their occupation, the Spanish had done little to develop the island. When the British arrived, the population was estimated at no more than 3,000, of whom at least a half were slaves (Sedgwick to Whitehall, "Situation of the Island of Jamaica," CO 1/14). [*Editor's note:* reference abbreviations are listed at the end of this chapter.]

For the first five years of the British occupation the colony remained under military rule, as the Spanish and some of their ex-slaves put up a strong guerrilla resistance (cf. Taylor 1965 for a comprehensive, if somewhat biased, account). In 1660, when the last of the Spaniards had finally left, civil government was established and an early attempt was made at developing a colony of settlement. Attempts at populating the colony with white immigrants persisted formally until well into the eighteenth century, but a combination of factors ensured the failure of such attempts less than thirty years after the occupation. For most Europeans the climate was not the most hospitable. Worse, malaria and other fevers, endemic in the island, took a heavy toll of newcomers. Further, the disruptive presence of the buccaneers, internal political strife, and constitutional conflicts with the mother country resulted in great insecurity, which was intensified by the frequent revolts of the blacks and, toward the end of the seventeenth century, several destructive raids by the French fleet under Du Casse. Acts of God also played their part. The culmination of these was the famous earthquake of 1692—one of the worst in recorded history—in which two thirds of the island's major commercial center sank beneath the sea, carrying nearly all its inhabitants with it (cf. Marx 1967; Parkhurst 1963).

But by far the most important set of factors leading to the failure of attempts at creating a colony of white settlers were the economic ones. The major portion of the cultivable land of the island was rapidly monopolized by a group of land-grabbing planters who sought to establish an economic system that was quite incompatible with pioneering, small-scale settlements. By the turn of the eighteenth century Jamaica was well on the way, not only to recovery from the economic failures of the early, unsettled, small-farming period, but to a recovery based on the large-scale monocrop plantation model. African slavery was the cornerstone of this system. Against it, the small, even middle-sized, planters, depending on their own labor or those of a few slaves, could not compete. Those who were unable or unwilling to seek employment as overseers, bookkeepers, or tradesmen on the large plantations had little choice but to migrate again (Patterson 1967:16–27, 33–51).

Between 1655 and 1661 over twelve thousand persons arrived in the island, yet hardly thirty-six hundred remained in 1662. In 1696 the white population was down to less than two thousand, and although this figure slowly increased in absolute terms during the eighteenth century, the ratio of whites to Negro slaves was to decline constantly, rarely exceeding 10 percent of the total population (Pitman 1917:Ch. 5; Gardner 1873:159).

By the second decade of the eighteenth century, the first group of successful planters had consolidated their fortunes and began to send their children to be educated in Britain, and later they themselves departed for the mother country, rarely to return to the place that was the source of their wealth (Ragatz n.d.; Patterson 1967:33–37). As the island approached its period of greatest prosperity, toward the end of the fourth decade of the eighteenth century, the wealthiest landowners, possessing well over three quarters of the island's property (including slaves), were all absentees, living in great style in Britain, where they married into the petty aristocracy and made up the greater part of the West India lobby, the most powerful interest group in British politics at that time (Williams 1964:91–97). In Jamaica, their affairs were managed, often with remarkable ineptitude—sometimes quite deliberate—by attorneys and agents who, with the few resident large-scale owners and the top echelons of the appointed officers, headed by the governor, made up the core of the local ruling class (Ragatz 1928:Ch. 1; Patterson 1967:Ch. 1, Sec. 3).

Politically, during the period of slavery, the island enjoyed a considerable degree of internal autonomy, having an elected House of Assembly, a governor—who was the Crown's representative in the island, and whose authority, after a long constitutional struggle, which culminated in 1728, depended largely on his strength of character and diplomatic skill—and a Council nominated by the governor. Whitehall, during the eighteenth century, remained a *deus ex machina,* which exercised its ultimate authority with considerable restraint so long as the colony remained His Majesty's "prizest possession" (Spurdle 1962, Whitsun 1929, Thornton 1956).

The British legal system was imported with a few modifications to meet local needs. For the whites, despite the gross lack of qualified legal personnel, the system worked well enough, guided as it was by the rugged individualism and democratic fervor that always, ironically, seem to characterize the elite castes of all oppressive colonial plantation systems.

For the nonwhite and particularly the nonfree, the legal system was a grim travesty. Traditional British law either completely neglected or, in the few cases where it obliquely touched on the topic, very clumsily handled, the problem of slavery or other states of unfreedom. The local masters preferred it this way. They made little attempt at formulating a slave code until the last quarter of the eighteenth century, and when they did, it was largely as an anti-abolitionist propaganda tactic and was rarely heeded in practice. For the nine tenths of Jamaicans who made up the slave population, the master was the law. In him rested the power of life and death. Occasionally, a white person might have had to pay a fine for murdering his slave, but in the majority of such cases no legal action could be taken even to inflict the mildest penalty, since a Negro could not give evidence against any white person (Patterson 1967:Ch. 3; Smith 1945).

Perhaps the most striking feature of the island during the first ninety years of British rule is the fact that it can only with difficulty be described as a society, if we take the latter term to denote, in the most general sense, a territorially based, self-sufficient collectivity possessing some reasonably coherent and consistent system of values, norms, and beliefs. At the most, we can describe it as a society in an acute state of anomie.

This was essentially a society of immigrants and transients —transients either longing for the day when they would have made their fortunes and returned to the mother country, or transients and forced immigrants whose sole ambition was escape from the horror of their enslavement, either through revolt or death. Unlike the slave systems of the American South or the majority of the Iberian colonies, there was here no ruling class who, infused with the pioneer spirit, were committed to the social well-being and cultural development of their community (Pitman 1917:1–2; Genovese 1961). For the resident white ruling class, the move to Jamaica was not an exodus involving a clean break with the past and visions of a glorious future and a new age of chivalry, but a hasty migration motivated by greed and endured with much impatience. The sociological consequence was a shambled patchwork of social relationships which, in its excessive commitment to the sole goal of quick profits, discarded all aspects of the social institutions that are generally considered as the basic prerequisites of normal social life: marriage, the family, education, religion (cf. Jelly 1826; Cundall 1939; Long 1774, II:246; Mahon 1839).

The white ruling class at least chose things this way. For the slaves there was not even the dubious advantage of such a choice. They came in great numbers from all over the coastal belt of West Africa. In 1703 there were about 45,000 of them on the island. Fifty years later the slave population had almost tripled, to an estimated 130,000 souls. In 1800 the number had increased to 300,939, and in 1834, when the Emancipation Act was ratified, the population stood at an estimated 311,070. This high rate of increase was achieved almost entirely by the importation of fresh Africans, since the estimated average annual rate of natural decrease was approximately 1.6 percent—so heavy was the mortality rate, especially during the first years of seasoning (Roberts 1957:36).

The area of West Africa from which these Africans came is characterized by a considerable degree of tribal and cultural diversity. While the range of tribal provenance was wide (and even included a few odd importees from as far east as Madagascar), we have elsewhere indicated that well over two thirds of the Africans who came to Jamaica derived from the areas now known as Ghana and Nigeria. During our period, however, slaves from Ghana constituted the single largest ethnic group and, for a short but not insignificant period (1700–25), slaves from Dahomey (then the Slave Coast) also made up a significant minority (Le Page and DeCamp 1960:Ch. 4; Patterson 1967:142–44). We have elsewhere argued that the ethnohistorical data strongly suggest that while elements of West African cultures did survive the process of enslavement (and would certainly have been most marked during our period), there was a general disintegration of the cultures of the imported Africans. Like their masters' culture, but for somewhat different reasons, the

Africans' beliefs, values, and ideas, not to mention the intricate structural contexts (which were of degrees of complexity varying from the loose segmentary organization of the Ibos to the formidable empire of the Ashantis) within which they functioned, rapidly collapsed under the vicious impact of slavery (cf. Patterson 1966).

During the first eighty-five years of the British colonization of Jamaica, then, we find this sorry sociological spectacle: a pseudo-society in which there were two quite distinct groups of people, both strangers to the land on which they met, both strangers to each other. Both groups were experiencing, in different ways, the dissolution of their traditional cultures. Both groups despised, distrusted, and loathed each other. Only the impulse of greed, the chains of slavery, and the crack of the cart whip kept them together. But such ingredients proved a poor social mortar. Without the welding force of some minimum set of shared values or collective sentiments, without any basis on consensus or agreement whatsoever, without a ruling-class ideology that, even in the vaguest way, purported to rationalize the system, what remained was a brittle, fragile travesty of a society, which lingered during these years constantly on the brink of upheaval and anarchy. Quite often it threatened to topple right over during the more dramatic moments of the revolts we shall presently describe, clinging as it did to the edge of order by the very slimmest of social threads.

This study has three objectives. First, to undertake a detailed survey of the revolts. No adequate historical analysis yet exists of this vital episode in West Indian history. Available accounts are either too inaccurate or superficial or ideologically biased, however well meaning. And invariably the same sources are employed, neglecting valuable contemporary accounts both in printed and manuscript form.

Second, an attempt will be made to explain these revolts in structural rather than purely historical terms.[2] That is, we shall place the revolts in comparative perspective, which will

[2] Sociohistorical analysis lies halfway between purely historical and purely sociological analysis of data on past social actions. Historical understanding is generally understood to be concerned largely with the uniqueness of the social actions studied (Dray 1964:8–10) and, insofar as this kind of understanding involves causal explanations at all, such explanations can never be *sufficient* in that only certain of the *necessary* conditions isolated from the immediate antecedents of the case being explained can be

allow for an isolation of the specific features of the Jamaican slave system that are necessary to and, to some extent, sufficient for, an explanation of the incidence of revolts.

And third, on the basis of our analysis, we hope to formulate a general hypothesis regarding the causes of slave revolts, which may act as a guiding principle in future research on the subject.

PART 2

In 1655, as their masters fled under the onslaught of the invading English soldiers, fifteen hundred slaves formerly belonging to the Spaniards suddenly found themselves with a precarious though avidly grasped freedom. During the next five years, as the remnants of the Spanish settlers continued to put up their last-ditch guerrilla resistance, the British conquerors repeatedly tried to woo them to their side by offering clemency and good treatment. While a few mulattoes took up the offer, the entire population of blacks maintained a careful distance between themselves and the strangers on the coast (Taylor 1965:101–2).

At first the blacks wandered uncertainly about the foothills of the parishes of St. Catherine and Clarendon, no doubt

---

known (ibid., Ch. 4, passim). A purely sociological interpretation of historical events, on the other hand, sees such events not in their uniqueness, but as kinds of action. They are, to use Popper's term, "means to certain ends"—those of generalization and hypothesis construction (Popper 1962, Vol. 2:263).

Sociohistorical analysis of the type employed in this study shares with history an interest in the uniqueness of the events studied. Unlike history, however, this approach seeks for more than a limited number of *necessary* conditions, which are inevitably selected on the basis of value judgments (see Becker 1959 and I. Berlin 1959). This it does by explaining the events structurally. But such structural explanations are only made possible by the use of certain working hypotheses, which are derived from a preliminary survey of similar kinds of events elsewhere—in short, by an initial comparative sifting of the data on the class of events within which the unique set of events being examined falls. These working hypotheses are also, to a limited extent, supplemented by deductions from relevant areas of sociological theory. The sociohistorian, however, does not go beyond such preliminary comparative sifting, for the major object of his inquiry is to explain the particular, the unique set of events. At the most, then, his work *illustrates* his hypotheses. It is the role of the sociologist to test such hypotheses.

trying to make some sense of the situation, and at the same time devising a strategy for maintaining their freedom. Eventually they formed themselves into three groups under elected leaders. One of these groups settled in the mountains overlooking Guanaboa Vale under the bold, astute leader called Juan Lubola (often referred to in the English records as Juan de Bolas) (ibid., 98–99; *CSP* 1661–68, No. 411). A second group established their village at Los Vermejales[3] under their leader Juan de Serras (ibid., 99). This group eventually came to be called the Vermahalis or Vermehaly band by the British. The third group remains obscure. A recent writer suggests that they took root somewhere in the valley running between the Clarendon plains and Porras (Porus) (ibid.).

Taking the view that, as far as whites were concerned, the known evil was always to be preferred to the unknown, the ex-slaves continued to associate with the Spanish guerrillas scattered about the mountains. It was, however, a relationship of equals. They were not, as a conservative Jamaican historian recently suggests, merely auxiliaries of the Spaniards but independent guerrillas who associated with their former Spanish masters when it suited their interests (ibid., 100). Indeed, the Spanish guerrillas were far more dependent on them than they were on the Spanish, since the latter relied entirely on them for their food supplies. Occasionally they offered their vastly superior guerrilla skills as mercenaries to their ex-masters, but at the same time they plundered and harassed the British to their own ends quite independently, and certainly far more effectively than the Spaniards did, as the British unequivocally admitted in their dispatches.[4]

[3] Los Vermejales was situated on a plateau in the mid-interior of Jamaica. Juan de Serras' band was referred to variously as the Vermejales, Vermehali, or Varmehaly Negroes. When the blacks moved some miles to the west of the original site they carried the name with them, and the new site later became known by the corrupted form of Vera Ma Hollis.

[4] The scattered references in the John Thorloe State Papers, Vol. 4, BM, which the author himself often quotes, flatly contradict this assertion. It is remarkable how Taylor, while throughout the work maintaining, rightly, a certain skepticism regarding the Spanish documents, on this one point is prepared to accept their word when it is clear that unlike the British, they had every reason to exaggerate their command of the situation and the continued dependence of the blacks.

In June 1658 the Spanish guerrilla band, under their stubborn and devoted leader Ysassi, suffered a disastrous defeat at Rio Nuevo and was forced to retreat from the fort they had erected there. Not long after this, the head of the English regiment stationed at Guanaboa discovered the richly cultivated village of Lluidas Vale, and instead of attempting to take it, sought an alliance with Lubola. The terms offered by the British were not disagreeable. In exchange for ceasing to support the Spanish, the freedom of Lubola and all his men would be recognized as well as his right to govern his people. Realizing that the Spanish were then on their last legs, anyway, and being unprepared to risk the destruction of his two hundred acres of carefully cultivated crops (at that time the largest single source of locally grown food), Lubola agreed to the terms offered (see Appendix, *JHA*, Vol. 1; also *CSP*, 1661–68, No. 411).

This, of course, spelled disaster for the Spanish guerrillas, who were now not only without their major supplier of food, but who were also faced with the prospect of a British ally who knew all their secret hideouts and who was more skilled in the techniques of guerrilla warfare. After that it was simply a mopping-up operation for the British soldiers. By 1660 the last of the Spanish had left.

Among the instructions given to the British commander in 1662 previous to the setting up of civil government was an order to "give encouragements as securely you may to such Negroes, natives, and others, as shall submit to live peaceable under His Majesty's obedience and in due submission to the government of the island" (Instructions [No. 11] to Colonel Doyley, Appendix, *JHA*, Vol. 1). The next year Lubola and his "Pelinco of negroes, about 150" were granted full civil rights, each man receiving thirty acres of land. Lubola was made a magistrate and his men formed into a "Black Militia" of "Lancers and archers." A few of the more adventurous even became private men of war (Appendix, *JHA*, Vol. 1).

The remaining black guerrilla bands had always viewed Lubola's alliance with the British with some suspicion. This was not allayed by his formal recognition and the remolding of his men into a black militia. When, however, Lubola's enthusiasm for the conquerors led him to assist them in searching for, and destroying, the blacks who continued to reject the British overtures, the latter realized that what may have begun as a slightly suspect, if understandable, act of *realpolitik,* had now degenerated into downright treachery. Sometime toward the end of 1663 he was killed as he attempted to lead a party on the Vermejales blacks (*CSP* 1661–68, No. 1038).

Juan de Serras continued to harass the British, who made several unsuccessful attempts to dislodge him. When further attempts to negotiate with him failed, the British lost patience and, in 1670, he and all his men were declared outlaws, with a price of £30 on de Serras' head and £20 on all his followers' heads. It was about this time that the term "Maroon" came to be applied to these black guerrillas.[5]

Under pressure from the British, the group retreated to the uninhabited northeastern section of the island. The whites were greatly relieved at their withdrawal and, since they were no longer molested by them, decided to leave them in peace. "In the course of years afterwards," a contemporary narrator informs us, "their companions were either dead or too old to guide parties to their haunts, the ways of them became utterly unknown to the white people and so they continued for many years" (Anon., "Account . . . ," op. cit.).

In the meantime, the newly arrived British settlers had begun to import their own slaves into the island. At first, most of these slaves came with the white migrants from Barbados and the other eastern Caribbean colonies (Patterson 1967: 135). Soon, however, slaves were coming directly from Africa. In 1662 there were about 550 blacks on the island. Two years later there were 8,000. During the brief period in which anything like a serious attempt at a white "colonie de peuplement" was under way—1664–90—the slave population, as one would expect, grew relatively slowly, there being only 9,500 slaves in 1673. Twenty years later, however, the slave population had quadrupled and, as we have noted above, there were 45,000 slaves on the island in 1703 (ibid., 95).

For this sudden influx of Africans the still-unsettled whites were quite ill prepared. The "pioneer" colonial system they sought to erect would soon collapse under the combined strain of land monopoly and African slave labor. There was

[5] Anon., "Account of the Maroons and the Late War. . . ." C. E. Long Papers, 12431, BM ms. The term "Maroon" is derived from the Spanish *cimarrón,* meaning a runaway or "unruly." See Cassidy 1961.

the more immediate problem, however, of how to control the newly imported slaves.

In 1673 the first blow was struck. In the thinly peopled parish of St. Ann, 200 slaves belonging to Major Sebly's plantation, nearly all of whom were Coromantee,[6] killed their master and about 13 other whites, then went on to plunder several smaller estates in the neighborhood, procuring all the arms and ammunition they could lay their hands on (Anon. "Account . . . ," op. cit.). By the time the whites had mustered a party, the rebels had all retreated to secure positions in the mountains around the borders of Clarendon, St. Elizabeth, and St. Ann. The first party of whites that went after them was "nearly destroyed," and this "not only discouraged other parties from going against them but also encouraged many other Negroes to rise, throw off their chains and join up with them" (ibid.). These groups of rebels formed the nucleus of what later became known as the Leeward band of Maroons.[7]

Five years after this uprising, in 1678, another serious rebellion took place. One Sunday afternoon, the slaves on Captain Duck's plantation, situated only four miles from the capital, St. Jago, noticing that the river, which ran between the plantation and the town, had risen so high that it appeared impassable, decided to seize the opportunity for freedom. The whites on the estate were attacked, Major Duck seriously wounded, and his wife killed. A black traitor swam the river and gave the alarm in St. Jago, whereupon a troop of horse, after crossing the river with some difficulty, counterattacked. Some of the rebels were killed, and those who were taken prisoner were "put to exemplary violent deaths" (Barham 1722).

Between 1685 and 1686 there were several revolts, the participants of which joined with the growing bands of rebels encamped in the leeward part of the island. In early August 1685 all the slaves belonging to a widow, Mrs. Grey, at Guanaboa rose in rebellion, along with the slaves from four neighboring plantations, altogether making a party of about 150. They seized all the arms on Grey's estate, then attacked

[6] The term "Coromantee" or "Coromantyn" was used by the Jamaican planters to describe slaves from the Gold Coast, more particularly, slaves of Akan-speaking origin.

[7] Not the revolt of 1690, as suggested by Dallas (1803, I:26) and Hart 1950.

another plantation, where they killed one white and wounded another. A detachment of 70 soldiers was beaten off by the rebels, who then sought the refuge of the hills. Once out of the range of the whites, they divided themselves into "2 or 3 parties." One party consisted of the "stoutest and best armed," who marched northward across the mountainous backbone of the island until they reached St. Ann. Pursued by the whites, they suddenly changed their course and headed east toward the parish of St. Mary, killing several whites and destroying their settlements on the way. In the end, of the 150 slaves who rebelled, 7 were killed in battle, 30 were captured, and 50 surrendered. The rest remained at large and were unsuccessfully hunted by Captain Davis and his party of imported Indian trackers. By September 1685, however, all the parties out against the rebels were recalled and paid off (Molesworth to Whitehall, CO 138/5, ff. 87; *CSP* 1685–88, Nos. 339–72).

This may have been the same rebellion led by the slave called Cuffee (Cofi: an Akan or "Coromantee" name). If so, they continued to harass the whites until April 1686, growing each day "more formidable than ever." In November 1685, £10 reward was offered for Cuffee and £5 for each of the "chiefest five others." When Cuffee was killed in April 1686, the number of parties out against them "were reduced to three" (*CSP*, 1685–88, Nos. 445, 560, 623).

By this time the different rebel bands had moved farther to the east, eventually taking up residence in the parish of St. George. Here they settled in three villages formed on the basis of tribal differences (Molesworth to Whitehall, CO 138/5; *CSP* 1685–88, Nos. 869, 883). While roaming the woods about the border of St. George and St. Mary, the rebel bands came upon another strange group of fugitives of whom no one had yet heard. Sometime between 1669 and 1670 a slave ship with an unusual cargo of slaves from Madagascar was wrecked near Morant Point at the eastern tip of the island. Those slaves who somehow managed to reach shore fled to the hills and later, in association with several runaways, set up a cluster of villages in the more remote areas of the eastern hinterlands (*CSP*, 1685–88, No. 883).

Joined now by the rebels formerly under Cuffee and possibly the parties from Guanaboa, they made up a formidable band, which often daringly descended in raiding parties on the plantations on the coastal plains. Three parties of whites were constantly out against them, scouring the parishes of St. George, St. Thomas, and St. Mary, but their failure to check the onslaught of the rebels proved "so discouraging to the poorer sort of people, that those of St. George," according to the governor, "unless relieved, are prepared to desert their settlements" (ibid.). The governor considered the situation sufficiently grave to necessitate the enforcement of martial law and stepped up the number and size of the parties. But they continued to have little success (*CSP*, 1685–88, Nos. 965, 1021, 543, 1286).

Four years later a new uprising broke out. In July 1690, 400 slaves, again mainly from the Gold Coast, belonging to Sutton's plantation in the parish of Clarendon, disposed of the person in charge of stores and, after seizing all the arms they could carry, proceeded to the next estate, where they killed the white overseer and set the house afire. The troops were called out, and 12 of the rebels were killed in the ensuing engagement. In the course of the following month, 60 women and children and 10 men surrendered. With 318 of them still at large, however, the Governor (Inchiquin) feared "that (it) will be very dangerous to the mountain plantations." This group of rebels eventually joined ranks with the Leeward gang already established in the mountains "and greatly strengthened their party, having good arms and plenty of ammunition" (Inchiquin to Lords, CO 138/7). Yet another rebellion took place in 1696 on the estate of Captain Herring, who was away at the time. His wife and some of his children died in the uprising, and the slaves, along with several more from neighboring estates, went off to join the Leeward group (Anon., "Account . . . ," op. cit.).

It is now time to take up the progress of the original group of former Spanish slave rebels. During the last thirty years or so of the seventeenth century, little had been heard of them. Runaway slaves who had made the mistake of seeking refuge with them were often treated so badly that the unfortunate fugitives sometimes fled back to their masters or, when they could, joined ranks with other, smaller bands of runaways. At the commencement of the eighteenth century, however, the group had a radical change of policy. This change was induced partly by the successes of the rebels during the past three decades, and partly by their shortage of women, arms, and certain other basic necessities, such as salt and meat. They therefore made contact with the rebel bands that had established themselves in their part of the island and, at the same time, started to treat runaways more hospitably, often using the latter as guides when they raided the plantation stores of the whites. At this time they were settled in the hills beween the north and southeastern part of the island. In addition to several scattered villages, there was a sizable town of about three hundred people with one hundred acres of land, "well planted in provisions" (ibid.).

Between August and September of 1702, four parties were out searching for them. Eventually, one of these parties, consisting of over twenty soldiers, came upon the main rebel town, and a battle was fought that lasted for nearly six hours. The defenders of the rebel town boldly resisted the soldiers and, in the words of the governor, "faced our men so long as they had ammunition." When their limited stock of ammunition ran out they were obliged to retreat, leaving three of the whites wounded. Several of the rebels were killed and a few taken prisoner. The settlement was burned. A party of whites was posted there while the remaining three parties continued to pursue the rebels. "I take this thing," commented the governor in his report on the matter, "to be of as much consequence as any I can think of at present" (Beckford to Lords, *CSP*, 1702, Nos. 912, 928).

This thing became of even greater consequence in the ensuing months—so serious, in fact, that by the next January rather desperate underhand measures were being resorted to: Captain Codler, a leader of one of the white posses, was known to have entertained the wife of Bulley, one of the rebel leaders (under what circumstances we do not know) in a vain attempt at enticing the woman to betray her husband (*CSP*, 1703, No. 203).

While the Windward rebels continued to harass the whites, another group of Coromantee slaves rebelled. Thirty of them "attacked two or three places, burnt only one house and wounded one man." Twelve were taken or killed and the rest made their escape to the hills, leaving the whites "more apprehensive of some bloody design from them than any other enemy," which was no mean tribute, in view of the fact that the War of the Spanish Succession was then being waged and the islands were open game for French warships (*CSP*, 1704–5, No. 484).

In the meantime, the Leeward group of rebels were involved in some internecine disputes. Sometime not long before 1720, a Madagascan slave had led an uprising on Downs' plantation. With the slaves from the plantation of his former master, the Madagascan established a rebel camp in the mountains behind Deans Valley, where he augmented the number of his group by actively encouraging slaves on nearby plantations to run away and join him. The Madagascan, however, was unable to hit it off with the main band of Leeward rebels under Cudjoe, which was encamped a little higher up. A power struggle ensued between the two leaders, and after several "bloody battles" the Madagascan was slain and his party incorporated with Cudjoe's (Anon., "Account . . . ," op. cit.).

In 1722 the resistance movement entered a new, critical phase. Since all available lands on the fertile southern coastal plains were taken up, the planters began to open up the area around the northeastern coast. These new estates cut off the communications of the Windward rebels from the coast, making the procurement of vital necessities even more difficult. To prevent further white expansion, the new settlements were systematically plundered, "murders were daily committed, plantations burnt and deserted, every person settled near the mountains in dread both of the Rebels and mutinies in their own Plantations" (ibid.).

Let us briefly take stock of the situation in the midtwenties of the eighteenth century, the time that is traditionally regarded as the formal commencement of the First Maroon War. There were two main bands of rebels: the Leeward band, found in the precipitous areas near the center of the island; and the Windward, or northeastern, band. Each band was divided into several settlements centered on a main town or village and were both well organized.

At about this time the Leeward band elected a chief called Cudjoe, "a bold, skillful and enterprising man," remarkably adept at the techniques of guerrilla warfare. He was a short, stocky, powerfully built man with a humped back. On the occasion of his celebrated confrontation with the whites who had come to his camp to sue for peace, he was dressed in knee-length drawers, an old ragged coat, and a rimless hat, and carried on his right side a cow's horn of powder and a bag of shots, and on his left a broad, sheathed machete, which dangled from a strap slung around his shoulder. His black skin, like those of his followers, was tinted red by the bauxite-rich soil found in the part of the island that he controlled (Dallas 1803, I:54).

Not all aspects of Cudjoe's character were, however, without blemish. He could be ruthless, even brutal, to his own men and, at times, unnecessarily selfish in his dealings with fellow guerrilla fighters. Worse, he was extremely ambivalent toward white people. He boldly resisted them as long as they sought to subdue him by the use of brute force and was generally highly suspicious of them. He was, however, all too easily seduced by their call for peace and friendship, and the account of his extraordinary behavior when he finally confronted the whites who had come to negotiate is still something of an embarrassment (ibid., 55–56; Anon., "Account . . . ," op. cit.).

Unfortunately, we do not know a great deal about the leaders immediately under Cudjoe's command, appointed by him to lead the outlying villages. Two of these were his brothers, Accompong and Johnny, and the other two captains were Cuffee and Quao. From their names it is clear that whatever the tribal composition of the followers, the leadership of the Leeward band was formed almost entirely of Coromantee slaves of originally Akan-speaking stock.[8]

At the head of the main settlement of the Windward band —Nanny Town—was Cuffee, who was as skillful and as shrewd a leader as Cudjoe, but unlike the latter, both he and his successors, especially Quao, seem to have been more psychologically liberated in their attitude toward the white planters. Cuffee ruled his band of three hundred or so men with iron discipline, distinguishing himself from the rest by wearing a silver-laid hat and a small sword. All defectors and other delinquents in the group were punished by the gun ("The Further Examination of Sarra, alias Ned, . . . ," October 1733, CO 137/21, f. 42).

There were many other leaders who attained distinction during the revolts. One of the most important was Kishee, "a great commander" of one of the northeastern groups who repeatedly outmaneuvered the whites in the region of the

[8] The names of the leading rebels of the Leeward group were: Captains Cudjoe, Accompong, Johnny, Cuffee, and Quaco; in the Windward group the leading figures were: Captains Cuffee, Kishee, and Quao. All, except Johnny, are names frequently found on the Gold Coast (now Ghana), especially among the Akan-speaking peoples.

Cotterwoods. He was eventually killed by a black traitor called Scipio (*JHA*, Vol. 3:121).

The most lengendary character of the wars, however, was Nanny, on whom, unfortunately, little is known positively. We know that she was the chief sorcerer or *obeah* woman of the main group of Windward rebels, and in this role exercised considerable influence over them. The whites dreaded her and when, in 1733, she was killed by a slave, Cuffee, they thankfully rewarded him for his deed. Nanny, who gave her name to the main rebel town, now exists more in legend than in fact, but there can be no doubt that she existed and that the role she played tactically and psychologically—not only in boosting morale but in maintaining loyalty by her highly sanctioned oaths of secrecy was of tremendous value (ibid.).[9]

Behind Nanny Town was another relatively large village called Guy's Town, after the name of its leader. It was well planted, contained about two hundred well-armed men, and even more women and children. The rebels of this village tended to play a passive role during the war, fighting mainly to defend their passes ("The Further Examination . . . ," op. cit.). Apart from their usual settlements, the rebels had patches of eddoes, plantains, and yams scattered in remote areas over the countryside, which they used only during periods of retreat and emergency. Some of the bands also had a sexually segregated pattern of settlement, which ensured the protection of their womenfolk and children from the savagery of the white raiding parties (*JHA*, Vol. 3:62).

The rebels relied not only on their guerrilla skills in compensating for the vastly superior weaponry of the whites, but also on a sophisticated intelligence system in which many of the slaves still on the plantations functioned, providing the rebels with information about the plans of the whites. A committee of the House of Assembly commented despairingly in 1733 that the rebels "are as well acquainted with our designs as we ourselves" (*JHA*., Vol. 3:210; cf. also Dallas 1803, I:34). Many other slaves, in addition, provided the rebels with ammunition and sometimes even harbored them on the estates. The rebels also took full advantage of the dependence of the whites on their slaves in their campaigns. In one case a large party of baggage Negroes was en-

[9] On the surviving legend of Nanny among twentieth-century maroons, see J. Williams 1938.

couraged to mutiny and desert with all their provisions by the two Coromantee interpreters who were accompanying the party (*JHA*, Vol. 3:155).

In the midtwenties the two main parties together "amounted to some thousands," the Windward group being "the most numerous," and not, as is commonly believed, the Leeward group (Anon., "Account . . . ," op. cit.). Regarding the tribal origins of the rebels, we do not, of course, know where the original band of Spanish ex-slaves came from, although the fact that ex-slaves from the Gold Coast eventually absorbed them would suggest that they too were from this area. The great majority of the rebels during the British era were Coromantee or Akan-speaking slaves from the Gold Coast. Another important group were also the Papaws, or slaves from the Slave Coast (now Dahomey).[10] It is significant that the two major groups of rebels came from the areas of the Guinea Coast where the great West African empires of Ashanti and Dahomey were at that time at the height of their imperial expansion (cf. Panikker n.d., esp. Ch. 8, and Claridge 1964, Vol. 1).

The situation, from the white viewpoint, became most critical in 1730 after repeated attempts at subduing the rebels had failed, and the rebels had become daily more bold and numerous. In June of that year, Governor Hunter told the House that:

> The Slaves in rebellion, from the increase of their numbers by the late desertions from several settlements, or from the bad success of common parties, are grown to that height of insolence that your frontiers that are no longer in any sort of security, must be deserted, and then the danger must spread and come nearer if not prevented [Hunter to Assembly, CO 137/18 of *JHA*, Vol. 3:708].

In the same address the governor told of the humiliating defeat and running away of a "grand party, consisting of 95 shots and 22 baggage Negroes, chiefly volunteers and detached men from the militia," when they had tried to take

---

10 Ashworth, one of the white commanders, in answering the charge against him that he maliciously refused to support Sambo, the black commander of one of the white parties, admitted that his opinion of the latter was lowered by the fact that Sambo, a Creole, could speak neither Coromantee nor Papaw (*JHA*, Vol. 3, p. 158).

the main rebel settlement (See "The Examination of Nicholas Physham," CO 137/18, ff. 84–85; also Hunter to Lords, ibid., f. 78.).

Panic soon began to set in among the white population. It was widely rumored that the rebels had communicated with the governor of the Spanish colony, of "Carcas," or "Cracas," offering to hand over the island to Spain when they had taken it over, on condition that the Spaniards guaranteed their freedom, a rumor that was not entirely without foundation.[11] Fear of the rebels largely accounted for a marked decline in the white population during this period, although the brutal treatment of indentured servants by their masters, in addition to the "low and languishing" state of the economy (due partly to severe drought and two recent hurricanes) were also responsible (Hunter to Assembly, *JHA*, Vol. 3, pp. 11–12). In response to the dismal picture of the colony painted by the governor, the British government sent two regiments of foot soldiers to the island from Gibraltar (CO 137/19, f. 19). Another large party was sent out from Port Antonio against the Windward rebels, but even before they had set out on their mission the governor expressed grave doubts about what they could achieve, in view of the incompetence of the commanding officers (ibid., f. 17). His fears were certainly not groundless, for the party was thoroughly routed by the rebels, and one of the commanding officers was later court-martialed (ibid., f. 30).

In November 1731 yet another large party set out against the rebels. At last the whites achieved some success. One of the villages was taken and burned after the inhabitants had abandoned it (ibid., f. 108). But the success was short-lived. Captain Thomas Peters, in command of the country party, withdrew a few days after taking the village. Whether this withdrawal was due to a counter attack by the blacks or just plain stupidity on Peters' part is unclear, but he was ordered to retake the town and failed to do so (*JHA*, Vol. 3:43). On the fourth of January, 1732, the Governor informed an emergency meeting of the Legislature of the "news of the bad success of the parties sent out against the slaves in re-

---

[11] "The deposition of John Tello," ibid., f. 98; also, "The Deposition of W. Quarrell," ibid., f. 100. "Carcas" or "Cracas" seems to be, from supporting evidence, a mistaken reference to Cuba, although Venezuela cannot be ruled out. See also, "Letter to James Knight. An Account of the Origins and Progress of the Revolted Negroes," ms., C. E. Long Papers, 12431, BM.

bellion on the north side of the island," and of his fears of a general uprising (ibid., 46–47). Knowing well the lack of discipline and foresight—even in matters so grave—of the local whites, he did not mince words in his assessment of the dangerous situation they were in:

> There never was a point of time which more required your attention to the safety of this island than at present; your slaves in rebellion, animated by their success, and others (as it is reported) ready to join them on the first favourable opportunity, your militia very insignificant, the daily decrease of the numbers of your white people and increase of the rebel slaves; these circumstances must convince you of the necessity of entering upon more solid measures than have been hitherto resolved upon for your security; all former attempts against these slaves having been either unsuccessful or to very little purpose [ibid.].

The governor passed on to the Assembly a suggestion made by the British government that a negotiated settlement be arrived at with the rebels "by which they are to agree to be transported to some of the Bahama islands," but no one took that seriously. So great was the fear of the rebels and the inability of the whites to resist them that a proposal by the governor to disband and settle the soldiers on favorable terms in the northeastern section of the island was tepidly received by them (ibid., ff. 47, 57). Since the defeat of the party in the early part of January 1731, numerous slaves had been encouraged to desert their masters and join the rebels, a matter that was of increasing concern to the whites. In addition, many of the baggage Negroes and black-shots deserted to the side of the rebels, taking arms and baggage with them (See Letter to Lords, CO 137/20, ff. 47, 54, 67). An attempt to halt this trend by offering freedom to every slave who killed or brought in a rebel met with little success (*JHA*, Vol. 3:51).

In March 1732, two large parties set out against both bands of rebels. One of them, consisting of 93 armed blacks and 5 white overseers, in addition to 4 columns of soldiers and 28 baggage Negroes, marched on the south side of the island against the Leeward band. The other party, consisting of 86 whites, 131 armed blacks, and 61 baggage Negroes, marched from Port Antonio against the Windward group of rebels (CO 137/20, f. 63; J.H.A., Vol. 3:77). The parties seemed to have met initially with some success, as three of the main settlements of the rebels, including Nanny Town, were taken. However, the counterattacks of the rebels, combined with "the desertion and backwardness of the baggage slaves"; the incompetence of the white commanding officers (one of whom, Leo, was killed; the other, Peters, was later recalled, "having manifestly misbehaved himself"); the extremely heavy rainfall during the engagement; and the exhausted state of the island's treasury, not to mention the general scarcity of currency—the last an endemic economic problem—meant that these successes could not be followed up (*JHA*, Vol. 3:77, 81). Four parties of blacks were sent out against the rebels, one of them under the most competent of the commanding officers in the service of the whites, the black freedman called, appropriately, Sambo (ibid, 99). However, in spite of the offer of freedom and spoils to the slaves in the party, they met with little success, taking only one of the plantain walks of the rebels. One source of failure was the high desertion rate of the blacks, which at one time became so serious that special guards had to be set up to cut them off (ibid., 81–82).

After the fall of Nanny Town, the main group of Windward rebels retreated toward Carrion Crow Hill, where they sought refuge with the Guy's Town group. Others scattered in small parties in the region of the Cotterwoods ("The Further Examination," op. cit.). Meanwhile, the main group of Leeward rebels set up a new town west of the recently destroyed one, in the parish of St. James. In November 1732 they suffered another setback when Whiles Town, a village not far from the main town, was taken by the whites, who started to make plans to set up a permanent base there (*JHA*, Vol. 3:104). Early in 1733, the dislodged Windward rebels reorganized themselves and, under Kissey's brilliant leadership, retook Nanny Town. Morrison and Ashworth, the white commanders holding the town, had intelligence of the intended counterattack but were so outclassed by the rebels that the knowledge was of little use to them (CO 137/20, f. 120; also *JHA*, Vol. 3:122, 154).

Perhaps the most impressive display of guerrilla warfare by the rebels was the second battle of Nanny Town, when they trounced the party sent out to retake it. In local terms this party was a formidable force. There were one hundred trained soldiers, taken from the two regiments sent from Gibraltar, a hundred local whites, and two hundred seamen from a warship then stationed at the island (Hunter to Lords, CO 137/20, f. 165). The party first divided itself into two divisions. The local whites made up one of these, and they were sent up to Carrion Crow hill, above Nanny Town, to cut the rebels off from the rear. They did not get very far. On the way they were ambushed by the rebels, and the entire division scrambled frantically back to Port Antonio without firing a shot.

The other division, which was supposed to have led the attack, placed the sailors at the front and the independent soldiers in the rear, an arrangement that in no way pleased the sailors. Two miles away from Nanny Town they were attacked by the rebels, and after several skirmishes in which they were utterly outclassed, the sailors fell into a panic and a large number of them fled to the soldiers in the rear with tall tales about the massacre of most of the commanding officers. When, therefore, reinforcements were urgently requested from the front, many of the soldiers refused to budge. In any event, those who sought to obey the order were unable to, since their black guide suddenly refused to show them the way through the woods. A fracas ensued in which the hysterical sailors turned on their own provisions and plundered them, possibly to ensure that they would not be able to carry out a sustained engagement against the dreaded guerrillas. Eventually, the entire party had to retreat in confusion. The guide who refused to lead the soldiers was later made a scapegoat, court-martialed, and shot (see "The Substance of Capt. Williams' Examination," CO 137/20, f. 154; "Extract out of Lieut. Swanton's Journal . . . ," ibid., ff. 192–93; also ibid., f. 180).

Conditions on the island had now grown really desperate for the planter caste. In August 1733 the rebels took possession of Hobby's plantation and easily repelled the parties sent out to relieve it (*JHA*, Vol. 3:195–96, 207). A planter wrote home to England in December 1733, "we are in terrible circumstances in respect to the rebellious Negroes, they got the better of all our partys, our men are quite despirited and dare not look them in the face in the Open Ground or in Equal Numbers" ("Paragraph in a letter from Jamaica," CO 137/21, f. 11). That same month Hunter, the governor, broke another "terrible" piece of news to the British government. Way over in Hanover parish, at the western end of the island, another group of blacks had risen in rebellion where the whites "had least expected it." The revolt of the blacks was now being waged at both extremities of the island as well as in the center (CO 137/21, ff. 16–17).

The war dragged on during 1734, with the planters getting the worst of almost all engagements. By now, however, "the greatest danger" for them was the remarkable number of slaves who were abandoning the plantations in order to join ranks with the main rebel bands or to set up their own guerrilla groups. In February alone, twenty-two slaves "pulled foot" from Port Antonio, while in St. Thomas forty "able Coromantines" did the same (ibid., f. 44). Encouraged by their successes and by the moral and active support of the enslaved population in their area, the Windward rebels now resumed the initiative in the struggle. The letters to Britain took on a new tone of even greater apprehension. One planter wrote in March,

> The Rebellious Negroes openly appear in Arms and are daily Increasing . . . they have already taken possession of three Plantations within eight miles of Port Antonio by which means they Cutt off any Communications between that Harbour by Land. . . . They have also attacked a place called the Breast Work where Several Men Armed were lodged to cover the workmen ["Extract of a Letter from Jamaica," ibid., f. 57].

Ayscough became governor after Hunter's death in March and continued to lead the whites' defenses as best he could, although he had grave doubts concerning the efficacy of the present methods employed against the rebels. Nonetheless, the whites persevered, and on the twentieth of April two large parties attacked the main town of the Windward rebels. After a battle lasting five days, in which eighty members of the white party were killed, Nanny Town was recaptured by the whites (Ayscough to Lords, CO 137/21, ff. 174–75). This victory, however, had been won at such great expense, and its implications were so slight, that the news was received with little enthusiasm by the white population. According to Ayscough, "the country had been at the Expense of one hundred thousand pounds within these five years and no Benefit received or relief had." He reported also that many of the "black shots" recruited by the whites were in communication with the rebels and were supplying them with arms. Later in the year he finally discharged all the parties. In October martial law was once more declared.

The Windward rebels, after retreating from their main town for the second time, now split up into two parties. In 1735, one of these, consisting of about three hundred men, women, and children, made an epic march of over one hundred miles across the densely wooded and precipitous mountain ranges of the island in order to join ranks with Cudjoe's Leeward band. The whites received intelligence of the march and hastily sent out parties to "oppose, disperse or destroy them," but the marchers "fought and forced their way on" (CO 137/22, f. 37; Anon., "Account . . . ," op. cit.). The march, apart from being a superb tactical maneuver, also paid certain psychological dividends in that the planters were left completely mystified and outwitted by it. "It is Supposed and feared," wrote Cunningham, the new governor, "they are Settling themselves in some Strong fastness and when that is done, will begin their ravages Again, in Such parts of the Island, as may be of more Mischievous Consequences than they have hitherto attempted" (CO 137/22, f. 40).

There is some uncertainty concerning what exactly transpired when the main body of Windward rebels met Cudjoe and his band. From all available sources, it would appear that Cudjoe received them anything but warmly. His response was a bitter blow for the Windward refugees. Cudjoe's reasons for his coolness, while understandable, were very revealing. First, he claimed that he did not have enough provisions for both parties. Second,

He blamed them for great indiscretion in their conduct before the parties were sent against them and told them it was a rule with him always not to provoke the white people unless forced to it and showed them several graves where he said people were buried whom he had executed for murdering white men contrary to his orders and said their barbarous and unreasonable cruelty and insolence to the white people was the cause of their fitting out parties who would in time destroy them all [Anon., "Account . . . ," op. cit.].

Even allowing for the patronizing esteem in which the chronicler, like most of the whites after the war, held Cudjoe, which may have overemphasized his Uncle Tom image, this alleged response is basically not inconsistent with the general pattern of the man's character or the way in which he conducted the war which, in contrast to the tactics of the Windward rebels, was essentially defensive.

Cudjoe's third reason, according to the above source, for rejecting an alliance with the Windward rebels was the fact that as absolute master of his own party he was not prepared to incorporate within his domain independent companies who held allegiance to other leaders. However, he did offer them temporary accommodation—for several months, it would appear—until they were in a position to return to their former quarters (Dallas 1803, 1:27; note, however, that Dallas is in error on the dating of this march).

At the beginning of 1736 there were three main rebel towns (Gregory to Lords, CO 137/22, f. 54). One was in St. George's parish, which in the early part of the year was the main abode of the remaining Windward rebels; another in St. Elizabeth under Accompong; and the third in St. James under Cudjoe. The largest of these towns was "supposed to contain in the whole about one thousand men, women and children" (ibid.). "Upwards of three hundred," who had not joined the main settlements, were scattered in small groups in the vicinity of the three great camps. Presumably Cudjoe's settlement in St. James was the largest party, since it attracted most attention during the first part of the year (see "A Journal of Proceedings in the Parties raised out of St. Ann and St. James . . . ," CO 137/22, ff. 57–58). The fact, too, that it was now accommodating the Windward refugees would have swelled the numbers to the size mentioned.

In the latter half of 1736 the rebels remained fairly quiet, especially during the last four months, but so much had the planters despaired of ever defeating them that they were content to let sleeping dogs lie. Governor Gregory wrote that he was at a loss to explain the relative quiet among the rebels for "the Success of our Partys has not been so considerable, nor their numbers so much lessened" (CO 137/22, f. 110). Clearly the Windward rebels at Cudjoe's camp were respecting his wishes, while those remaining in the northeast were biding their time as they recouped their losses and waited for the right opportunity to retake their beloved Nanny Town. Cudjoe as usual was playing his defensive game. All this, combined with the general view of the whites that "it would be advisable not to disturb them unless we could do it with some visible prospect of Success," accounted for the relative calm of the last months of 1736.

But it may have been the proverbial calm before the storm. The band of Windward refugees who had sought refuge with Cudjoe decided that they had had enough of his grudging hospitality and, in May 1737, set out on the grueling march back home to recover their lands. Gregory "had some intelligence of their design" but was unable to exploit it, for although he "took all precaution . . . to prevent it . . . their march was so silent and expeditious, and (his) orders so ill-executed that . . . (they) did not succeed" (ibid., f. 141). Having failed to stop them, Gregory decided that the whites had better swallow their pride and sue for peace. He made this suggestion to the Assembly, but they would have none of it (ibid.). Clearly, with their usual lack of foresight, the whites had been lulled into a false sense of security by the relative inactivity of the last months.

However, during the course of that year and the one that followed—1738—the Windward rebels began to reassert their claims to both freedom and land in the form of raids, ambushes, and strong defenses of their positions, the pattern and outcome of which were strikingly similar to those of previous years. The white population gradually came around to Gregory's view that nothing could be gained in the battle bush and that a treaty appeared to be the only way of settling the matter.

In February 1739, Colonel Guthrie, an able, popular planter-commander who had long been pressing for negotiations, was finally given the go-ahead by the governor, Trelawny. After surviving a few ambushes in which several men were lost, Guthrie and a party of the Independent Company under Captain Sadler finally contacted one of Cudjoe's commanders. The whites did everything to allay the strong suspicion of the rebels. Not only did they offer gifts and hostages, but the governor himself made the long and arduous march to a place hardly twenty miles from the main Maroon town to make himself available for the immediate ratification of the proposed treaty (Anon., "Account . . . ," op. cit.).

At a well-chosen defile, selected by the Maroons, Cudjoe finally met Guthrie under the protective eyes of the former's armed, hidden sentries. Cudjoe approached Guthrie, shook hands and, it is claimed, "threw himself to the ground, em-

bracing Guthrie's legs, kissing his feet, and asking his pardor
He seemed to have lost all his ferocity, and to have becom
humbly penitent and abject. The rest of the Maroons, follow
ing the example of their chief, prostrated themselves, and ex
pressed the most unbounded joy at the sincerity shown on th
side of the white people" (Dallas 1803, 1:56; also Anon., "A
count . . . ," op. cit.).

On the first of March, 1739, a fifteen-point peace treat
was signed between the Leeward Maroons and the white
(*JHA*, Vol. 3:457). The treaty ensured the liberty and free
dom of Cudjoe and all his followers and their right of owner
ship of all lands in the vicinity of their towns to the amour
of fifteen hundred acres. They were to remain in the area bu
could hunt wild hogs wherever they wished, except withi
three miles of any white settlement. Runaway slaves wh
had joined Cudjoe within the past two years were offered th
choice of returning to their masters with full pardon and ir
demnity or of remaining with the Maroons. Further, the Ma
roons were at liberty to sell their cash provisions in the mar
kets of neighboring towns as long as licenses were obtainec
If their rights were infringed by any white person the
could apply to any commanding officer or magistrate fc
justice; likewise, any Maroon who injured a white person ha
to be delivered to the white authorities for trial.

During their lifetime, Cudjoe and all his successors wer
given full powers to punish all offenders within their camp
except those guilty of murder. To facilitate communicatio
and "friendly correspondence," the Maroons were required t
cut roads between their towns and the coastal settlements c
the planters, and two white men, appointed by the governo
were to reside among them constantly.

Apart from the recognition of their freedom and land right
however, perhaps the most important parts of the treaty wer
those clauses that required the Leeward Maroons to assist th
whites in repelling not only external enemies, but "to tak
kill, suppress, or destroy . . . all rebels wheresoever they b
unless they submit to the same terms"; and further, that a
future runaways who sought refuge among them or were cap
tured by them, were to be returned to the whites, for whic
service the Maroons were to be compensated.

The implications of the treaty as a whole, but particularl
of the last two clauses, were not lost on all of Cudjoe's follow
ers, nor on the slave population. They were extremely embit

tered by what they could only interpret as a completely unnecessary sellout. In the act of ratifying his own freedom, Cudjoe had sealed the fate of future freedom-fighters, for with the Maroons on the side of the whites, no slave could hope to escape the tyranny of his master, either by running away or by rebellion.

While the whites rejoiced at the way they had succeeded in doing, in a single act of negotiation, what years of fighting had failed to accomplish, disgruntled and outraged elements from among both Cudjoe's camp as well as the slave population began to make plans for a last-ditch stand that would nullify the effects of the treaty. The first move was made by several of Cudjoe's "chief men," who got in touch with the slaves on neighboring plantations and incited them to revolt (see "Cudjoe's Fidelity," C. E. Long Papers, 12431). The plot was nipped in the bud by Cudjoe, who arrested the four ringleaders and sent them to the governor. They were tried, two of them were condemned to death, and the other two were ordered to be transported. The governor, however, as an act of goodwill, pardoned them and returned them to Cudjoe. But Cudjoe would have none of it. At least it could be said of him that he was a man of his word, however contemptible that word. He hung the two who were condemned to death and sent the other two back to the governor, insisting that they be transported. The governor granted his request and, like the rest of the white population, was doubtless very impressed with his zealous new ally (ibid.).

The slave population, however, was not prepared to take the treaty lying down. A mood of restlessness ran like a quake through it. They complained, with cutting irony, that freedom had been granted to those who had rebelled, while the mass of the loyal continued to suffer enslavement. More directly, they viewed with great alarm the elimination of the only real avenue of escape from the barbarity of their masters. Dissatisfaction "grew to such a height among them" that throughout the island, but especially in Spanish Town (St. Jago), they gathered into groups, where they made preliminary plans for revolt. The restive and mutinous spirit increased in intensity with each moment. Whites were everywhere openly being abused (ibid.).

Taking action just in time, the governor ordered a troop of horse against one of the larger groups of plotters and, in order to strike terror in the rest of the slave population, punished and executed most of them brutally, and transported the rest. The technique had the desired effect, and gradually the islandwide mood of unrest lessened (Anon, "Account . . . ," op. cit.).

In the meantime, attempts were being made to bring the Windward rebels to terms, although the latter showed little taste for the matter, stubbornly continuing with the resistance. Colonel Guthrie very reluctantly assumed the responsibility once more of negotiating a treaty, and assisted by the Maroons of Cudjoe's party, set off for St. George's parish. On his way he was "seized with a most violent griping pains in the bowels" and died a little after reaching his destination. It was strongly suspected that he was poisoned by one of the many slaves who "were in the utmost despair" over the settlement with Cudjoe and the prospect of a further treaty with the Windward Maroons (ibid.).

With the Leeward Maroons pledged to fight against them, and with their own party reduced in size, harassed and weary from bearing the brunt of the war against the whites for the past ten years, the Windward rebels, under their leader Quao, the last of the leaders before the end of the war (possibly Kissey's successor), had little choice but to sign a treaty similar in all but three respects to the one agreed with Cudjoe (ibid.). The atmosphere at the signing of the treaty was quite different from that at the agreement with the Leeward rebels. The Windward Maroons never ceased to be suspicious of the whites and made it quite clear that the treaty was signed with great reluctance and out of sheer necessity.

The white hostage who was left in their midst during negotiations complained later that the hatred that the Maroons bore for him and all whites was so great that even the children who gathered curiously around him poked his breast, with their fingers pointed as if they were knives, as they mockingly shouted: *"buckra, buckra"* ["white man, white man"]. His nervousness was not abated by the sight of the women who crowded around him, adorned with necklaces strung with the teeth of white men (Dallas 1803, 1:73).

At the end of the war there were four principal maroon towns, two on the Leeward side of the island, the other two on the Windward side. At the Leeward end there were Trelawny Town in St. James parish and Accompong Town in St. Elizabeth. The Maroons of the northeastern end of the island were settled mainly in Charles or Crawford Town in St. George's parish and Moore Town in Portland, formed when the rebels retreated from Nanny Town after it fell for the second time.

PART 3

How do we account for this remarkable tradition of revolt among the slaves of Jamaica? Certainly, as slave societies go, this is an unusual, perhaps unique record. One initially might be tempted to explain this record in largely psychological terms.[12] Such an attempt, however, would be not merely erroneous but irrelevant. Even if it could be proved that the Jamaican slave population was more prone to revolt than slaves from other societies, say the American South, we would still be left with the problem of explaining why they were thus more prone. The view, however, that a slave population can be more or less psychologically prone to revolt or, conversely, to dependence and docility, is, we think, without foundation, and rests on a highly simplistic view of slave personality, indeed, of human personality in general.

[12] For the best-known statement of this view, see Elkins 1959. See also Genovese 1967. I cannot agree with Genovese that Elkins does not equate childishness with docility. He does not simply "give such an impression"; it is clearly implied in the thesis. Nor do I find anything "subtle" or elusive in the idea that Sambo is employed to account for "most forms of day-to-day resistance." No one who has heard, say, West Indian middle-class housewives discussing "the maid problem" could find anything remotely subtle in this. Servile recalcitrance is by no stretch of the imagination the same thing as resistance, even if qualified as "day-to-day." Elkins, to justify the subtlety that Genovese so generously endows him with, would have had to show that the slave was actively role-playing, consciously duping the master, rather than behaving in a manner that came naturally. Apart from merely noting the possibility of such a distinction in a footnote, Elkins shuns the subject. The issue may seem irrelevant to white historians. For modern black historians, aware of the ideological implications of their work, and their intellectual responsibilities to their primary audience, it is a matter of the utmost importance. Of some interest is the exchange between Genovese and Herbert Aptheker in *Studies on the Left,* Vol. 6, No. 6, 1966. While I am in sympathy with many of the points raised by Professor Genovese in this exchange, I agree with Professor Woodward's contention that they need further substantiation. See also A. Sio's comments on the Elkins thesis in *Social and Economic Studies,* Vol. 16, No. 3, 1967.

Slavery is a denial of all freedom and, as such, is a denial of humanity, of the very essence of the human condition, for it is an attempt at objectification, at making the person a thing, a chattel. Hence, it is an absurd denial.[13] Faced with such an attempted denial, the slave, under certain conditions, may have appeared to acquiesce. Such apparent acquiescence may even, to a superficial observer, have seemed like an essential feature of the modal personality syndrome of the slave. This view is not only demonstrably one-sided, but fails largely in its inability to recognize, as Genovese points out, the all-too-human quality of contradiction. Stanley Elkins' "Sambo," the acquiescing, submissive slave, no doubt existed on one level, but along with it—we might even add, implied by it—was hatred of the master and the urge to destroy him.

For one thing, "Sambo," even on the shallow level interpreted by Elkins, was found in all slave systems and was certainly not a "peculiarly American" phenomenon. It was a commonplace in Jamaica, this most rebellious of slave systems, and in the island there was even a name for it, "Quashee" (Patterson 1967:174–81; see also Genovese 1967: 294–98). The fact that "Sambo" could be found in Jamaica not only disproves Elkins' claim that it was a peculiarly American phenomenon but questions the very basis of his interpretations of the so-called syndrome.

This is no place to undertake the much-needed task of properly analyzing the personality of the black slave (insofar as this is at all permitted by the available data). Our point here is to stress the irrelevance of psychological factors in the analysis of slave revolts. There is no correlation whatever between the modal personality of a slave population (whatever this may be) and the incidence of revolts among that population. This view is best supported by glancing briefly at one of the major personalities of the First Maroon War: Cudjoe. Cudjoe fully exhibits the kind of contradiction, mentioned earlier, that is the essence of the slave's personality, a contradiction necessitated by the existential absurdity and sociological depravity and oppression of his condition. The dis-

---

[13] For philosophical arguments likely to support what may be called the existential absurdity of slavery, see G. Marcel's very stimulating work, *The Existential Background of Human Dignity;* also Albert Camus' *The Rebel* and *The Myth of Sisyphus;* see also Hegel's highly suggestive discussion in his 1931:229–40.

cipline, skill, shrewdness, courage, and spirit of independence shown by Cudjoe throughout the wars is a model of the heroic man, incapable of being crushed by tyrannical conditions or overwhelmed by uneven odds. Up to the moment of his confrontation with Guthrie he seems to be the very antithesis of Elkins' "Sambo." Yet suddenly, faced with the white officer suing for peace, he undergoes what appears to be an amazing metamorphosis of character. The gallant, rebellious hero becomes a groveling fawn kissing the feet of his enemy. The poverty of Elkins' analysis becomes quite clear at this point, for there is no way in which it can explain this extraordinary behavior.

And yet, Cudjoe's *volte-face* is hardly surprising. In its contradictory way it was quite consistent. Furthermore, even as he groveled at the feet of the great white "massah," one suspects that there is more to this extravagant show of humility than meets the eye. Is it perhaps the perfect *coup de grâce* of the rebel slave? Could it be that the real meaning of Cudjoe's extraordinary act was an expression of contempt for the white master by the very slavelike psychological technique of diverting the contempt on himself? There is no way, really, of knowing. But there is much in modern psychology to support this view.[14] And certainly it is more in keeping with the facts of history than the simplistic deductions of the "Sambo" thesis.

The personality of the Jamaican slaves, then, while of considerable intrinsic interest, is of little explanatory value in the interpretation of the causes of the revolts narrated above, for as Eugene Genovese so well expresses it in his critique of Elkins (1967), ". . . Sambo existed wherever slavery existed . . . he nonetheless could turn into a rebel, and . . . our main task is to discover the conditions under which the personality pattern could become inverted and a seemingly

---

[14] Cf. the brilliant analysis of schizoid personality by British existential psychoanalyst R. D. Laing in his *The Divided Self*, where he explains the "eccentricity and oddity" of schizoid persons in terms of their tendency to express their hatred through identification and excessive compliance with the wishes of the hated person, then finally giving vent to this hatred through "compulsive caricature" of the internalized hate-object. "The individual begins by slavish conformity and compliance, and ends through the very medium of this conformity and compliance in expressing his own negative will and hatred" (109).

docile slave could suddenly turn fierce." Or, we may add, a hostile slave suddenly seem to turn docile.

Before seeking to discover these conditions, however, one nagging explanatory problem peculiar to the type of historical data surveyed above needs to be resolved. It is the extent to which we should distinguish between Maroon and slave revolts and the role of Maroon activity, per se, as an explanation of those revolts of the blacks still on the plantation. In other words, it may be argued that, first, the Maroons were not strictly slaves and, as such, the rebellions cannot be regarded as slave revolts, and second, that the very presence of the Maroons contributed to the climate of revolts in that their existence was living proof of the vulnerability of the whites and encouraged the slaves to challenge the system. Hence, while the Maroons partly explain revolts on the plantations, a separate set of explanations is required for the presence and activity of the Maroons themselves.

Clearly, the important factor here is the extent to which the revolts delineated above are related to each other and have their roots in the slave situation. The matter can be settled by answering three questions. First, were the revolts cumulative? Second, what was the nature of recruitment to the Maroon camps—was it primarily through reproduction or immigration of plantation slaves? And third, how did the original band of Spanish ex-slaves who were obviously not derived from rebel activity on the plantations but were the product of a unique historical experience (the English capture of the island) figure in the revolts during the British period?

On the first question, if the different revolts were completely unrelated, or more specifically, if the groups that earlier established themselves in the hills had been little influenced by later rebels, then one could reasonably hold that they were a factor in explaining later rebellions. This, however, was not the case. As we have seen, the revolts form a meaningful series of events. There were no historical discontinuities—no period marked a break in the sequence of events during which a separate Maroon identity was formed. The rebels of each revolt joined one or another of the major bands or were closely related to them. Obviously, the presence of rebel gangs stimulated slaves on the plantations to revolt and join them, but this does not justify the view that the Maroons should be treated separately, any more than we are justified in regarding the early phases of the Thirty Years' War as causes of that war in spite of the fact that what took place then considerably influenced later developments. All social processes at some time become self-reinforcing. The important thing is to recognize the beginning and the end of the process and its essential features. The data indicate that an essential feature of the Maroons was the fact that they were merely one aspect of the revolt of the slaves. Indeed, one may go further and suggest that all sustained slave revolts must acquire a Maroon dimension, since the only way in which a slave population can compensate for the inevitably superior military might of their masters is to resort to guerrilla warfare, with all its implications of flight, strategic retreat to secret hideouts, and ambush.

The second question is closely related to the first. It may be argued that a generation of Maroons born in the hills outside of slavery had a separate identity from the slaves, that to the extent that the Maroon population was composed of members born in the camps there would have been the kind of discontinuity which, it could be argued, would justify the distinction between their struggles with the whites and those of the plantation slaves. There are two replies to this argument. First, even if the Maroon population at any given time after, say, 1700, was composed mainly of those born in the camps, one would still be justified in regarding the resistance as slave revolts. In the first place, there is no reason why participants in a slave revolt need only be masters and plantation slaves. In the eyes of the masters, the Maroons were runaway slaves who had to be brought to subjection. In the eyes of the slaves on the plantation, the Maroons were simply successful rebel slaves (hence the ironical observation by many of them at the end of the wars that those who had challenged the system were given their freedom). And in the eyes of the Maroons (that is, those already in the hills), the slaves were all potential allies on whom they depended for provisions, arms, and intelligence.

In the second place, while the data are slight, it would appear that at any given moment after a second generation of Maroons became possible (after about 1700), the great majority of Maroons were nonetheless ex-slaves. If one compares the total population of the four major Maroon towns given by Long in 1749 with that suggested by the data on the Second Maroon War nearly half a century later, one finds that the natural rate of increase during times of peace was very low. One would hardly expect the natural increase of the population to be any higher during times of war. Indeed, the rigors of guerrilla warfare would place a strong curb on child-bearing, not to mention the artificially increased mortality rate of the adult population. The perennial scarcity of women among the older generation of Maroons—it was, indeed, one of the main reasons for the early plantation raids of the Maroons—would seem to reinforce our view that the Maroon population hardly reproduced itself. The Maroon population, then, was primarily an ex-slave population, for its rapid increase during the first quarter of the eighteenth century can only be explained in terms of recruits from runaway slaves.

Finally, there is the question of the original band of Spanish ex-slaves. As the data indicate, however, this group was of no influence whatever on the slave revolts of the seventeenth century, since they deliberately cut themselves off from the rest of the island. If anything, they were a disincentive, since they treated those runaways who wandered in their camps so badly that few ventured anywhere near to them. During the eighteenth century, however, they did become the more formidable group. But this was only after they had changed their policy toward rebel slaves. And as we have seen, this change was occasioned by the success of the rebels in the Leeward section of the island. It was the slaves who swelled the ranks and the arms of this originally small group (whose numbers were declining because of a scarcity of women), allowing them to become the major threat to the whites. What is more, Quao, the most important leader of the Windward band, who eventually negotiated the treaty of peace, was a Creole. It would seem reasonable to regard the revolts described above as slave revolts.

PART 4

The conditions favoring revolts in Jamaica were both social and cultural, and while, naturally, these two sets of conditions were closely related, for purposes of analysis they will be considered separately. There were five or six features of the social structure of the Jamaican slave system accounting for the rebellions.

First, there was the master-slave ratio. We have seen how,

over a very short period of time, the slave group came to outnumber the ruling class by nearly ten to one. Sheer numbers, then, made adequate security measures impossible. There were simply not enough whites to ensure proper surveillance of the slave group. The comparative data on slavery in the New World and in antiquity clearly indicate a correlation between low master-slave ratio and high incidence of revolts. Mendelsohn, for instance, states that the great numerical superiority of the master class throughout the Ancient Near East accounts for the complete absence of slave revolts in that area (1949:121).[15] And the famous revolt of the Helots (assuming that they were slaves, a controversial issue) has been partly explained by the fact that "they outnumbered the free population on a scale without parallel in other Greek communities" (Finley 1960).

The second feature favoring revolt was the ratio of local (or Creole) to foreign-born (in this case, African) slaves. It would appear reasonable, and the available comparative literature lends support to the hypothesis that the higher the proportion of slaves recruited from outside the system, the greater was the probability of rebellions taking place (ibid.; in all the societies discussed in the works referred to in note 15, foreign slaves far outnumbered those locally born during the periods of revolt). Clearly, people socialized within the slave system would have been more adapted to such a system, more aware of the risks involved in revolting, and less inclined to bring down the known wrath of the ruling caste upon themselves than would slaves recruited as adults to the system. Joseph Vogt in his classic work on slave revolts in antiquity, *Structur der antiken Sklavendriege,* claims the Poseidonios and other writers of antiquity "quite rightly" emphasized the role of slaves who were formerly freemen in the famous Sicilian slave revolts (Vogt 1957:12).

Furthermore, the hatred of the Creole slave for his master would have been less single-minded than that of his African counterpart. All kinds of personal ties with members of the master caste—as a sexual partner, as a childhood playmate, as a favorite, even as a kinsmen—would have corrupted and blurred the passionate desire for vengeance and the sense of

[15] The correlation is fully supported by the comparative data on slave revolts of classical antiquity: See Vogt 1957; Westermann 1955a:8–10, also his 1955b, an impossibly written but still important work, esp. Ch. IX; Mommsen 1878–1905, Vol. 3:308–9, 380–81.

injustice, if not of freedom. Personal ties, too, with other slaves would have operated in this direction—the fear of retaliation against a lover, child, or friend, for example. It is the old revolutionary story of which group had more to lose. A locally bred slave population might think that it had more than its chains to lose. A foreign-born slave population literally had only its chains.

The fact, then, that the great majority of Jamaican slaves during this period were of African origin—certainly no less than four fifths—would have added a further element in favor of revolt. It may be contended that we are here assuming that the great majority of Africans enslaved in Jamaica were freemen before being captured, although many eighteenth- and nineteenth-century pro-slavery writers have suggested quite the contrary.[16] We have no reason, however, to believe that the majority of slaves from Africa were not freemen, and besides, even if they were not originally free, the argument would hardly be affected, since it is well known that slavery in West Africa at that period, as in most traditional societies, was of the household type, entirely different in nature from the industrial slavery that existed in the plantation systems of the New World. Enslavement would have been as much of a shock, and the sense of outrage no less intense, for an African household slave as it would have been for the average African freeman (cf. Forde 1941; M. G. Smith 1954; Siegel 1945).

A third feature of the society favoring revolt were the opportunities for leadership and political organization that the system permitted. It was common knowledge among the planters—as indeed among all slave-owning castes—that it was a dangerous practice to recruit too many slaves from any one region or ethnic group, for the simple reason that this offered a basis for solidarity and communication among

[16] See Mungo Park's famous work, *Travels in the Interior Districts of Africa in the Years 1795, 1796 and 1797.* It has been claimed, however—and the internal stylistic evidence in addition to the known alterations of the original text by Park strongly supports the claim—that the proslavery Jamaican planter-historian, Bryan Edwards (author of *The History, Civil and Commercial, of the British Colonies in the West Indies,* 3 vols., 1807) had a considerable influence which he unscrupulously exploited by persuading the young traveler to exaggerate the extent to which Africans exported from the Guinea Coast to the New World were already slaves.

a section of the enslaved group. As early as the late fourth century B.C., "the peripatetic author of the *Oeconemica* made the sensible recommendation that neither an individual nor a city should have many slaves of the same nationality" (Finley 1960:66; cf. also Aptheker 1969:63–64, 369).[17]

In other words, the observance of this rule was an essential precondition of the well-known policy of divide and rule. But this was a rule the Jamaican planters refused to follow once they came to believe in their own stereotype that certain groups of Africans (especially Coromantees) made much hardier slaves after being seasoned or broken into the system.[18] Facilities for detribalization and seasoning at this time, however, were very poorly developed (if they were ever really effective), and in the mad rush for profits, slaves, among whom must have been warriors and leaders of considerable experience, were hastened into the fields long before they had been in any way subdued.

During these eighty-five years Coromantee, and to a lesser extent Papaw, slaves made up a significant sector, perhaps more than half, of the slave population. However, not only were they the two largest single groups of slaves, but they were precisely the groups that were likely to be most dangerous, for it was during this period that the expansion of the relatively advanced political systems of Ashanti and Dahomey, with their strong militaristic traditions, was taking place. Coming mainly from the forest belt of West Africa, their normal method of combat would have been jungle warfare (cf. Claridge 1964, esp. Vol. 1, Pts. 3 and 4; Dalzell 1793; B. Davidson 1966:Chs. 18–19).

Add to this a fourth significant feature of Jamaica—its wild, forested countryside, with tall, rugged mountains, narrow defiles, precipitous slopes, and countless hidden valleys, all ideally suited to guerrilla warfare—and one immediately

[17] Spartacus, who led the most famous of the slave revolts of the late Roman Republic, was of Thracian origin and was able to exploit ethnicity in mobilizing his enslaved countrymen for revolt. The Thracians were joined by the major ethnic group—the Gauls—in this revolt. The parallel between the role of these two groups and that of the Coromantees and the Papaws in Jamaica is striking. See Vogt 1957:17, 36–37.

[18] There is a curious parallel between the reputation of Gold Coast slaves among Jamaican planters and that of Syrian slaves among the Roman latifundia owners of Sicily and Italy during the period of the late Republic.

realizes what a powder keg the planters were constantly sitting on (cf. Dallas 1803, I:39–45).[19]

Another important feature of the society—perhaps the most important—conducive to revolt was the high incidence of absenteeism among the master caste. Absenteeism constantly creamed off the most successful and, presumably, most efficient members of the ruling caste, leaving the island in the hands of a group of attorneys and overseers whose treatment of the slaves was not even mitigated by proprietorial self-interest. A resident owner could, at least, have been expected to be constrained by the brute fact that a wasted slave was wasted capital. No such constraint was imposed on managers who, being paid largely on a commission basis, had a vested interest in increasing profits (and also in compensating for their notorious managerial incompetence) by depleting the major capital asset of the property in their charge, namely, the slaves. There is even evidence from a later period of the society that many of the overseers and attorneys—"swallowers up of estates," one owner called them—deliberately reduced their estates to bankruptcy in order to purchase them cheaply from their absentee employers (Patterson 1967: 43–44; cf. also Address of Assembly to Crown, 1750, CO 137/25, and *Marley* 1828:23).

Related to this is the fact that large-scale plantation agriculture, regardless of the incidence of absenteeism, was itself a direct spur to harsh treatment of slaves, since the marginal value of each individual slave was thereby lessened, making him more dispensable. It takes, however, only one angry and inflamed slave with the right qualities of leadership to incite a revolt, whatever the size of the plantation. The shift to absenteeism and large-scale monocrop plantations, then, coming at the turn of the eighteenth century, when the relationship between the castes was still unsettled, inevitably created a situation where extreme brutality and, more important, inconsistency of treatment were prevalent.

Earlier, we mentioned the general state of cultural disintegration prevailing among both masters and slaves, es-

---

[19] See also the aerial photograph and description of the cockpits in Robinson 1969; this book includes many photographs of eighteenth-century artists' impressions of maroon leaders as well as eighteenth-century maps of Jamaica, which the interested reader may wish to consult. The text, however, was intended for the nonspecialist. For a modern account of the site of Nanny Town and the difficulties involved in reaching it even today, see, Teulon n.d.

pecially the latter, at this time. Several features of this cultural situation were particularly conducive to revolt. One was the lack of social commitment, the nearly complete absence of a cohesive set of collective sentiments among the masters. Clearly, since they saw their stay on the island as a temporary one, they would hardly be inclined to take unnecessary risks in defending it. The slaves obviously had, somehow, to be kept in submission, but hardly anyone was prepared to lay down his life doing so. Indeed, even simple routine security tasks such as militia duties were considered unduly irksome and, apart from periods of crisis, the militia remained a largely defunct body. In a petition to the Duke of Newcastle in 1734, the Council and Assembly of the island unfairly tried to place the entire blame on "the cowardice and treachery" of the parties and the militia, "which mostly consisted of tradesmen and indentured servants" (*JHA*, Vol. 3:229). They failed to mention, however, the utter selfishness of what one war-weary white petitioner referred to as "persons of the best property," who refused to perform militia duties, and regarding whom he went on to say "that means be found for the compelling them to do so" (ibid., 223). Perhaps the best example of the near total lack of public spirit, of a sense of shared concern for the fate of the society they ruled, was the outright refusal of many of the planters in the parish of Portland, where the rebels were most active, to allow their slaves to help in the building and replacing of barracks for the soldiers. Others would only provide slaves if they were compensated by the government, which they knew was bankrupt, largely because they themselves had refused to pay their taxes (ibid., 31).

One structural factor contributing to this lack of cultural cohesiveness and social will was the highly imbalanced sex ratio of the white population. White women constituted no more than 30 percent of the total white population (Long 1774, 1:376; also *Marley* 1828:117, 210–11). Jamaican slave society was no place for the fair sex, and the evidence indicates that those white women who survived were hardly the fairest specimens of their race (Patterson 1967:41–42).[20]

[20] At the height of the revolts the white community was shaken by the divorce proceedings of one of the leading planters, whose adulterous wife not only had several "criminal conversations" (illicit sex) with her husband's white friends, but, as it transpired, with not a few of her own slaves (*JHA*, Vol. 3:493). It is not without significance that the most famous legend surviving the

In the absence of wives, mothers, daughters, and sisters, the Jamaican great-house never became the sanctified fortress of southern "gynocracy" (Cash 1960:85–89, 115–26). The inflammatory thought of white women being raped by rebelling black slaves seeking racial vengeance rarely spurred men on to gallant deeds. Indeed, there is not one recorded case of rape during the revolts, though several white women were killed.

At the bottom of this lack of social commitment, of course, was the absence of any integrative cultural mechanisms, such as a shared group of locally created values and beliefs. And without succumbing too much to the old anthropological adage that "women are the carriers of culture," we may suggest that the failure of a creole colonial culture (similar to southern culture) to develop was largely due to the high [male: female] sex ratio of the white population. Whatever the cause, it is certain that this cultural poverty indirectly contributed to the climate of revolt, in that the African slaves brought over to the island had to go through all the agonies of culture loss and detribalization without the mitigating condition of an alternative cultural pattern to which they could accommodate, which could at least offer some crumb of meaning to counteract their total sense of meaninglessness and loss. In Jamaica, there were no Catholic priests or zealous fundamentalists to tell them that they had just been saved from the pangs of eternal darkness. There was not even an ideology of racial superiority, which could offer, if even to the more feeble-minded, the message of the white man's burden. It is strikingly ironical that, in this most brutal and materialistic of slave societies, the ruling caste was too busy with the business at hand—making money—to concern itself with rationalizations and nice theories of biological superiority. The absence of a viable, cohesive culture among the ruling caste therefore not only meant that the will of the rulers to defend their society was, ipso facto, lessened, but also by offering no alternative to the newly arrived slave increased the likelihood that his prolonged state of normlessness would resolve itself in desperate acts of violence. This is

period of slavery concerns the diabolical sex murders of a beautiful, nymphomaniac, white witch, who not only consumed six of her husbands but countless sable beaus to boot. See H. G. DeLisser's novel, *The White Witch of Rosehall*, London: E. Benn, 1929; Also C. Black's entertaining folk history, *Tales of Old Jamaica*, London: Collins, 1966.

quite unlike the situation in slave systems such as the American South, those of the Ancient Near East, and ancient India (apart from the Oligarchy), where there were highly cohesive cultures to which the slave population could adjust.[21]

Closely related to the cultural poverty of the ruling caste was their failure to supplement the use of force with a minimum of consensual mechanisms. No system of total power can ever hope to rely solely on naked force for the maintenance of order. A ruling class must somehow find a way of buttressing its use of force with some minimum common denominator of values shared by both rulers and ruled (see Parsons 1953, and Parsons and Shils 1951, esp. p. 24). The literature on the limitations of total power indicates that force is most effective in preventing single acts of disobedience (see Wittfogel 1957 and Sykes 1966, esp. Chs. 3 and 6). It becomes less effective in *inducing* people to perform tasks, as the notorious inefficiency of prison and labor camps demonstrates. When, however, these tasks are of a complex nature (as was the case in Jamaica, where the scarcity of white artisans impelled reliance on the slave population for the performance of skilled and semi-skilled tasks), total reliance on force soon becomes dysfunctional.

The Jamaican planters were therefore faced with a socioeconomic vicious circle. Their large-scale monopolistic farming practices drove most of the white lower and artisan class from the island. This created a situation in which there were not only fewer whites to defend the slave regime but, more seriously, the development of a colonial settlement community and, consequently, a viable, congruent creole culture were prevented. The whites, then, were forced to rely on their slaves for the performance of many complex tasks. But the very factors that created this dependence also militated against the development of an accommodated artisan group

[21] On the American South, see Phillips 1929. Once it is recognized that enculturation does not necessarily imply social and psychological satisfaction with the donor group, Phillips' work can still be regarded as one of the best treatments of the subject. On the Near East, see Mendelsohn 1949, esp. p. 122. Significantly, the sole reference to unrest and revolt among the slaves of ancient India relates to the Oligarchy, during the period of the Buddha, the only period when the masters had a cultural system that was "closed" to the mass of culturally alien slaves. See Chanana n.d.:62, Ch. 5, passim.

among the slaves, which further meant that force had to be used to induce this group to work which, in turn, was economically and politically disastrous.

In the present work we have employed the following working hypothesis in explaining, sociohistorically, the causes of the First Maroon War. Stated crudely, the hypothesis may be put as follows:

In systems of slavery where the following conditions prevail, there will be a high tendency, increasing with the conjunction of such conditions, toward slave revolts:

(1) Where the slave population greatly outnumbers that of the master class.

(2) Where the ratio of local to foreign-born slaves is low.

(3) Where the imported slaves, or a significant section of them, are of common ethnic origin.

(4) Where geographical conditions favor guerrilla warfare.

(5) Where there is a high incidence of absentee ownership.

(6) Where the economy is dominated by large-scale, monopolistic enterprise.

(7) Where there is weak cultural cohesiveness, reinforced by a high [male:female] sex ratio among the ruling population.

It is possible, however, on the basis of our knowledge of slave society, to considerably refine the above hypothesis, in that several of the conditions are known to be contingent on others. Hence, condition (1) is invariably implied by the existence of conditions (5) and (6) in that the latter two conditions are mutually exclusive, with the conditions ensuring a large settlement of free, small-scale farmers. Condition (2) is also contingent on conditions (5) and (6) due to the absence of proprietorial self-interest, the relatively low marginal value of each slave, and the tendency, due to endemic inefficiency (though not necessarily unprofitability), toward the equation of marginal cost with price of product by the depletion of capital (mainly slaves) in slave societies where (5) and (6) prevail. This same set of factors will also mean that the demand for slaves will be so great that purchasers will be in no position to pick and choose, hence the strong likelihood of condition (3) being contingent on (5) and (6). The same is true of condition (7) in that the unsettled and transient state of the ruling class and its high sex ratio—both implied by (5) and (6)—are the major factors explaining the failure of a viable creole culture to develop among them.

We may now restate the hypothesis as follows:

Large-scale, monopolistic slave systems with a high rate of absenteeism will, geographical conditions permitting, exhibit a high tendency toward slave revolts.[22]

KEY TO REFERENCES

CO = Colonial Office Records, Public Records Office, London.
CSP = Calendar of State Papers (Colonial; America and West Indies).
JHA = Journals of the House of Assembly, Jamaica.
BM = British Museum.

REFERENCES NOT CITED IN GENERAL BIBLIOGRAPHY

Barham, H.
    1722 "The Most Correct and Particular Account of the Island of Jamaica." British Museum, Sl. Ms. 3918.
Becker, C.
    1959 "What are Historical Facts?" *In* H. Mererhoff (ed.), *The Philosophy of History in Our Time.* Garden City, N.Y.: Doubleday.
Berlin, I.
    1959 "What Are Historical Facts?" *In* H. Mererhoff (ed.), *The Philosophy of History in Our Time.* Garden City, N.Y.: Doubleday.
Cash, W. J.
    1960 *The Mind of the South.* Vintage.
Cassidy, F. G.
    1961 *Jamaica Talk: Three Hundred Years of the English Language in Jamaica.* London: Macmillan.
Chanana, D. R.
    n.d. Slavery in Ancient India.
Claridge, W. W.
    1964 *A History of the Gold Coast and Ashanti.* London: F. Cass.
Cundall, F. (ed.)
    1939 *The Journal of Lady Nugent.* London.
Dalzell, A.
    1793 *History of Dahomey.*

[22] The author is now conducting research toward the purely sociological end of testing this hypothesis as well as its subsumed theory of large-scale system.

Davidson, B.
1966 *A History of West Africa.* Garden City, N.Y.: Anchor Books.

Dray, W. H.
1964 *Philosophy of History.* Englewood Cliffs, N.J.: Prentice-Hall.

Finley, M. I.
1960 "Was Greek Civilization Based on Slavery?" *In* M. I. Finley, *Slavery in Classical Antiquity.* Cambridge: Cambridge University Press.

Forde, Daryll
1941 *Family and Marriage Among the Yako.* London.

Gardner, W. J.
1873 *The History of Jamaica.* T. Fisher Unwin.

Genovese, Eugene D.
1961 "The Slave South: an Interpretation." *Science and Society,* 25.

Hegel, G. W.
1931 *The Phenomenology of Mind.* London: J. Baillie.

Jelly, Thomas
1826 *Remarks on the Condition of the Whites and Free Coloured Inhabitants of Jamaica.*

Mahon, B.
1839 *Jamaica Plantership.* London.

Marley, or the Life of a Planter in Jamaica.
1828 Glasgow.

Marx, Robert F.
1967 *Pirate Port.* New York: World.

Mendelsohn
1949 *Slavery in the Ancient Near East.* New York.

Mommsen, T.
1878–1905 *The History of Rome.* Scribner.

Panikker, K. M.
n.d. *The Serpent and the Crescent.* New York: Asia Publishing House.

Parkhurst, T.
1963 *The Truest . . . Account of the Late Earthquake in Jamaica.* London.

Parsons, Talcott
1953 "A Revised Analytic Approach to the Theory of Stratification." *In* R. Bendix and S. M. Lipset, *Class, Status and Power: A Reader in Social Stratification.* New York: The Free Press.

Parsons, T. and Shils, E. A.
1951 *Toward a General Theory of Action.* Cambridge: Harvard University Press.

Patterson, Orlando
1966 "Slavery, Acculturation and Social Change." *The British Journal of Sociology* 17(2).

Phillips, U. B.
　1929 *Life and Labor in the Old South*. Boston: Little, Brown.
Pitman, F. W.
　1917 *The Development of the British West Indies*. New Haven.
Popper, Karl
　1962 *The Open Society and Its Enemies*. London: Routledge.
Ragatz, L.
　1928 *The Fall of the Planter Class in the British Caribbean, 1763–1833*. New York: Century.
　n.d. *Absentee Landlordism in the British Caribbean, 1750–1833*.
Roberts, G.
　1957 *The Population of Jamaica*. Cambridge: Cambridge University Press.
Siegel, B. J.
　1945 "Some Methodological Considerations for a Comparative Study of Slavery." *American Anthropologist* 47 (3).
Smith, M. G.
　1954 "Slavery and Emancipation in Two Societies." *Social and Economic Studies* 3(3).
Smith, R. W.
　1945 "The Legal Status of the Jamaican Slaves Before the Anti-Slavery Movement." *Journal of Negro History* 30.
Spurdle, F. G.
　1962 *Early West Indian Government*. New Zealand.
Sykes, G. M.
　1966 *The Society of Captives: A Study of a Maximum Security Prison*. New York: Atheneum.
Taylor, S. A. G.
　1965 *The Western Design*. Institute of Jamaica, Historical Society.
Teulon, A. E.
　n.d. *Report on Expedition to Nanny Town, July 1967*. Mimeo, pamphlet. Institute of Jamaica.
Thornton, A. P.
　1956 *West India Policy Under the Restoration*. Oxford: Clarendon Press.
Vogt, H. C. J.
　1957 *Struktur der antiken Sklavendriege*. Akademie der Wissenschaften und der Literatur.
Westermann, W. W.
　1955a "Slave Maintenance and Slave Revolts." *Classical Philology* 40.
　1955b *The Slave Systems of Greek and Roman Antiquity*. The American Philosophical Society.
Whitsun, A. M.
　1929 *The Constitutional Development of Jamaica 1660–1729*. Manchester.

Williams, E.
  1964 *Capitalism and Slavery*. Andre Deutsch.
Wittfogel, Karl
  1957 *Oriental Despotism: A Comparative Study of Total Power*.
  New Haven: Yale University Press.

PART SIX

The Guianas

For three centuries, the Guianas have been the classic setting for maroon communities. Though local maroons in French and British Guiana were wiped out by the end of the eighteenth century (see the bibliographical note to this section), the maroons of Surinam, known as "Bush Negroes," have long been the hemisphere's largest maroon population, boasting (with the possible exception of Haiti) the most highly developed independent societies and cultures in the history of Afro-America. Unlike the countless maroon communities elsewhere, which were brought to their knees by an overpowering force of arms, or those which, by gradual assimilation into the general population, are disappearing as sociocultural entities, the Bush Negro tribes can still be said to be vigorous, flourishing societies, in many respects still "states within a state."

The ancestors of the largest Bush Negro tribes escaped from the plantations of coastal Surinam in the late seventeenth and early eighteenth centuries and, after a half century of brutal guerrilla warfare against colonial and European troops, signed peace treaties with the government in the 1760s. The late eighteenth century witnessed new hostilities, culminating in the formation of still another independent tribe. For the next hundred years these societies were allowed to develop more or less in isolation, remaining dependent, however, on coastal society for certain manufactured items, from cloth and pots to axes and guns. (During the

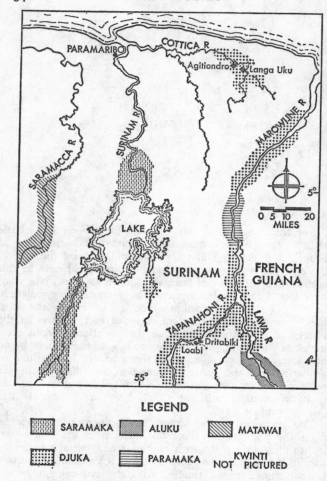

LEGEND

SARAMAKA	ALUKU	MATAWAI
DJUKA	PARAMAKA	KWINTI NOT PICTURED

Figure 4: Bush Negro tribes of Surinam and French Guiana (indicating the Djuka villages mentioned in Chapters 19 and 20).

wars, such goods had been obtained by raiding plantations; following the treaties, the government instead supplied them as periodic "tribute," allowing in addition brief trading trips to the coast; during the last hundred years, Bush Negroes have instead engaged heavily in logging and coastal wage labor.) Today, depopulation due to the emigration of men to the coast has become a problem, Christian missions have brought education and medical care to some remote areas, and there are even some scores of Bush Negroes living, working, and continuing their education in the Netherlands. Nevertheless, of all maroon societies, those of the Bush Negroes have been most successful in forging their own destinies. It would not be hard for a casual visitor in many Bush Negro villages to imagine himself a full continent and several centuries away.

Today, there are six Bush Negro tribes: the Djuka and Saramaka (each fifteen thousand to twenty thousand people), the Matawai, Aluku, and Paramaka (each closer to a thousand), and the Kwinti (only a few hundred). Tribal territories are shown in the sketch map (Fig. 4). These basically similar societies, though formed under like historical and ecological conditions, nevertheless display small but significant variations in everything from language, diet, and dress to patterns of marriage, residence, and migratory wage labor. From a cultural point of view, the greatest differences seem to be between the Saramaka and Matawai on the one hand, and the Djuka, Aluku, and Paramaka on the other.

To generalize broadly: Villages, which average a couple of hundred people each, consist of a core of matrilineally related kinsmen plus some spouses and some descendants of lineage men. Villages have headmen and assistant headmen, who are responsible to their tribal chief; the influence of these officials is to some extent limited by the importance of oracles, spirit possession, and other forms of divination in political and social control. Matriliny dominates descent ideology, with "matriclans" and "matrilineages" (the exact definitions of which vary from tribe to tribe) forming the basic units of the formal social structure. These peoples enjoy an extremely rich ritual life, and the complex series of shrines and cults serve as foci for groups of residentially dispersed kinsmen. Their economy has long been based on a combination of periodic male wage labor on the coast and swidden horticulture and hunting and fishing; material culture includes both selected coastal imports and a wide variety of products fashioned by local techniques. Unusually skillful artists, performers, and orators, Bush Negroes in general exhibit a strongly aesthetic approach to life.

Today, Bush Negro societies are facing pressures for sociocultural change. While it may once have been easy for them to maintain a world view rooted in isolationism and in a belief in their superiority over both whites and coastal blacks, the recent rise in the standard of living on the coast has made them increasingly aware that their societies have, in some respects at least, been left behind. The construction by Alcoa and the Surinam government of a giant hydroelectric project, which flooded almost half of Saramaka tribal territory in the 1960s, was only the most dramatic of many recent events to stress to Bush Negroes the need for more effective accommodation to the outside world. Having now become involved, almost in spite of themselves, in the party politics of Surinam, and finding themselves dependent on the decisions of corporations based thousands of miles away, some Bush Negroes are beginning to realize that their traditional isolationist strategy holds little promise for the future. At the same time, it seems clear that, while beginning to make the difficult adjustment to a new role as part of a larger, developing nation, Bush Negro societies are still managing to retain (and will continue to maintain for a long time to come) much of their traditional individuality and vitality.

The following selections offer a variety of perspectives on the history, society, and culture of the Guiana Maroons.

It seems fitting to give the first word to Johannes King, a literate Bush Negro of the Matawai tribe who, during the nineteenth century, set down this traditional, oral account of early guerrilla warfare and of making the peace (see, for biographical information on King, King 1973, and Voorhoeve and Lichtveld 1974). Captain J. G. Stedman, a British soldier who fought against the newly formed rebel groups in the late eighteenth century, left a vivid and insightful description of the rebels, the war itself, and the remarkable colonial society from which they fled; and an excerpt dealing with the wars is presented here as the second selection. The last of these historical selections is a rare, firsthand description of his own community by a young recaptured French Guiana rebel belonging to the independent band of André, offering an invaluable glimpse of the earliest (but also the final) years of one small group (see the bibliographical note for Part Six for more on this community).

The next two selections examine Bush Negro culture and society from an anthropological perspective, demonstrating in the realms of kinship and religion the extent to which Bush Negroes have evolved highly developed sociocultural systems that are truly their own. First, Professor A. J. F. Köbben, of the University of Amsterdam, describes the powerful role of kinship as an organizing force in Cottica Djuka society; then Dr. W. van Wetering, a Dutch anthropologist who worked in a different region of the same tribe, presents a vivid analysis of the role of witchcraft accusations in that society.

The final selection brings this book full circle. In late 1970, as part of a political bargain involving Surinam party politics, the tribal chiefs of the Djuka, Saramaka, Matawai, and Paramaka were sent by the national government on a visit to West Africa, retracing the journey their slave ancestors had made three centuries before. Dr. Silvia W. de Groot, a Dutch scholar who has written extensively on Bush Negro history, was the official escort for the chiefs and kept a diary of this historic trip, parts of which are excerpted here.

Suggestions for further reading on the Guiana Maroons are presented in the bibliographical note for Part Six.

CHAPTER SIXTEEN

Guerrilla Warfare:
A Bush Negro View

JOHANNES KING

Here is the story of our ancestors and of their difficulties while they were at war with the *bakra* ["whites"[1]]. At that time they suffered severe shortages and were living under dreadful conditions, but the lack of food was their worst problem. They didn't even have time to clear and plant gardens to produce food. The whites were always pursuing them and attacking. Whenever they did manage with great difficulty to clear an area, they would fell the trees; then, when they planted food and it began to ripen, the whites would always be on them again with more fighting. Whenever the soldiers arrived in one of the camps, some of the women, frightened by the noise of battle, would run and take a rice mortar, heft it onto their shoulders, and flee with it into the forest. They would run on until the crisis subsided a little, when their heads would clear and they would realize that instead of their children they had brought with them nothing but pieces of wood. Well, listen to this: As soon as those soldiers got into one of our ancestors' camps and saw some young child, they would take that child, put him in a mortar and beat him with pestles, just as people mash bananas. That child would be

From Johannes King, Skrekiboekoe. Ms., 1885. This fragment is a rather free translation (by R. and S. Price) of parts of the original Sranan text, which may be found, together with a Dutch translation, in Ursy M. Lichtveld and Jan Voorhoeve (eds.), *Suriname: Speigel der vaderlandse kooplieden*, Zwolle: W. E. J. Tjeenk Willink, 1958, pp. 90–119.
[1] In this selection we gloss *bakra* as "whites," though it refers in general to "Westerners," both white and black.

completely crushed. And then they would burn the whole settlement and cut down all the banana trees and throw away any other food they saw. They slashed the crops to bits, ruining everything that they saw. They set fire to everything they found that they didn't want to carry off with them. Well, that enraged our early ancestors against the whites. And they swore a blood oath, vowing to take proper revenge against those whites for the blood of the slaves that the whites had spilled on their plantations, at the time when there were still no Bush Negroes.

. . . Well, by the time the war had dragged on for five years [sic; actually more than a half century], this strenuous life had begun to wear very heavily on our ancestors. There was no food to eat. But some of the seeds that God had put in the forest helped them, and they ate many of these sweet seeds of the forest instead of regular food [rice]. But there was no lack of game and fish, not at all. Animals and birds were not scarce; these were very abundant, and there were many fish too. This helped them greatly, because these things were not difficult to find. But there was a real shortage of salt. They were even forced to make "bush salt" with the various kinds of trees whose trunks contain salt.

. . . The women made giant clay pots to cook things in. Likewise, they made big clay pans and big tubs that could hold a lot of water. . . . And they made water jugs, big ones and little ones. As for iron pots, large or small, these our ancestors had to capture from the enemy. And when the fighting got hard, sometimes the soldiers saw that the bush people were killing too many of them and ran back to save their lives. Then they could not carry all their big pots back with them. Often they ran off and abandoned everything. Our ancestors would sometimes take these and wipe out the entire detachment of soldiers. They would spare only two soldiers so that they could carry the message back to the city to tell the government, to let them know that all the soldiers in that detachment were gone, that it was all over for them, that they had all been killed. In this way our ancestors would obtain more iron pots as well as guns and machetes, gun powder, bullets, everything. And some of the rest of them would go sack a plantation, taking away many Negroes and all kinds of goods. They took men and women, children and adults, and killed any slaves who refused to go off to the bush. Then they would take all that they could carry and go back with it into the forest. In this way our ancestors got things in the bush to help them survive during those five [sic] years while the fighting was going on, until the whites finally made peace with them.

. . . [In the course of the wars] when the Bush Negroes had killed too many whites and destroyed plantations one after another, and when the whites saw that they were losing even more slaves over and above the original ones and that the government soldiers were dying in vain, they decided to send a white to the Matawai tribe to make a truce with the Matawai people. When the whites arrived, those people replied to the whites that it was good, that they would make peace with them just as the whites suggested, and that they would put an end to the fighting. They said, yes, that was good for them too. And they discussed the whole thing together. Then the whites gave the Bush Negroes presents.

They brought lots of cloths and many other things to give them as presents. Well, the Bush Negroes took all the presents. But then they did not do the right thing. Those people acted dishonorably and tricked the whites. At this first treaty, they thought that the whites were coming to deceive them and that the treaty that the whites were offering could not be in good faith. And that is why the Bush Negroes tricked the whites at the outset. Each one took a soldier as his *mati*,[2] to sleep in his own hut. This is how they divided up the soldiers, but some of the blacks were left over because there were more of them than whites. Well, during the night, each one killed his *mati*. And that is how they killed all the soldiers; they spared just two of the whites to send them to the city to bring the news to the government.

Well, after that the government tried sending another detachment to the Djuka people to ask them if they wanted to make a treaty with the whites. But how did they make that request? A house slave who knew how to write a little had run away to the forest. The whites wrote a letter and left it on one of the Bush Negroes' paths. When they found the letter, they had the man read it. That is how they learned that the whites wanted to come make peace with them. And then

---

[2] *Mati* is a relationship of formal friendship, a form of ritual kinship still common among Bush Negroes (see the introduction to this book).

the Djukas said yes, they wanted it. So the Djukas went to meet the whites and told them everything that they needed in order to live. Then they swore an oath with the whites; they made peace together; they made an agreement. With that, they drank a blood oath. The whites said they would not go shoot the Negroes or fight with them anymore. But they too must cease their fighting with the whites and must no longer raid plantations or take more of the whites' slaves back to the bush. And whenever a plantation slave ran off to join them, they must not harbor him; they must bring him back to the whites. And if a slave from the city ran off to them, they must return him to the whites and the whites would pay them for that. The government's forests were all open to them, and the Bush Negroes along the upper courses of the rivers could do whatever they wanted. In other words, they were free to clear the underbrush, cut lumber, fell trees, make horticultural camps, clear gardens, and plant crops. They could do any work they were able to do and bring things to sell in the city. The government allowed them to do all these things. But the government did not give the Bush Negroes permission to do as they liked along the lower course of the rivers, where the tide was still visible and where the whites themselves worked. Upstream, from where the rapids begin, the government has continued to allow them a free hand to this very day.

. . . The government closed this treaty with a solemn oath, requiring the Bush Negroes to renew the oath every three years. They would bring lots of goods to distribute among them.

That is: salt and cloth, guns, powder, bullets, shot, beads, pots, knives, cutlasses, axes, grindstones, two types of adzes, razors, shovels, scissors, mirrors, and nails to nail things, screwdrivers, tinderboxes and flintstones, large griddles for making cassava cakes and pans for cooking fish, cloth to make hammocks, hammers, cowrie shells, bells, cockle shells, barrels of rum, barrels of salt meat, barrels of bacon, and barrels of salt cod. Well, such was the agreement the early whites made with our early ancestors in the bush. The Bush Negroes were satisfied with the agreement and the whites were satisfied too. It was good for them all. The whites took a knife and cut their hands, drawing a little blood. They wiped it onto the inside of a glass. And then the blacks took a little blood the same way and put it in the glass. The whites then swore upon the blood of the blacks, and the blacks swore upon the blood of the whites. Then they mixed a little wine with the blood and "drank the oath." Well that's how the whites and the Bush Negroes made the very first peace treaty.

[King here recounts the similar stories of how the government made peace with the Saramakas and then with the Matawais.]

. . . The government said that if they honored the agreements, every three years they would send many goods to distribute among the three tribes. . . . Every three years they had to drink an oath all over again. The whites did indeed hold to the agreement and the oath. For more than a hundred years they kept giving goods. And they drank a blood oath every three years, for more than a hundred years. Even up to my, Johannes King's, lifetime when I was a little boy, the government kept sending presents to give to the three tribes of Djuka, Saramaka, and Matawai. But by the time I saw the distribution of presents for the second time, I was already pretty big. They again drank an oath. That was the last time whites and Bush Negroes ever drank a blood oath. After that, the government sent goods again to distribute to the three Bush Negro tribes. By then I, Johannes King, had already become a young man. I could already do everything like a man. After that, whites and Bush Negroes never drank a blood oath again. The whites and the Bush Negro chiefs gave each other their hand; they shook hands together to make peace; it was over. And the whites gave presents, which the Bush Negroes received with joy.

. . . The story of how our forefathers honored God and their early ancestors when they came to receive the presents and then returned to their villages:

When they got back safely to their villages, they fired many salutes for the people who had waited at home. These people came to the bank of the river singing, to escort them to shore. They played drums, danced, blew African trumpets, and sang, danced and celebrated the whole afternoon until nighttime and the whole night until morning. In the morning, they took a piece of white cloth and they raised a white flag to Gran Gado or Masra Gado [the supreme deity] in the heavens. Then they all touched their knees to the ground and gave Masra Gado thanks for all that he had done for them and for the strength that he had given them against the many hardships they encountered in the bush. Moreover, Masra Gado had helped them and given them strength in the forest to fight and win a major war against the whites. Now the whites themselves were bringing them peace and many goods. And for that, everyone knelt down on the ground to give Masra Gado thanks. They put all their children with their bellies to the ground, and even many of the adults threw themselves with their bellies to the ground to show Masra Gado respect and to give him thanks for the good things that he had done for them. Then they got up, took their guns, and shot many salutes for Masra Gado, to honor him. And finally they were finished.

Then they raised another flag with a black cloth. This they did to honor the former warriors, those who had fought and won against the whites. Then they all came together under the flag; this was also to give thanks to the warriors and to honor their name and to blow African trumpets, which the Africans had made out of wood in Africa, and which they loved to blow whenever they went off to battle and with which they talked to one another. These early people who lived in the bush really loved to blow those trumpets! Whenever they blew such a trumpet, they would shoot many salutes, play drums, sing, dance, and play *sanga* drums. And the adults would *sanga* all over the place. That word, "*sanga*," means many people with guns, machetes, and spears in their hands running all over the place exactly the way that the warriors used to fight in Africa itself, and with many war cries. And the older men showed the youths and young girls how they fought with the whites and how the warriors raided and destroyed white plantations, carrying off people to the forest. While they were running around like this, they would shoot many, many salutes, just like the [government] soldiers do in the city square. Then many people would shout together: "Battle! Battle! The battle's on!" And then they would fire guns, play drums, and blow horns, like warriors going off to raid a plantation. And if someone were far off who didn't know about this, he would think that a real battle was taking place on a plantation, there were so many cries and guns shooting. And they played drums so! When they were finished, they would bring a bush drink that they made from sugar cane juice, and which is called bush rum.

They would pour a libation on the ground. That was in order to give thanks to God and the ancestors. After that they would play for the *obeahs* and for the other gods who had helped them fight.

CHAPTER SEVENTEEN

Guerrilla Warfare:
A European Soldier's View

CAPTAIN J. G. STEDMAN

At ten o'clock we met a small party of the rebels, with each a green hamper upon his back; they fired at us, dropped their bundles, and taking to their heels ran back towards their village. These we since learned were transporting rice to another settlement for their subsistence, when they should be expelled from Gado-Saby (the name of this settlement) which they daily expected, since they had been discovered by the gallant Captain Meyland. The green hampers, which they call *warimbos*, were very curiously plaited with the manicole leaves. And when our men cut them open with their sabres, there burst forth the most beautiful clean rice that I ever saw, which was scattered and trampled under foot, as we had no opportunity of carrying it along. A little after this we perceived an empty shed, where a picquet had been stationed to give notice of any danger, but they had precipitately deserted their post. We now vigorously redoubled our pace till about noon; when two more musket shot were fired at us by another advanced guard of the enemy, as a signal to the chief, Bonny, of our approach. Major Medler and myself, with a few of the van-guard, and a small party of the rangers, at this time rushing forward, soon came to a fine field of rice and Indian corn: we here made a halt for the other troops, particularly to give time for our rear to close up, some of whom were at least two miles behind us; and during

From Captain J. G. Stedman, *Narrative of a five-years' expedition, against the revolted Negroes of Surinam . . . from the year 1772, to 1777*. London: J. Johnson and J. Edwards, 1796, Vol. 2, pp. 105–14.

which period we might have been cut to pieces, the enemy, unknown to us, having surrounded the field in which we were, as we were afterwards informed.

In about half an hour the whole body joined us, when we instantly proceeded by cutting through a small defile of the wood, into which we had no sooner entered, than a heavy fire commenced from every side, the rebels retiring, and we advancing, until we arrived in the most beautiful field of ripe rice, in the form of an oblong square, from which the rebel town appeared at a distance, in the form of an amphi-theatre, sheltered from the sun by the foliage of a few lofty trees, the whole presenting a *coup-d'œil* romantic and en-chanting beyond conception. In this field the firing was kept up, like one continued peal of thunder, for above forty min-utes, during which time our black warriors [the government's rangers] behaved with wonderful intrepidity and skill. The white soldiers were too eager, and fired over one another at random, yet I could perceive a few of them act with the ut-most coolness, and imitate the rangers with great effect; amongst these was now the once-daunted Fowler, who being roused from his tremor by the firing at the beginning of the onset, had rushed to the front, and fully re-established his character, by fighting like a brave fellow, by my side, until the muzzle of his musket was split by a shot from the enemy, which rendered it useless; a ball passed through my shirt, and grazed the skin of my shoulder; Mr. Decabanes, my lieu-tenant, had the sling of his fusee shot away: several others were wounded, some mortally, but I did not, to my surprize, observe one instance of *immediate* death—for which seeming miracle, however, I shall presently account.

This whole field of rice was surrounded and interspersed by the enemy with the large trunks and roots of heavy trees, in order to make our approach both difficult and dangerous; behind these temporary fortifications the rebels lay lurking, and firing upon us with deliberate aim, whilst their bulwarks certainly protected them in some measure from the effects of our fire, we having vast numbers of these fallen trees to scramble over before we could reach the town: but we still advanced, in defiance of every obstacle, and while I admired the masterly manœuvres of their general, I could not help pitying them for their superstition. One poor fellow, in particular, trusting to his amulet or charm, fancied himself invulnerable; he mounted frequently upon one of the trees that lay near us, discharged his piece, descended to re-load, and then with equal confidence and the greatest deliberation returned to the charge in my full view; till at last a shot from one of my marines, named Valet, broke the bone of his thigh, and he fell crawling for shelter under the very same tree which had supported him just before; but the soldier instantly advancing, and putting the muzzle of his musket to the rebel's ear, blew out his brains, while several of his countrymen, in spite of their spells and charms, shared the same fate.

Being now about to enter the town, a rebel captain, wearing a tarnished gold-laced hat, and bearing in his hand a torch of flaming straw, seeing their ruin inevitable, had the resolution to stay and set the town on fire in our presence, which, by the dryness of the houses, instantly produced a general conflagration, when the firing from the woods began gradually to cease. This bold and masterly manœuvre not only prevented that carnage to which the common soldiers in the heat of victory are but too prone, but also afforded the enemy an opportunity of retreating with their wives and children, and carrying off their most useful effects; whilst our pursuit, and seizing the spoil, were at once frustrated both by the ascending flames, and the unfathomable marsh, which we soon discovered on all sides to surround us. . . .

I must indeed confess that within this last hour the continued noise of the firing, shouting, swearing, and hallooing of black and white men mixed together; the groans of the wounded and the dying, all weltering in blood and in dust; the shrill sound of the negro horns from every quarter, and the crackling of the burning village; to which if we add the clouds of smoke that every where surrounded us, the ascending flames, &c. &c. formed, on the whole, such an uncommon scene as I cannot describe. . . .

In short, having washed off the dust, sweat, and blood, and having refreshed ourselves with a dram and a bit of bread till the flames subsided, we next went to inspect the smoking ruins; and found the above town to have consisted of about one hundred houses or huts, some of which were two stories high. Among the glowing ashes we picked up several trifles that had escaped the flames, such as silver spoons and forks, which we supposed, by the marks BW, to have been pillaged from the Brunswick estate in Rio Cottica. We found also some knives, broken china and earthen pots; amongst the latter one filled with rice and palm-tree worms fell to my share: as this wanted no fire to dress the contents, and as my appetite was very keen, I emptied it in a few minutes, and made a very hearty meal. Some were afraid this mess had been left behind with a view to poison us; but this suspicion, proved however, fortunately for me, to be without foundation.

The silver plate I also purchased from the men that picked it up, determined to carry it off as a trophy, and I have used it ever since. Here we likewise found three skulls fixed upon stakes, the mournful relics of some of our own brave people, who had been formerly killed; but what surprized us most, were the heads of two young negroes, which seemed as if fresh cut off, these we since learned had been executed during the night of the 17th, when we heard the hallooing and the firing, for speaking in our favour.

Having buried all these remains promiscuously in one pit, we returned to sling our hammocks, under those beautiful and lofty trees which I have already mentioned; but here I am sorry to add, we found the rangers shockingly employed, in playing at bowls with those very heads they had just chopped off from their enemies. . . .

They related that upon reconnoitering the skirts of the surrounding forest, they had found quantities of human blood in different places, which had flowed from the dead and wounded bodies the rebels had carried away during the action.

To reprimand them for this inhuman diversion would have been useless, as they assured us it was *"Condre fassee,"* the custom of their country; and concluded the horrid sport by kicking and mangling the head, cutting off the lips, cheeks, ears, and noses; they even took out the jaw-bones, which they smoke-dried, together with the right hands, to carry home, as trophies of their victory, to their wives and relations. That this barbarous custom prevails amongst savages is a well-known fact, which originates from a motive of insatiable revenge. And though Colonel Fourgeoud might have prevented their inhumanity by his authority, in my opinion he wisely declined it; observing, that as he could not do it by persuasion, to do it by power, might break their native spirit, and produce no other effect than alienating them from the service, so necessary were they to us, though so savagely revengeful, and so bloody.

About three o'clock, whilst we were resting from our fatigue, we were once more surprised by an attack from a party of the enemy; but after exchanging a few shots they were repulsed. This unexpected visit, however, put us more upon our guard during the night, so that no fires were allowed to be lighted, and double sentinels were placed around the camp. Thus situated, being overcome by excessive toil and heat, I after sun-set leaped into my hammock, and soon fell fast asleep; but in less than two hours my faithful black boy Quaco roused me, in the midst of pitch darkness, crying, *"Massera, massera! boosee negro, boosee negro!"*—"Master, master! the enemy, the enemy!" Hearing, at the same moment, a brisk firing, with the balls whistling through the branches, I fully concluded that the rebels were in the very midst of our camp. Surprised, and not perfectly awake, I suddenly started up with my fusee cocked; and (without knowing where I ran) first threw down Quaco, and next fell down myself, over two or three bodies that lay upon the ground, and which I imagined to be killed. When one of them, "d--ning me for a son of a b--ch, told me, if I moved I was a dead man; Colonel Fourgeoud having issued orders for the troops to lie flat on their bellies all the night, and not to fire, as most of their ammunition had been expended the preceding day." I took his advice, and soon discovered him by his voice to be one of our own grenadiers, named Thomson. In this situation we lay prostrate on our arms until sunrise, during which time a most abusive dialogue was carried on indeed between the rebels and the rangers, each party cursing and menacing the other at a very terrible rate; the former "reproaching the rangers as poltroons and traitors to their countrymen, and challenging them next day to single combat; swearing they only wished to lave their hand in the blood of such scoundrels, who had been the principal agents in destroying their flourishing settlement. The rangers d--n'd the rebels for a parcel of pitiful skulking rascals, whom they would fight one to two in the open field, if they dared but to shew their ugly faces; swearing they had only deserted their masters because they were too lazy to work." After this they insulted each other by a kind of war-whoop, sung victorious songs on both sides, and sounded their horns as signals of defiance; when the firing commenced once more from the rebel negroes, and continued during the night, accompanied by their martial voices, at intermissions resounding through the woods, which echo seemed to answer with redoubled force.

At length poor Fourgeoud took a part in the conversation, myself and Serjeant Fowler acting as his interpreters, by hallooing, which created more mirth than I had been witness to for some time: he promised them life, liberty, victuals, drink, and all they wanted. They replied, with a loud laugh, that they wanted nothing from him; characterised him as a half-starved Frenchman, who had run away from his own country; and assured him that if he would venture to pay *them* a visit, he should return unhurt, and not with an empty belly. They told us, that we were to be pitied more than they; that we were *white slaves*, hired to be shot at and starved for four-pence a day; that they scorned to expend much more of their powder upon such scarecrows; but should the planters or overseers dare to enter the woods, not a soul of them should ever return, any more than the perfidious rangers, some of whom might depend upon being massacred that day, or the next; and concluded by declaring that Bonny should soon be the governor of the colony.

After this they tinkled their bill-hooks, fired a volley, and gave three cheers; which being answered by the rangers, the clamour ended, and the rebels dispersed with the rising sun.

Our fatigue was great; yet, notwithstanding the length of the contest, our loss by the enemies fire was very inconsiderable, for which I promised to account; and this mystery was now explained, when the surgeons, dressing the wounded, extracted very few leaden bullets, but many pebbles, coat-buttons, and pieces of silver coin, which could do us little mischief, by penetrating scarcely more than skin deep. We also observed, that several of the poor rebel negroes who were shot, had only the shards of Spa-water cans, instead of flints, which could seldom do execution; and it was certainly owing to these circumstances that we came off so well, as I have mentioned before; yet we were nevertheless not without a number of very dangerous scars and contusions.

. . . The Rebels of this settlement being apparently subdued and dispersed, Colonel Fourgeoud made it his next business to destroy the surrounding harvest; and I received orders to begin the devastation, with eighty marines and twenty rangers. Thus I cut down all the rice that was growing plentifully in the two above-mentioned fields; this being

one, I discovered a third field south of the first, which I also
emolished, and made my report to Fourgeoud, with which
e appeared highly satisfied. In the afternoon Captain Hamel
vas detached, with fifty marines and thirty rangers, to recon-
oitre behind the village, and to discover, if possible, how the
ebels could pass to and fro through an unfathomable marsh,
vhilst we were unable to pursue them. This officer at length
erceived a kind of floating bridge amongst the reeds, made
f maurecee-trees, but so constructed, that only one man
breast could pass it. On this were seated astride a few rebels
o defend the communication, who instantly fired upon the
arty, but were soon repulsed by the rangers, who shot one
f them dead, but he was carried away by his companions.

On the morning of the 22d, our commander ordered a de-
achment to cross the bridge and go on discovery, at all haz-
rds. Of this party I led the van. We now took the pass with-
ut opposition; and having all marched, or rather scrambled
ver this defile of floating trees, we found ourselves in a large
blong field of cassava and yams, in which were about thirty
ouses, now deserted, being the remains of the old settlement
alled Cofaay. In this field we separated into three divisions,
he better to reconnoitre, one marching north, one north-west,
nd the third west. And here, to our astonishment, we dis-
overed that the reason of the rebels shouting, singing, and
iring, on the night of the 20th, was not only to cover the re-
reat of their friends, by cutting off the pass, but by their un-
emitting noise to prevent us from discovering that they were
mployed, men, women, and children, in preparing warim-
oes or hampers filled with the finest rice, yams, and cassava,
or subsistence during their escape, of which they had only
eft the chaff and refuse for our contemplation.

This was certainly such a masterly trait of generalship in a
avage people, whom we affected to despise, as would have
one honour to any European commander, and has perhaps
een seldom equalled by more civilized nations.

CHAPTER EIGHTEEN

Rebel Village in French Guiana:
A Captive's Description

[*Editor's note:* By the mid-eighteenth century, groups of maroons had been living for some years in the forests to the west of Cayenne, near the so-called Lead Mountain (see Henry 1950:112–17). After an abortive attempt by a Jesuit priest to get them to give themselves up in return for pardon, the government declared open season on them, offering rewards for their capture dead or alive. Military detachments, which included Indians brought from the eastern part of the country, were sent after the maroons and succeeded in killing many and capturing most of the others. Among the captives was Louis, a fifteen-year-old born a slave, who gave the following testimony before the criminal lieutenant of Cayenne in 1748.]

INTERROGATION OF THE NEGRO, LOUIS[1]

Declaration and explanation drawn up by M. Le Tenneur, criminal lieutenant of Cayenne, about the interrogation of Louis, Negro slave belonging to M. Gourgues l'Aîné, who is about fifteen years of age and was brought to Cayenne by the detachment of Monsieur de Préfontaine on the twenty-sixth of the present month of October, 1748, from the maroon village above Tonnégrande to the west of Cayenne, after having had the aforesaid Louis swear to tell the truth in return for a promise of leniency.

[1] The original copy of this document is in the French *Archives Nationales* (Colonies C14/20, f⁰ 317–21). This translation utilized the version published in Sylvie Mirot, "Un document inédit sur le marronnage à la Guyane Française au XVIIIe siècle," *Revue d'Histoire des Colonies* (Paris) 41:245–56 (1954).

FIRSTLY.

He declared and admitted that he has been a maroon for about eighteen moons with Rémy, his father, and other Negroes belonging to his above-mentioned master; that Rémy, having displeased the said M. Gourgues and having been whipped by him, had planned this marronage, having first gotten a supply of food together without absenting himself from work; and that he left two days later with the said Louis his son, Claude, Louis Augé, and Paul, his brother, in a small fishing canoe belonging to M. Sébastien Gourgues; that they passed in front of Roura and from there, with the tide, near Brugeon's land into the forest of Cavalay; that they did not stop in any houses along the way, since they had brought cassava and bananas for the trip; that the said Paul and Louis Augé decided to return to their masters and went back to Compté in the same small fishing canoe; that after an unknown number of weeks, a certain André, accompanied by Sébastien and Michel, came upon them in a canoe, which he claimed to have taken from the landing at Pataoüa, where he then brought them and found them a place to sleep at the house of Copena, who was living with his wife Mariette, with whom he had a son and a daughter and who was then ill; that after they had spent the night there, the said André instructed them to leave early in the morning with the said Sébastien and Michel and go to the maroon village; that they passed by the old estate of M. de la Mathérée but did not come upon any other plantations along the way, since they traveled through the forest by means of innumerable detours; and that they were supplied with food that had been prepared at Cavalay, namely, bananas and smoked fish; that toward noon of the first day of their journey, they found a container with five cassava cakes, which the said André, Sébastien, and Michel had hidden earlier to be eaten when they would pass that way again; that they slept in the forest that first day and arrived at the village on the following day at about noon, after having taken several detours and passed many streams and mountains; that they did not know who owned the canoe that André had provided for their transportation from Cavalay to Pataoüa, but that they left it tied up at the aforementioned landing at Pataoüa before leaving for the village; that in the said village there are twenty-seven houses and three open sheds—ten in the old gardens, which had been cleared several years earlier and about the number of which he is unsure, and sixteen in those cleared last year, with another belonging to a certain Augustin in a garden that he had cleared about a league from last year's, and in addition, three open sheds in the three gardens burned this year, which had already been planted; that the said houses belong to and are or were inhabited by twenty-nine strong male Negroes *pièces d'Inde* [fully productive workers], twenty-two female Negroes who are also fully fit, nine Negro boys, and twelve Negro girls, making in all seventy-two slaves. . . . [For the list of slaves and their owners, deleted here, see Mirot 1954.]

The said Luis noted that Couacou takes care of wounds, as does André, and that Couachy repairs the muskets.

That Sébastien and Jeanneton bleed people.

That Bernard, nicknamed Couacou, baptizes with holy water and recites daily prayer.

That all the Negroes and Negresses are equipped with axes and machetes and that there are spares that had belonged to Léveillé, killed by Ramassiny.

That André has two small griddles for making cassava, and Augustin the same, which are used by the whole troop.

That Sébastien possesses the bottom part of a roucou kettle, which he uses to cook cassava, that other Negroes have flat rocks used for the same purpose, and that all own cooking pots.

That the said André, Louise, Rémy, and Félicité, wife of the deceased Léveillé, are all being treated with herbs in their houses, to wit André for yaws, Rémy for pain in his foot, which he attributes to sorcery [*sort*], Félicité for pains throughout her body, which she also attributes to a spell, and Louise for sores on her nose and throat. It is Couacou who is the herbalist.

That no member of the troop has died during the past two years.

That the captain's orders are obeyed perfectly; it is in his yard that prayers are recited in the morning and evening, as they are on well-run plantations; those who are sick recite their prayers in their houses.

That André either whips or has whipped those who deserve punishment.

That they have two small rivers in their various gardens,

which seem to flow to the west and to originate in the mountains behind Montsénnery.

That André and some of his trusted followers make sorties from time to time to recruit new members in the area of Tonnégrande. He used to take shelter in the house of the said Copena of Pataoüa. It is from there that he summoned the Negroes belonging to Messrs. Gourgues and Boudet, and using a canoe that he found at the landing at Pataoüa and that he later returned, took the Negroes to sleep at Copena's house and the next day led them to the village.

That they can clearly hear the cannon shots fired at Cayenne, and thus know when an emergency has arisen. That on the feast of Corpus Christi, at the first cannon shot signaling that the Blessed Sacrament has been carried outside of the church, they fall to their knees and form a procession around their houses, singing hymns, and the women carrying crosses. All of which would seem to indicate that their village is located directly to the west of Cayenne.

That no whites ever entered the village, nor any Negroes other than the ones who are recruited by the said André, Augustin, and Sébastien during their periodic trips outside, and who promise never to betray them nor run away, under penalty of being hunted down and killed. They are brought to the village in the same manner as was the witness Louis and his companions, by way of numerous detours and without going on any real paths, so that once they are there, they cannot find their way back; and if they escaped, it would be by pure chance, and after several days' journey, during which they would risk dying of hunger, since the area does not appear to contain any houses nor to be inhabited by any Indians, at least as far as Louis was able to tell.

Whenever new maroons arrive, food is furnished them by the other members, until they have cleared a space for a garden and their crops are ready to be eaten.

That whenever land has to be cleared, everyone works together, and that once a large area has been burned, everyone is allotted a plot according to the needs of his family to plant and maintain.

That the wild pigs that they kill frequently are divided among them, as is other large game, even fish that they drug when there are large numbers of them; and that the only fish in their rivers are *patayayes, yaya blancs, oeils rouges,*

Brobro, and occasional *coulans;* and that there are few deer but all sorts of other game, and many jaguars, which they catch in traps and which they leave in the forest without skinning them, since, having no way of exporting the skins, they have no use for them.

That there is no road nor path whatsoever leading to Couroux or any other place, and that they are guided only by the path of the sun and by the rivers whose courses are known to André and other maroon leaders.

That he knows of no correspondence they might have; and that they maintain and repair their arms themselves, keeping them in good condition at all times, but that when having hunted a great deal they are without powder and shot, except for a little powder kept for emergencies, they use tiny stones, which are very hard and found in abundance in the area instead of shot.

That neither André nor any person representing him visited their house during the night; that they have no more than five dogs, and only Couachy keeps fowl; they have no cats; many of the Negroes eat rats; that lacking powder, they hunt pacas, armadillos, and other land animals with arrows, dogs, and traps.

That he heard absolutely no talk of fleeing at the news that the detachment was in pursuit; that it was André who had learned of the detachment's arrival at Montsénnery from the information gathered by Copena, who had accompanied André along with the present witness and Rémy, his father; that the news did not cause them to flee though they remained always on their guard, to the extent that whenever a tree happened to fall to earth they would imagine they heard musket shots and were ready to run into the forest in the direction of the setting sun.

That it was Augustin, Sébastien, and Michel, who, while searching for arrows, came upon the trails made by the detachment and ran to warn the village, upon which the same Augustin, Michel, Matador, Mathieu, and Jean de Maranne left to reconnoiter the area of the Montsénnery plantation; that both Augustin and Mathieu were armed with loaded muskets, having saved a few rounds of powder that had not been used up hunting; that Matador and Michel were armed with arrows and Jean de Maranne with a harpoon.

That ever since the above-mentioned five Negroes had left the village to search for this detachment, he had neither seen them nor heard that they had returned; and that several of the maroons had hidden their best possessions in the forest for fear of a surprise attack.

That this summer they have cleared three gardens at about a league's distance from the old ones, and that the said Augustin has a house there where he spends most of his time; that in the same new gardens there are three large sheds, which the detachment did not discover; that these three gardens, along with the houses and sheds, are still in existence; that these gardens are located on flat land and are almost completely filled with manioc, millet, rice, sweet potatoes, yams, sugar cane, bananas, and other crops, and a lot of cotton, since it rained a great deal during the summer.

That the women spin cotton when the weather is bad and work in the fields in good weather.

That Couachy, Augustin, and Bayou weave cotton cloth, which serves to make skirts for the women and loincloths for the men; that this cotton material is woven piece by piece and then assembled and decorated with Siamese cotton thread.

That they have no special sign of recognition (password) for when they return from reconnaissance missions and other expeditions; that they have neither killed nor caused the death of any person, nor do they place any watchmen or scouts near their village; that the only news they receive of the outside is furnished by their leaders when they go on their sorties, usually near Tonnégrande.

That he had not heard that the blacksmith of the [Jesuit] Fathers of Kouroux had done any repairs for them nor furnished them with objects made of iron.

That they maintain strict observance of Sundays and feast days by refraining from work and reciting the rosary in addition to their usual prayers.

That they get salt from the ashes of the Maracoupy palm.

That they make a beverage out of sweet potatoes, yams, bananas, plantains, and various grains, in addition to their *Nicou* and *Cacheiry* [manioc beer].

That the witness Louis had been captured by surprise and without violence as he was returning from Augustin's former gardens, by Saint Germain, Oreste, and Scipion, one of whom is a mulatto and two free Negroes; that his father Rémy and Couachy, who were with him, escaped into the forest, without a single shot being fired, and that they apparently warned their other companions, who also took flight.

That it is Marion and Jacqueline, her sister, who act as midwives.

That he has never heard of Claire, Mme. Meunier's Negress, nor of M. Trouillard's Negroes, nor that Chrétien, belonging to M. Jean-Baptiste Tisseau, had visited Marion, his mother, who belongs to M. Pierre Boudet.

That if someone should be missing in the evening, they make an extensive search for him.

That land for this year's gardens was burned about two moons ago, and planting was begun right away.

That they store all their belongings in *pagarats* [basketry containers] and that they have no tools other than a few files, gimlets, and hammers; that they have no saws or adzes.

That they had at the said village two Negro drums, which they played on certain holidays.

That Mathieu, his sister Madelon, Lizette, Rémy and his daughter, and Madelon Le Roux have asked permission to return to their masters, but that André was opposed to this and kept them in the village by force and threat of violence.

And after several readings and reiterations of the above testimony, made over a period of several days, the said Louis having upheld and affirmed that all that he said here was true and that he had nothing to change nor add to these facts, he was returned to the custody of the jailer's guard pending further orders.

At Cayenne, this thirty-first day of October, 1748.

(Signed): Le Tenneur Ardibus

[*Editor's note:* Most of the maroons captured with Louis were pardoned, being returned to their masters without further punishment (Henry 1950:115). But those who had temporarily evaded recapture were to meet a different fate. In 1752, an expedition was launched against a large band of maroons who were under the leadership of this same André. The troops included three officers, twenty soldiers, an unspecified number of Indians, and nine mulattoes and free blacks. They found and destroyed several settlements and many gardens, and captured several prisoners including Copena, who was put in prison pending trial, "weighted down with shackles on his feet and hands and with the iron collar around his neck" (Henry 1950:116). During Copena's trial in 1752, he testified that he had first run away some years before, had been captured and been punished by having both ears cut off, that after receiving thirty lashes he again escaped, leaving behind his wife and two children, and finally that he joined André's band. The final sentence of Copena and his companions, quoted directly from the records of the trial (see Henry 1950:116–17), speaks for itself.

Copena, charged with and convicted of marronage; of bearing firearms; of invading and pillaging, along with other maroons, the house and plantation of [M.] Berniac from which they stole various expensive furnishings, silver and a musket, and carried off many of his slaves; of mistreating him; and of committing other excesses. Copena is sentenced to having his arms, legs, thighs, and back broken on a scaffold to be erected in the Place du Port. He shall then be placed on a wheel, face toward the sky, to finish his days, and his corpse shall be exposed. Claire, convicted of the crime of marronage and of complicity with maroon Negroes, shall be hanged till dead at the gallows in the Place du Port. Her two young children Paul and Pascal, belonging to M. Coutard, and other children—François and Batilde, Martin and Baptiste—all accused of marronage, are condemned to witness the torture of Copena and Claire.]

CHAPTER NINETEEN

Unity and Disunity:
Cottica Djuka Society
as a Kinship System[1]

A. J. F. KÖBBEN

1. *Introduction.* The Djuka, one of the Bush Negro
tribes of Surinam, live in the interior of this vast country
along the Tapanahony, Marowijne, and Cottica rivers [see
Fig. 4]. Their precise number is not known, but it probably
amounts to about fifteen thousand. They live in villages
averaging some hundreds of inhabitants; they practice shifting cultivation, in addition to which they have of old earned
money through rendering transport services on the rivers.
Nowadays many young Djuka leave their homeland temporarily to work as migrant laborers in the capital (Paramaribo) or elsewhere. The tribe has a Paramount Chief
(*Gaaman*), who lives in the village of Dritabiki on the
Tapanahony River. There his power is preponderant (Thoden van Velzen 1966b:Chs. 6–9, 12, 13), but in the Cottica
region, which will be the subject of this paper, his influence
is negligible, although his name is held in high esteem. For

Reprinted with the permission of the author and publisher from
Bijdragen tot de Taal-, Land- en Volkenkunde 123:10–52 (1967).
[1] The field work on which this paper is based was carried out
from August 1961 to July 1962, mainly in the village of Langa
Uku on the Cottica River. In the same period Mr. (now Dr.) and
Mrs. Thoden van Velzen worked in Dritabiki, the village of the
Paramount Chief on the Tapanahony River. The Netherlands Or-
ganization for Scientific Research in Surinam and the Netherlands
Antilles made this field work financially possible. The translation
was done by Mrs. M. J. van de Vathorst-Smit.

all practical purposes, therefore, in this region there is no tribal political power that exceeds the village level.

2. *Djuka society as a kinship system.* In this paper Djuka society is analyzed as a kinship system. It may well be described from other points of view, but in a sense kinship is basic in that almost all relations within the village—legal, political, economic, and religious ones—are expressed in terms of kinship. Such other relations only exist by definition and not as separate parts of the social structure.

The inhabitants of a Djuka village will say: "We are all kinsmen," and in most cases this is actually true, at least if affines are also regarded as kin. The 176 adult inhabitants of the village of Langa Uku, for instance, may all be fitted into one diagram (see Figure 5. [Ed. note: unlike the full kinship

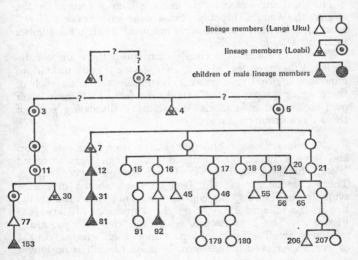

Figure 5: Inhabitants of Langa Uku and Loabi who are mentioned (by identifying number) in text.

diagram in the original article, this diagram shows the genealogy of *only* those individuals mentioned by identifying number in the text]). Ba Apetina (no. 153), for example, is the momomomomosidadadasoso of Sa Pobieng (no. 207), and thus her classificatory brother (*bala*).[2] Although she cannot, without consulting others, state the precise nature of the relationship, she knows quite well that he is a classificatory brother, and she behaves accordingly toward him.

The Djuka are matrilineal. The nucleus of the village is formed by the matrilineal descendants of the ancestress Afo Tesa (Fig. 5, no. 2). They are, to use the graphic Djuka expression, the *bé-sama*, "the people of the belly." A second group in the village are the "fathers-made-them-children" (*dada-meke-pikin*); descendants of men of the matrilineage, who are, therefore, not themselves members of the lineage, yet live in the village. This is by no means an insignificant group, neither in position nor in numbers: Forty-six adult inhabitants of the village belong to this category, as opposed to eighty-five adult "belly people."

The third and last category in the village is formed by the affines, the *konlibi*, literally "those who have come to live," most of them men but also some women.[3] Their total number in Langa Uku is forty-five.

The Djuka themselves clearly distinguish these three categories. Whenever the village crier (*basia*) goes around to announce a ritual or a palaver, he loudly summons each of these groups separately. They do, in fact, each have their own rights and obligations. We shall be discussing each of these three groups in turn.

3. *The matrilineage.* Matrilineal kin form a corporate group and have a name. The kingroup of Langa Uku is called "Pata." Langa Uku, however, is not the only *Pata* village. Those descendants of Afo Tesa who are shown in dotted symbols on Figure 5 [as well as many not indicated there] live in the village of Loabi on the Tapanahony River (see Figure 4). The Pata people, with their two villages, are a relatively small kinship group. Other such groups consist of five, six, or even ten villages. In those cases it is no longer

[2] *Ba* (lit. brother) and *Sa* (lit. sister) are terms for (young) man and (young) woman, respectively. The following genealogical conventions are used throughout this chapter: mo=mother['s], fa=father['s], br=brother['s], si=sister['s], so=son['s], da=daughter['s], hu=husband['s], wi=wife['s]. Thus, for example, "mobrwi" means "mother's brother's wife."
[3] In Figure 5 [and in the original, more complex version in Köbben 1967b] these affines are omitted in order not to render the figure illegible.

possible to trace actual kinship lines: Such matrilineal groups consist of several "bellies" (matrilineages), together forming one *lo* (matriclan).

So far the picture does not differ materially from that of matrilineal societies in West Africa. In one respect, however, these matriclans are unique: Each one originated (roughly during the first half of the eighteenth century) from a particular group of runaway slaves of a particular plantation or group of plantations, from which they also derive their names.

Thus the Dju-*lo* (literally the Jew-*lo*) goes back to a group of runaways from plantations owned by Portuguese Jews. The ancestors of the Pinasi-*lo* were the slaves of a planter called l'Espinasse; those of the Ansu-*lo* belonged to a Mr. Amsingh, the owner of the plantation called "Meerzorg," near Paramaribo (Wong 1938:310–16).

According to Wong (1938:313), the Pata group derive from the Maagdenburg plantation on the Tempati River (a tributary of the Surinam River), which belonged to a Mr. Pater. This statement, meanwhile, is not in agreement with the map of de Lavaux (1731). This shows all the existing plantations with their names and those of their owners. According to this map the plantations on the Tempati (or Tamapati) were already deserted at this time and none of them ever belonged to Pater. The latter did however own a plantation on the Commewijne River as well as one on the upper Cottica. If the ancestors of our Pata people really came from this Cottica plantation, this would lend a certain piquancy to the situation, since in that case they settled as free people, after many wanderings, almost exactly on the same spot where their ancestors formerly lived as slaves.

It is unlikely that the runaways from any one plantation were all related, let alone matrilineally related to one another. Still, that is how the Djuka represent the situation. If a *lo* consists of, for instance, five "bellies" (matrilineages), they say that the ancestresses were five sisters. This is a phenomenon known from many other societies: When people live in close proximity to one another like kinsmen, they tend to address and treat one another as kinsmen and to end up regarding each other as such. Social ties, in short, are more important than ties of the blood.

I do not claim hereby to have shown how these kinship groups were actually formed. Unfortunately, this process is definitely lost in the past. The anthropologist would be interested to know how these people came to choose a consistent matrilinear system. Undoubtedly their West African heritage played a part, but this cannot be considered a sufficient explanation, since the runaways did not all originate from matrilineal societies. The influence of the matrilineal Akan tribes is unmistakable, but so is that of patrilineal tribes. Were there discussions about how to reckon descent? Did the one group impose its will on the other? If they imitated what they remembered from Africa, how are we to explain the significant differences between the Akan and Djuka matrilineal systems? Do these differences date right from the beginning, or did they develop later? We shall never know the answers to these questions.

History of the Pata lineage. During the second half of the eighteenth century the Pata people probably migrated to the Tapanahony River together with the main body of the Djuka. According to informants, they built their first village in the upper Tapanahony district near Godoholo, on the Sliba Creek. This information agrees with a report by post holder Schachtruppe dating from 1830, which mentions a Pata village on that spot, a certain Andries being its head (Wong 1938:310–11). Later, probably during the second half of the last century, the Pata people migrated in little groups to the Cottica region, which offered better economic possibilities. The original village fell into decay. Eventually only Ma Komfo (Figure 5, no. 3) remained on the Sliba Creek with a granddaughter, Ma Neni (no. 11), the latter's husband, and their five children.[4] Around 1900 Ma Lena (no. 15) came from the Cottica district to visit the Sliba Creek village. Ma Komfo asked her to stay and settle there: "I don't want to stay on here by myself just with my granddaughter, and it would be a bad thing if all the Pata people left the Tapanahony region where the ancestors lie buried." Ma Lena responded to the appeal. Even so the village was too small in the end to be viable, so the inhabitants decided to move to nearby Loabi, a small village of the Pinasi-*lo* on the Tapanahony.

And such is still the situation at the present time, Pata

[4] *Ma* (lit. mother) is the term for elderly woman.

and Pinasi people living together in Loabi, although in separate quarters and each with their own headman. The village has only one ancestral shrine (*fagatiki*) and one mortuary house (*ké-osu* or *gáwan-osu*), built by the Pinasi lineage, but also used by the Pata people. The latter are not satisfied with their dependent position and have recently requested the Chief (*Gaaman*) of the tribe to be allowed to found a village of their own again.

Other clans similarly have their original village on the Tapanahony, with in addition one or more villages on the Cottica.

Although it takes ten days to reach Loabi from Langa Uku by canoe, travelers having to negotiate the formidable Marowijne and Tapanahony falls, there is regular contact and a feeling of solidarity between the two villages. Whenever people from Langa Uku have to go to Dritabiki to see the Paramount Chief, they go to nearby Loabi to stay for a while in the village of their kinsmen. A few years ago they came in great numbers to attend the mortuary feast (*booko dé*) for the captain of Loabi, Da Agi (Figure 5, no. 30).[5]

Da Nosu (no. 77) was appointed as Da Agi's successor, although he had been living in Langa Uku for years. Langa Uku is regularly visited by people from Loabi, who may come for a brief stay but may also remain there for as long as they wish, or even settle there permanently. The people of both villages know one another well enough for plenty of gossip both ways.

The Djuka have a good memory, since, if children are counted, the [Pata] genealogy includes no less than nine generations. As elsewhere, social structure determines what and how much of the past is remembered. Of the first generation only two persons are known, and it is no accident that these two are remembered: Da Abuta (no. 1) was a village head, and Afo Tesa (no. 2) is the link between the people of Langa Uku and those of Loabi. If her name had been forgotten, it would no longer be possible to show the relationship between the two villages.

Who came before them? Their names have been lost, for they are not needed to account for present-day kinship ties. According to some informants the two persons named were

[5] *Da* (lit. father) is the term for elderly man.

the first ancestors, meaning that they were the leaders of the runaways (*lowè sama*) from the plantation and the founders of the Pata lineage. Considering, however, that the group must have been formed at least 225 years ago, this cannot be true. Oral tradition tends to draw the moment of liberation (running away) closer in time: This act is simply attributed to the oldest generation of which names are remembered. It is not surprising, therefore, to find that about 35 years ago, when Wong (1938:313) asked the then captain of Langa Uku for the name of the Pata ancestress, the name given was not the same one that is given by the villagers today.

History, to these people, serves to account for and to justify the present, and as such it interests them—or at least some of them—greatly. But they feel no urge to establish "*wie es wirklich gewesen ist*," to use Von Ranke's famous expression. This is evident from what has just been said, and is also illustrated by the following incident. In the genealogy, Alali (no. 4) and Fisama (no. 5) are shown as brother and sister. My informant on this point asserted at first that Fisama was Alali's *mother*. I remarked that this made Alali, the second captain, and Aki (no. 7), the third captain, brothers with one and the same mother. But that is contrary to Djuka rule (see below). Therefore the reaction was prompt: "That won't do, so he must have been her brother, not her son."

A lineage is a unit, but not an undivided one. It is subdivided into *segments*, each having its own quarter (*pisi*) in the village. In Langa Uku there are five such segments, the respective ancestresses of which are indicated in Figure 5 by the numbers 16, 17, 18, 19, and 21. In matters of inheritance and succession the segment as a group plays an important part, as we shall see below.

Solidarity is greater among the members of a segment than among those of the matrilineage as a whole.

After a nocturnal séance two young men quarrel about some trivial matter and come to blows. In no time the whole crowd is fighting, each of the youths receiving assistance from the members of his own segment, who take sides without even knowing the reason for the fight. A *basia* (village headman's assistant, village crier) tries to calm people down by saying: "Stop it, go and sleep, tomorrow we'll sort things out." But the following day the matter is quickly dismissed. Everyone agrees it was only child's play, and allowance is made for the fact that both parties had had a few drinks.

Usually there is no obvious division between the various quarters, and for an outsider they are hard to distinguish. But the village people know precisely where the territory of each segment ends, and if a member of segment A wishes to live in that of segment B, he must ask for permission to do so.

In the village of Ajumakonde a man wanted to build a hut on a particular spot. A woman took exception to this: He had no business there, she said, for he belonged to a different segment and, besides, she herself was planning to build a hut just there. During the ensuing quarrel she struck the man in the face. This led to a general fight, both parties being assisted by their own closest relatives. Bystanders put an end to it, but during the next few days they exchanged blows again on two occasions. The man's group lost, and after much discussion they left and built a settlement of their own not far from the village.

Vis-à-vis the outside world, however, the matrilineage does act as a unit. This unity is manifested in religion. The lineage has a deity of its own as well as its own ancestors (*gán-jóka*) and, in addition, one or more avenging spirits (*kunu*).

The lineage deity. The deity of Langu Uku, Majombe, may serve as an example. He possesses powers enabling him to locate persons who get lost in the forest.

October 7. Some young men from Agitiondo arrive in Langa Uku with the news that a boy went out hunting yesterday and did not return in the evening; they have come to ask Majombe for help. An offering is made to the deity and a bundle of medicine (*obia*) is tied to a man's wrist, after which an attempt is made to work him into a state of trance with drums and chanting. *October 8.* An official delegation arrives from Agitiondo. A palaver (*kutu*) is held to discuss the matter. This takes several hours. In the evening there is a séance: Six men dance until they go into a trance. They fall down and *obia* water is spat over them. Early the next day they go out to search. *October 13.* The boy still hasn't been found, "but Majombe says he isn't dead yet." The search is continued. *October 14.* Shouts of exultation: He has been found. The village crier goes around to make the good news known. A messenger is sent to Agitiondo. The news has already reached that village, but the official message should come from Langa Uku, as if from Majombe himself, "for he is the one who found him." *December 15.* The Great Deity (*Sweli Gadu*)—the most powerful of Djuka deities—who dwells in Agitiondo has sent some of his priests to Langa Uku with six bottles of beer to thank his "colleague" Majombe for the latter's assistance. *January 4.* The boy who was lost comes to Langa Uku with his father to be ritually washed in Majombe's little temple.

The village people say: "When we ran away from the plantations we carried the knowledge of Majombe with us in our hearts. In the forest we built a small temple for him. Later we took him with us when we moved from Sliba Creek to this place." Loabi (the other Pata village) only has an unimportant subsidiary shrine (*bakaman*) to Majombe.

The ancestors. Each village has a shrine to the ancestors (*faga-tiki*), where libations are made on occasions of illness or misfortune, or before starting on some important undertaking, such as leaving the village for some length of time. The ancestors make no distinctions: They will help a stranger who lives in the village and makes them an offering, even a member of another tribe or a white man.

They are believed to be generally well disposed toward their descendants, but once their anger is roused by some improper action they can bring illness or death to a member of the lineage, not necessarily always the person against whom their anger is directed.

In the village of Pikin Santi a woman is seriously ill. What is the cause? The oracle is consulted and intimates that the ancestors have made her ill. The people of her deceased husband's village did not treat her well when she stayed there as a widow. Her younger brother, instead of siding with her and avoiding the village in question, married a woman from that very village and went to live there. To show their displeasure at this action the ancestors caused the illness in the woman.

The avenging spirits. The fear inspired by the avenging spirit (*kunu*) is far greater than that felt for the ancestors.

The *kunu* concept is reminiscent of the Furies of classical Greece: It is the doom a lineage brings on itself by killing someone unjustly. The dead person's spirit enters the head of a member of his own or his murderer's lineage, manifesting itself at irregular intervals. When the "bearer" of the *kunu* dies, the spirit is inherited by another member of his matrigroup. The *kunu* tries to take revenge for the injustice suffered, causing the illness or death of members of the guilty lineage.

Not every person who is murdered by the lineage actually becomes a *kunu*. A few years ago two women beat an old woman to death in a quarrel. "The old woman's spirit plays nasty tricks on the two women who killed her, for instance by frightening them when they are alone in the forest to relieve nature. But it is not a real *kunu* yet, for it has not manifested itself in anyone so far. The two women are being treated by the priests of the Great Deity to prevent it from turning into a real *kunu*."

Not only a murdered Djuka but a Creole, a white man, a Javanese—anyone who falls by a murderer's hand can become a *kunu*.

The *kunu* is not possessed by blind vengeance, however; he only takes action when provoked. He is an upholder, albeit a very strict one, of the moral order. He deals out punishment when someone speaks ill of his lineage in front of strangers; or when there is jealousy or rancor between members of the matrigroup (*fio-fio, buja*); or when a person does something against the express wish of his lineage; or, finally, in cases of incest.[6] The Djuka do believe, though, that living persons can defend themselves against the *kunu*, at least to some degree. They may mollify it by regular offerings and supplications and by showing their gratitude as long as all goes well. After a mortuary feast that has passed without dissonance, the Djuka never fail to thank the *kunu* for keeping aloof. As such the belief is an example of the *do ut abeas* idea. It is significant to note, however, that there also is evidence at times of a *do ut des* attitude: a feeling that this hostile *kunu* may be profitable to the lineage—though

---

[6] W. F. van Lier (1940:179) emphasizes this last aspect of the *kunu* belief stronger than my informants do.

reluctantly and, as it were, contrary to its real nature—if only it is properly served.

Like the ancestors, the *kunu* does not necessarily punish the actual offender, but rather just any members of the lineage. An informant commented: "We people of today (*baka kio sama*) can't approve of that any longer. The *kunu* should not kill innocent people! For what will their spirits do? They will be filled with vengeance in their turn to kill still other members of the matrigroup. In that way there's no end to it." These words show that the younger generation no longer views the lineage as a homogeneous unit. Collective responsibility is no longer a matter of course for them.

The *kunu* is greatly feared, even by those who have been influenced by Western religious ideas. One such informant told me: "I have become a Christian, so I need not be afraid of anything any longer, except of course the *kunu*." Actually, the person in question was also afraid of witchcraft and of the Great Deity. Nevertheless, his remark illustrates the central position of the *kunu* belief.

Kunu is not just associated with danger. If a member of lineage A is killed by lineage B and becomes B's *kunu*, he simultaneously becomes a good genius for lineage A. In addition, the situation gives lineage A a certain amount of power over lineage B.

The Pinasi lineage once murdered a Pata man. His spirit became a *kunu* for the Pinasi. It first manifested itself in a Pinasi man and later entered the head of a Pata woman ("he returned to his own lineage"). The Pinasi people now must treat this woman in particular and the Pata lineage in general with deference.

A Pinasi man was married to a Pata woman. He suspected her, with good reason, of being unfaithful, but she would not admit her guilt. He dared not insist too strongly on a confession for fear of the *kunu* in question.

It is not permitted for a man of a third lineage to be married to a Pata woman and a Pinasi woman at the same time. If such cowives were to quarrel it might, again, arouse the *kunu*'s anger, resulting in illness or death.

The Pata woman in whose head this *kunu* dwells acts as his priestess. She has his shrine in her hut and it is one of the most sacred places in the village. At times of illness or other misfortune the Pata people come here to ask for aid. The priestess derives prestige from her position. Once when some young men had stolen the crops she had harvested she went into a trance and the *kunu* spoke threatening words through her lips. The elders reproached the miscreants and warned them of the danger they incurred.

4. Exogamy. Unilineal groups of the type outlined are exogamous in most societies, in fact so frequently so that most theorists include exogamy as an element in their definition of "clan" and "lineage." Does this apply also for the Djuka? In former times their society was strictly exogamous, marriage to even the farthest-removed clan sister being forbidden.

According to W. F. van Lier (1919:76): "If a man has sexual relations with his own sister the *kunu* will punish, but it does not take action in less serious cases (sexual contact with a distant clan sister); it will never, however, condone a marriage between such persons and they may not live together." This is in accordance with what my informants tell me of "former times."

Recently, however, things have changed. In most Cottica villages intralineage marriages (*bé anga bé,* lit. "belly with belly") are permitted now, on condition that the partners must not belong to the same matri*segment.* At present there are seven such marriages in Langa Uku, including those of the captain and his two *basia.*

Nevertheless, such marriages are not yet a matter of course. No one in this village really opposes them, but they are still a subject of lively discussion. Some still don't think it quite right: "Formerly the gods would have punished such persons, but nowadays people just do as they like and the gods are more easygoing." Significant is the fact that the village captain at first kept his own intralineage marriage concealed from me, apparently believing I would think it blameworthy or indecent. Others, however, express enthusiasm at the change and advance good arguments in defense of it: "If you marry someone of another lineage the children are not for yourself, but if your wife is of your own 'belly' the children are too." A man who has two wives, one a lineage sister and the other a stranger, said: "That first one lives with me here in the village, both of us can continue to live at home. My things also stay in my own village. But look at my other wife: I have a hut in her village, everything I possess there is lost, for I am only a stranger in that place. In the past you were not allowed to marry a 'sister'; if you tried, people would beat you. But nowadays it is permitted, thank goodness!"

With respect to this matter there is no clear difference between the generations. Young people are heard to defend such marriages, but so, too, is the oldest man in the village. It's a question of personal interests. This village eldest wished to marry a lineage sister himself some years ago, and therefore he takes the "progressive" point of view.

The former headman, who died six years ago, vehemently opposed such marriages for many years. The people of the village still give colorful descriptions of the way he used to rail at those who had the impudence to start an affair with a lineage sister. It is interesting to note that his arguments, according to his son (who is now some sixty years old himself), were based not only on tradition or the gods, but also on practical grounds. "If everyone married inside the village, we wouldn't have any more affines (*konlibi*) coming to live in the village. *And then who would mediate in conflicts?* Suppose a Pata man quarreled with another Pata man and there was no outsider to mediate between them. The mediator then would *have* to be a third Pata man. If he decides in favor of the first man against the second, what will people say? They won't say that the first one was really right, but they'll say that he has a preference for that first man!" As we shall see, affines do mediate in conflicts between members of a lineage. The headman's argument testifies, therefore, to a considerable amount of insight into his own society.

Toward the end of his life, when he realized that there was no way to prevent such marriages, the headman surrendered: "A few men may marry lineage sisters, but not all. That way there will still be affines." Even today most people agree with this. As one informant commented in an almost Lévi-Straussian mood: "Suppose everyone married within the 'belly,' we wouldn't have any contact with other villages and there would only be a few people present on such occasions as mortuary feasts, only people from our own village, and that wouldn't be right."

We should like to know where and when and in what circumstances such intralineage marriages first took place.

Probably the change came about gradually and without spectacular conflicts, for the present-day Djuka, or at least my informants, couldn't tell me anything about it. And we must allow for the fact that the process is not yet completed. Among the Djuka of the Tapanahony River, for instance, such marriages are still exceptional (cf. Thoden van Velzen 1966b:33–34). Oddly enough, the Cottica people quote the authority of the *Gaaman* (Paramount Chief), who lives on the Tapanahony, to sanction these marriages. When I asked what the *Gaaman* thought of the matter, an elder replied: "It was actually a former *Gaaman* who instituted these marriages. He said there was no objection to them, not even in the case of children of full sisters." Needless to say, this is an apocryphal statement.

On the Cottica River too we find "progressive" and "conservative" villages. In the big village of Agitiondo, a few hours by canoe from Langa Uku, there are only two instances of intralineage marriage, and even those are scarcely thought decent. This conservatism is due to the fact that Agitiondo is the residence of the Great Deity (*Sweli Gadu*), the deity whose priests are the most important power group in the society. They are suspicious of this sort of innovation, which they usually manage to check in an effective manner, at least in their own village.

The village headman of Langa Uku is married to a clan sister, as we saw above, and this is in no way detrimental to his position. Compare what happened to Da Atonsé in the village of Agitiondo. This man is an important elder. Since the death of the village headman, which occurred some years before, he was acting headman, meanwhile carrying on intrigues to ensure his definite appointment. At the same time he had a clandestine affair with a distant clan sister and made her pregnant. In Langa Uku the matter would have been settled quickly with the sanction of the normal marriage ritual. Here, however, it was treated as a case of incest. The (priests of the) Great Deity imposed on Da Atonsé a heavy fine, namely a demijohn of *tafia* (an inferior type of rum), twelve bottles of beer, and one sheet. In the past the man himself had several times whipped others who had affairs with clan sisters. "That is why it is necessary for the Great Deity to humiliate him now in this way."

It should be noted that this punishment by the priests was also a political maneuver. They did not want the man in question to become village headman, and this affair gave them an opportunity to campaign against him. As a matter of fact, the affair did obliterate his chances of obtaining the office. Interestingly enough, the people of Langa Uku, where he was also disliked, displayed great moral indignation when they heard of the affair. "It is true we also marry lineage sisters," they said, "but he does so in Agitiondo, and that's a different thing. That is very bad."

One *result* of intralineage marriage is increased disunity between the various matrisegments within the village. The solidarity of the segments is stressed at the expense of that of the village as a whole.

Ba Mansooi (Figure 5, no. 206) recently married his lineage sister Sa Meina (no. 180), his momomomosidadadada. He decides to build a new hut in the quarter of his own lineage segment. This is not to the liking of Sa Meina's grandmother and foster-mother Ma Faandi (no. 46). She demands that the hut be built in her quarter. The result is a violent quarrel, which finally involves all the members of the two lineage segments concerned. The cause of the quarrel is less futile than it might seem. If the hut is built in the man's quarter it counts as his property, if in the woman's, as hers. If the young couple were to divorce—and divorce is common in this society—then the location of the hut decides to whom it will go, to the man or to the woman.

To settle the dispute a palaver (*kutu*) is finally held, which produces a verdict intended more or less to humor both parties and which is an example of the kind of compromises the Djuka are so fond of. Ba Mansooi is allowed to finish his hut, but later, at some unspecified date, he must also build one in Sa Meina's quarter.

These intralineage marriages are an example of recent change. Are they also an instance of acculturation? In other words, did this change come about as the result of (direct or indirect) external influences? This seems a plausible enough supposition, but we cannot be sure. Note that the matrilineal Ashanti of West Africa, although their society is infinitely more Westernized, still adhere to the rule of exogamy (cf. Fortes 1950:259).

5. *Succession*. For the principal political offices, those of the Paramount Chief (*Gaaman*) and the village headman (captain), succession is strictly matrilineal. In the following exposition we shall limit ourselves to the village headman.[7] When such a functionary dies, which member of the lineage succeeds him? According to Djuka rules, the new headman must belong to the next generation and preferably not to the dead man's matrisegment. The explanation the Djuka themselves offer for the latter requirement is that in this way the various segments of the lineage in turn may reap the profits (*njan*, lit. "eat") of captainship: a sort of spoils system. As West Europeans, we know from dynastic history the rule that the successor must be the closest relative of the defunct ruler, regardless of whether or not he happens to be capable. Here we have a system where the successor must, on the contrary, be a *distant* relative.

There are considerable differences between this matrilineal system of succession and that of the West African Akan peoples. There the successor should preferably belong to the same generation as the dead man, if possible be a (real or classificatory) brother. There is no circulation of the office among the segments. For the inheritance of goods too, we may already note at this stage, the rules differ. Among the Akan, in principle, one person is the inheritor. Among the Djuka the inheritance is divided among as many individuals as possible (see below). I mention this to illustrate my statement that Djuka culture is no copy of any West African example.

Even taking into account the two limitations mentioned, a large number of lineage members are eligible for the office. By what means does the final choice come about? A headman who feels that his death is near usually indicates who is his favorite. He prepares the latter for the office by transmitting to him the esoteric knowledge of the group's history. But only what happens after his death is decisive. The Djuka believe that the dead man's spirit definitely appoints

[7] As to the succession of the Paramount Chief, cf. Thoden van Velzen 1966b:64–68 and Ch. XV.

his successor. The spirit is consulted in the following way. The dead man's hair is shaved off and tied together in a bundle on a paddle. During the burial rites two bearers walk around with it, each carrying one end of the paddle on his head. The belief is that the dead man's spirit has gone into his hair, which thus becomes a sort of oracle. It is asked a number of questions, the answer being contained in the movements of the bearers carrying the paddle with the bundle of hair. They either nod affirmatively or shake their heads.

Burial of the captain of Ricanaumofo. 4 P.M.: The men carrying the paddle approach the circle of elders. These show respect, those wearing a cap or hat take it off. The spirit is greeted by a clapping of hands and is addressed as "*Da*" (father). The atmosphere carries no trace of *mysterium tremendum.* People around are talking and joking and show no particular interest in what is happening. The spirit is asked questions: Is the feast to his liking? Are the offerings big enough? Such a person has come with such a gift, does that please him? The bearers nod "Yes" but show some uneasiness. This is interpreted as meaning: "I am content, but a bottle of *tafia* should be offered to the ancestors or else they will be angry." The request is immediately complied with. A little later the bearers are wildly running about: The spirit is showing his annoyance. The reason is that an important affine (*konlibi*) has not yet given anything for the burial. In a palaver arranged on the spot the man is sharply criticized.

In a similar way the spirit is asked to appoint his successor, but this takes place a year or more after the burial, at the great three-day feast that concludes the period of mourning (*pu na blaka*). The elders ask him: "Who is it to be? This man . . . or this one . . . or this one . . . ," until the spirit nods.

Not every official is chosen in this way. Deputy headmen and *basia* (headman's assistants, village criers) are appointed by living persons. Priests of some deities are chosen by their predecessors. The appointment may receive extra confirmation by the deity manifesting itself through "calling in his head" (possession).

[According to] Durkheim's theory, religious beliefs are symbolic representations of society itself (Durkheim 1912: 97–121, 293–334). As a general theory this has been repeatedly and rightly rejected (for example, Lowie 1924: Ch. VII; Norbeck 1961:22), but in this case it is applicable. *The will of the deity* (the dead man) *represents public opinion.* Or at least the part of public opinion that predominates in the group. This last addition is essential, for only rarely is there complete agreement about the person of the new headman. Often there are endless intrigues by the various candidates and their supporters.

Where does this public opinion come in when the dead man is questioned? At first I thought of the bearers who carry the paddle around. It is not on them, however, that the decision depends; they are picked more or less at random, and at the various séances of one mortuary feast they are not the same individuals.

In actual fact, it is the interrogators who make the decision, a handful of elders, virtuosos in the art of suggestive questioning. "Is this man to be the new headman?" "No." "Or that one?" "No." "*Or what about him?*" "Yes."[8] Is this prompting recognized as such, might it even be a case of conscious deception? Yes and no. Oddly enough, people deny this on their own part but quite readily ascribe it to their opponents.

Many years before his death, Da Baja, the formidable captain of Agitiondo who lived to a great age, had promised the headman's office to Folikè. He taught him all about the lineage and the tribe and even advised him to send a few sisters' children to school so that they might be able to help him later in writing letters. Many, however, grudged him the office. One of Folikè's sisters' sons told me: "After Da Baja's death, when his spirit was questioned about his succession, the people involved were all enemies of Folikè. It was a perfidious business. That's how someone else came to be designated." This criticism was expressed in private, but in the following case it was done more openly. Six years ago when Da Mankilo, village headman of Ricanau died, there were many candidates for his

[8] Cf. also Thoden van Velzen 1966b:66–67. On the other hand, van Lier (1919:59) is of the opinion that it is the bearers who play the decisive role.

succession. During his lifetime Mankilo himself had chosen a comparatively young man, because the older men had behaved disloyally toward him. But to everyone's surprise and even amusement, the spirit when questioned initially designated Da Sokoda. Now he is held in very low esteem by his fellow villagers: "He can't do anything, not even beget a child." True enough, even to an outsider the person in question seems quite unfit for any leading position. His designation was explained as the work of Da Lankoi, headman of the neighboring village of Lantiwé, who had recently married Da Sokoda's mother and wished to do the old woman a favor. "*He* arranged for Sokoda to be appointed." After much bickering and several days of palavering, the captain of yet another village declared the designation invalid. The dead man's hair was carried around once more, and this time the choice did fall on the man Mankilo had chosen during his lifetime.

But, as I said before, people deny any cheating on their own part, and they do so in good faith. A few days before a new headman was to be designated by his predecessor's spirit, the most influential elder of the village told me that he had already decided who it was to be. With seeming artlessness I asked him whether he had informed the bearers, so that they would not nod "Yes" at the wrong moment. His reaction was peevish and indignant: "No, that would be cheating. It is not the bearers who move the hair, it's the hair that moves the bearers." Didn't I know that by now? Didn't I believe it? Then I should have a go at carrying the paddle myself!

This elder does not see anything contradictory in what he says. He believes if an important person like himself wants something and asks it on behalf of the whole village (or at least on behalf of the most powerful faction in the village), the deity himself will want that too.

In certain cases, therefore, the dead man's decisions may be repudiated, but only if this is known to be in accordance with the *communis opinio,* not if the action would incur the opposition of a majority or a powerful faction.

Tabigi is convinced that his failure to be appointed was the work of his enemies: "That was the work of human beings, a treacherous business." Couldn't he try to have the decision canceled, I ask him. "No, the dead man has spoken. They have forced the decision on him against his will, but if I were to contest it now he would cause my illness or death. Even if *Gaaman* (the Paramount Chief) said that I ought to be headman, I still wouldn't accept."

Thus we see that what is regarded as the will of the deity is in fact public opinion, or at least a part of public opinion. But at the same time it is more. The supernatural sanction accompanying the appointment will, if not prevent, at least discourage dispute. Nor does this function remain unperceived by all the Djuka, judging by a remark made by one of them: "Voting might be a better way of appointing a headman than letting the ancestors decide . . . but there would certainly be more quarrels then."

I have already mentioned the two principles that have to be observed in matters of succession. The successor must belong to the next generation and be a member of the same lineage as the dead man but of a different lineage *segment*. These rules, however, are not always strictly followed. People will try to deviate from them, especially if they are in conflict with their personal interests.

Napang opposes Abinte's candidacy for the headmanship of Agitiondo, basing his objections on the second principle: "Abinte is too closely related to the late captain." At the same time he is concerning himself with the succession in Lantiwé, where his own father was headman. For this position he is recommending a man . . . who is very closely related to his late father: "How proud my father ('s spirit) will be." His attention having been called to this inconsistency, he says: "Those other segments have been asking for it, they've always obstructed him. Anyhow, they haven't anyone suitable."

Although sickness and death are thought to be the possible result, occasionally someone is appointed who does not fulfill the requirements mentioned. The Djuka are incorrigible pragmatists: They always try to find out how far they can go. If no one falls ill and no one dies, the gods have evidently acquiesced! All the same, they will never omit to "ask the gods' pardon." In the village of Pinatjaimi, a man who was the previous headman's mother's sister's son was appointed to the office. When he died, after only a few years, the villagers interpreted this as a sign that they had overstepped the mark. In *his* succession the rules were once more strictly observed.

The successor must be a man of a younger generation, but this by no means implies, with such a large kinship group, that he will be a young man. A very old man will not easily be appointed, nor will a very young one. Actually, the opinions are divided on this subject. The appointment of a man of about thirty-five or forty in one village gave rise to some discussion. Some considered him too young: "A captain ought to be gray-haired and know about the things of the past. He must be old enough to dare put people in the wrong." But others opposed this. As one of them said: "They should take young men, who can hold the office for many years and learn to do the job well." The same man, on being shown a photo of John F. Kennedy and learning what function he held, showed the photo to a lot of people to lend force to his arguments: "Look how young that man is!"

Although the system of succession outlined above is still very much alive for the Djuka, some people do criticize it. As someone remarked: "We Djuka are stupid. We shouldn't carry around this hair, we should be doing the choosing ourselves. We shouldn't take a man from a particular segment but simply elect whoever's best." I tried to comfort this man by telling him about our hereditary monarchy, in which, after all, even the smallest element of choice is lacking.

An implicit assumption in what has been said so far is that the office of headman is a much coveted one. And so it is. It provides some small income, a certain, though small, amount of power and, especially, status. All this amply outweighs any drawbacks.

But this is something never expressed in public. On the contrary, the elders in particular will often emphatically state that nothing in the world would induce them to take on the job of headman. "Imagine the trouble, the loss of time, the gossiping, and the evil things (witchcraft) you'd be exposed to!" When a person is designated as headman, he will lament and protest: "Oh, why me, there are so many others both older and wiser." Sometimes the headman-to-be will hide in a forest camp and will only allow himself to be persuaded to return to the village after endless *pourparlers*. During the period intervening between appointment and installation (which may be many months again), nobody is permitted in his presence to allude to his future office on pains of incurring his grave indignation.

This behavior is highly institutionalized and contains histrionic elements. The prospective holder of the office should not appear too eager. "If he did he would fall ill and perhaps die before long." Yet the Djuka are well aware this is no more than make-believe. On one occasion, when someone rejected the headmanship in categorical terms, one of the bystanders whispered: "Just wait, in the end he'll bite. Actually there's no one who wouldn't want to be headman."

We have seen that a period of one year at least—but this may become three or four—passes between the death of one headman and the debut of his successor. During this interegnum the office is filled by a deputy, who is preferably not a member of the matrilineal group himself, though closely connected with it, that is, a "father-made-him" child, a son of a male member of the group. The guiding motive here is the consideration that such a person can have no claim to becoming the "real" captain, and thus will not be able to exploit his position as acting headman in canvassing for his own election. This is not only the anthropologist's interpretation but the one given by the people themselves. In Agitiondo a man who was appointed acting headman did, contrary to the custom, belong to the matrilineage of the village. When he started intriguing for his own appointment, the prompt reaction was: "Their own fault, they should have taken a father-made-him child."

6. *Inheritance of goods.* While the inheritance of offices is strictly matrilineal, as we have seen, this is not true of the inheritance of goods. These are divided among a large number of persons. The ideal is that "everyone" should share in the inheritance, the dead man's matrilineal kin but his children too and sometimes others as well. Before his death a man may give instructions: "My hut is for this man, my gun for that one," and these wishes will mostly be taken into account when the inheritance is divided.

When a person dies, his hut, containing all his possessions, is closed under supervision of a matrilineal relative—for instance, a brother. Division does not take place until the end of the mourning period, after at least twelve months. How much goes to the deceased's children and how much to the matrilineal kin depends on the situation. Sons who live in their father's village and have worked with him, as happens in a minority of cases, will receive the largest portion, but in other cases the sons get less or even nothing at all.

In the numerous cases in which the deceased after his death proves to have been a witch, the procedure is different. His possessions are confiscated and fall to the Great Deity and his priests. The latter take whatever they fancy and graciously return the remainder to the family.

My informants all agree that "formerly" the inheritance went exclusively to the matrilineal kin, and that it is only recently that a man's own children have been getting a share. The strange thing is, though, that this is pictured as an accomplished fact, as a change completed without any conflict. And what is "formerly"? The old men say: "That was when we were children," but such a statement is hard to check. This brings us face to face with the difficulty of all research into the processes of change in tribal societies, namely the fact that we are insufficiently informed about the zero point. It is quite possible that no change took place at all, or nothing much to speak of, and that formerly too the children of the deceased shared in the inheritance. Matrilineal inheritance is the ideal, and perhaps they merely impute this ideal situation to the good old times.

Even stranger is the fact that the Djuka, who will quarrel about almost anything and who are very acquisitive, rarely quarrel about the division of the inheritance among matrilineal and nonmatrilineal relatives. It hardly ever figures as a subject of conversation. If it did, it would not have escaped me, since I more or less expected to find conflicts of this sort and even asked some impudently suggestive questions in this direction—this on account of my previous experiences with the matrilineal Agni (West Africa), where jealousy and disputes among a man, his sons, and his sister's sons are the order of the day (cf. Köbben 1956:28–36). These types of conflicts, as a matter of fact, are found in many other matrilineal societies as well (cf. Köbben 1964:25–37).

How is it that the Djuka are an exception? The explanation may perhaps be found in the principle of division, by which each individual receives only a trifle. The West African Agni, as well as other Akan tribes, have a family treasure, which is considered sacred and which is left as much as possible intact to pass on to the next generation.

In such a society, therefore, the matrilineal group is more apt to feel wronged if some part of the inheritance goes to the sons.

A confirmation, to some extent, of this explanation is provided by one of the rare cases that did give rise to dispute about an inheritance. Two brothers, older men, had put all their money into a tractor. They announced that they wished their sons (the only men who could handle the tractor) to be sole inheritors. In this case the inheritance, consisting as it did of one piece only, could not be split up, and the matrilineal group felt wronged. Maybe the comparative wealth of these men is also a factor. They were the only Djuka to have purchased such an expensive machine. From the literature we know that conflicts of the type outlined tend to grow more virulent in matrilineal societies as the differences in income incease. Among the Djuka, differences in income are, on the whole, still very slight.

Apart from material goods, spiritual goods, too, may be inherited, especially the "ownership" of a lesser deity. The inheritor receives the shrine and cult objects of the deity, together with the esoteric knowledge. He becomes its priest, and often the deity will manifest itself in him (possession). Such an heir may be a matrilineal kinsman, but equally well the deceased's son. The latter possibility is definitely no recent development, for W. F. van Lier (1940:204), whose data derive largely from the early twenties of this century, already mentions it. Such a deity does not only serve the interests of his priest; in principle he is there for the whole matrigroup. Suppose No. 2 in Figure 6 inherits a deity from his father. The deity has thus moved outside No. 1's lineage. On account of his special connection with his father's matrilineage, No. 2 may still act as a priest on behalf of this lineage. The ties between No. 2 and his father's lineage are of a personal nature, however, which means that, if after No. 2's death the priesthood were to devolve on No. 4 or No. 5, the deity would be considered lost to the original matrilineage. In such a case there may be two heirs, for instance No. 4 or No. 5 *and* No. 3. An additional shrine is built, a sort of branch of the existing one, and it is inaugurated with suitable ritual.

In most matrilineal societies there is a special relationship between ego and his mother's brother, the locus of authority being with the mother's brother. With the Djuka, however,

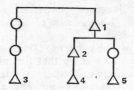

Figure 6: Inheritance of deity.

a young man should show a certain deference before *all* fellow villagers of the ascendant generation, including, for instance, a father's brother. While it is true that he will often have more dealings with his mother's brother than with other members of his lineage, this kinsman is not a special category. I assume that this is connected with the fact that ego is not specifically his mother's brother's heir—neither of his dignities nor of his goods.

7. *Residence.* The Djuka have no hard-and-fast rule or custom prescribing the individual's residence in a certain place or in a particular village. In this respect there is ample room for choice and manipulation, even though there are limits to this choice, and regularities may be detected in the way it comes about. Table 1 gives a picture of the residence of all the marriages of one lineage (in this case the Pata lineage).

uxorilocal	20
ambilocal	19
virilocal	8
autolocal	15
endolocal	30
neolocal	3
	95

Table 1: Residence of 95 marriages.

Uxorilocal are those marriages in which the married couple reside in the wife's village. *Ambilocal:* The couple reside alternately in the man's and in the woman's village. *Virilocal:* The couple reside in his village. *Autolocal:* Husband and wife each remain in their own village, now and again one going to stay with the other (the husband usually visiting the wife). *Endolocal:* These are intravillage marriages, husband and wife living together, both in their own village. *Neolocal:* The couple settle permanently in a locality that is new for both husband and wife.

A system may be detected in these figures only if we take the time factor into account—that is, if we look at the life histories of individuals. Let us take as our starting point a young man who marries a girl from another village. He is expected to build a hut for her in her own village and to settle there, at least for the time being (*uxorilocality*). He must clear a plot of land for her, and in addition perform services for his parents-in-law, as a way of showing his appreciation for having acquired rights in the woman.

Murdock (1949:213–14) argues that in a tribal society it is practically impossible for an adult man to settle in a new community, since this would oblige him to master an entirely new environment. "All the knowledge he has gained . . . concerning the location of trails and landmarks, of superior stands of timber, of the haunts of game . . . becomes largely useless, and must be painfully accumulated afresh." Uxorilocality could, therefore, occur only with local endogamy.

In the case of the Djuka, however, many young men settle uxorilocally in a new village without any great problems. This is simply explained by the fact that the physical environment into which they move is of the same nature as at home. Asosié is a young man from Agitiondo who has been given a girl from Langa Uku in marriage. He hasn't so far built a hut in Langa Uku, nor does he live with her yet. He has now come for the first time to stay for a while in Langa Uku, and he is going to build a cooking hut for his mother-in-law. He asks a man from the village: "Where in the forest do I find *pina* leaves (for thatch)? And where are such-and-such sorts of lianas?" The other man tells him in a few sentences, and that's that.[9]

All this does not mean that such an uxorilocally married young man loses touch with his village of origin. On the contrary, he will often stay there for longer or shorter periods of time—for instance, to attend a mortuary feast. As he grows

[9] Cf. Kloos 1963:854–62 for an adequate explanation of why uxorilocality and local endogamy are correlated.

older he is more and more drawn toward his own village, where his position is growing in importance. That is why at a certain moment he builds a hut of his own in his own village. The ties linking husband and wife are not as close as in Western society, so a man may without difficulty go and stay in his own village by himself for a week or so. If these periods grow longer, however, his wife begins to accompany him: The marriage has become *ambilocal*.

The nineteen cases of ambilocality in Table 1 are not all identical. Some of these couples move back and forth frequently; others (when the two villages are a long distance apart) change residences at longer intervals. Some couples spend about the same amount of time in both villages; others live predominantly in one. There is a smooth transition from uxorilocal to ambilocal, so much so that in some cases the investigator finds it hard to decide whether *still* to class the marriage as uxorilocal or *already* as ambilocal.

If a man obtains some high position in his village—for instance, if he is appointed headman, or assistant headman, or if he becomes a priest of some important deity—he will settle permanently in the village and his wife will come to live with him there: The marriage becomes *virilocal*. The husband's position, though, is not the only decisive factor in the choice of residence. It is no coincidence that all five sisters of the headman of Langa Uku are living in their own village (four with their husbands, one divorced), although they, as well as their husbands, are middle-aged by now. They share in the prestige of headmanship, and that is what keeps them in the village. There may be other reasons, too, that cause an older couple to decide on uxorilocality.

Ma Jeje (no. 91) has lived most of her life in Pikin Santi, to which village she is attached by a twofold bond: It is the village of her father, and she herself married a man from this village. When one of her children died she was accused—not openly, but plainly enough—of having bewitched him. She on her part accused those of Pikin Santi of the same crime. After a quarrel she left the village and went with her husband and all her descendants back to her own matrivillage, where they now form a separate matrisegment.

Autolocality has as its main cause polygyny, which occurs frequently among the Djuka. Of seventy-eight married men, twenty have two and three even have three wives (which means that 28 percent are polygnously married). Of the group of middle-aged and older men, half have more than one wife. In the Cottica region, cowives never live in the same village (though they sometimes do along the Tapanahony). If they did, it would only give rise to conflicts, as the Djuka rightly say. Thus a man with two wives has two households in different villages, staying alternately at one or the other. A village notable will have one wife living with him in his own village, and now and again visit the other. The first marriage is virilocal, the second autolocal.

The headman of Langa Uku is married to a lineage sister who lives with him in the village and is always near him. Only after I had been in the village for a month did I learn that he has a second wife as well, who lives in Petondo, about eight hours by canoe from Langa Uku. From August 1961 to August 1962 he visited her only twice, each time staying about a week. Both times the reason for his visit had nothing to do with her. The first time it was a mortuary feast in her village, the second time a divorce case in which, as a headman, he was involved. During these same twelve months the wife in question visited Langa Uku only once, staying there a few days on her way to Agitiondo to consult the oracle of the Great Deity. The position and way of life of such a woman do not differ much from those of a widow or a divorced woman.

A second type of autolocal marriage is that of an older man marrying an older woman (often a widower marrying a widow) from a neighboring village. Both remain in their own village, visiting one another at intervals. Four of the fifteen autolocal marriages in Table 1 are of this type.

In the cases of virilocality, the couple concerned are nearly always older people, the husband being an elder in his own village. If such a man has high status and prestige, his children will often stay in their father's village and continue to live there once they are grown up, when they will build their huts close to their father's. Such groups, of a father and his children living close to him, are perhaps the closest-knit units existing in Djuka society. These "father-made-them" children, moreover, greatly strengthen their father's position.

Examples are the deputy headman, Daose (no. 45 in Figure 5) with two grown-up sons, the village eldest (no. 20), with five adult children, and nos. 92 and 56 with seven and five children, respectively.

When such a prominent man dies, his widow will usually return to the village of her own lineage. His children, who have grown up in the village and feel at home there (have *gwenti*), will often continue to live there. They may marry and have children of their own, and *these* too may stay in the village.

In other cases, however, the children of a prominent man leave the village one after the other after their father's death. Take, for example, Da Songe (no. 55), who died a few years ago. His five children all still have a hut in Langa Uku, and one of them still lives there permanently. The others, however, have built huts in their own lineage village and spend part of their time there. The eldest had a quarrel in Langa Uku and scarcely shows his face there any more. The roof of his hut is leaking and the rain comes in, but he won't be fixing it.

Settling in a "strange" village, especially one far removed from one's own, is thought of as disagreeable. Through special marriages the Djuka try to prevent such situations. In the first place, there are quite a number of marriages with mates from the two villages closest to Langa Uku, respectively five minutes and fifteen minutes by canoe. Even if he settles in his wife's village, a man can in these cases fully take part in the activities of his own lineage village.

Da Daianen is an elder of Langa Uku. He is one of the mortuary priests[10] there, and in addition priest to Majombe (see above). He regularly takes part in the palavers of his "belly" village. Yet he does not live in Langa Uku, and even has no hut there. He is married to a woman from the neighboring village, where he resides. If he is needed in Langa Uku, he is fetched.

There are no technical difficulties; still he is annoyed at having no hut in his own village—he feels it detracts from his prestige. For this reason he is preparing to build a hut in Langa Uku.

The only perfect solution is offered by *endolocal* marriage, in which case both husband and wife stay "home." The

[10] About mortuary priests see Thoden van Velzen 1966b:239–44.

easiest way to achieve this is by marrying a member of one's own lineage. As we saw, this is permitted nowadays. In Langa Uku there are seven such marriages (see Table 2).

	male lineage members	sons of male lineage members	strangers (men)
female lineage members	7	13	28
daughters of male lineage members	4	6	3
strangers (women)	23	11	—

Table 2: Marriages of residents of Langa Uku to kinsmen and strangers.

An elegant further possibility is the marriage of a "father-made-him" son living in his father's village with a girl of his father's lineage. Marriage to an actual father's sister's daughter is not permitted. The Djuka regard this as a form of incest; it is, as they say, "too close." Marriage to a classificatory father's sister's daughter, however, is regarded with favor. This is clearly a preferential marriage rule. Although the Djuka generally leave the choice of a mate to the persons concerned, parents or other kinsmen not infrequently take the initiative to force a marriage of this type (*kisi gi ju*). There are thirteen instances of such a combination in Langa Uku (see Table 2 and Figure 7a).

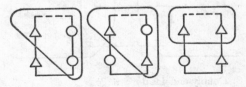

Figure 7a: classificatory patrilateral cross-cousin marriage. 7b: classificatory matrilateral cross-cousin marriage. 7c: classificatory parallel-cousin marriage.

"It is a good marriage," the Djuka say, for such a man has been begotten by the lineage and now he, in turn, begets children for the lineage: "He plants back." In this way, furthermore, the lineage establishes a close bond with its "child." The opposite, the marriage of a woman with a man of her father's lineage—classificatory matrilateral cross-cousin marriage—also occurs, but less frequently (four times; see Table 2 and Figure 7b). The last possibility, finally, is a marriage between two "father-made-them" children, that is, a classificatory parallel-cousin marriage (see Figure 7c). This is found six times in Langa Uku.

Some marriages are, we might say, doubly endolocal. For example, a couple has two huts, one in village A and one in village B, and they live alternately in one or the other. In village A *she* is a member of the lineage and *he* is a "father-made-him" child; in village B it is the other way around (see Figure 8). The Djuka consider this a most recommendable type of marriage.

The last category in our Table 1 are the *neolocal* marriages. I use this term for those cases where the couple settle permanently in a place that is new to both of them, that is, outside the tribal villages—for instance, in a camp near the mining town of Moengo. This is the situation of three members of the Pata lineage. A more usual situation, however, is for a couple to live temporarily outside the tribal area. This temporariness is indicated by the fact that they continue to have a hut in the village and are considered to fall under its jurisdiction.

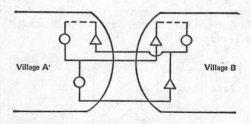

Figure 8: Doubly endolocal marriage.

Sa Lomina, a woman from Langa Uku, is married to Ti Valisi. For over three years they have been living on the Commewijne River, where the husband is working on a timber concession. All this time they haven't been back to the village, although in the meantime her father has died and the woman herself has had a child.

nts-in-law. His conduct toward his *mother*-in-law, in par-
icular, should be respectful; he must not shout or stamp his
feet in front of her and especially not use obscene language
—of which the Djuka on the whole are very fond.[11]

Fanaili is employed full-time by the anthropologist.
He is given four days off to clear a plot of ground but
doesn't get very far. On his way he happens to meet one
of his fathers-in-law, who demands his assistance for moving some timber. This takes three days. The fourth day he
loses more time yet by another father-in-law claiming his
help (this is his second wife's mother's second husband,
whom she has divorced). Only after a lot of talking does
he succeed in putting him off.

At dawn on the day of Da Saleng's mortuary feast, the
village crier goes through the village calling the affines
(*konlibi*): "*Konlibi-ooo!* Get up, get up. Bring the *konlibi*
drink! Get up, get up!" About twenty bottles of liquor are
brought in, obviously far too little, many classificatory affines, especially, failing to meet their obligations. Some
notables fulminate against the (absent) defaulters: "What
sort of men are these, they bring disgrace on us, let us
give our daughters to other men, they'll be sorry. . . ."
Not that this helped one bit, though.

As is already evident from what we have seen, a man does
not have just one set of parents-in-law but he may have
many, particularly as a result of polygyny and divorce.

More important from the structural point of view is the
fact that all members of the ascendant generation in the
wife's village count as classificatory parents-in-law to the
husband, for instance, ego's wimobr is a "father-in-law"
and his wife is a "mother-in-law"! With respect to distant
classificatory parents-in-law, of course, the relationship outlined above exists only in a rudimentary form. It is only on
special occasions that such persons prove to belong to the
category of ego's parents-in-law.

Sa Bobi has been unfaithful to her husband, Ba Anaki;
at least there are strong indications that she has. While

---

[11] With real and classificatory *sisters*-in-law, however, a man has a
joking relationship, in which very obscene language may be exchanged. Joking may also occur between a man and his wimomo.

the matter is still pending, Ba Anaki comes into the village one day and catches two brothers, Ba Asapoti and Ba Aleki, speaking disparagingly of him and of his lineage: "What he says about Sa Bobi is probably all lies; anyway, his whole family is no good, his grandmother was a witch, and his mother very likely has an evil heart too." Ba Anaki is furious and gives them the rough side of his tongue. When the two brothers attempt to go off in their boat, Ba Anaki takes his machete and hews at the boat for all he is worth to stop them. Others arrive on the scene and take the infuriated man away. Two days later there is a palaver about the case. From an objective point of view, Anaki was right. Such gossip about another man's lineage (*kosi mama pima*) is a serious offense. All the same, Anaki is put in the wrong; he has to beg forgiveness and pay a fine of one bottle of liquor. Asapoti and Aleki go scot free. They are lineage brothers of Anaki's father-in-law, and so his classificatory fathers-in-law, whom he should treat with respect. As "fathers-in-law" *they* may, on the other hand, take all sorts of liberties toward *him*. After the court session a few men, including Anaki, are talking about the affair. Anaki gives vent to his annoyance: "In actual fact I was right, nevertheless I have to pay, only because they are my 'fathers-in-law.' Perhaps that was thought proper in former times, but we, people of these times, don't want this anymore!" But Ba Anaki's father consoles him: "You'll get your bottle of liquor back soon; think of Ba Buli! They have planted bananas!" The banana is an annual plant, but after the first year new shoots come up in unexpected places; so the expression means: "They did not realize the consequences of their action." Ba Buli (a brother of Asapoti and Aleki) wants to marry a woman who is a (classificatory) sister of Ba Anaki's. When Ba Buli comes to ask for her hand in marriage, Anaki will make sure he is present and the roles will be reversed: *He* will be one of the bride-givers and can have his revenge.

During a mortuary feast Ba Mongi retires with Sa Jolina in the latter's hut. Although she is no older than he, she is a classificatory mother-in-law, being his wimobrwi. They are caught by Ba Mongi's cross cousin, who raises the alarm but without disclosing the culprit's name, on account of the special relationship. Ba Mongi gets away by a bold leap through the roof, which is made of leaves. He mingles with the dancers again and even joins in the search for Sa Jolina's assailant. He also helps to repair the roof. Nevertheless, his secret leaks out, or at least rumor points more and more in his direction. He hides a few days near the river by the landing stage of the boat to Paramaribo (the capital), and when the boat calls, he climbs aboard at the last moment when it is too late for other people to stop him. "He'll be staying in town one or two years; after that the affair is dead and he can come back." If anyone runs into him in town he won't make trouble, for in town the law is different. Mongi's wife and Jolina's husband both declare they won't have anything more to do with their respective mates. Sa Jolina has left and gone to her father's village. Ordinarily, people are not ashamed of sexual adventures. But in this case, because of the special relationship between the persons in question, everyone denounces them.

Affines who misbehave may be expelled from the village. Actually, though, expulsion is often threatened but rarely carried out, and even then it is usually only temporary. Ostensibly it is "the village" that decides to expel a person, the wife in question seemingly having no say in the matter. In actual fact, however, her opinion is decisive. If she doesn't wish to lose her husband the divorce does not go through, and conversely, if she wants to get rid of him she gets her divorce, even if the man's presence is appreciated by "the village."

Sa Posu is seriously ill. The people of her lineage attribute her illness to machinations on her husband's part (the couple recently had a serious quarrel). In a palaver he is upbraided by the elders, while some matrilineal kinsmen of his who similarly live in the village as affines also get their share of abuse. The man returns to his own village. Sa Posu is pregnant, however, and at such a time a woman should preferably not be without a husband. What is more, she does not really want to lose him. Quite soon efforts at reconciliation are being made. The man says (to save his face): "All right, I will come back and stay until the child is born, but then I will go away for good." But he does not really want the divorce either, and after the child is born he stays on in the village. "We're keeping a good eye on him now," say the villagers. The other affines whisper that the man's conscience is clear: "The elders accused him so loudly only to conceal the evil done by the wife herself." They hint that the woman herself is a witch ("her grandmother and her aunts were both witches") and that it was the Great Deity (*Sweli Gadu*), persecutor of witches, who made her ill.

As far as their relations with the "belly people" are concerned, the affines are more or less a solidary group. If an affine is the defendant in a palaver he is represented by other affines, even if these are not his kinsmen. An affine will also try to avoid having to give evidence against another affine. There are even proverbs referring to this.

The affine's position changes as he grows older. He becomes a *gankonlibi* (lit. a great affine), an elder. Such a man may make offerings to the ancestors on behalf of the village; he may even represent the village vis-à-vis the outside world. These older affines, in particular, are the mediators referred to above. In a fight between lineage members it is their job "to pull them apart; to separate them; to put an end to the fight" (*pu den, pati, tapu*). But in regular palavers, too, especially in those between members of one matrisegment, they act as mediators. They are closely involved with this matrisegment but they do not belong to it; hence are preeminently fitted for this task. The presence of this element in the social structure is important, since the village headman cannot use physical force and thus has no means of imposing peace. Structural position alone, of course, does not make a man a good mediator. Some *konlibi* are more prominent in this respect than others simply because their personalities make them more suitable.

The reader will perhaps remark that there are few such "great" *konlibi* in the village, since influential older men usually live in their own village. True, but they too will on occasion spend one or more weeks in the bride-giving village, for instance to attend a mortuary feast. During these periods they have ample opportunity to exercise their mediating function, for especially at such feasts all sorts of conflicts may arise.

In conclusion, a few words about *female affines*. It is regarded as a special favor on the part of the bride-giving village if the wife is permitted to live with her husband in the latter's village. Her position, therefore, is a sheltered one. Referring to her, people say, "We must look after her, help her, and meet her wishes. We cannot expel her unless she does something very wrong, such as having an affair with her husband's brother or practicing witchcraft." All the same, she feels a stranger in her husband's village, as is evident from the fact that she associates preferably with other female members of her lineage also living as affines in the village.

11. *Kinship terminology.* On several points the kinship terminology of this society differs from what one would expect. The system is remarkable for its symmetry, kinsmen on the father's side being called by the same terms as those on the mother's side, matrilinearity notwithstanding. In a unilineal system such as this, one would, as a matter of fact, sooner expect bifurcate merging than a lineal terminology, as is found here in the ascendant generation. Nor would one expect Hawaiian Cousin terminology, since this means that ego uses one and the same term ("sister") both for a classificatory mobrda and for a lineage sister. Yet the former is a preferential marriage partner, while marriage with the latter is, or at least used to be, prohibited. Once more, it may be observed that the correlations between kinship system and kinship terminology as established by Murdock (1949:Ch. 7) are no more than statistically significant correlations and are not true for every individual case. I am unable, meanwhile, to provide an explanation for these unexpected terminological features.[12]

The terms used by female ego are the same as those used by male ego; the term for husband is *man;* the term for co-wife is *meti* which is, remarkably enough, also the term used by a male ego to refer to his wisihu (there is no special term for husihu).

Note, finally, that father-in-law and son-in-law use polar terms vis-à-vis one another, as do mother-in-law and daughter-in-law.

[12] The Djuka language is a so-called creolized language, its vocabulary being of African, Portuguese, English, and Dutch provenance, although many of its syntactic features are West African. The reader will recognize several words in Figure 11 and might suppose that the terminology of lineal type derived from European kinship terminology. This seems, however, improbable, as the kinship structure itself is not at all modeled on a European example.

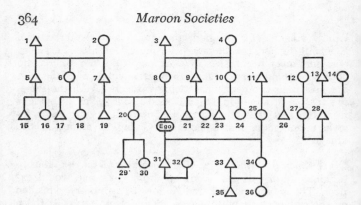

Figure 11: Kinship terminology.

1. ganda	10: tia	19: bala	28: meti
2: ganma	11: (gan) pai	20: sisa	29: sisapikin
3: ganda	12: mai	21: bala	30: sisapikin
4: ganma	13: (gan) pai	22: sisa	31: (man) pikin
5: tiu	14: mai	23: bala	32: mai
6: tia	15: bala	24: sisa	33: (pikin) pai
7: da (pápa)	16: sisa	25: uman; mujé	34: (uman) pikin
8: ma (máma)	17: bala	26: swagi	35: ganpikin
9: tiu	18: sisa	27: swagi	36: ganpikin

12. *Unity and disunity.* The Djuku village, as a composite of kinsmen, would seem to be preeminently a community or a *Gemeinschaft*-like group. One may ask if the characteristics that some anthropologists attribute to the community are present in the Djuka village. Murdock (1949:38), for instance, describes these as follows:

> United by reciprocal relationships and bound by a common culture, the members of a community form an ingroup, characterized by internal peace, law, order, and cooperative effort. Since they assist one another in the activities that gratify basic drives . . . there develops among them a collective sentiment of group solidarity and loyalty.

In the same spirit Sahlins (1965:147, 149, 151) writes:

> Kindred goes with kindness. . . . It is in regard to people of the household, camp, hamlet, or village that compassion is required. . . . Close kin tend to share, to enter into generalized exchange, [whereby] the expectation of a direct material return is unseemly. At best it is implicit.

And Hurault (1961:134–35) says about the Boni, which is also a Bush Negro tribe:

> *Ce n'est pas en vain qu'à l'intérieur du lignage les hommes se disent frères; les obligations qu'ils ont les uns vis-à-vis des autres sont acceptées par tous avec joie, et chacun met à remplir le meilleur de lui-même.* [Roughly: It is not without reason that within the lineage, men call themselves brothers; the obligations they have toward one another are accepted joyfully by all, and each person tries to give of himself to the fullest.]

On the face of it Djuka society seems in many ways to conform to this image. Ideologically, for instance: "Together we are one big family," people say, "we should do everything together." Expressions and exhortations to this effect are often heard, for example, at palavers. There is a proverb that says: "Belly members shouldn't quarrel two mornings." In other words, a quarrel with a lineage member should be made up within twenty-four hours. Outwardly the reputation of the village must be upheld, no washing of dirty linen in public and no behavior that might damage its reputation. These rules of conduct have a religious foundation, too, as we have seen: At any breach of them the *kunu* and the ancestors will take action. Nor is all of this mere ideology. Something of the "generalized exchange" mentioned by Sahlins is to be seen, for instance, in the division of a large hunting catch, when all the elders and the older women of the hunter's lineage receive their share. Similarly in the building of a hut.

March 11. This morning Ba Mansooi starts building his new hut. Yesterday he asked only one man to come and help him, though he needs five or six for the job. But no worry: *Every man who passes gives a hand, for a few hours or half the day. A village elder sits and watches, offering a bit of advice here and there, though no one pays any attention to him. Eleven o'clock:* Da Pé comes by, *stops and watches for a moment, and wants to go off again. The elder rebukes him for leaving. The man apologizes: He has hurt his hand. Even so, he hasn't the courage to leave, and hangs around for at least another hour. The village headman also arrives to lend a hand. 5:30 P.M. Ba Mansooi fetches a bottle of* tafia, *and everyone present is rewarded with a good swig of the liquor. He whispers some derisive remarks about old Da Saité, who always arrives to "help" at the very moment drinks are being handed around.*

But it is not true that the device of all for one and one for all is an absolute rule in this society. In some respects, as a matter of fact, individual interests come to the fore more than in Western society, and certain transactions that would be noncommercial with us have a commercial side for the Djuka. A woman uses a sewing machine belonging to her (full) brother for one day and owes him Sf. 0.50 ($0.28) for this. A man asks his (full) sister for a few miserable fish or some oranges, and she makes him pay for them. A man sells some timber to his brother-in-law, and they ask an impartial third person to inspect and value it. In short, the Djuka are acquisitive. Theirs is a nought-for-nought culture.

What I want to demonstrate is not just that there is a discrepancy between ideal and reality, that goes almost without saying, and Sahlins (1965:157–58) too points this out. More significant is the fact that this acquisitiveness is *a theme*[13] in Djuka culture side by side with, and opposed to, the theme that stresses the solidarity of the group. It is considered understandable and wise for a person to put something aside and to keep it for himself.

These two themes combined cause people to conceal with great care whatever goods they may acquire. They pretend to be even poorer than they are. Conspicuous consumption and conspicuous giving are alien to Djuka culture, at least until recently (cf. Köbben 1968:86–87). There are sayings in support of this attitude, such as "Not everything is for

[13] I use the term in Opler's (1962) sense.

the public eye" (*Ala sani na de fu gaanda*) and "A wise man conceals himself."

According to Van der Veen (1971), every society has institutions promoting cooperation side by side with other institutions that allow individual interests to be expressed. Whether this is a universal rule I cannot say, but for Djuka society the theory certainly holds good.

Late one evening, when everyone has left my hut, old Ma Dow surreptitiously enters. "Uncle, have you got a piece of tobacco for me, without tobacco I can't sleep. And please have you also got a piece of paper to wrap it in, or someone will see it and I'll have to share it with them."

Old Da Amoksi is sitting near his hut with a dozen men of the village. In passing I remember having bought a stool from him for which I haven't paid yet. With my purse in my hands I approach him to settle my debt. General horror, almost as if I had made some improper noise. I am tactfully but firmly reprimanded: What I have offered him for the stool is nobody else's business, and by making it publicly known I am embarrassing and insulting the old man.

Concomitant phenomena of this situation are gossip, suspicion, and jealousy, which often give rise to accusations of witchcraft.[14]

Ti Valisi has returned to the village after an absence of three years, the proud owner of a boat with an eighteen-horsepower outboard motor. He derives more trouble than pleasure from it, however. People who have to go somewhere, for instance to Moengo (two hours with an outboard motor, eight hours paddling) ask to go with him, or will even say: "Take me there, will you?" Valisi proposes starting a daily service to Moengo for a modest fixed price. General indignation! He should at least have kept up an outward pretense of rendering his services free of charge while privately demanding some payment.

Da Tengi has been buying timber in various villages for a number of years. He is an intelligent man with a com-

[14] For a general discussion of witchcraft in Djuka society, see van Wetering n.d.

mercial talent, and when he starts supplying a big factory his transactions grow to a comparatively great volume. He is careful not to change anything in his way of life. His hut remains just as sober as everyone else's. He discharges his kinship obligations more than generously. All the same, people are jealous, for they can see that he is rising considerably above them financially, and they somehow feel it is at their expense. Tengi feels the hostile sentiments and thinks himself threatened by witchcraft. When one of his grandchildren dies and another takes ill soon afterward, he stops his timber transactions for a few years.

Thus Djuka society is a combination of loyalty and disloyalty, of unity and disunity, of solidarity and dissension, and as such it is very human.[15]

REFERENCES NOT CITED IN GENERAL BIBLIOGRAPHY

Durkheim, E.
  1912 *Les formes élémentaires de la vie religieuse.* Paris.
Fortes, M.
  1950 "Kinship and Marriage Among the Ashanti." *In* A. R. Radcliffe-Brown and D. Forde (eds.), *African Systems of Kinship and Marriage.* Oxford: Oxford University Press.
Junus, Uma
  1964 "Some Remarks on Minangkabau Social Structure." *Bijdragen tot de Taal-, Land- en Volkenkunde* 120:293–326.
Kloos, Peter
  1963 "Matrilocal Residence and Local Endogamy: Environmental Knowledge or Leadership." *American Anthropologist* 65: 854–62.
Köbben, A. J. F.
  1956 "Le planteur noir." *Études Eburnéenes* 5:7–190.
  1964 *Van primitieven tot medeburgers.* Assen: Van Gorcum.
  1967 "Why Exceptions: The Logic of Cross-Cultural Comparisons." *Current Anthropology* 8:3–32.
van Lier, W. F.
  1919 *Iets over de Boschnegers in de Boven Marowijne.* Paramaribo: H. van Ommeren.
  1940 "Aanteekeningen over het geestelijk leven en en de samenleving der Djoeka's in Suriname." *Bijdragen tot de Taal-, Land en Volkenkunde* 99:131–294.
Lowie, R. H.
  1924 *Primitive Religion.* New York: Boni and Liveright.

[15] For obvious reasons pseudonyms have been used for some individuals.

Murdock, George Peter
   1949 *Social Structure.* New York: MacMillan.
Norbeck, E.
   1961 *Religion in Primitive Society.* New York: Harper and Row.
Opler, M.
   1962 "Themes of Culture." *In* W. Bernsdorf and F. Bülow (eds.), *Wörterbuch der Soziologie.*
Sahlins, M. D.
   1965 "On the Sociology of Primitive Exchange." *In* M. Gluckman and F. Eggan (eds.), *The Relevance of Models for Social Anthropology.* London.
van der Veen, K. W.
   1971 "Ambivalence, Social Structure and Dominant Kinship Relationships: a Hypothesis." *In* Hsu, F. L. K. (ed.), *Kinship and Culture.* Chicago: Aldine.
Wong, E.
   1938 "Hoofdenverkiezing, stamverdeeling en stamverspreiding der Boschnegers van Suriname in de 18e en 19e eeuw." *Bijdragen tot de Taal-, Land- en Volkenkunde* 97:295–362.

CHAPTER TWENTY

Witchcraft Among the Tapanahoni Djuka

W. VAN WETERING

[*Editor's note:* The following account of Djuka witchcraft is adopted, with the author's permission, from a much longer, theoretically oriented paper. For the full and stimulating sociological analysis and for numerous case histories omitted here, see the original.]

The Djuka understand by witchcraft (*wisi*) the ability to harm others by supernatural means. The witch (*wisiman*) is believed to act out of sheer maliciousness, without just cause, consciously and deliberately. The power to bewitch is not inherited. Witchcraft is believed to take various forms. The witch may change into a vampire (*azeman*) . . . or he may use magical techniques (in which case he should more technically be called a "sorcerer"). The most important witchcraft technique represents a perversion of established religion: the invoking and bribing of a mischievous bush spirit (*baku*) to induce it to enter the intended victim as a tormenting spirit.

In the course of about one year I obtained data on eighty witches (people denounced as witches after their death); fifty-one were women, twenty-nine men. In the period between October 1961 and October 1962, the Paramount Chief in Dritabiki was notified of thirty-two deaths of adults in the

Reprinted with extensive editing from W. van Wetering, "The Dynamics of Witchcraft Accusations in Tapanahoni Djuka Society." *In* Peter Kloos and A. J. F. Köbben (eds.), *Structure, Function and Process: Contributions of Dutch Anthropologists.* Assen: van Gorcum 1972.

Tapanahoni villages, and in thirty of these cases the supernatural cause of death was clearly stated: No less than twenty-one of the deceased were condemned as witches (thirteen of the fifteen women and eight of the fifteen men). These figures certainly suggest that witchcraft beliefs and accusations play an important role in Djuka society.[1]

It is commonly assumed by sociologists and anthropologists that witchcraft accusations reflect tensions between the accuser and the accused or, more generally speaking, that they indicate the existence of social tension between certain categories of relatives. Without denying the value of these and similar views for some specific cases, I doubt whether they are the key concepts in terms of which witchcraft beliefs and behavior in general can be explained. I would suggest, with Turner (1964), that our observations should be extended to encompass the entire social field in which the phenomenon of witchcraft occurs, for suspicions and accusations are only incidents in a complex social process. The development of a reputation for witchcraft, from the first suspicion via insinuations to an overt accusation, is (like the opposite case when the accused, finding support, is finally exonerated) a process that must be viewed as a whole. Important are not only the persons mentioned as accuser and accused, victim and accomplice, but also the reactions of the others around them. To the accused person's group it matters greatly from what source the accusation springs. As we shall see, insinuations from some sources are simply ignored, and the kinsman or neighbor is defended; while a suspicion from another source will strike root, and people in the accused's immediate vicinity will either sustain the accusation or keep aloof.

The course of Djuka witchcraft dramas is influenced by three major social groupings, and a few words must be said about each at the outset.

The localized lineage or village quarter. The central social group relevant to Djuka witchcraft is the localized lineage or village quarter. This is, in fact, "the natural arena of witchcraft belief" (to borrow a phrase from Marwick [1965:

[1] The field work on which this article is based was carried out from June 1961 to November 1962, mainly in the village of Dritabiki on the Tapanahoni River, under the auspices of the Netherlands Organization for Scientific Research in Surinam and the Netherlands Antilles.

95]). Most Djuka villages include two quarters or wards (*pisi*)—although in large villages like Dritabiki, the residence of the Paramount Chief, there are more than two quarters and, because of labor migration to the coastal region, some villages have decreased in numbers to such an extent that these subdivisions are no longer viable units and the villagers act as if there were only one quarter. As a rule each ward is made up of three categories of inhabitants. The members of the localized matrilineage (*bee*) form the core of its population, and they are joined by resident affines (the spouses of members of the matrilineage) and by patrilateral relatives (that is, children of male matrilineage members). Some statistics can highlight the relative importance of these groups in witchcraft accusations. Out of thirty accusations I recorded, thirteen were directed at coresidents of the ward, of whom twelve were matrilineal relatives and one an affine. Of the seventeen people accused in other quarters, eleven were affines and six nonrelated people; the latter six accusations, affecting neither kin nor neighbors, derived from a fear of being bewitched by a rejected lover or, in one case, a rival. I have data also on sixty-seven relationships between witch and victim. In fifty-six of these cases the witch is supposed to have picked his victim from among the members of his own village quarter. No less than forty-four victims were matrilineally related to the alleged witch, four patrilaterally—people bewitched by their father—and eight affinally. Finally, I have data on nineteen relationships between witch and accomplice. In all but one of these cases, the witch and accomplice were pictured as living in the same quarter, and in seventeen of them the witch and accomplice were matrilineally related. Only in eleven cases were the witch's victims believed to have been selected from among the residents of other wards; in six cases the relationship between the witch and victim was affinal; in the other five they were not related at all. Furthermore, I know of only one case in which an inhabitant of another quarter was mentioned as an accomplice, namely the witch's husband. To sum up: It may be said that the Djuka fear most of all those kinsmen who live nearby.

The priests of the Great Deity. The cult of the Great Deity (see Thoden van Velzen 1966b, 1972) is closely connected with witchcraft beliefs. The priests pursue a consistent policy in witchcraft matters, on the one hand invalidating accusa-

ons directed at living persons, and on the other increasing
he number of charges against dead persons. They have their
easons. Both the Paramount Chief (*Gaanman*) and the
illage headmen or captains (*kabiten*) receive a salary from
he Surinam government. The main standard the govern-
nent uses in gauging the Djuka officials' competence is their
uccess or failure in preventing physical violence. Since the
'aramount Chief and the high priest of the Great Deity cult
vere at the time of our field work one and the same person,
t is not hard to see why the priests do their utmost to sup-
>ress witchcraft accusations, which often lead to fighting.

The method they employ is simply to declare such accu-
ations unfounded. The opportunity for this arises whenever
a patient known to be suspected of witchcraft comes to con-
ult the oracle. The priests will bring up the topic of the
existing suspicions, show them to be false, and proceed to
ebuke the patient's kinsmen, not infrequently accusing the
atter of having caused the illness by their malicious slander.
t is believed that the ancestors, angered by any sort of dis-
:ord among relatives, will terminate the victim's life rather
han let him suffer the humiliation of further insinuations of
witchcraft. Accusations directed at dead persons, however,
:an only bring profit to the priests. When someone is post-
humously condemned as a witch, the inheritance devolves to
the priests. Moreover, such a condemnation "explains" their
failure to restore a patient's health—it is one of the tenets of
the cult that the Great Deity does not give help to witches—
so the priests are particularly anxious that incurable cases
brought before the oracle be branded as witches after their
death. Village captains are obliged to report every demise,
stating the supernatural cause of death to the oracle priests,
who may endorse or repudiate the verdict. By this means the
priests of Dritabiki are at all times well informed about all
that happens in other villages.

The grave diggers. After death every Djuka above the age
of about ten years is subjected to a trial designed to discover
whether or not he was a witch. To this end the corpse is
tied to a litter and carried about by two people. The spirit of
the deceased is supposed to direct the movements of the bier.
From these movements, in answer to questions put by the
elders, the supernatural cause of death is ascertained. The
inquest is mainly conducted by the grave diggers, a sodality
that recruits its members from all villages. The grave diggers

who cooperate for one particular inquest and funeral usuall
come from a number of neighboring villages. For the de
tailed procedure followed at the inquest and a sketch of the
sodality, see Thoden van Velzen (1966b, Ch. X).

In arriving at their judgment, the grave diggers are largel
guided by the opinion prevailing in the deceased's villag
quarter. "The lineage has the final say," a grave digger onc
assured me. He added: "If we have difficulty in interpretin
the clues given by the deceased's spirit, and his own kinsme
think he is a witch, we can hardly decide otherwise." Th
relatives get every opportunity to be heard; the corpse i
carried around at least once by kinsmen among the grav
diggers, and the inquest is always attended by members c
the deceased's village quarter. In Dritabiki as well as in th
neighboring villages, the grave diggers are inclined to le
the wishes of the oracle priests prevail. The priests, in fac
hold prominent positions in the hierarchy of grave diggers.

This does not imply, however, that the grave diggers an
the others involved are cynics; every Djuka is firmly con
vinced that at most inquests it really is the spirit of the de
ceased that pronounces the verdict. Nevertheless, people al
low for the fact that some bearers at some occasions ma
have tried to influence the course of events. But in general
the religious tenet that lies at the root of the ritual is no
challenged or consciously belied.

This, then, is the social context in which Djuka witchcraf
dramas take place. By presenting a number of case histories
I hope next to shed light on the dynamics of witchcraft ac
cusations, on how they grow and spread among the variou
groups concerned. (The cases are set in different village
along the Tapanahoni River. For simplicity's sake the name
of the villages are not mentioned except Dritabiki, the vil
lage I know best.)

ACCUSATIONS WITHIN THE VILLAGE QUARTER

Case 1: *An accusation and a fight*

Ma Luma, whose son has recently died, accuses ar
older member of her lineage, Ma Aswiti, of having be
witched her son. In a ritual state of trance, Luma hurl
this accusation in the old woman's face and at the sam
time physically attacks her, supported by some neigh
bors. She knows in advance that she can count on th

approval of the quarter and village headman. Aswiti gets a beating but lodges a complaint in Dritabiki, and the priests declare the accusation unfounded (cf. Thoden van Velzen 1966b:144, Case 19).

Case 2: *A lynching*

In the early 1950s eight inhabitants of a certain village quarter, four men and four women, killed an old man called Doglasi. The men were classificatory sister's sons and two of the women classificatory sister's daughters of the victim; the other two women lived in the same quarter. The inhabitants of the quarter had for a long time been complaining about Doglasi; people alleged that they had seen him in their dreams "doing strange things," and it was said that he had been caught tampering with other people's food. In general, his behavior and actions were considered suspicious.

The eight accusers started by hurling invective at the old man, and followed this up with their fists and a whip until he remained lying half dead on the ground. The other inhabitants of the village, those who did not belong to this quarter, pretended to see or hear nothing and did not intervene. That night Doglasi was hanged, not having had the strength to get away in time. The next day the eight executioners asserted that Doglasi had died by his own hand, implying that he was a witch, for more often than not a suicide is believed to be a witch. But the other villagers refused to believe this. "You cannot hang yourself," they argued, and notified the Paramount Chief in Dritabiki. There the case was later tried (cf. Thoden van Velzen 1966b:217, Case 33).

In every case of this type the rule holds that witchcraft accusations between neighbors are an internal matter, the quarter preferring to straighten out its own affairs. The accuser makes sure he has the moral support of his group, including the head of the quarter. Fellow villagers not belonging to the same quarter, or people in other villages, do not play a role in decision-making, although they may gossip a great deal. Nor do they attempt to intervene, even when people get killed. However, the views of the Paramount Chief and the other priests of the Great Deity are relevant. No matter how much such action is resented, the priests can and do interfere in the internal affairs of the quarter.

ACCUSATIONS BETWEEN AFFINES LIVING IN DIFFERENT QUARTERS

Accusations of affines differ from those directed at neighbors. While a neighbor is usually accused only in a state of trance, a charge against an affine is pronounced rather easily. Affines have little feeling of solidarity; in quarrels they do not feel obliged to keep up an appearance of harmony, nor is the possible consequence of a serious conflict, the severing of all relations, considered a very grave matter. Accusations of affines, therefore, are on one level often merely a pretext to pick a quarrel and do not arise from any real fear of being bewitched. The accuser may get support from his own quarter in the form of new accusations directed at the same person, sometimes without waiting for a new illness or other occasion. With an inhabitant of the same quarter, more care is taken that no accusation is pronounced without sufficient reason. In Case 3 below, the new accusation merely signifies support for the neighbor who first made the accusation, that is, it is purely "political."

Case 3: *Metamorphosis*
Da Asopa is accused by his wife of turning himself first into a fireball and then into a jaguar. Two young men from the wife's village, members of her lineage, support her accusation with the story that once when out hunting they stalked a peccary, but when they got within range it turned into a human being, namely, Asopa.

[*Editor's note:* In the original, van Wetering next presented several cases, omitted here, to demonstrate that] . . . the idea that a neighbor is a witch is not accepted when it originates from an outsider. As long as a person is above suspicion in his own quarter, he will be protected by the other members of his group. If the conviction that he is a witch exists also in his group, the position is somewhat, but not essentially, different. While the group will not feel obliged to defend the subject's reputation they will, on the other hand, not make use of this support from outside. The accusation will provoke no visible reaction: Whether secretly gloating or not, the group will not make common cause with the outsider, nor even adopt a more aggressive attitude toward the accused. . . .

Formerly, witchcraft accusations by people in different quarters often gave rise to outbursts of physical violence. If a person was thought to have died as a result of witchcraft by an affinal relative, usually the surviving spouse, the people of the quarter would organize an expedition of revenge called *boto-feti* ("fight by canoe"). The affines were beaten up, their houses and possessions destroyed, and their fruit trees cut down. Nowadays the Djuka authorities usually manage to prevent such reprisals. The priests of the Great Deity summon the accusers, declare the accusation unfounded, and often pronounce the deceased himself guilty of witchcraft and his death a punishment by the Great Deity. But whether the revenge is actually carried out or not, the fact that the need is felt indicates a high degree of solidarity in the village quarter.

All that has been said so far concerning affines and their mutual accusations is true only of affines living in different quarters. Those affines, however, who take up residence in the wife's or husband's quarter and only visit their original village on very rare occasions, throw in their lot with the inhabitants of the new quarter. For them a severing of ties is a far more serious matter. In the course of time their presence in the new home becomes such a matter of course that they are regarded as kinsmen. Even in witchcraft matters they are treated as members of the quarter, and that is how they feel themselves. They are not afraid of being openly accused, like normal affines, but rather of being secretly bewitched by neighbors. "Where you eat is where you can expect evil," the Djuka say. Moreover, they will not easily accuse a person born in the quarter. If such an accusation has to be pronounced, the resident affine will prefer to leave it to his or her spouse.

Case 4: *The sudden death of a hunting dog*

Da Dowsu had settled in his wife's village. When his hunting dog suddenly died, he suspected witchcraft, for which he believed his wife's mother, who was already suspected by the whole quarter, to be responsible. It is worth noting that Dowsu does not come out with a new suspicion, but adopts an already current idea. It is not out of personal or emotional need that he utters his suspicion. He wonders what could have caused the dog's death, and it occurs to him that perhaps a witch is trying to get at him in this way. If it is a witch, then it must be the person who is suspected by everyone in the quarter and who happens to be his mother-in-law. Dowsu voices his suspicions only in private, though as a rule accusations come easily to the lips of affines. In his position as resident affine, he feels it would be improper publicly to accuse a member of the local lineage. He prefers to leave it to his wife. She will have to stand up for him in this case, and she does. Early one morning about a fortnight later, having felt herself threatened by the witch during the night, she shouts her accusation into the silent village: "Witch, I know who you are even though I don't name you. You have annoyed my husband. If you do it again I shall divorce him, so that you won't be able to kill him. But if you force him to go back to his own village, I shall know where to find you". Everyone in the village knows it is her mother she is referring to.

When resident affines die, the grave diggers have not one but two quarters to contend with, those of "orientation" and of "procreation." The lineage always keeps a certain amount of authority over its members, however loose the ties may have grown: *"Fow fé, ede na fu doti,"* say the Djuka: A bird may fly where he likes, but eventually he will end up on the ground. No person can altogether detach himself from his lineage.

Case 5: *Where did the witchcraft come from?*

Ma Bewani had lived many years in Dritabiki, her husband's village. After her death the usual inquest was held to discover the cause of death. Even before the kinsmen of the deceased had arrived from her own village, the people of Dritabiki started with the first round of carrying the bier. After this they had to wait, however. It was not until two men of the deceased's lineage had taken their turn as bearers that the result of the first trial was announced and corroborated: The old woman was a witch. Neither her neighbors nor her matrilineal kinsmen felt any desire to save her reputation. One of the deceased's kinsmen, a grave digger, would have

liked to keep Bewani's witchcraft a purely Dritabiki
affair, as if to show that all ties between Bewani and the
village of her birth had been severed. By pronouncing
her a disciple and accomplice of a local witch, he hoped
to hurt the people of Dritabiki. He even declared that
Bewani could not possibly have been made a witch in
her own village, for witchcraft did not occur in the
lineage. This arrogance roused the anger of the other
members of the grave diggers' committee, including those
from other villages. During the second test the bier
stopped in front of a house formerly inhabited by another woman from Bewani's village. She, too, had died
a witch. The grave diggers asked why the litter stopped
here, but no matter what questions they tried, the litter
did not respond. Finally an elder from another village,
one of the men who had been so indignant at the arrogance displayed by the deceased's lineage, loudly
suggested that the witch who used to live here might
have been the evil spirit who had made Bewani her
accomplice. At this remark the bier immediately started
moving; it moved straight up to the speaker and nudged
him. "That is right," others now exclaimed: "That is
what she wanted to tell us." So Bewani had after all
been turned into a witch by a member of her own lineage. Her intended victims, however, declared the grave
diggers, were neighbors, her husband's sister's sons.

As is evident from this case, there is a strong tendency to
regard a lineage member permanently residing in another
village as a member of the other group. The old woman was
involved in the witchcraft affairs of the village she lived in;
she was named as an accomplice of someone who lived in the
same village though belonging to her own lineage, and for
her victims she was said to have chosen neighbors. Lineage
membership does remain important, however, for the verdict
of the inquest has to be endorsed by the lineage of the deceased. Case 5 shows that the influence of the elders is not
inconsiderable, for it was such a noninvolved elder who gave
the matter a decisive turn.

In the cases described so far we have seen that the inhabitants of a ward tend to support one another, both as accused and as accusers, against outsiders. Suspicions and
accusations spread more readily within the quarter than out-

side it. There is little chance that they will fall on fertile s
outside the quarter of their origin, for the attitude towar
ideas coming from outside is hostile, or, at most, indifferen
Normally, different quarters will not try to make commo
cause in witchcraft accusations, not even against a commo
enemy. When neither accuser nor accused belongs to th
quarter, the attitude is strictly neutral. In deciding who is
witch and who is not among its inhabitants, the quarter en
joys a certain autonomy; an autonomy, that is to say, wit
respect to other quarters, not to the priests of the Great De
ity. The latter repeatedly succeed in their attempts to in
fluence decision-making within the quarter.

From suspect to witch. We have yet to discuss the back
ground of witchcraft accusations within the quarter—how
such accusations spread and which factors promote or im
pede their spreading. Social relations within the quarter ar
often disturbed by all sorts of differences between persons o
groups, and only rarely is there general agreement o
whether someone is a witch. Usually different opinions con
tinue to exist side by side. The inquest, however, requires
unanimous verdict. Below, I shall describe some of th
maneuvers employed to enforce conformity to majority opin
ion.

In a number of the cases described so far, old people wer
suspected and accused (Cases 1, 2, 4, 5). It is often hard to
say what gave rise to the suspicion, and it is rarely possible
to find out who first uttered it and how it spread. These old
people are often railed at, not infrequently threatened with
a beating, and sometimes even murdered. Everything they do
is found suspicious. Insinuations and accusations come at
them from all sides, for when a number of lineage members
are convinced someone is a witch, resident affines, too, feel at
liberty to blame their misfortunes and illnesses on these scapegoats. In this way suspicion spreads, growing more serious
all the time. There is little chance for old people who are
suspected by the whole quarter of being acquitted at the
inquest. Of twenty-one old people who died in 1962, seventeen were condemned as witches. During their lifetime they
are to some degree protected by the priests of the Great
Deity, but this is no longer necessary after their death, when
the danger of illegal violence is past. Even if these suspects
seek protection with the oracle and are acquitted, their position in their own group does not improve. Their presence is

often felt as a burden: "They eat but they do not work," I
was told.

The significance of power. The relative power and influence of the individuals involved are important factors in determining the spread of accusations.

Case 6: *Ambition*

The suspicions concerning Da Pakila are at least as serious as in the cases of the old people just described. But
however much scandal is spread about Pakila behind his
back, in his presence no one would dare to impugn his
reputation. On the contrary, he is treated with respect.
In the meantime, the suspicions grow more and more
serious. The reasons are, briefly, as follows: Pakila is an
obiaman (medicineman) and, like many Djuka, the
medium of a guardian spirit. This spirit, however, is
generally assumed to be an evil one, assisting him in his
witchcraft. Two of his wives in succession accused him
of witchcraft, both declaring that he turned himself into
a jaguar. These stories cropped up again when one of
the two captains of the village died and a successor had
to be found. Pakila, a younger brother of the deceased,
openly showed his ambition to be appointed. The village
was buzzing with rumors: Was Pakila a witch? Would
he be village captain? For outsiders this gossip offered a
welcome diversion, but for Pakila's quarter the situation
was awkward, since the choice of a successor was in the
first place their concern. A thing that counted heavily
against Pakila was that even as the former captain lay
ill he had been to see the authorities in Albina, a coastal
town, supposedly to recommend himself as a successor.
At the inquest the spirit of the deceased captain declared
he was murdered, and of course everybody thought
Pakila guilty. The quarter hesitated between dislike of
Pakila and fear of revenge by the deceased on the one
hand, and on the other hand fear of Pakila's anger and
revenge if he was not chosen. The other captain preferred not to have Pakila as a colleague and had another
candidate in mind, namely one of the deceased's classificatory brothers. The latter, however, dared not accept
the appointment for fear of Pakila's vengeance. The
quarter eventually decided that there was nothing to do
but appoint Pakila. Actually public opinion had never

shown itself definitely opposed, and on the occasion of Pakila's installation only one or two individuals privately voiced their displeasure. The general mood turned against Pakila, however, once it became apparent that the chief and the oracle priests opposed his appointment. At the tribal installation in Dritabiki most of Pakila's quarter were absent. But when the chief declared that Pakila would be installed in spite of everything, and requested the quarter to accept him as a captain, they complied. (cf. Thoden van Velzen 1966b:260, Case 51). Now they were obliged to recognize him and treat him as headman of both village and quarter.

A short time later, a woman from Pakila's lineage, but now living in Dritabiki with her husband, came to the oracle for help in an illness. The oracle told her that she had done wrong in not attending the installation of Pakila, a member of her own lineage. The priests advised her to go and pray to the ancestors at the shrine in her own village and to get Pakila to intercede for her, since it was for her neglectfulness toward him that the ancestors had made her ill. This shows that it is important to keep up to date about fluctuations in people's reputations. Those who fail to keep up with the latest developments, at least in their own group, are liable to be reprimanded.

The suspicions gradually lost their topical significance, and some people even began to wonder if there had ever been any foundation for them at all. It may well be that in due time the difficulties surrounding Pakila's installation will be forgotten and have no influence on the outcome of the inquest when he dies, for only rarely is a captain condemned as a witch at his inquest. It is worth noting that Pakila suffered little damage from the suspicions. On the contrary; it was fear of his supernatural powers that prompted his rival to refuse the appointment. Pakila made use of this reputation to intimidate others, making the most of the fear he inspired in them.

The important difference between Pakila and most suspects is that Pakila is a person of consequence and the others are not. Pakila is shown respect because the possibility that he may become village captain has to be taken into account. Pakila has power and influence and is in a position to avenge insults. This is not possible for old women living on the charity of their quarter. Most middle-aged men have some influence and are not easily made into scapegoats. On the other hand, once it becomes clear that a man's career of power and influence is over, either because he has withdrawn from social life or because he is incurably ill, his neighbors are no longer afraid to show their feelings [see Cases 15 and 16 in the original].

In general, it seems that in Djuka he who openly pronounces an accusation must be quite certain of the strength of his own position or of the support of influential persons; in other words, he must be convinced that the accusation is politically "realistic." But in Djuka society there is relatively little difference in power between individuals, so that not many people are in a position regularly to accuse others. For this reason it is only rarely that we find comparatively powerful or influential persons defending or trying to improve their position by means of such accusations. Remember also that when the accuser and the accused belong to different quarters (usually being affines), the factor of personal power is far less important. Then they count on the solidarity of the other members of the group, and it is a trial of strength not so much between individuals as between groups.

The significance of personal feelings. Although power is an important consideration, it does not altogether dominate the picture of witchcraft accusations within the quarter. A suspicion may spread among most or practically all members of a compartment, but it rarely happens that a suspect is abandoned by the entire group. The suspect's children, for instance, often find it hard to accept that their father or mother (usually the latter) was a witch. This does not mean they doubt the truth of the grave diggers' findings, for it seems that in a large number of cases the witch is actually believed guilty. In public at least, they will pretend to accept the verdict. To help resign themselves to the idea that their beloved mother was a witch, a son or daughter will, for instance, cast about for extenuating circumstances. When Ma Atuku, whose case will be related below, was condemned as a witch, her eldest son found it hard to accept. Outwardly he was cheerful, but the loss of his mother meant a lot to him. He regarded his mother's witchcraft as a weakness, into which she had been misled by the gossip of her neighbors: "Those women put it into her head that she was being slighted in favor of her cowives, and made her jealous," he repeatedly said.

Sometimes the children of a witch are convinced the inquest was fraudulent. They regard the verdict as the outcome of a conflict in which they themselves came off the losers. The grave diggers give expression to the opinion of the majority in the quarter; if he is alone in his conviction that the accusation is unjust, the child of a witch cannot sufficiently influence the verdict. Persons in this situation do not usually voice their objections in public, in the first place because it is no use anyway, and in the second place because it would make their own position precarious. The other people in the quarter closely watch the reactions of the deceased person's children. If one of them appears not to accept the majority verdict without question, they will try to intimidate him. There is an excellent method for this: A person who is loyal to the witch is named as either victim or accomplice.

By accusing someone of being the witch's accomplice, the grave diggers clearly indicate that this person had better omit all demonstrations of loyalty toward the witch. To be named as a victim has a similar import but is comparatively less serious for the person in question. The grave diggers frequently name as a victim the person who was most loyal to the suspect and looked after her most faithfully during her illness. They are less concerned with children who showed less interest in the suspect's welfare when he was still alive, for they are not likely to oppose the verdict.

Sometimes a son or daughter, feeling an accusation of complicity to be forthcoming, will in order to avoid this join in with the accusers. This is what Ma Bewani's daughter did (see Case 5) when she saw the litter move toward her house and stop in front of it. She felt that it could mean only one thing. Immediately she began to make inarticulate noises, indicating that her mother had made an evil spirit enter into her. Thus presenting herself as a victim, she admitted that her mother was a witch.

In other cases, the mutual feelings cherished by close relatives, for instance by parents and children, serve to impede the spreading of an accusation throughout the quarter. The maneuver of naming dissidents as victims and accomplices is a kill-or-cure remedy to enforce conformity to majority opinion. And it is these maneuvers that at least partly explain why victims and accomplices so often turn out to be close relatives of the witch.

The next, and final, case illustrates the way in which an accusation can change direction because of external circumstances, or as a result of changes in the distribution of forces in the social field. The relatives initially acquiesced in the verdict pronounced by the priests. It was only some years later, when circumstances had drastically changed in their favor, that they publicly rejected the outcome of the inquest and the priests' interpretation of it.

Case 7: *Jealous cowives*

Ma Atuku lived in her husband's village, no longer visiting her native village at all. Being the high priest's first wife, she naturally turned to the oracle priests for help when she fell ill. She depended on them for medical assitance and was entirely at the mercy of the oracle, much more so than other persons who maintain regular relations with their own lineage. As long as there was hope of recovery, Atuku's last illness was ascribed to a conflict with one of her cowives. When it became clear that she was dying, however, the priests began to consider the possibility that she was a witch herself, and was being punished by the Great Deity for that reason. She supposedly resorted to witchcraft because she feared being ousted from her husband's favors. At the inquest in December 1961 she was denounced as a witch.

In 1964 Atuku's husband, the Paramount Chief, died, and the situation changed accordingly. The priests could no longer be expected to support the personal views of their dead chief as a matter of course. Atuku's relatives now got a chance to be heard. In other words, a change had taken place in the social field of the parties concerned, and this found expression in a reinterpretation of Atuku's death.

In 1965 a woman, Misajee, from Atuku's lineage died in Dritabiki where, like Atuku, she had lived for many years. Atuku's husband had acted as Misajee's foster father when she was young but later, when she was grown up, he started a sexual relationship with her and made her pregnant. To the Djuka this is a sin; a man who has sexual relations with two women of one lineage incurs the wrath of the ancestors. Atuku, who was still alive at the time, was much distressed by the affair. After her husband's death Atuku's relatives asserted that she had died of grief, the Great Deity had taken her away out of pity. She did not die a witch's death, *wisi-dede*, but rather *misi-dede*, death because of sin (not her own but her husband's).[2] This new interpretation was revealed in the verdict, which stated that the woman with whom the chief had committed adultery had died "through sin," killed by Atuku's spirit. Since Atuku herself had been killed by the Great Deity, those her spirit kills now also die "through sin." Atuku's spirit had become an avenging spirit to her husband's lineage, loosed by the Great Deity to play havoc among the lineage members of *Gaanman* Akontu.

The verdict is accepted by the lineage in question; and in their conduct toward the mourners they show that they are aware of their guilt.

At the time of Atuku's death it was possible for her to be denounced as a witch because of the particular power constellation existing then. When the tide turned, the accusation had to make way for an interpretation more acceptable to the other party.

CONCLUSION

Witchcraft beliefs in Djuka are a social idiom in which many kinds of conflicts are fought out. In spite of certain common anthropological explanations of witchcraft that view it largely as a reflection of social tensions existing between the accuser and the accused, we have seen that many aspects of Djuka witchcraft can be understood only by stressing the group membership of the persons involved, the whole social field. As we have seen, many accusations are prompted by feelings of solidarity or opposition between groups rather than by actual tension in the relations among individuals. Witchcraft involvements are transmitted easily from one social relationship into another. What starts as a feeling of being be-

[2] According to the Djuka, the Great Deity can terminate a person's life for one of two reasons: on account of witchcraft (*wisi-dede*), or on account of sin (*misi-dede*). In the second case the one who suffers may die in punishment for the sins of another member of his quarter, usually a member of his lineage.

witched may be communicated to others and taken over and elaborated upon. Yet there are barriers that check the spread of the accuser and the suspect are an important influence on insinuations may spread quite rapidly; yet coming from outside the village quarter, an accusation will meet with resistance. Moreover, we have seen that the power positions of the accuser and the suspect are an important influence on whether a suspicion will turn into an open accusation and whether the accusation will find an echo. A strong power position is a good basis to accuse and find support and may grant a certain degree of immunity. Conversely, a weak position does expose one to witchcraft accusations and severely limits one's capacity to act as an initiator of an accusation.

Witchcraft within the quarter and between different quarters have been shown to be not quite the same thing. We might almost say that there are two types of witchcraft in Djuka, each characterized by its own complex of sentiments and actions. Among members of the same quarter, fear of being bewitched is often rife but comes to the surface only rarely in the form of accusations. On the other hand, accusations directed at people resident in other quarters (mainly affines) are usually prompted not so much by a fear of being bewitched as by animosity between the groups concerned and by the need to declare one's solidarity with a member of one's own group. Within the quarter, witchcraft is marked by a dominance of fear and a relative absence of overt aggressive behavior. Between quarters it shows the opposite picture: a dominance of overt aggressive behavior and a relative absence of fear. As stated above, most accusations—seventeen out of thirty—are directed at people in other quarters, yet in fifty-six out of sixty-seven cases the witch is supposed to have picked his victim from among the inhabitants of his own village quarter.

Of course, not all witchcraft accusations can be explained as having a "social" origin. Some originate merely as expressions of a cognitive desire to determine the cause of an illness or other misfortune. But even in such cases, it seems clear that the course taken will depend on the forces operating in the social field. In twentieth-century Djuka society, witchcraft remains a major idiom of social organization. Studying the dynamics of witchcraft accusations provides important insights into the fundamental nature of Djuka society.

REFERENCES NOT CITED IN THE GENERAL BIBLIOGRAPHY

Marwick, M. G.
  1965 *Sorcery in Its Social Setting*. Manchester: Manchester University Press.
Turner, V. W.
  1964 "Witchcraft and Sorcery: Taxonomy versus Dynamics." *Africa* 34:314–24.

CHAPTER TWENTY-ONE

The Bush Negro Chiefs
Visit Africa: Diary
of an Historic Trip

SILVIA W. DE GROOT

Several times, the Tribal [or Paramount] Chiefs (Gran-mans) of the Bush Negroes had expressed a wish to journey to West Africa, the land of their origin, in order to re-establish contact. . . . The journey [described here] was offered them by the Government of Surinam and made during three weeks in November 1970.

On Saturday, November 7, the Granmans arrived from Surinam at Schiphol [Amsterdam] Airport. They were given a VIP reception. To greet them, high dignitaries such as Minister Polanen and Minister Bakker were present. After the initial reception, they were taken to the press room and, aided by Minister Polanen and the interpreter, they answered questions from the press. They were agreeably surprised but not at all overwhelmed by the great interest shown. Their answer to the question of how they liked being in Holland was, understandably, that they found it delightful, although they had seen nothing yet but the inside of Schiphol. . . .

A telecast was organized. The problem of the "transmigration" [the forced displacement of some six thousand Saramakas by a hydroelectric project during the 1960s] entered

From Silvia W. de Groot, "Vier Surinaamse Groot-Opperhoofden op zoek naar hun oorsprongen," *Vrij Nederland* 31, December 26, 1970:1, 19, 27; January 2, 1971:1, 17, 18. The editor expresses his gratitude to *Vrij Nederland* and the author for their permission to use this diary portion of a forthcoming book *Retour Africa*.

into the discussion. Granman Aboikoni, in whose territory the lake was constructed and where the transmigration occurred, stated that he had not been informed about the plans and that he was dissatisfied about their execution. But all this, he said, referred to the actions of the previous administration; the present administration was trying to effect improvements. Chairman Lachmon [of the current majority party of Surinam], who was present, confirmed this contentedly. Aboikoni concluded by saying that he had not come to talk about internal matters, that he wanted to avoid political considerations and wished to consider this journey as a pleasure trip.

R. Dobru, poet, writer, and revolutionary [Surinam] nationalist, answered [before the TV cameras] a question about what he thought of the Granmans' trip.

What is happening now and what will surely be of great influence on them is that here they will be taken to the Queen and the Princess, etc., and that they will be made much of by their colonial rulers. But when they get to Africa, they will be exposed to aware, revolutionary Africans, and that is going to change a lot of ideas they have acquired about the colonial government in Surinam.

[And in fact,] their visit to Queen Juliana and Princess Beatrix was for the Granmans a high point of their stay in the Netherlands. . . .

At the departure from Schiphol for the hotel it appeared that the Surinam Government had not provided the Granmans with winter clothing. They put on borrowed coats, and at the hotel I quickly drew up a list of things they would need during their visit in Holland. I phoned Hollenkamp [a department store], asked to have five sales clerks at our disposal, and drove to the store with the Granmans. There we bought hats, overcoats, gloves, winter suits, warm underwear, shirts, socks, and also some tropical clothing. . . . The Granmans were entranced with their new acquisitions. They were to insist, when they were ready to return to Surinam, on taking along all the newly acquired winter clothes. Granman Aboikoni wore his long woolen underwear throughout the African trip. The bill went to the Surinam Government. . . .

Several days later, we were finally ready to leave for Africa. My companions were:

Granman Aboikoni, Chief of the Saramakas, an older gentleman with arthritis in both knees, supported by a cane and by one of the interpreters. This handicap caused us little trouble, however, and for the rest he was strong as an ox. His natural dignity, his eloquence, and his traditional formality caused him to be treated with respect everywhere.

Granman Gazon, Chief of the Djukas, about sixty years old and also an outstanding speaker, a master at finding the appropriate imagery and in offering libations, and possessing a great sense of humor.

Granman Aboné, Chief of the Matawais, and Granman Forster, Chief of the Paramakas, both somewhat simpler in their ways, but also well-spoken, quick to laugh and like the two other Granmans, always equal to any situation.

[Finally, there were] Rudi Amsdorf, first interpreter, a Saramaka by birth, now teaching school in Amsterdam West while studying for a higher degree . . . [and] Richène Libretto, second interpreter and "third foot" of Granman Aboikoni, a member of the party from Paramaribo at the special request of the Granmans.

Wednesday, November 11. Departure from Schiphol. Sendoff by [Minister] Polanen and his staff, the ambassador of Nigeria, and the first secretary of the Ghanaian Embassy. At the entrance of the airplane we were frisked and our carry-on luggage thoroughly inspected. Gazon proved to have a hunting knife with him, which we had to leave with the stewardess.

Thursday, November 12. At 8 A.M. we arrived at the Ghana-Kotoka Airport and were met by, among others, the *chargé d'affaires* for the ambassador, Mr. Vos, the chief of protocol of Ghana, Mr. Ephson, and representatives of the Ministry of Foreign Affairs, television, and press. Gazon said with emotion, "We stand on African soil." It appeared that Ghana was receiving the Granmans and those accompanying them as official guests. We were put up at the Hotel Continental. . . . The official receptions started at ten o'clock that morning. The Granmans declared themselves unwilling to don their [official Surinam] uniforms for the occasion: They had seen that those strikingly resembled the uniforms of the hotel porters who opened the taxi doors. Unfortunately, they had not brought along their own traditional attire . . . due to

misunderstandings. From then on all official visits were car
ried out in business suits.

After being received by the Minister of Foreign Affairs, w
went to the Prime Minister *pro tem* (K. A. Busia wa
abroad), who presented us with photographs of Busia
Granman Gazon presented a (carved) paddle. . . . Address
ing the Granmans in an emotional speech, the Acting Prim
Minister said [in English]:

> We feel that accidents of history always have thei
> bright sides too, and its providential consequences. We ar
> happy that these accidents of history have not made then
> forget their origins. Had I not been told that they had com
> from Surinam as much as I have seen from them now,
> would have identified them as coming from Ghana. So tel
> them that they have come home and that here at home we
> regard them as our chiefs. Thus the respect we pay to ou
> chiefs will be the same respect we pay to them. The centra
> concepts in our chieftaincy is that the chiefs should reflec
> the very best in our way of life. And therefore it is the
> responsibility of every citizen to make the chief show thei
> very best. So let them know that everything we Ghanaian:
> can do to help them to show their people their very best
> we will try to do.

This address can be considered typical of those we were t
hear. . . .

Following the offering of a drink of welcome, with both
parties pouring libations to the gods and ancestors, Aboikon:
pronounced words of gratitude, referring to the fact that hi:
ancestors were taken across the ocean as slaves, but that they,
the descendants, had the good fortune of being in a positior
to greet this beautiful country and its people. He invoked
God's blessing over the land, and concluded with a prayer in
"Kromanti," a sacred language [of the Bush Negroes] in
which the Almighty, Nana Kediapon, is invoked. This caused
great emotions, for the same Supreme Ruler is invoked in
Ghana. The Prime Minister presented the Granmans with an
Ashanti stool, and explained that this was the symbol of a
chief's authority, a symbol that expresses their entire cultural
heritage as well as the power of their ancestors. . . . The
Granmans presented the Prime Minister with a decorative

plank on which the Surinam coat of arms was engraved, surrounded by carved Bush Negro Motifs.

Then came a luncheon given by the Minister of Foreign Affairs at which many chiefs from Accra and its surroundings were present, all dressed in splendid and colorful togas. At a quarter to four we left for Larteh (about an hour's drive), the site of one of the most important sanctuaries, the Akonede.

Friday, November 13. Departure by plane for Kumasi, accompanied by a protocol official, Dugblé. Luncheon with the district commissioner and many chiefs. Visit to the sanctuary of Kumasi, where we were received by drums and singing women. A priest danced a welcoming dance, his body daubed with white clay (also used in Surinam on ritual occasions). Then a reception by the Asantehene, Otumfuo Opoku Waré II. He was the recently appointed leader of the Ashanti Empire, direct successor to the founder, King Osei Tutu, who founded the empire at Kumasi at the end of the seventeenth century. It was a grandiose reception and an impressive spectacle. In a large courtyard the Asantehene was enthroned in a covered space, surrounded by his immediate counselors and a number of fly chasers. Outside, two groups of chiefs were seated to the left and right, each group in three rows; a third group enclosed the square. At the other end of the courtyard, facing the Asantehene, also in a covered space, were many drums, two of which, talking drums, were being played; they repeated the words of the Asantehene. In front of the chiefs on the one side were hornblowers and drummers, on the other side a row of "amen-sayers" who after every sentence pronounced by the Asantehene stood up and cried out "Syong." They wore black caps with large decorated golden disks. The Granmans were seated to the left of the chiefs. The Asantehene addressed the district commissioner, who translated the speech into English. Rudi Amsdorf translated it for the Granmans, passing it on to the "Bassia." The Granmans were greatly impressed, as was clear from their answers. They declared that finally they had found their true king again. Taking turns, each of them stood up close to the Asantehene and addressed him with great emotion. Aboikoni, trembling with emotion, sang a Kromanti song while kneeling before the Asantehene. . . . The Granmans presented paddles. The chiefs approached in long lines to greet the Granmans ceremoniously, in the same way as customary in the Surinam interior. . . .

In the evening in the hotel the Granmans began to expre their first impressions. The manner in which they were bei received made a great impression on them and exceeded the expectations, but still they were in no way overwhelme After all, they were and felt themselves to be Paramou Chiefs. Moreover—and this appeared also from later rea tions—they were of the opinion that their ancestors had bee taken away as slaves with the collaboration of their ov brothers, and so they felt that some retribution was owe them. On a later occasion, for example, Granman Gazo speaking in the form of a parable, was to remark: "A dog driven away from his yard. His master does not notice it o at least, pays little attention to it and does not go looking f him to bring him back. When the dog finally gets hungry, l tries to find the way back home." As he explained his mea ing, "Both the dog and his master (here the king) had falle asleep for three hundred years. Now the dog is awake an has also awakened its master."

Monday, November 16. We visited the old fortresses alon the coast from which, in the seventeenth, eighteenth, an nineteenth centuries, the slaves were transported in ship . . . The visit to the subterranean dungeons in which tl slaves were piled up before they were stowed in boats b way of narrow doors which gave directly on the sea cause deep emotion in the Granmans.

Tuesday, November 17. Very early by plane to Lomé i Togo. At the airport of Lomé the Granmans were receive with salvos of salutes, and by many high officials and th press. A reception took place at the home of the mayor, M dame Sivoney, where many chiefs were present. Afterward reception by the *chef-supérieur de la ville*, M. Joseph Adal Dadzié. There was a welcoming orchestra with drums an horns, and fireworks. The Granmans were pleasantly su prised by the fireworks as well as the salutes fired to welcom them. . . . Here also many words of fraternity and refoun friendship were spoken, and libations poured out for god and ancestors. Prayers were pronounced. . . .

Wednesday, November 18. In the morning, we left by ca for Palimé, to the northwest of Lomé. At the entrance of tl town we were awaited by the *chef de circonscription*, M. Ag bounou, and the mayor, who accompanied us to the *che*

supérieur of the town, Apétor II. A large crowd was present
to welcome us. In front of his house was the chief in full
regalia, surrounded by drummers, hornblowers, singing
women, and dancing fetish men with amulets and statues of
the ancestors. On the threshold, the throat of a he-goat was
cut, and the doorstep was sprinkled with blood, as well as
the hat of the fetish man. After that we were given permission to enter. Having arrived in the courtyard, we were again
welcomed with song and dance under the direction of a master of ceremonies, who was dancing about wildly. M. Ag-
bounou and I took charge of the translations of the welcoming words by Apétor II. The women then danced by us and
embraced us to everyone's joy, crying, just as in Surinam,
"Atuueee." Amsdorf [the interpreter] became enthused and
danced along, cheered on by the crowd. A woman fainted
and was carried off. Palm wine was poured, also as a libation.
Granman Gazon gave a speech, and Granman Aboikoni again
sang a Kromanti song. At our departure official photographs
were taken. . . .

Tuesday, November 24. [Following an exciting few days in
Dahomey, we drove to Lagos,] where we were hurriedly installed in the Ikoyi Hotel, from which we left immediately
to go to a cocktail party given by the Netherlands ambassador. . . . It appeared that the Nigerian Government too was
going to receive the Granmans as guests of the state.

Wednesday, November 25. [In the morning, we visited]
. . . the Paramount Chief of Lagos, Oba Oyekan. Here
again we were received in the grand style. Many chiefs were
present; the Oba conducted us through his palace and
showed us his sanctuary. Women sang to us, drummers beat
out a welcoming song. Afterward the entire company settled
down in the garden, and after words of greeting from both
sides, dances were performed: "Bata" dances in honor of
Shango, the thunder god, another welcoming dance, and a
performance by an acrobatic dance group. The Oba presented a beautiful box, ornamented with beads, for cola nuts,
which (after I had consulted with him through an inter-
mediary) he designated as a present for the Prime Minister of
Surinam. . . .

Thursday, November 26. In the morning, we left by plane
for Ibadan. . . . At the [official] luncheon, lukewarm cham-
pagne was offered and consequently when the bottle was
opened about half of the contents burst out. Comment from

Granman Gazon: "This is a worthy sacrifice to African soil." Then we were received by the Paramount Chief, Oba Oluba dan of Ibadan, and his chiefs. We were welcomed by a large band, part of which was formed by policemen in uniforms of English cut who blew trumpets. The Oba was seated on a beautiful throne flanked by two enormous elephant tusks . . . The Granmans and their three escorts then received a cola pot each (beautifully sculpted gourds in which cola nuts are kept; these nuts were offered, among other things as a welcoming snack). The Oba stated that he would like to keep the Granmans here permanently, but that he supposed they had wives in Surinam and so would not let themselves be persuaded. The Granmans answered that, alas, this was so, but that the temptation, with so many beautiful African women present, certainly was great. After this visit we were conducted through the television studio of the Western Nigerian Broadcasting System, where a "chat with four Paramount Chiefs from Surinam" was held.

Friday, November 27. From Ibadan we went to Ife, where we were lodged as guests of the university, in the elegant guest house on campus, in this important traditional center of Yorubaland. . . . In the afternoon, the University of Ibadan historians organized a meeting with the Granmans to discuss history. The Granmans asked some aggressive questions about the background of the delivery of slaves. The historians were unable to extricate themselves in a satisfactory manner, neither in their own opinion nor in that of the Granmans. In the evening the vice chancellor of the university gave a cocktail party for them.

Saturday, November 28. [Toward the end of our luncheon with the Timi of Ede] . . . Gazon came out with a remark that we did not translate. "It is a fine meal," he said, "probably paid for with the money that was earned by selling us as slaves." But then he concluded with a lyrical thank-you speech, in which he also referred to the women who had done the cooking. After lunch we returned to Ibadan. . . .

Monday, November 30. . . . It was the last day of our stay, and it was concluded with a dinner given by the Federal Minister of Information, His Excellency Enahoro. Also present were his very beautiful wife . . . and a few chiefs. Before we sat down at the table, the minister spoke a word of welcome. For the occasion, he took an unopened whiskey bottle in his hand, turned the cork till it came out, pulled off his right shoe and sock, sprinkled his large toe with whiskey, and pronounced a blessing in English. His wife uttered a frightened little cry. Next he offered the bottle to the Granmans. When Aboikoni got it, he also pulled off his shoe and his sock and followed suit. But of course he pronounced the blessing in Saramaccan, and afterward in Kromanti.

The whole ceremony was carried out with many expressions of satisfaction by those present. During dinner an interesting discussion occurred about mutual cultural customs: burial rites, the naming of children, initiation rituals, marriage customs, etc. Granman Aboikoni requested an explanation of how it was possible that Africa had managed to preserve its ancient traditions yet at the same time grow to be a modern state. Enahoro's answer was that Africa had been accustomed since earliest times to mixing many different cultures and to absorb of each culture that which was most valuable. They had also absorbed from European culture many things that might contribute to the progress of their own country. He added that in the matter of the slave trade it is not only the white people who should be blamed. The Negroes themselves promoted it. Now, however, was the time, he said, to make up for some of that. Then Granman Gazon gave a speech in which he again used some of his elegant imagery. "The same wind," he said, "that drove us against our will from Africa, has now aided us to find the way back." Expressions of hope for continued contact were exchanged with much emphasis. Just as in Ghana, the Granmans now presented a sculpted board with the Surinam escutcheon, to be given to the head of state, General Jacubo Gowon.

Tuesday, December 1. The day of departure from Africa. Before leaving the hotel each of Granmans was presented with a statue in the name of Enahoro. At the airport . . . the farewells were emotional. Goodbye, Africa!

On their final day in the Netherlands [before returning to Surinam], I asked the Granmans again about their impressions. Apart from the shock of recognition of their country of origin, they were deeply impressed by the expanse of the region visited, the many large towns, the enormous number of villages, the chain of large marketplaces, and especially— even more than by the air flights we took—by the enormous distances we covered by car in Africa. They were happy about the often-pronounced sincere wish of the African countries to have more contact with Surinam, a land whose existence was hardly known to them before this visit. They were proud of the fact that this wish was expressed on all levels, by governments, universities, and traditional chiefs.

The wish of the writer Dobru, expressed on November 7 at their departure from the Netherlands, that the Granmans would have contact with revolutionary Africans, and through this that they would acquire a whole new set of ideas, seemed to have been fulfilled. The Granmans declared with great assurance that without wanting to give up their traditions they would strive for modern development, and that they would make a beginning by founding more schools, and schools on a better level, in the interior of their own country.

BIBLIOGRAPHICAL NOTES

PART ONE: Students seeking further readings on maroons in Hispanic America would do well to begin with Guillot's readable and comprehensive overview of sixteenth-century slave rebellions and maroon communities throughout the hemisphere (1961; see also Acosta Saignes' introduction to archival materials for the same broad area [1969]). The Spanish territories boast a large body of particularistic scholarship on maroons, some of high quality. I list what I have found to be the more interesting of these, by area.

For Cuban maroons and their communities, the best survey (listing sites, dates, and so forth) is Franco 1968; Pérez de la Riva (1946) and Ortiz (1916: Ch. 22) contain additional background information. Franco has written in more detail on three particular communities (1964); Dalton has described the prisons used for nineteenth-century maroons in Havana (1967), and Estéban Montejo, the centenarian Cuban ex-maroon, has sensitively recounted his life as a slave and runaway during the waning days of Caribbean slavery (1968; cf. also Salkey 1971).

Venezuelan scholars have succeeded admirably in setting local maroons in the sociohistorical context of slavery; the two basic works are Acosta Saignes 1967 (in particular Chs. 13 and 14) and Brito Figueroa 1961 (see also his 1966). Arcaya (1949) and Felice Cardot (1952) have each written histories of major rebellions, and Palacios de la Vega, an eighteenth-century missionary, has left a number of firsthand observations on maroon communities that he encountered in his Venezuelan travels (1955).

Colombia still lacks a comprehensive analytical overview. Arrazola (1970) pulls together many of the major documents on maroons, and is a rich historical source. Escalante's monographic study of the *palenque* of San Basilio (1954; see also Bickerton and Escalante 1970) remains the best available ethnohistorical work for this country. T. Price 1954 and Arboleda 1952 survey the state of Afro-Colombian studies in general, but contain little on maroons. Arboleda devotes several pages to maroons in his thesis (1950:82–88).

For Mexico, the major primary sources are listed in Davidson's comprehensive survey (1966, reprinted here), and in Guillot

(1961). Pérez de Ribas (1896, I:282–94) is among the richest of the original accounts. In addition, Aguirre Beltrán has written an ethnographic monograph on the West Coast town of Cuíjla tracing continuities with its original, maroon founders (1958).

For Panama, the region that witnessed the most intensive maroon-pirate collaboration, Diez Castillo (1968) provides the most comprehensive coverage, but it is often unreliable. Masefield covers much of this same ground in his popular and readable book (1925). Fortune has written several shorter popular works on the maroons of the Isthmus (1951, 1954, 1956, 1958). Aguado includes important documentation on Bayano's kingdom (1919, in particular Vol. II:183–231). And Nichols provides interesting contemporary descriptions of maroons and pirates in the area (1653). A useful annotated bibliography on Afro-Panamanians in general has been compiled by Arosemena Moreno (1969).

Maroons in the remainder of the Spanish Americas have received only sporadic scholarly attention. Díaz Soler discusses slave rebellions and the lack of maroon communities (though not of maroons and laws against runaways) in Puerto Rico (n.d.:Ch. 9); and Carvalho-Neto briefly discusses maroons in Uruguay (1965:94–96, 243–60), as does Millones for Peru (1971).

Finally, I mention a research possibility that has never, to my knowledge, been explored: comparison of Afro-American revolts and maroon communities in the Hispanic Americas with similar phenomena among American Indians. In the so-called Caste War of Yucatan, for example, Maya Indians retreated to the Yucatecan hinterlands, formed themselves into guerrilla bands that fought courageously against colonial troops and built new, syncretistic forms of religious, political, and social organization (see Reed 1964). Such comparisons might well lead to greater analytical exactness in assessing the relative influence of environment and culture on early Afro-American maroon groups throughout the hemisphere.

PART TWO: The two major works on maroons in the French colonies, written from contrasting ideological perspectives, are Debbasch 1961/62 and Fouchard 1972. Both range over many aspects of marronage and include impressive documentation as well as suggestions for further reading. Debien 1966a and Debien *et al.* 1961–67 include biographical data on many hundreds of individual maroons, with tribal origins, sex, occupation, and so forth, suggesting how much remains to be done with archival materials; parts of Fouchard 1972 carry this approach further for Saint-Domingue. The role of maroons in the Haitian revolution is assessed by, among others, James 1963, Debien 1966b, Fouchard 1972 (which presents the most compelling case to date for their prominence as revolutionaries) and Brutus n.d. [1972], which is a particularly striking example of the current glorification of maroons underway in Haiti itself.

On the Black Carib of British Honduras, who were mentioned briefly in the introduction, the basic modern monographs are Taylor 1951 and González 1969 (cf. also Conzemius 1928, 1930, and Coelho 1955); two relevant historical accounts are La Borde 1704 and Young 1795.

References on maroons in French Guiana will be found in the bibliographical note for Part Six.

PART THREE: For the United States, Mullin's recent book on flight and rebellion (1972) is the best modern study, taking up controversial theoretical questions and relating marronage to ongoing debates about the nature of North American slavery. Among the many works on American slave revolts, one might mention Carroll 1969, Kilson 1964, and Aptheker 1969 (which contains considerable additional bibliography); the introduction to this book gave references for many of the recent re-evaluations of the prevalence of nonviolent or more subtle resistance to slavery in the United States.

There is a large and growing literature on the immensely complex relations between maroons and Indians on the southeastern frontier, some of whose descendants are today scattered as far away as Texas, Oklahoma, Mexico, and even the Bahamas. One might begin with the various papers by K. Porter (1932, 1941, 1943a, 1943b, 1945, 1946, 1956), Goggin (1946), and the ongoing research of Willis (1963, 1970).

PART FOUR: The selections reprinted in this book list most major references on maroon communities in Brazil. To repeat only a few: For Palmares, the basic documents, including firsthand descriptions, are found in Carneiro 1947 (only the Portuguese edition has the documentary appendix) and Ennes 1938; the best general monograph remains Carneiro 1947 (Spanish edition 1946); Ennes has pulled together materials about the final years of this "republic" (1948); and Bastide offers his own perspective on Palmares in his book on African religions in Brazil (1961:114–26).

Many of the major sources on other *quilombos* are listed in Bastide's survey in this book, but there are a number of more recent books by Brazilians that broaden and deepen our knowledge; for example, Goulart 1972 and the revised edition (1972) of Moura 1959, which are comprehensive surveys of revolts, marronage, and *quilombos* for the whole of Brazil; Almeida Barbosa 1972 on the *quilombos* of Minas Gerais; and Goulart 1971, a detailed description of the punishments and tortures inflicted upon Brazilian slaves. For general background on Afro-Brazilians, and on the major "tribal" rebellions of the early nineteenth century, see Nina Rodrigues 1935 (especially pp. 65–150), Ramos 1939 (especially pp. 24–53) and Pierson 1942.

PART FIVE: The standard histories of the Jamaican Maroons to the end of the First Maroon War are Dallas 1803, Edwards 1796, and Long 1774 (II:338–83, 440–75). Modern treatments of this same period include Hart 1950, Robinson 1969, and P. Wright 1970. On the events of 1795 and the deportation to Nova Scotia and West Africa, see Brymner 1895, Crawford 1858 (III:1–146), Dallas 1803, Edwards 1796, Furness 1965, Winks 1971 (pp. 78–95, which contains considerable additional bibliography), and A. Porter 1963. Kopytoff 1972 is the most comprehensive modern analysis of the whole sweep of Jamaica Maroon history.

A number of anthropologists and folklorists, amateur and professional, have sojourned briefly with the Maroons during the twentieth century. Their descriptions include Beckwith 1929 (pp. 183–97), Dunham 1946, Hurston 1938 (pp. 34–53), Scott 1968, and Williams 1938. Linguistic field work has been carried out by Le Page and DeCamp (1960:97–103, 143–79) and by Dalby (1971).

Marronage and maroons as literary themes have been handled with particular sensitivity by Jamaican novelists, for example, Reid 1949 and Patterson 1972. Among the more interesting of the other novels on the English-speaking Caribbean that make use of the theme of marronage are Behn 1688 and Marshall 1969. Other fiction in English, in addition to Faulkner's frequent references to periodic truancy in the plantation South, includes a number of novels dealing with slave rebellion and marronage, for example, Bontemps 1936, Styron 1967, and, more recently, translated from the French, Schwarz-Bart 1973. I would note that poems, dramas, and novels treating maroons in non-English-speaking Afro-America also form a rich and rewarding body of literature, but it is beyond the scope of this book to list them here.

PART SIX: The specialized literature on the Guiana Maroons is vast, including many hundreds of items, and I have written a comprehensive review of it elsewhere (R. Price 1974; cf. also R. Price 1972). Here, I mention just a few of the works with which a student interested in further exploration of Bush Negro societies might begin.

In depicting the society from which the original rebels fled, as well as early Bush Negro history, Stedman (1796) is still the best available primary source in English. More recent historical studies include de Groot 1963, 1965, and 1969, all on the Djuka. From an ethnographic perspective, Herskovits and Herskovits (1934) present a sympathetic (if romantic) overview of Bush Negro life in the 1920s (cf. also Herskovits and Herskovits 1936). More recently Köbben, who worked with the Cottica Djuka, has written excellent papers on sociocultural change (1968), social roles (1969a), law (1969b), and the field work experience (1967a), as well as a brief general ethnography (n.d.). The Thoden van

Velzens, who worked in the village of the Djuka tribal chief on the Tapanahony River, have produced full-length monographs on political organization (Thoden van Velzen 1966b, currently being translated into English [see also his 1972]) and witchcraft (van Wetering n.d.) and papers on aspects of religious and domestic organization (Thoden van Velzen 1966a, van Wetering 1966). My wife and I carried out general ethnographic research among the Saramaka on the Pikilío between 1966 and 1968, which has resulted to date in a monograph on social structure (R. Price 1973c) and papers on emigration and social change (R. Price 1970a), the naming system (Price and Price 1972b), the arts (R. Price 1970b, 1972, Price and Price 1972a and 1973), religious organization (R. Price 1973a), and language history (R. Price 1973b); we are currently working both on a general descriptive ethnography of Saramaka and on a historical reconstruction of the society in the eighteenth century. And Jean Hurault has written three major works on the Aluku (Boni) tribe: one on social structure and religion (1961), another on material culture and economy (1965), and the third on art (1970).

Finally, for a fuller picture of André's community in French Guiana, see Henry 1950 (112–17); and for accounts of the attempts by slaves in British Guiana to form maroon communities, see the English translation of Hartsinck (1958–60) and Rodway 1891 (I:171–214).

GENERAL BIBLIOGRAPHY

Acosta Saignes, Miguel
    1967 *Vida de los esclavos negros en Venezuela.* Caracas: Editorial Hesperides.
    1969 "Introducción al estudio de los repositorios documentales sobre africanos y sus descendientes en América." *América Indígena* 29:727–86.
Aguado, Fray Pedro de
    1919 *Historia de Venezuela.* Madrid: Real Academia de la Historia.
Aguirre Beltrán, Gonzalo
    1946 *La población negra de México, 1519–1810.* Mexico: Ediciones Fuente Cultural.
    1958 *Cuijla: esbozo etnográfico de un pueblo negro.* Mexico: Fundo de Cultura Economica.
Almeida Barbosa, Waldemar de
    1972 *Negros e quilombos em Minas Gerais.* Belo Horizonte.
Aptheker, Herbert
    1939 "Maroons Within the Present Limits of the United States." *Journal of Negro History* 24:167–84.
    1969 *American Negro Slave Revolts.* New York: International Publishers.
Arboleda, José Rafael
    1950 "The Ethnohistory of the Colombian Negroes." Unpublished M.A. thesis, Northwestern University, Evanston.
    1952 "Nuevas investigaciones afro-colombianas." *Revista Javariana* 37 (184):197–206.
Arcaya, Pedro M.
    1949 *Insurrección de los negros en la serranía de Coro.* Caracas: Instituto Panamericano de Geografía y Historia, Comisión de Historia.
Arosemena Moreno, Julio
    1969 "Documentacion relativa al negro en Panama." *Lotería,* II época 14 (164): 49–60.
Arrazola, Roberto
    1970 *Palenque, primer pueblo libre de América.* Cartagena: Ediciones Hernandez.

Bastide, Roger
1961 *Les religions Africaines au Brésil.* Paris: Presses Universitaires de France.
1967 *Les Amériques noires: les civilisations africaines dans le nouveau monde.* Paris: Payot.
1972 *African Civilizations in the New World.* New York: Harper & Row [trans. of Bastide 1967].

Bauer, Raymond and Alice Bauer
1942 "Day-to-day Resistance to Slavery." *Journal of Negro History* 27:388–419.

Beckwith, Martha W.
1929 *Black Roadways: A Study of Jamaican Folk Life.* Chapel Hill: University of North Carolina Press.

Behn, Aphra
1688 *Oroonoko or the royal slave: a true history.* London: W. Canning.

Bickerton, D. and A. Escalante
1970 "Palanquero: A Spanish-based Creole of Northern Colombia." *Lingua* 24:254–67.

Blassingame, John W.
1972 *The Slave Community: Plantation Life in the Antebellum South.* New York: Oxford University Press.

Bontemps, Arna
1936 *Black Thunder*, new edition. Boston: Beacon Press, 1968.

Brito Figueroa, Federico
1961 *Las insurrecciones de los esclavos negros en la sociedad colonial.* Caracas: Editorial Cantaclaro.
1966 *Historia económica y social de Venezuela.* Caracas: Universidad Central.

Brutus, Edner
n.d. [1972] *Révolution dans Saint-Domingue.* Les Editions du Panthéon (Belge).

Bryce-Laporte, Roy Simon
1971 "Slaves as Inmates, Slaves as Men: A Sociological Discussion of Elkins' Thesis." *In* Ann Lane (ed.), *The Debate on Slavery: Stanley Elkins and His Critics.* Urbana: University of Illinois Press, pp. 269–92.

Brymner, D.
1895 "The Jamaica Maroons: How They Came to Nova Scotia—How They Left It. *Transactions of the Royal Society of Canada* (second series) 1 (2): 81–90.

Buve, R.
1966 "Gouverneur Johannes Heinsius: de rol van van Aerssen's voorganger in de Surinaamse Indianenoorlog, 1678–1680." *Nieuwe West-Indische Gids* 45:14–26.

Carneiro, Edison
1946 *Guerras de los Palmares.* Mexico: Fondo de Cultura Economica.

1947 *O quilombo dos Palmares, 1630–1695.* São Paulo: Editora Brasiliense Limitada (2nd ed., 1958; 3rd ed., 1966).

Carroll, Joseph Cephas
1969 *Slave Insurrections in the United States, 1800–1865.* New York: New American Library (new edition).

Carvalho-Neto, Paulo de
1965 *El negro uruguayano (hasta la abolicion).* Quito: Editorial Universitaria.

Coelho, Ruy
1955 "The Black Carib of Honduras." Unpublished Ph.D. dissertation, Northwestern University, Evanston.

Conzemius, Eduard
1928 "Ethnographical notes on the Black Carib (Garif)." *American Anthropologist* 30:183–205.
1930 "Sur les Garif ou Caraïbes Noirs de l'Amérique Centrale." *Anthropos* 25:859–77.

Crawford, A. W. C. L., Lord Lindsay
1858 *Lives of the Lindsays.* London (2nd ed.).

Curtin, Philip D.
1969 *The Atlantic Slave Trade: A Census.* Madison: University of Wisconsin.

Dalby, David
1971 "Ashanti Survivals in the Language and Traditions of the Windward Maroons of Jamaica." *African Language Studies* 12: 31–51.

Dallas, R. C.
1803 *The History of the Maroons.* London: T. N. Longman and O. Rees.

Dalton, Margarita
1967 "Los depositos de los cimarrones en el siglo XIX." *Etnología y Folklore* 3 (enéro–junio): 5–29.

Davidson, David M.
1966 "Negro slave control and resistance in colonial Mexico, 1519–1650." *Hispanic American Historical Review* 46:235–53.

Debbasch, Yvan
1961–62 "Le marronnage: essai sur la désertion de l'esclave antillais." *L'Année Sociologique,* 3e série, 1961:1–112; 1962: 117–95.

Debien, Gabriel
1965 "Les marrons autour du Cap en 1790 et en 1791." *In* Debien, et. al., 1961–67, pp. 755–99.
1966a "Les esclaves marrons à Saint-Domingue en 1764." *Jamaican Historical Review* 61 (1 and 2):9–20.
1966b "Le marronage aux Antilles Francaises au XVIIIᵉ siècle." *Caribbean Studies* 6(3):3–44.

Debien, G.; Houdaille, J.; Massio, R.; and Richard, R.
1961–67 "Les origines des esclaves des Antilles." *Bulletin de l'Institut Français d'Afrique Noire* 23, Sér. B:363–87 (1961);

26, Sér. B:166–211 (1964); 27, Sér. B:319–69 (1965); 27, Sér. B:755–99 (1965); 29, Sér. B:536–58 (1967).

Diaz Soler, Luis M.
n.d. *Historia de la esclavitud negra en Puerto Rico (1493–1890)*. Madrid: Ediciones de la Universidad de Puerto Rico.

Diez Castillo, Luis A.
1968 *Los cimarrones y la esclavitud en Panamá*. Panamá: Editorial Litografica.

Dunham, Katherine
1946 *Journey to Accompong*. New York: Henry Holt and Company.

Edwards, Bryan
1796 "Observations on the disposition, character, manners, and habits of life, of the Maroon Negroes of the island of Jamaica." In Bryan Edwards, *The History . . . of the West Indies*. London (1807): Vol. I, Appendix II, pp. 522–76.

Elkins, Stanley M.
1959 *Slavery: A Problem in American Institutional and Intellectual Life*. Chicago: University of Chicago Press (new edition 1963).

van der Elst, Dirk Hendrik
1970 "The Bush Negro Tribes of Surinam, South America: A Synthesis." Unpublished Ph.D. dissertation, Northwestern University, Evanston.

Engerman, Stanley L.; Fogel, Robert W.; Genovese, Eugene D.; and Gutman, Herbert
1972 "New Directions in Black History: A Symposium." *Forum* 1(2):22–46.

Ennes, Ernesto
1938 *As guerras nos Palmares (subsidios para sua historia)*. São Paulo: Edições de Companhia Editora Nacional.
1948 "The Palmares "Republic" of Pernambuco: Its Final Destruction, 1697." *The Americas* 5:200–16.

Escalante, Aquiles
1954 "Notas sobre el palenque de San Basilio, una communidad negra en Colombia." *Divulgaciones Ethnologicas* 3(5):207–359.

Felice Cardot, Carlos
1952 *La rebelión de Andresote*. Caracas.

Fortune, Armando
1951 "Como don Pedro Ursúa sometió e hizo prisionero a Bayano." *Diario El Día (Panamá)*, Dec. 1:4.
1954 "Marron King Bayano was Foremer [sic] of Emancipation of Slave in Panama." *The Nation (Panamá)*, Nov. 28:2.
1956 "Estudios sobre la insurrección de los negros esclavos, los cimarrones de Panama." *Lotería, II época*, 1:(5) 61–68, (6) 46–51, and (9) 44–67.
1958 "Corsarios y cimarrones en Panama." *Lotería, II época*, 3(33):77–97.

Fouchard, Jean
  1972 *Les marrons de la liberté.* Paris: Editions de l'Ecole.
Franco, José Luciano
  1961 *Afroamérica.* La Habana: Publicaciones de la Junta Nacional de Arqueología y Etnología.
  1964 "Palenques del Frijol, Bumba y Maluala [with the cooperation of Rosario Franco]." *In* José L. Franco, *Placido: Una polemica que tiene cien años y otro ensayos.* Havana: Ediciones Union / Ensayo, pp. 27–41.
  1968 "Cuatro siglos de lucha por la libertad: los palenques." *In* J. L. Franco, *La presencia negra en el nuevo mundo.* Havana: Casa de las Americas, pp. 91–135.
Frederickson, George and Lasch, Christopher
  1967 "Resistance to Slavery. *Civil War History* 13:315–29.
Friederici, Georg
  1960 *Amerikanistisches Wörterbuch und Hilfswörterbuch für den Amerikanisten.* 2. Auflage. Hamburg: Cram, de Gruyter & Co.
Furness, A. E.
  1965 "The Maroon War of 1795." *Jamaican Historical Review* 5:30–49.
Gage, Thomas
  1958 *Travels in the New World.* Norman: University of Oklahoma Press.
Genovese, Eugene D.
  1967 "Rebelliousness and Docility in the Negro Slave: A Critique of the Elkins Thesis." *Civil War History* 13:293–314.
Goggin, John M.
  1946 "The Seminole Negroes of Andros Island, Bahamas." *Florida Historical Quarterly* 24:200–6.
Gonzalez, Nancie L. Solien
  1969 *Black Carib Household Structure.* Seattle: University of Washington Press.
Goulart, José Alípio
  1971 *Do palmatória ao patíbulo: castigos de escravos no Brasil.* Rio de Janeiro: Conquista.
  1972 *Da fuga ao suicídio: aspectos de rebeldia dos escravos no Brasil.* Rio de Janeiro: Conquista.
Goveia, E. V.
  1965 *Slave Society in the British Leeward Islands at the end of the Eighteenth Century.* New Haven: Yale University Press.
de Groot, Silvia W.
  1963 *Van isolatie naar integratie: de Surinaamse Marrons en hun afstammelingen.* Verhandelingen van het Koninklijk Instituut voor Taal-, Land- en Volkenkunde 41. 's-Gravenhage: Martinus Nijhoff.
  1965 "Migratiebewegegingen der Djoeka's in Suriname van 1845 tot 1863." *Nieuwe West-Indische Gids* 44:133–51.
  1969 *Djuka Society and Social Change.* Assen: van Gorcum.

1970–71 "Vier Surinaamse Groot-Opperhoofden op zoek naar hun oorsprongen." *Vrij Nederland* 31, December 26, 1970:1, 19, 27; January 2, 1971:1, 17, 18.

Guillot, Carlos Federico
1961 *Negros rebeldes y negros cimarrones (perfil afro-americano en la historia del Nuevo Mundo durante el siglo XVI).* Montevideo: Fariña Editores.

Hart, Richard
1950 "Cudjoe and the First Maroon War in Jamaica." *Caribbean Historical Review* 1:46–79.

Hartsinck, J. J.
1958–60 "The story of the slave rebellion in Berbice, 1763" [trans. from J. J. Hartsinck, *Beschrijving van Guyana*, 1770, Amsterdam]." *Journal of the British Guiana Museum and Zoo of the Royal Agricultural and Commercial Society* (Dec. 1958–Sept. 1960), Nos. 20–27.

Helms, Mary W.
1971 *Asang: Adaptations to Culture Contact in a Miskito Community.* Gainesville: University of Florida Press.

Henry, A.
1950 *La Guyane française: son histoire 1604–1946.* Cayenne: Paul Laporte.

Herlein, J. D.
1718 *Beschrijvinge van de volk-plantinge Zuriname.* Leeuwarden: Meindert Injema.

Herskovits, Melville J.
1958 *The Myth of the Negro Past.* Boston: Beacon (orig. edition 1941).

Herskovits, M. J. and Herskovits, F. S.
1934 *Rebel Destiny: Among the Bush Negroes of Dutch Guiana.* New York: McGraw-Hill.
1936 *Suriname Folk-lore.* New York: Columbia University Press (*Columbia Contributions to Anthroplogy* 27).

Hodges, H. Eugene
1971 "How to Lose the Hounds: Technology of the Gullah Coast Renegade." In *The Not so Solid South,* J. Kenneth Morland (ed.), *Southern Anthropological Society Proceedings* 4: 66–73.

Hurault, Jean
1961 *Les Noirs Réfugiés Boni de la Guyane Française.* Mémoires de l'Institut Français d'Afrique Noire (Dakar) 63.
1965 *La vie matérielle des Noirs Réfugiés Boni et des Indiens Wayana du Haut-Maroni.* Paris: Office de la Recherche Scientifique et Technique Outre-Mer.
1970 *Africains de Guyane: la vie matérielle et l'art des Noirs Réfugiés de Guyane.* La Haye-Paris: Mouton.

Hurston, Zora Neale
1938 *Tell My Horse.* Philadelphia: Lippincott.

James, C. L. R.
    1963 *The Black Jacobins: Toussaint L'Ouverture and the San Domingo Revolution* (2nd ed., rev.). New York: Vintage.
Kent, R. K.
    1965 "Palmares: An African State in Brazil." *Journal of African History* 6:161–75.
Kilson, Marion D. de B.
    1964 "Towards Freedom: An Analysis of Slave Revolts in the Unites States." *Phylon* 25:175–87.
King, Johannes
    1958 "Skrekiboekoe" (selection). *In* Ursy M. Lichtveld and Jan Voorhoeve (eds.), *Suriname: Spiegel der vaderlandse kooplieden;* Zwolle: W. E. J. Tjeenk Willink, pp. 92–119.
    1973 *Life at Maripaston,* H. F. de Ziel (ed.). The Hague: Martinus Nijhoff.
Klein, Herbert S.
    1967 *Slavery in the Americas: A Comparative Study of Cuba and Virginia.* Chicago: University of Chicago Press.
Köbben, A. J. F.
    1967a "Participation and Quantification: Field Work Among the Djuka (Bush Negroes of Surinam)." *In* D. G. Jongmans and P. C. W. Gutkind (eds.), *Anthropologists in the Field.* Assen: van Gorcum, pp. 35–55.
    1967b "Unity and disunity: Cottica Djuka society as a kinship system." *Bijdragen tot de Taal-, Land- en Volkenkunde* 123:10–52.
    1968 "Continuity in Change: Cottica Djuka Society as a Changing System." *Bijdragen tot de Taal-, Land- en Volkenkunde* 124:56–90.
    1969a "Classificatory Kinship and Classificatory Status: The Cottica Djuka of Surinam." *Man* (*N.S.*) 4:36–49.
    1969b "Law at the Village Level: The Cottica Djuka of Surinam." *In* Laura Nader (ed.), *Law in Culture and Society.* Chicago: Aldine, pp. 117–40.
    n.d. "Of freedom and bondage: the Cottica Djuka of Surinam." Ms.
Kopytoff, Barbara Klamon
    1972 "The Incomplete Polities: An Ethnohistorical Account of the Jamaica Maroons." Unpublished Ph.D. dissertation, University of Pennsylvania, Philadelphia.
La Borde, Sieur de
    1704 "Voyage qui contient une relation exacte de l'origine, moeurs, coûtumes, religion, guerres, et voyages des Caraïbes." *In* R. P. Hennepin, *Voyage curieux.* Leide: P. van der Aa, pp. 517–604.
Lane, Ann (ed.)
    1971 *The Debate on Slavery: Stanley Elkins and His Critics.* Urbana: University of Illinois Press.

Le Page, R. B. and DeCamp, David
  1960 *Jamaican Creole*. London: Macmillan.
van Lier, R. A. J.
  1971 *Frontier Society: A Social Analysis of the History of
  Surinam*. The Hague: Martinus Nijhoff.
Lindblom, Gerhard
  1924 *Afrikanische Relikte und Indianische Entlehnungen in der
  Kultur der Busch-Neger Surinams*. Göteborg: Elanders Bok-
  tryckeri Aktiebolag.
Long, Edward
  1774 *The history of Jamaica*. London: T. Lowndes.
Mannix, Daniel P. and Cowley, Malcolm.
  1962 *Black Cargoes: A History of the Atlantic Slave Trade*. New
  York: Viking.
Marshall, Paule
  1969 *The Chosen Place, the Timeless People*. New York: Har-
  court, Brace & World.
Masefield, John
  1925 *On the Spanish Main* (4th ed.). London: Methuen.
Millones, Luis
  1971 "Gente negra en el Perú: esclavos y conquistadores."
  América Indígena 31:593–624.
Mintz, Sidney W.
  1971 "Toward an Afro-American History." *Cahiers d'Histoire
  Mondiale* 13:317–32.
——— and Price, Richard
  1973 *An Anthropological Approach to Afro-American History*.
  Andover, Mass.: Warner Modular Publications.
Mirot, Sylvie
  1954 "Un document inédit sur le marronnage à la Guyane
  Française au XVIIIe siècle." *Revue d'Histoire des Colonies*
  41:245–56.
Montejo, Esteban
  1968 *The Autobiography of a Runaway Slave* (Miguel Barnet,
  ed.). New York: Pantheon.
Moreau de Saint-Méry, Médéric Louis Elie
  1958 *Description . . . de la partie française de l'isle Saint-
  Domingue*. New edition revised from the original ms. by
  B. Maurel and E. Taillemite. Paris: Société de l'Histoire des
  Colonies Françaises.
Moura, Clovis
  1959 *Rebeliões da senzala: quilombos, insurreições, guerrilhas*.
  São Paulo (2nd ed. 1972, Rio de Janeiro: Conquista).
Mullin, Gerald W.
  1972 *Flight and Rebellion: Slave Resistance in Eighteenth-
  Century Virginia*. New York: Oxford University Press.
Nassy, David de Ishak Cohen, et al.
  1788 *Essai historique sur la colonie de Surinam . . .* Paramaribo.
  (Facsimile reprint, Amsterdam: S. Emmering, 1968).

Nichols, Philip
    1653 *Sir Francis Drake Reviv'd.* London: Nicholas Bourne.
Nina Rodrigues, Raymundo
    1935 *Os Africanos no Brasil* (2nd ed.). São Paulo: Bibliotheca Pedagogica Brasiliera.
Ortiz, Fernando
    1916 *Hampa Afro-cubana: los negros esclavos.* Havana: Revista Bimestre Cubana.
Palacios de la Vega, Joseph
    1955 *Diario de viaje entre los indios y negros de la Provincia de Cartagena en el Nuevo Reino de Granada, 1787–1788.* (G. Reichel-Dolmatoff, ed.). Bogotá: Editorial A.B.C.
Parry, J. H. and Sherlock, P. M.
    1965 *A Short History of the West Indies* (2nd ed.). London: Macmillan.
Patterson, Orlando
    1967 *The Sociology of Slavery.* London: MacGibbon and Kee.
    1970 "Slavery and Slave Revolts: A Socio-historical Analysis of the First Maroon War, 1655–1740. *Social and Economic Studies* 19:289–325.
    1972 *Die the Long Day.* New York: Morrow.
Pérez de Ribas, Andrés
    1896 *Corónica y historia religiosa de la provincia de la Compañia de Jesús de México en Nueva España.* Mexico: Imprenta del Sagrado Corazón de Jesús.
Pérez de la Riva, Francisco
    1946 "El negro y la tierra, el conuco y el palenque." *Revista Bimestre Cubana* 58(2, 3):97–139.
    1952 *La habitación rural en Cuba.* La Habana: Contribución del Grupo Guamá, Antropología No. 26.
Peytraud, Lucien
    1897 *L'esclavage aux Antilles françaises avant 1789.* Paris: Hachette.
Philalethes, Demoticus
    1856 *Yankee Travels Through the Island of Cuba.* New York: D. Appleton and Co.
Pierson, Donald
    1942 *Negroes in Brazil.* Chicago: University of Chicago Press (2nd ed., Carbondale, 1967).
Pinckhard, G.
    1806 *Notes on the West Indies.* London: Longman, Hurst, Rees and Orme.
Pope-Hennessy, James
    1969 *Sins of the Fathers: A Study of the Atlantic Slave Traders, 1441–1807.* New York: Capricorn.
Porter, Arthur T.
    1963 *Creoledom: A Study of the Development of Freetown Society.* Oxford: Oxford University Press.

Porter, Kenneth W.
1932 "Relations Between Negroes and Indians Within the Present Limits of the United States." *Journal of Negro History* 17:287–367.
1941 "Abraham." *Phylon* 2:107–16.
1943a "Florida Slaves and Free Negroes in the Seminole War, 1835–1842." *Journal of Negro History* 28:390–421.
1943b "Three Fighters for Freedom." *Journal of Negro History* 28:51–72.
1945 "Notes on Seminole Negroes in the Bahamas." *Florida Historical Quarterly* 24:56–60.
1946 "John Caesar: Seminole Negro Partisan." *Journal of Negro History* 31:190–207.
1956 "Negroes and Indians on the Texas Frontier, 1831–1876." *Journal of Negro History* 41:185–214, 285–310.

Price, Richard
1970a "Saramaka Emigration and Marriage: A Case Study of Social Change. *Southwestern Journal of Anthropology* 26:157–89.
1970b "Saramaka Woodcarving: The Development of an Afroamerican art." *Man* (*N.S.*) 5:363–78.
1972 "The Guiana Maroons: Changing Perspectives in 'Bush Negro' studies." *Caribbean Studies* 11(4):82–105.
1973a "Avenging Spirits and the Structure of Saramaka Lineages." *Bijdragen tot de Taal-, Land- en Volkenkunde* 129:86–107.
1973b "Kikoongo and Saramaccan: a reappraisal." *Journal of African Languages* 12(1).
1973c *Saramaka Social Structure: Analysis of a "Bush Negro" Society.* Rio Piedras: Institute of Caribbean Studies of the University of Puerto Rico.
1974 *The Guiana Maroons ("Bush Negroes"): A Bibliographical Introduction.* Ms. in final stages of preparation.
——— and Price, Sally
1972a "*Kammbá:* The Ethnohistory of an Afro-American art." *Antropologica* 32:3–27.
1972b "Saramaka Onomastics: An Afro-American Naming System." *Ethnology* 11:341–67.
1973 "Secret Play Languages in Saramaka: Linguistic Disguise in a Caribbean creole." *In* Barbara Kirshenblatt-Gimblett (ed.), *Speech Play on Display.* The Hague: Mouton.

Price, Thomas J.
1954 "Estado y necesidades actuales de las investigaciones Afro-Colombianas." *Revista Colombiana de Antropología* 2(2):13–36.

Ramos, Arthur
1939 *The Negro in Brazil.* Washington: Associated Publishers.

Rawick, George P.
  1972 *From Sundown to Sunup: The making of the Black Community*. Westport, Conn.: Greenwood Publishing Company.
Reed, Nelson
  1964 *The Caste War of Yucatan*. Stanford: Stanford University Press.
Reid, Vic
  1949 *New Day*. New York: Knopf.
Rivière, Peter
  1969 *Marriage Among the Trio*. London: Oxford University Press.
Robinson, Carey
  1969 *The Fighting Maroons of Jamaica*. Kingston: William Collins and Sangster (Jamaica) Ltd.
Rodway, James
  1891 *History of British Guiana from the year 1688 to the present time*. Georgetown.
Salkey, Andrew
  1971 *Havana Journal*. Baltimore: Penguin.
Schuler, Monica
  1970a "Akan Slave Rebellions in the British Caribbean." *Savacou* 1(1):8–31.
  1970b "Ethnic Slave Rebellions in the Caribbean and the Guianas." *Journal of Social History* 3:374–85.
Schwartz, Stuart B.
  1970 "The Mocambo: Slave Resistance in Colonial Bahia." *Journal of Social History* 3:313–33.
Schwarz-Bart, André
  1973 *A Woman Named Solitude*. New York: Atheneum.
Scott, Clarissa S.
  1968 "Cultural Stability in the Maroon Village of Moore Town, Jamaica." Unpublished M.A. thesis, Florida Atlantic University, Boca Raton.
Southey, Robert
  1817–22 *The History of Brazil*. London: Longman, Hurst, Rees, Orme and Brown.
Staehelin, F.
  1913–19 *Die Mission der Brüdergemeine in Suriname und Berbice im achtzehnten Jahrhundert*. Herrnhut: Vereins für Brüdergeschichte in Kommission der Unitätsbuchhandlung in Gnadau.
Stedman, Captain J. G.
  1796 *Narrative of a Five-years' Expedition, Against the Revolted Negroes of Surinam . . . from the year 1772, to 1777*. London: J. Johnson and J. Edwards.
Stewart, J.
  1823 *A View of the Past and Present State of the Island of Jamaica*. Edinburgh: Oliver and Boyd.

Styron, William
1969 *The Confessions of Nat Turner.* New York: Random House.

Synnott, Anthony
1971 "Slave Revolts in Guyana and Trinidad: A History and Comparative Analysis. Ms. Sir George Williams University, Montreal.

Taylor, Douglas MacRae
1951 *The Black Carib of British Honduras.* New York: Viking Fund Publications in Anthropology No. 17.

Thoden van Velzen, H. U. E.
1966a "Het geloof in wraakgeesten: bindmiddel en splitzwam van de Djuka matri-lineage." *Nieuwe West-Indische Gids* 45: 45–51.
1966b *Politieke Beheersing in de Djuka Maatschappij: een Studie van een Onvolledig Machtsoverwicht.* Leiden: Afrika-Studiecentrum.
1972 "Some Aspects of Power Exertion in Tapanahoni Djuka Society." *In* Peter Kloos and A. J. F. Köbben (eds.), *Structure, Function and Process: Contributions of Dutch Anthropologists.* Assen: van Gorcum.

Voorhoeve, Jan
1971 "Church Creole and Pagen Cult Languages" *In* Del Hymes (ed.), *Pidginization and Creolization of Languages.* Cambridge: Cambridge University Press.
―――― and Lichtveld, Ursy M.
1974 *Kriorodron: An Anthology of Creole literature in Surinam.* New Haven: Yale University Press (in press).

van Wetering, W.
1966 "Conflicten tussen co-vrouwen bij de Djuka." *Nieuwe West-Indische Gids* 45:52–59.
n.d. "Djuka Witchcraft Beliefs: A Sociological Approach." Ph.D. dissertation, University of Amsterdam (in press).

Williams, Joseph J.
1938 "The Maroons of Jamaica." *Anthropological Series of the Boston College Graduate School* 3(4):379–480.

Willis, William S., Jr.
1963 "Divide and Rule: Red, White, and Black in the South East." *Journal of Negro History* 48:157–76.
1970 "Anthropology and Negroes on the Southern Colonial Frontier." *In* James C. Curtis and Lewis L. Gould (eds.), *The Black Experience in America.* Austin: University of Texas Press, pp. 33–50.

Winks, Robin W.
1971 *The Blacks in Canada: A History.* New Haven: Yale University Press.

Woodbury, George
1951 *The Great Days of Piracy in the West Indies.* New York: Norton.

Wright, Irene
1929 *Spanish Documents Concerning English Voyages to the Caribbean, 1527–1568* (2nd series). London: Hakluyt Society.
1932 *Documents Concerning English Voyages to the Spanish Main, 1569–1580* (2nd series). London: Hakluyt Society.
Wright, Philip
1970 "War and Peace with the Maroons." *Caribbean Quarterly* 16(1):5–27.
Young, Sir William
1795 *An Account of the Black Charaibs in the Island of St. Vincent's.* London: J. Sewell.

INDEX

420